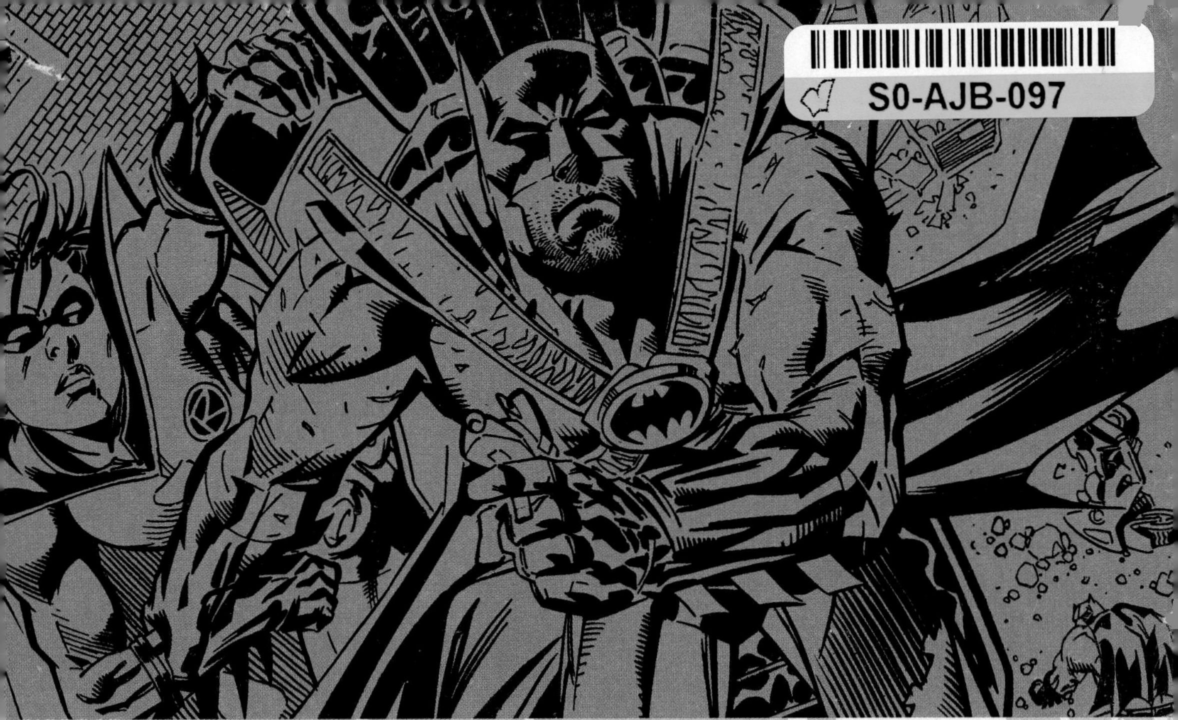

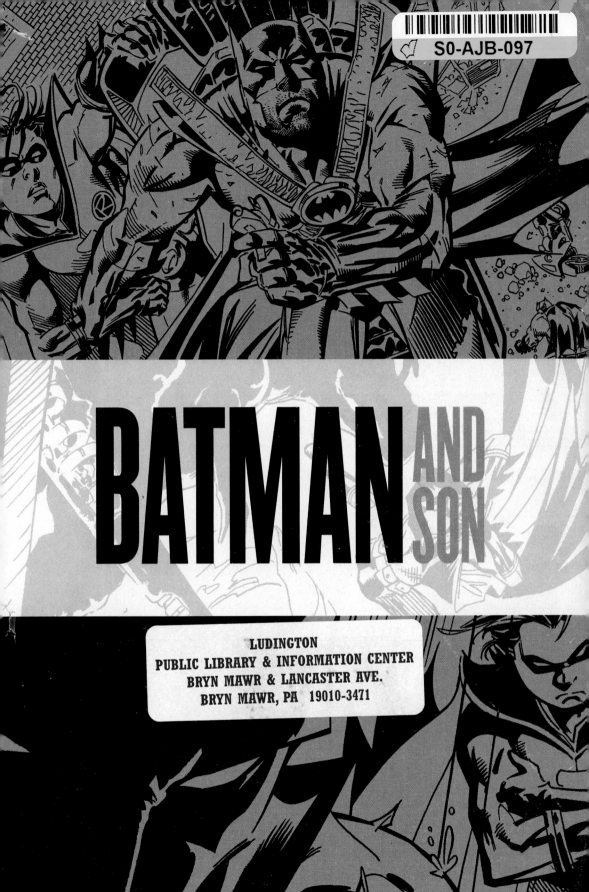

BATMAN AND SON

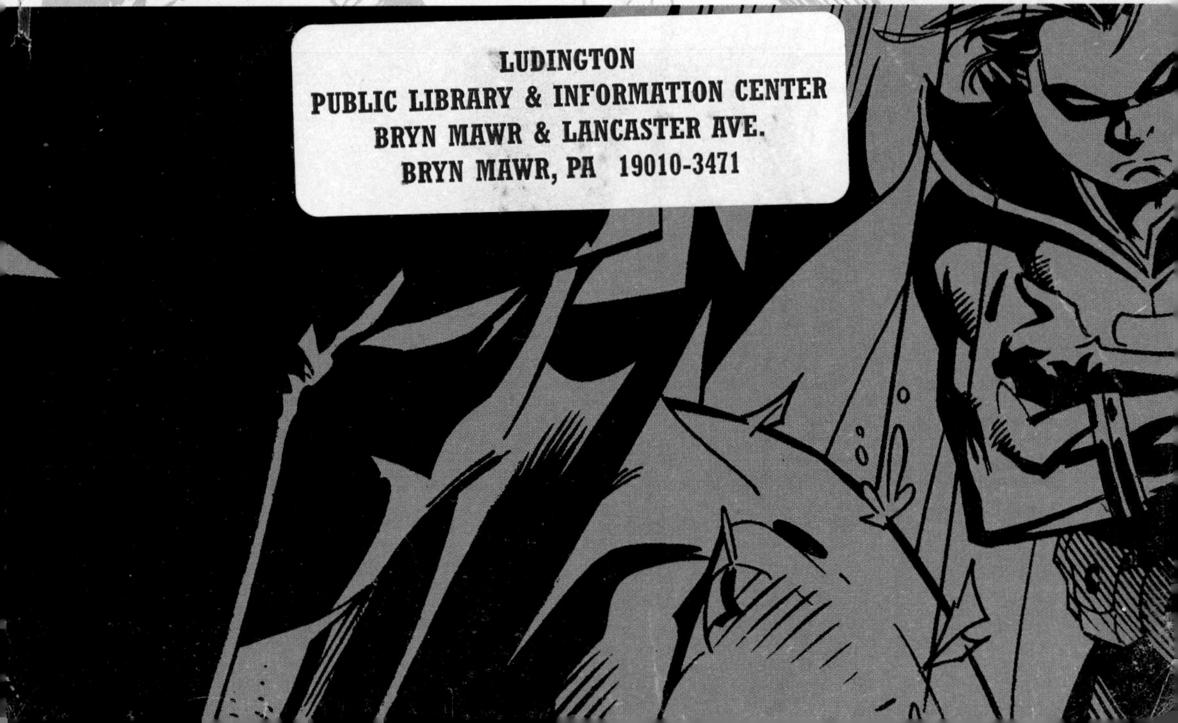

Dan DiDio Senior VP-Executive Editor   **Peter J. Tomasi** Senior Editor-original series   **Michael Siglain** Associate editor-original series   **Elisabeth V. Gehrlein** Assistant Editor-original series
Bob Harras Editor-collected edition   **Robbin Brosterman** Senior Art Director   **Paul Levitz** President & Publisher   **Georg Brewer** VP-Design & DC Direct Creative
Richard Bruning Senior VP-Creative Director   **Patrick Caldon** Executive VP-Finance & Operations   **Chris Caramalis** VP-Finance   **John Cunningham** VP-Marketing   **Terri Cunningham** VP-Managing Editor
Alison Gill VP-Manufacturing   **Hank Kanalz** VP-General Manager, WildStorm   **Jim Lee** Editorial Director-WildStorm   **Paula Lowitt** Senior VP-Business & Legal Affairs
MaryEllen McLaughlin VP-Advertising & Custom Publishing   **John Nee** VP-Business Development   **Gregory Noveck** Senior VP-Creative Affairs   **Sue Pohja** VP-Book Trade Sales
Cheryl Rubin Senior VP-Brand Management   **Jeff Trojan** VP-Business Development, DC Direct   **Bob Wayne** VP-Sales

Cover art by Andy Kubert   Publication design by Amelia Grohman

BATMAN AND SON

BATMAN AND SON

GRANT MORRISON WRITER   ANDY KUBERT PENCILLER   JESSE DELPERDANG INKER

GUY MAJOR DAVE STEWART COLORISTS   JARED K. FLETCHER ROB LEIGH NICK J. NAPOLITANO LETTERERS

"THE CLOWN AT MIDNIGHT" Grant Morrison WRITER   John Van Fleet ART   Todd Klein TYPE DESIGN

BATMAN created by Bob Kane

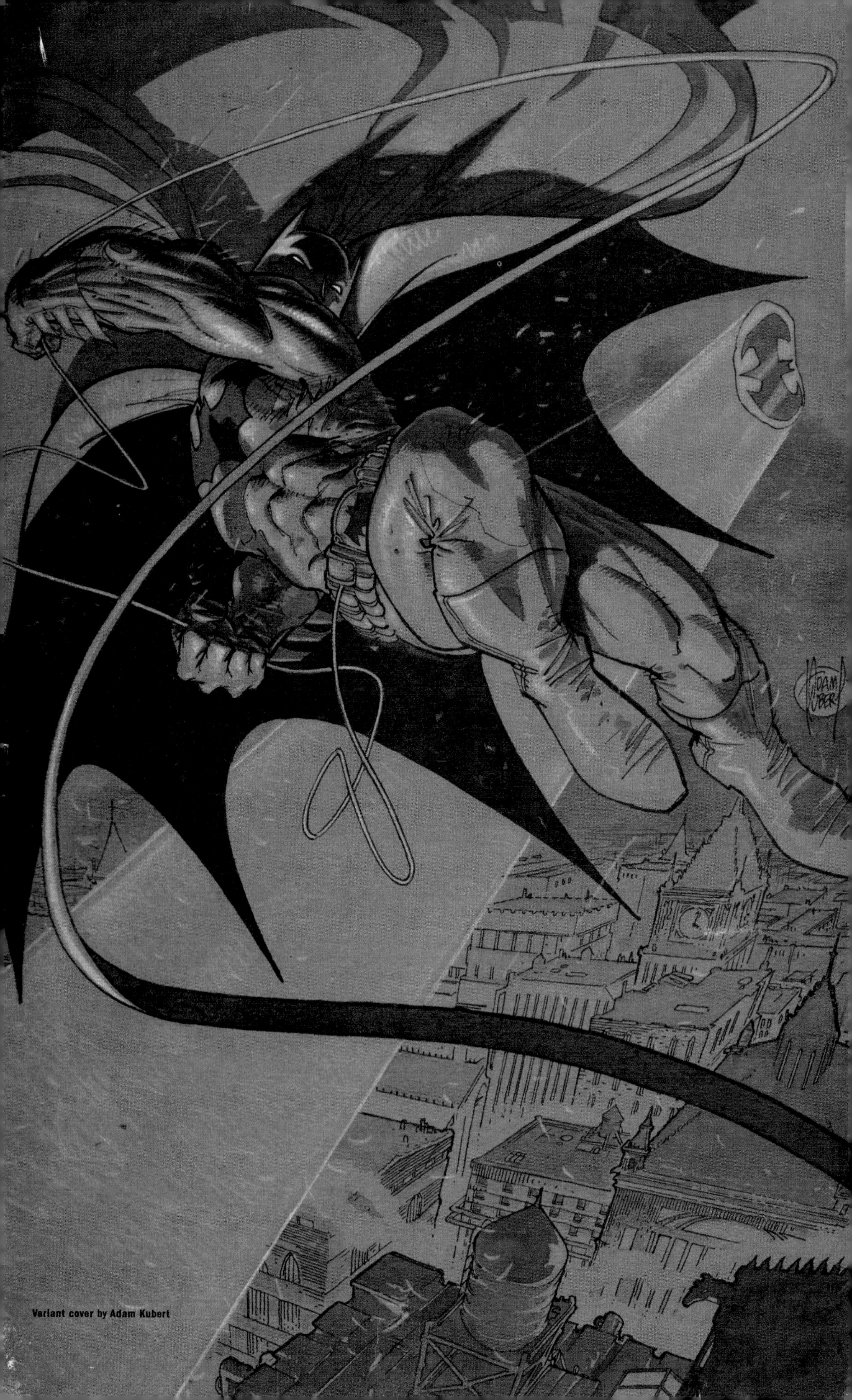

Variant cover by Adam Kubert

CHAPTER ONE

BUILDING A BETTER BATMOBILE

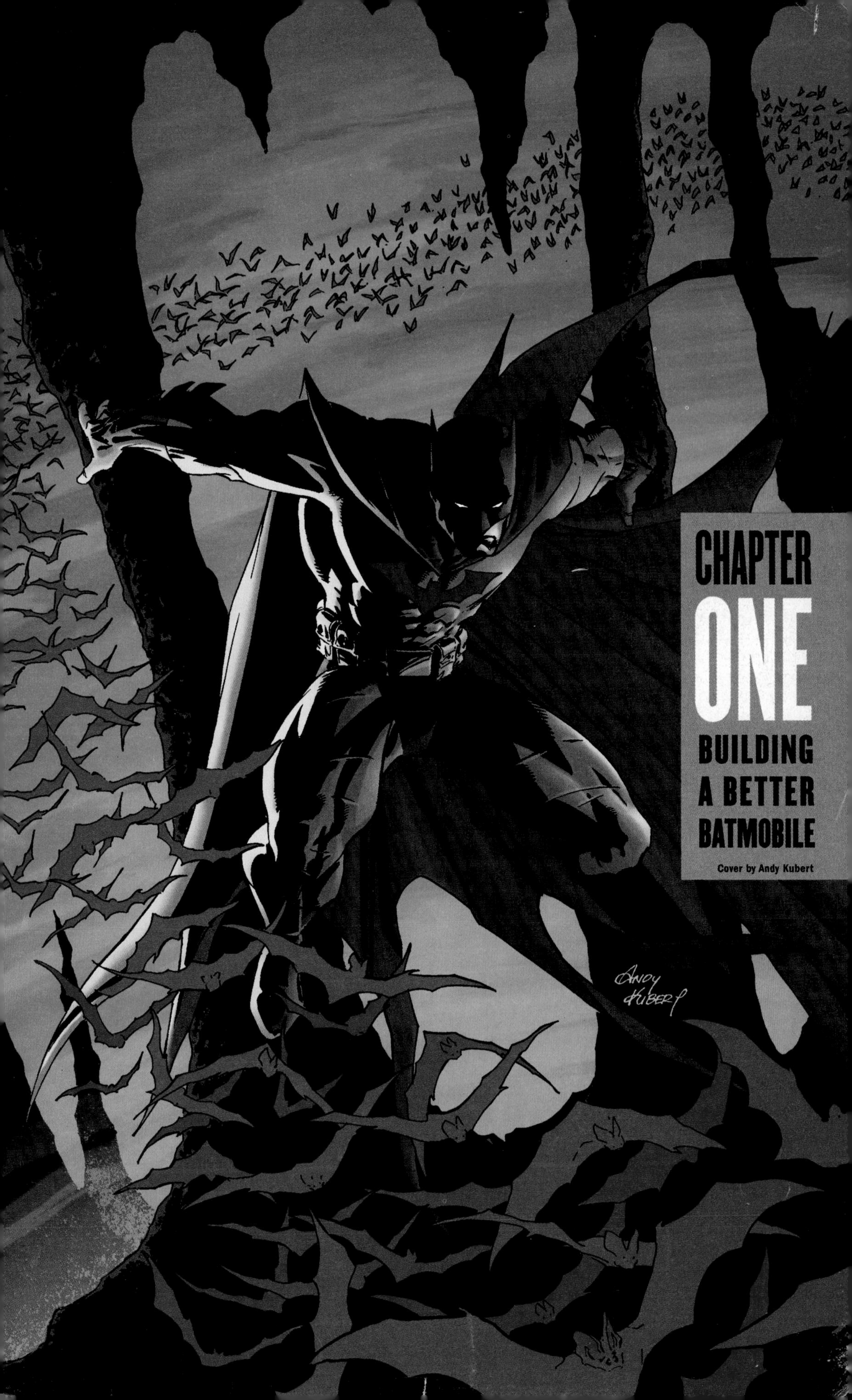
ANDY KUBERT

Cover by Andy Kubert

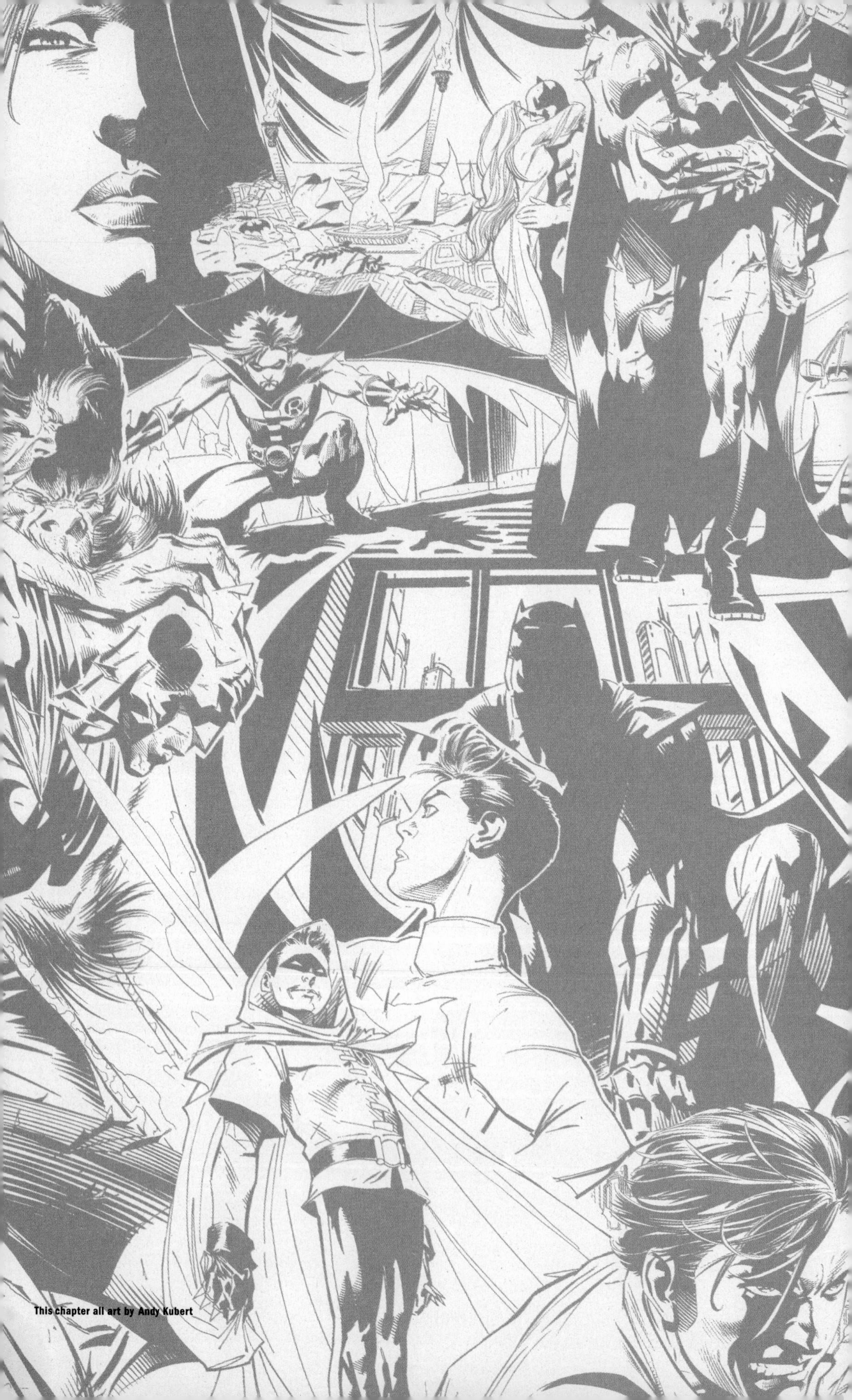

This chapter all art by Andy Kubert

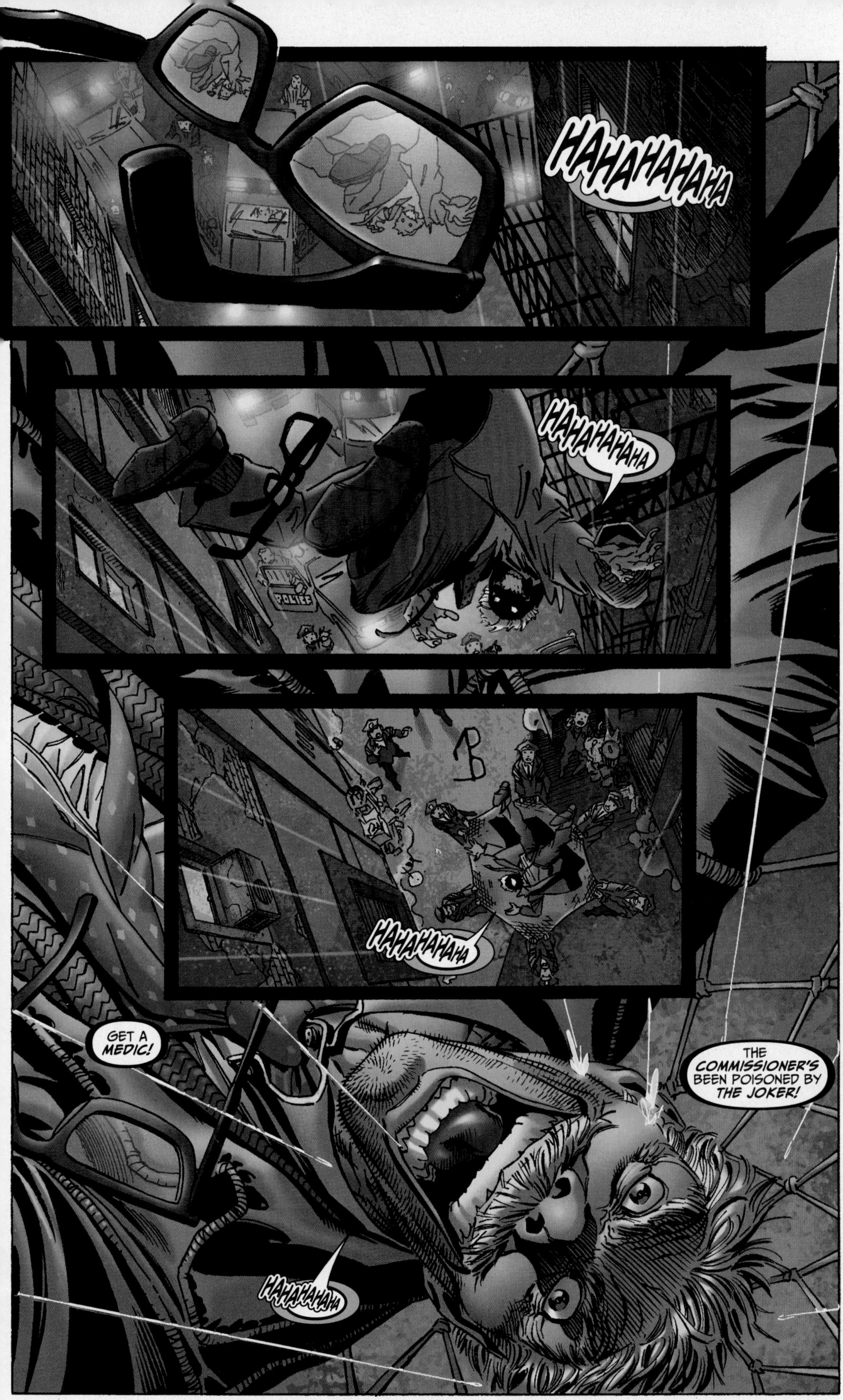
HAHAHAHAHA
HAHAHAHAHA
HAHAHAHAHA
GET A MEDIC!
THE COMMISSIONER'S BEEN POISONED BY THE JOKER!
HAHAHAHAHA

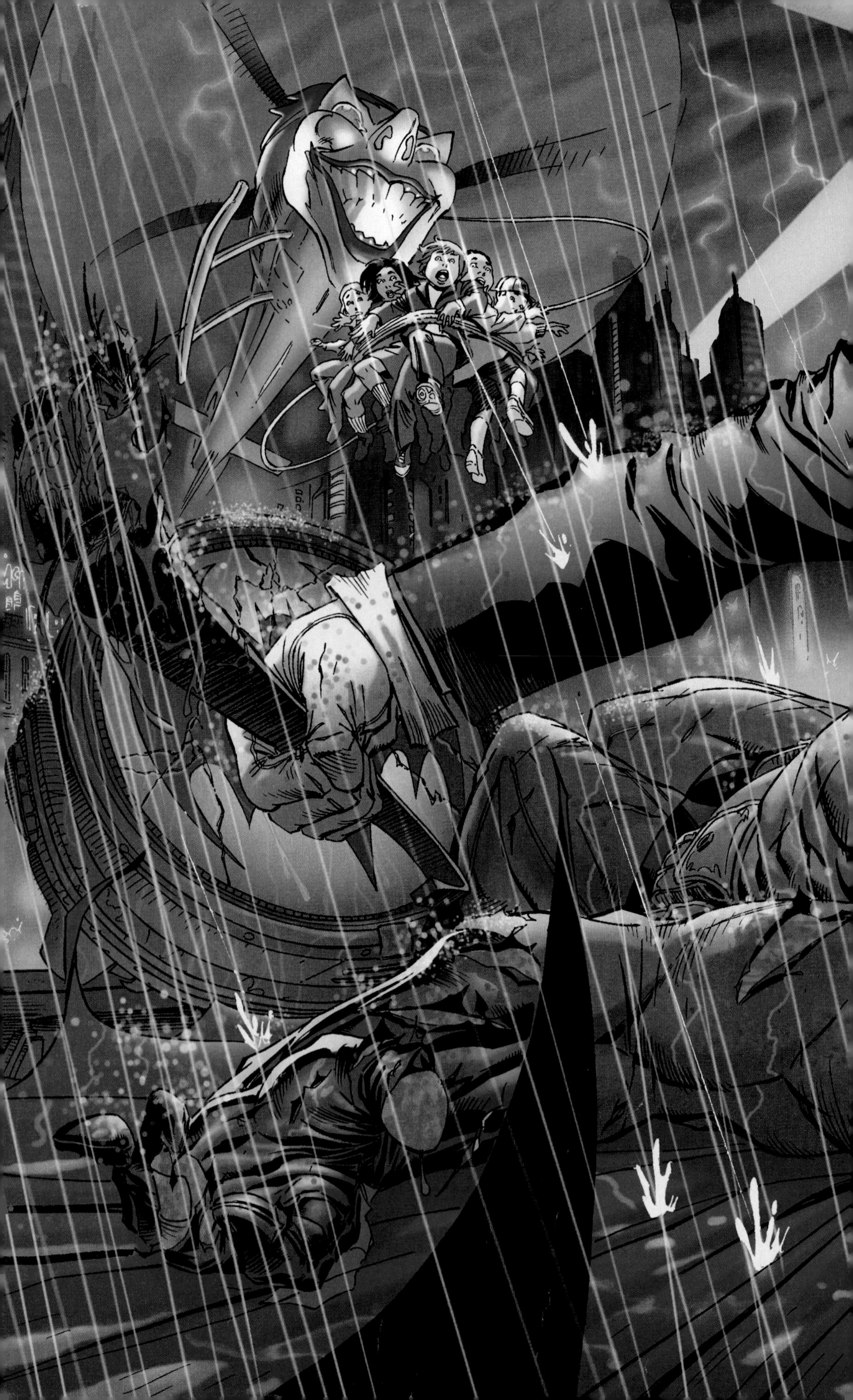

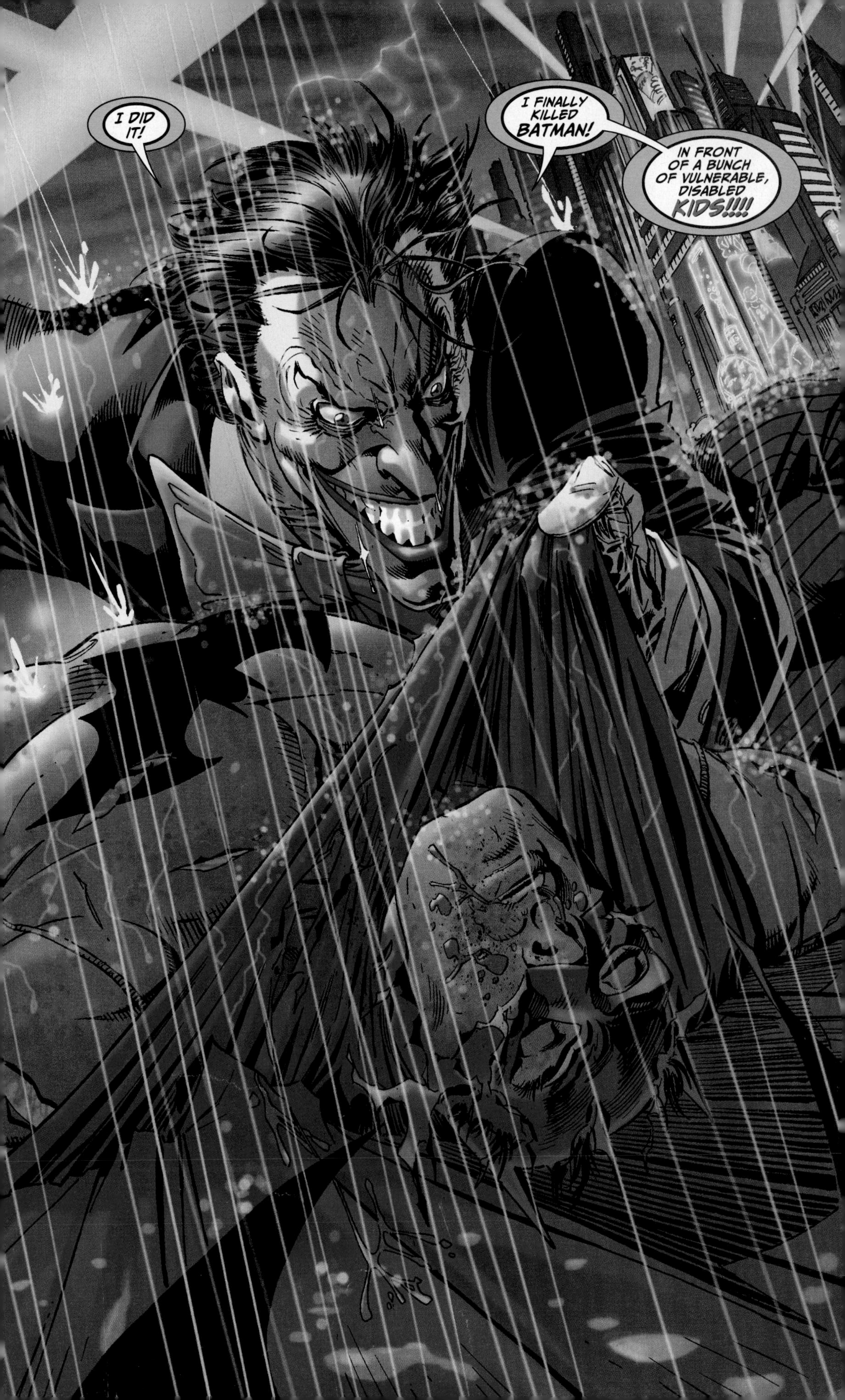
I DID IT!
I FINALLY KILLED BATMAN!
IN FRONT OF A BUNCH OF VULNERABLE, DISABLED KIDS!!!!

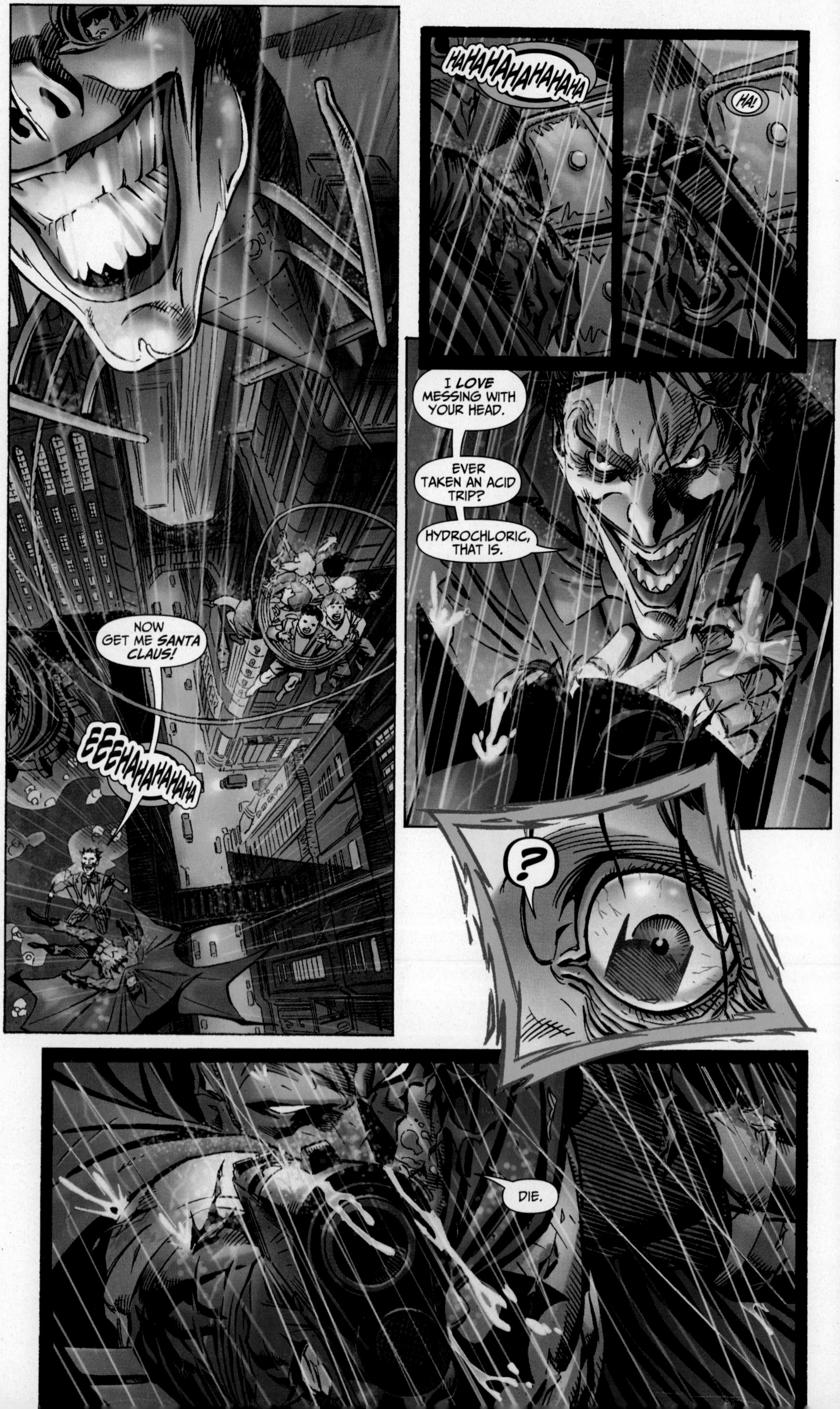

NOW GET ME SANTA CLAUS!
EEEHAHAHAHAHA
HAHAHAHAHAHAHAHA
HA!
I LOVE MESSING WITH YOUR HEAD.
EVER TAKEN AN ACID TRIP?
HYDROCHLORIC, THAT IS.
?
DIE.

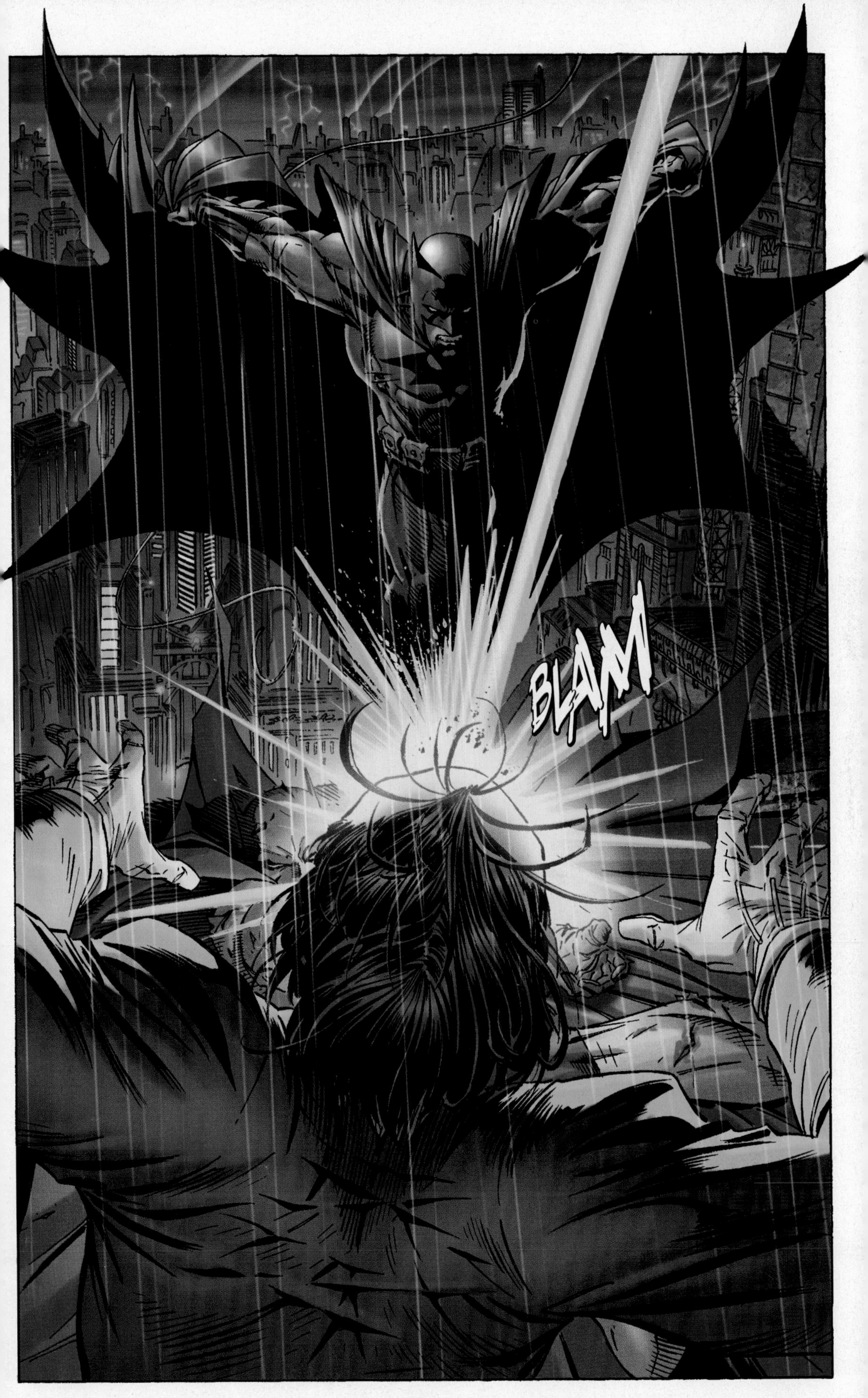
BLAM

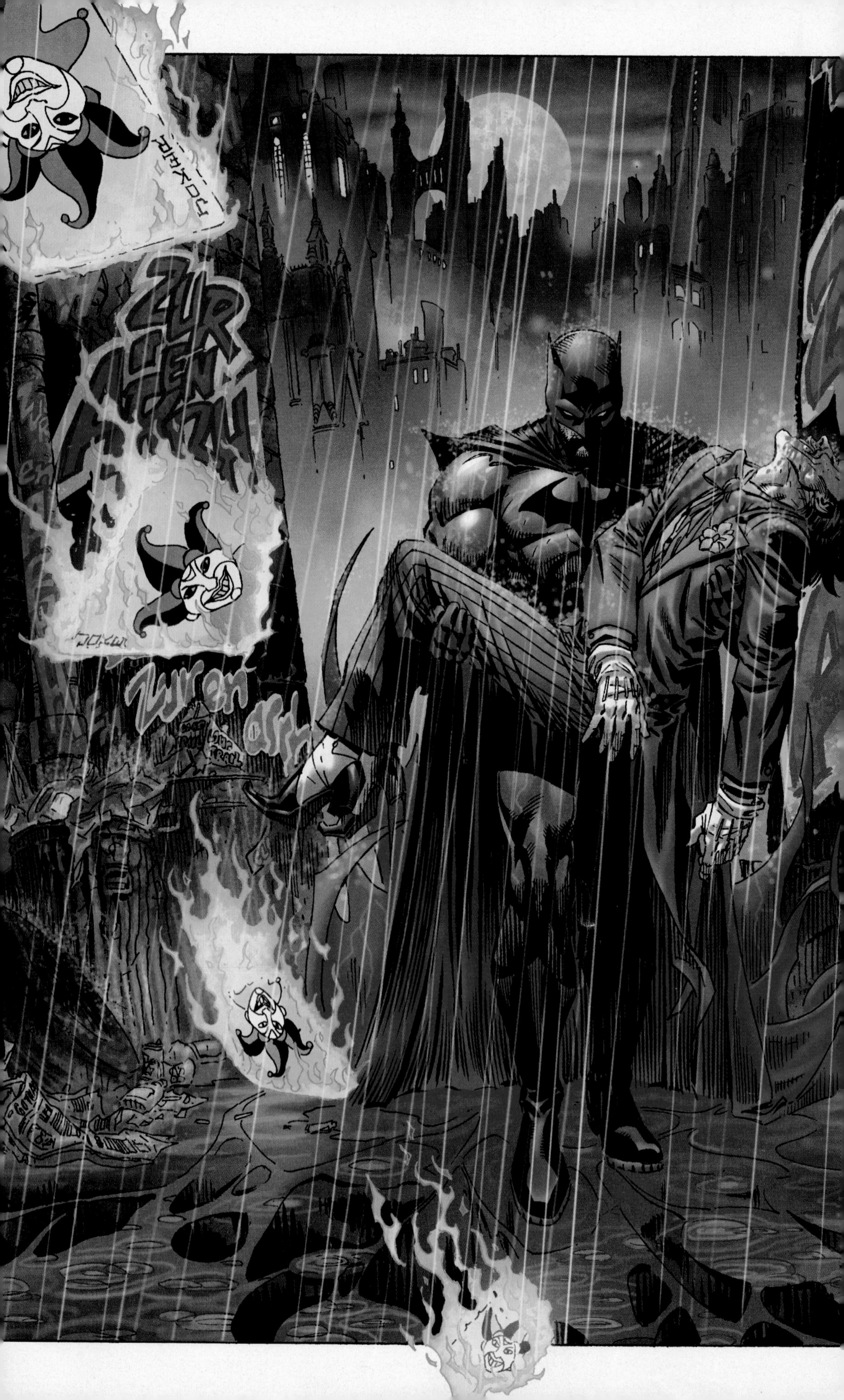
ZUR EN ARRH
Zur en arrh

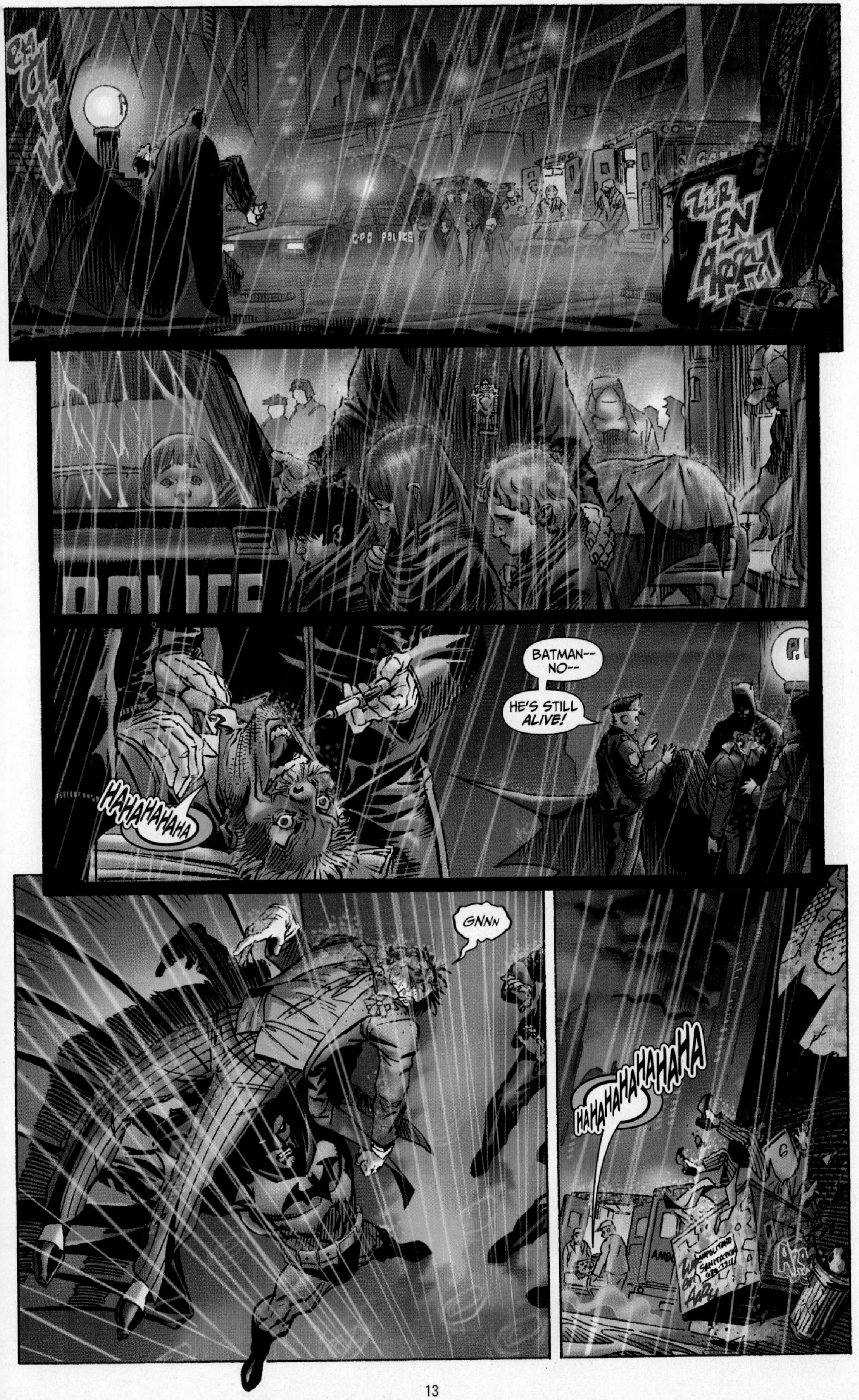

BATMAN--
NO--
HE'S STILL ALIVE!
HAHAHAHAHA
GNNN
HAHAHAHAHAHAHAHA

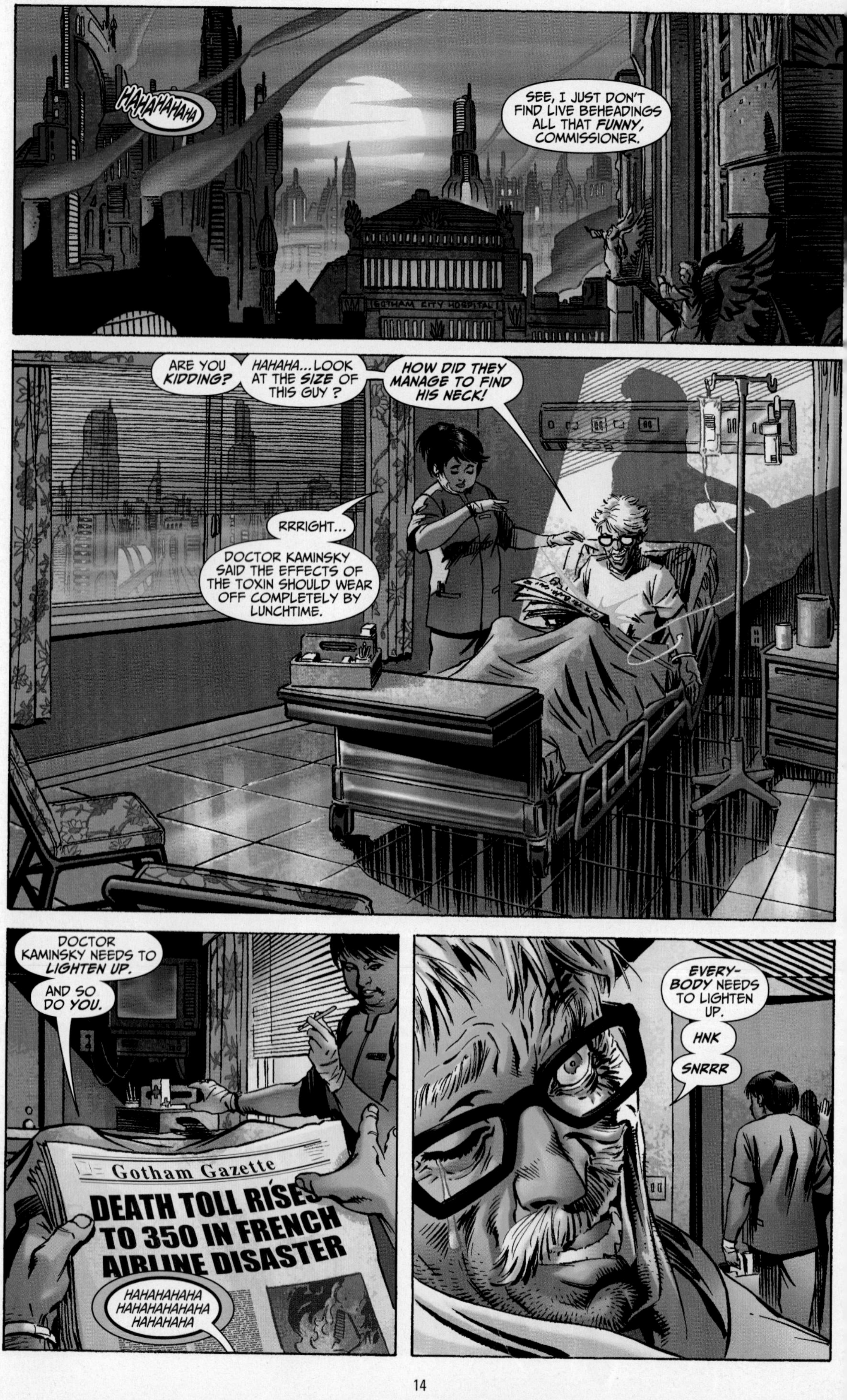
HAHAHAHAHA
SEE, I JUST DON'T FIND LIVE BEHEADINGS ALL THAT FUNNY, COMMISSIONER.
GOTHAM CITY HOSPITAL
ARE YOU KIDDING?
HAHAHA... LOOK AT THE SIZE OF THIS GUY ?
HOW DID THEY MANAGE TO FIND HIS NECK!
RRRIGHT...
DOCTOR KAMINSKY SAID THE EFFECTS OF THE TOXIN SHOULD WEAR OFF COMPLETELY BY LUNCHTIME.
DOCTOR KAMINSKY NEEDS TO LIGHTEN UP.
AND SO DO YOU.
Gotham Gazette
DEATH TOLL RISES TO 350 IN FRENCH AIRLINE DISASTER
HAHAHAHAHA HAHAHAHAHAHA HAHAHAHA
EVERYBODY NEEDS TO LIGHTEN UP.
HNK
SNRRR

JIM.

UH.

IS THAT REALLY YOU? HAS ANYONE EVER TOLD YOU HOW RIDICULOUS YOU LOOK IN THAT GETUP?

THEY DON'T USUALLY GET THE CHANCE.

THOSE KIDS OWE YOU THEIR LIVES, JIM.

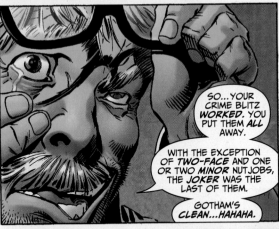

NAH.

NAH, IT WAS THE OTHER GUY, THE NUT IN THE BATMAN SUIT.

EX-COP. SEEMS LIKE HE JUST SNAPPED AND TOOK IT ON HIMSELF TO CLEAN UP THE CITY.

JOKER THOUGHT HE HAD YOU.

FUNNY WHEN YOU THINK ABOUT IT.

EVERYTHING'S FUNNY WHEN YOU THINK ABOUT IT...

...SNICKER...

..SO FUNNY IT HURTS...

SO...YOUR CRIME BLITZ WORKED. YOU PUT THEM ALL AWAY.

WITH THE EXCEPTION OF TWO-FACE AND ONE OR TWO MINOR NUTJOBS, THE JOKER WAS THE LAST OF THEM.

GOTHAM'S CLEAN...HAHAHA.

SO WHAT DO YOU DO NOW?

HAHAHAHA

WHAT DO YOU DO NOW, BATMAN?

HH.

HOW DID THEY FIND HIS NECK?

THAT'S WHAT I JUST SAID.

...DOES THIS MEAN I'M GETTING BETTER OR WORSE?

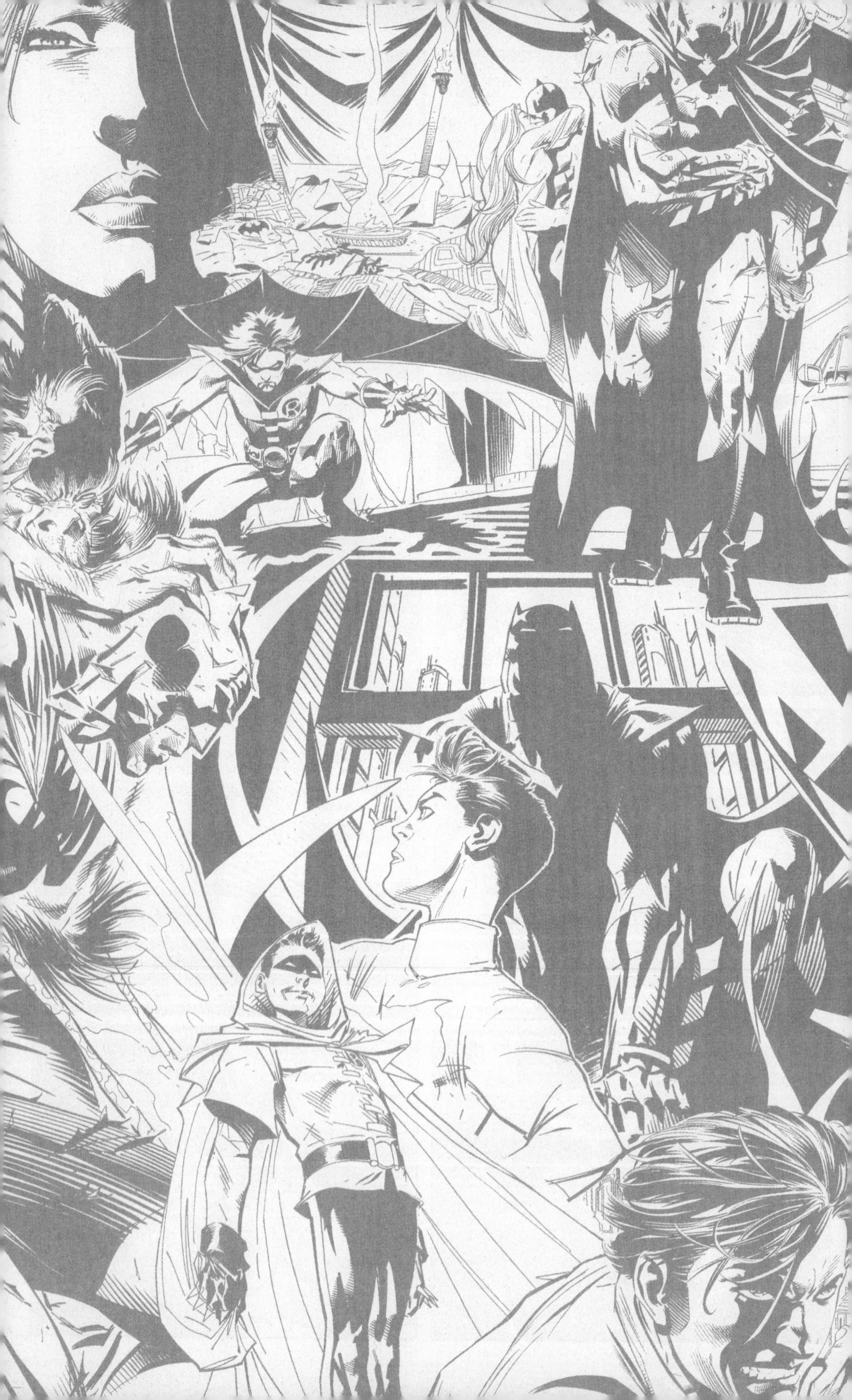

3 PM

5 PM

7 PM

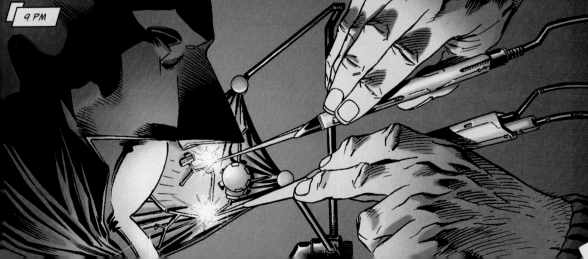

9 PM

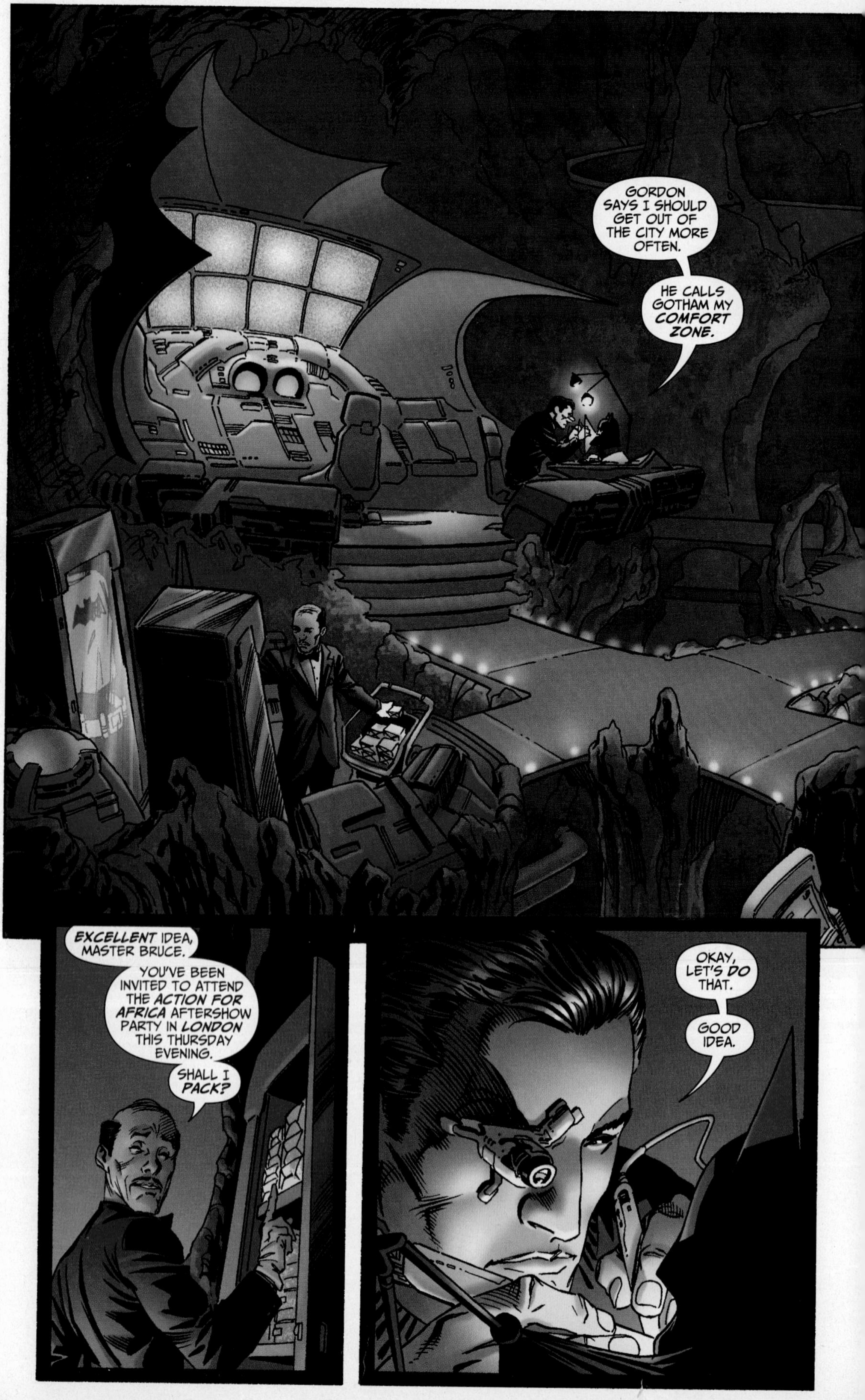
GORDON SAYS I SHOULD GET OUT OF THE CITY MORE OFTEN.
HE CALLS GOTHAM MY COMFORT ZONE.
EXCELLENT IDEA, MASTER BRUCE.
YOU'VE BEEN INVITED TO ATTEND THE ACTION FOR AFRICA AFTERSHOW PARTY IN LONDON THIS THURSDAY EVENING.
SHALL I PACK?
OKAY, LET'S DO THAT.
GOOD IDEA.

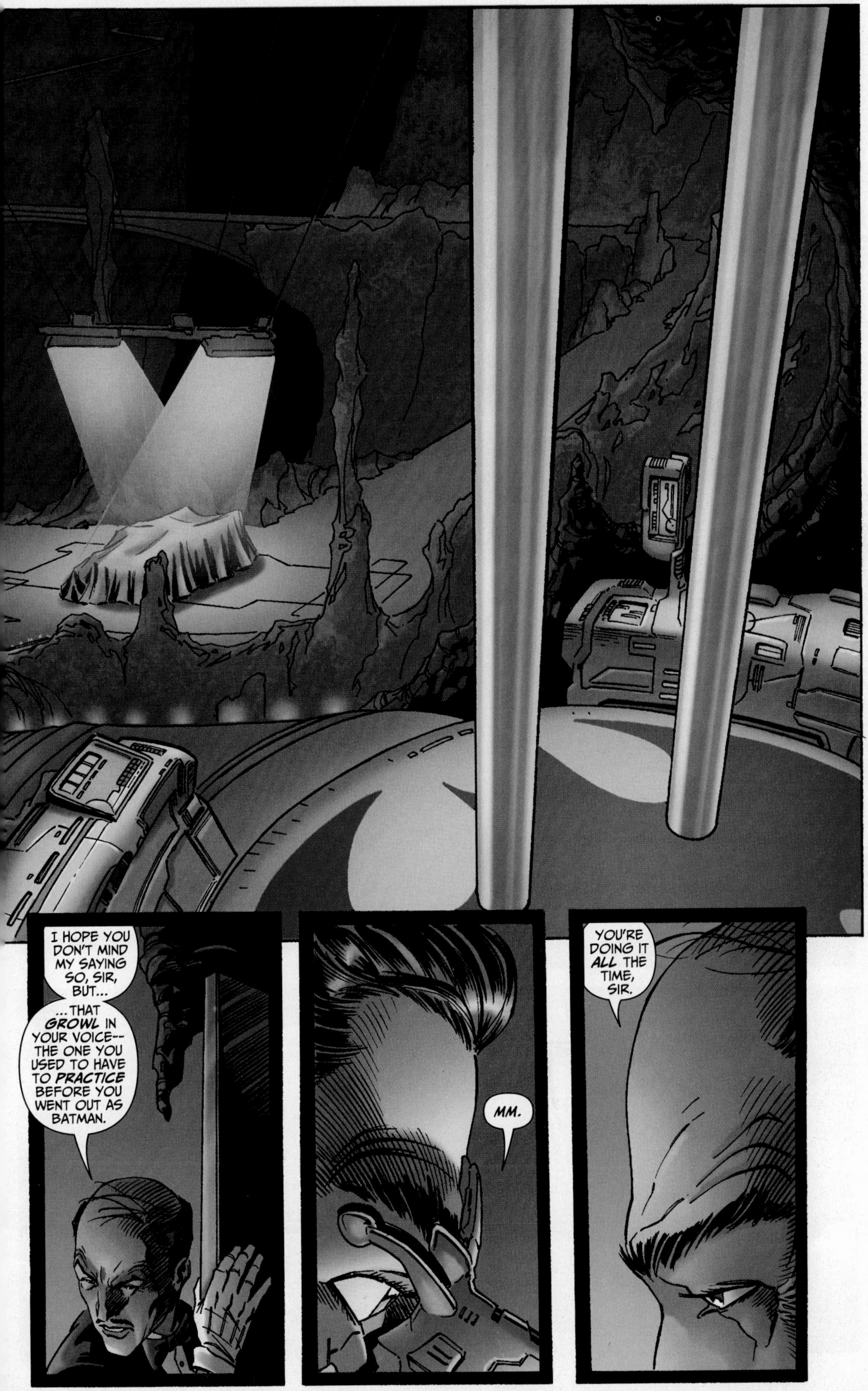
I HOPE YOU DON'T MIND MY SAYING SO, SIR, BUT...
...THAT GROWL IN YOUR VOICE-- THE ONE YOU USED TO HAVE TO PRACTICE BEFORE YOU WENT OUT AS BATMAN.
MM.
YOU'RE DOING IT ALL THE TIME, SIR.

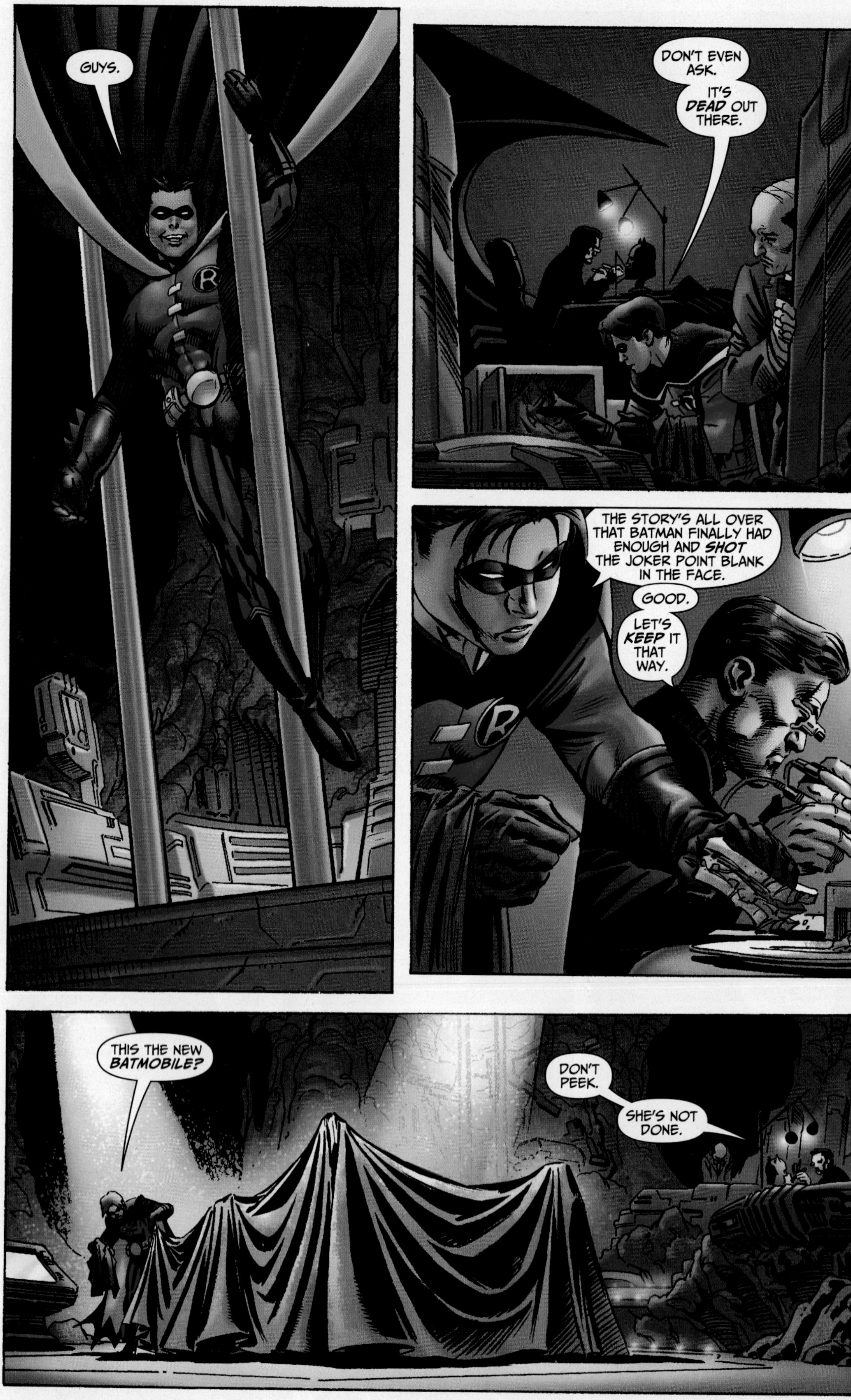

GUYS.
DON'T EVEN ASK.
IT'S *DEAD* OUT THERE.
THE STORY'S ALL OVER THAT BATMAN FINALLY HAD ENOUGH AND *SHOT* THE JOKER POINT BLANK IN THE FACE.
GOOD.
LET'S *KEEP* IT THAT WAY.
THIS THE NEW *BATMOBILE?*
DON'T PEEK.
SHE'S NOT DONE.

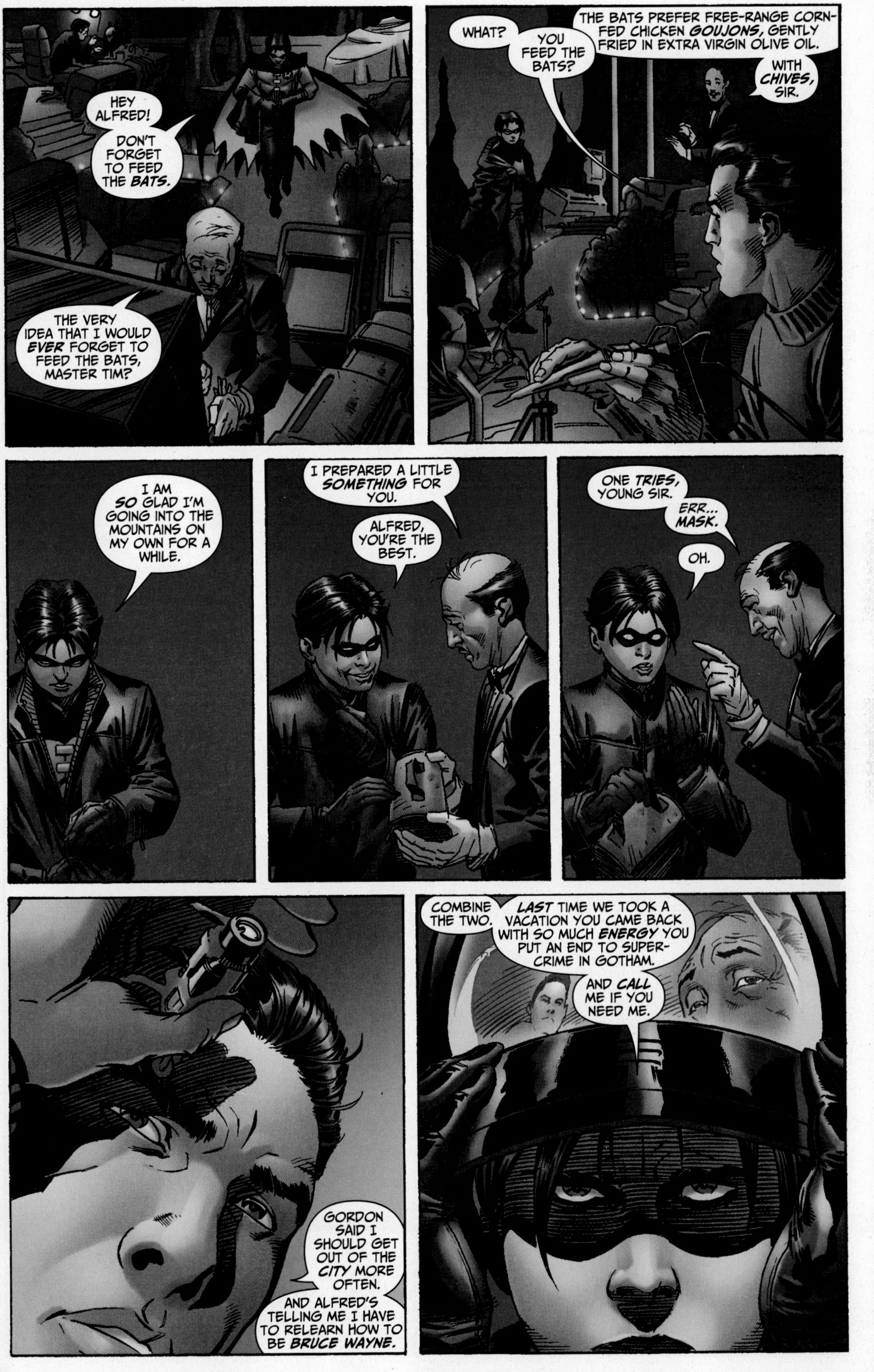
HEY ALFRED!
DON'T FORGET TO FEED THE BATS.
THE VERY IDEA THAT I WOULD EVER FORGET TO FEED THE BATS, MASTER TIM?
WHAT?
YOU FEED THE BATS?
THE BATS PREFER FREE-RANGE CORN-FED CHICKEN GOUJONS, GENTLY FRIED IN EXTRA VIRGIN OLIVE OIL.
WITH CHIVES, SIR.
I AM SO GLAD I'M GOING INTO THE MOUNTAINS ON MY OWN FOR A WHILE.
I PREPARED A LITTLE SOMETHING FOR YOU.
ALFRED, YOU'RE THE BEST.
ONE TRIES, YOUNG SIR.
ERR... MASK.
OH.
GORDON SAID I SHOULD GET OUT OF THE CITY MORE OFTEN.
AND ALFRED'S TELLING ME I HAVE TO RELEARN HOW TO BE BRUCE WAYNE.
COMBINE THE TWO.
LAST TIME WE TOOK A VACATION YOU CAME BACK WITH SO MUCH ENERGY YOU PUT AN END TO SUPER-CRIME IN GOTHAM.
AND CALL ME IF YOU NEED ME.

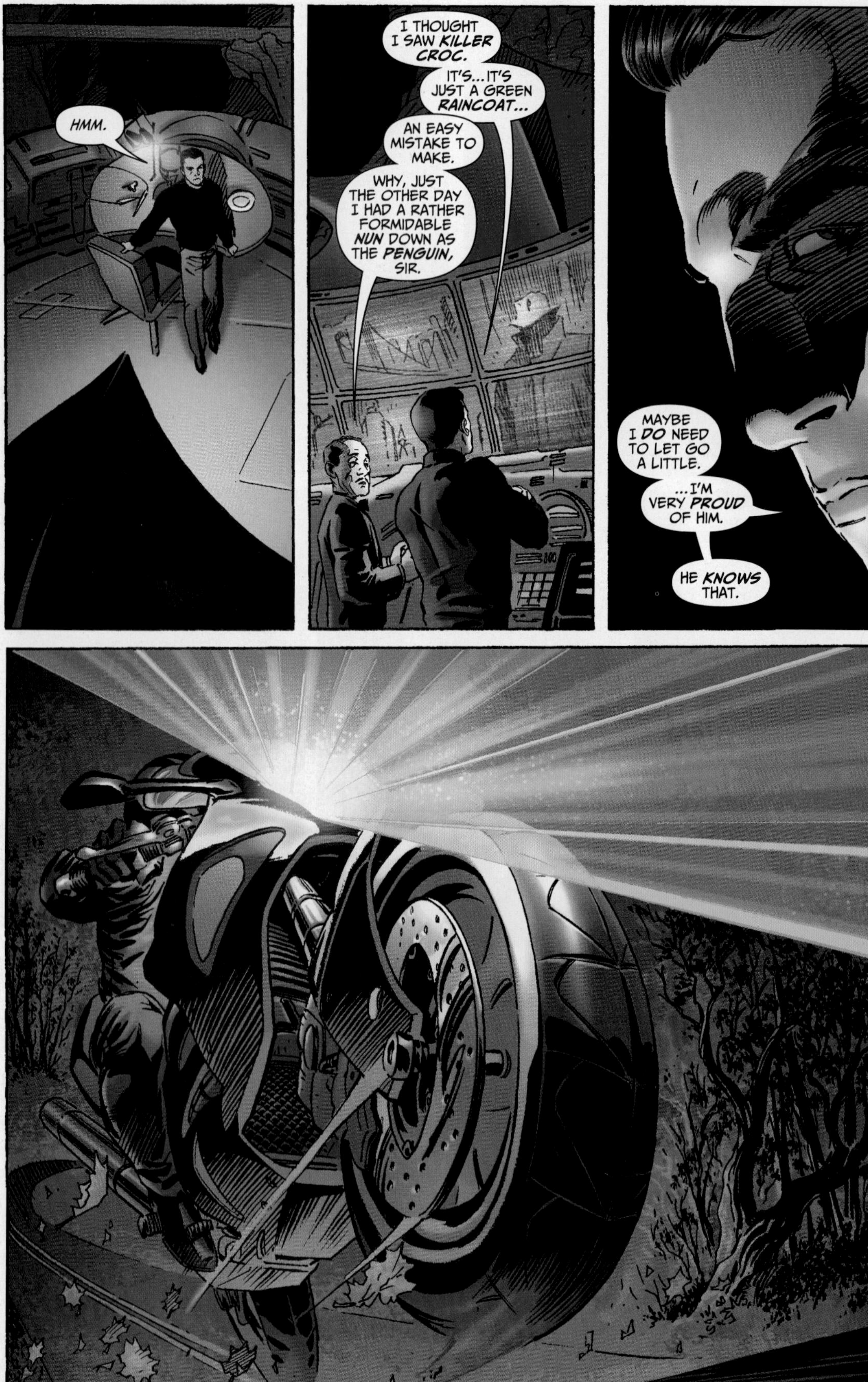
HMM.
I THOUGHT I SAW KILLER CROC.
IT'S...IT'S JUST A GREEN RAINCOAT...
AN EASY MISTAKE TO MAKE.
WHY, JUST THE OTHER DAY I HAD A RATHER FORMIDABLE NUN DOWN AS THE PENGUIN, SIR.
MAYBE I DO NEED TO LET GO A LITTLE.
...I'M VERY PROUD OF HIM.
HE KNOWS THAT.

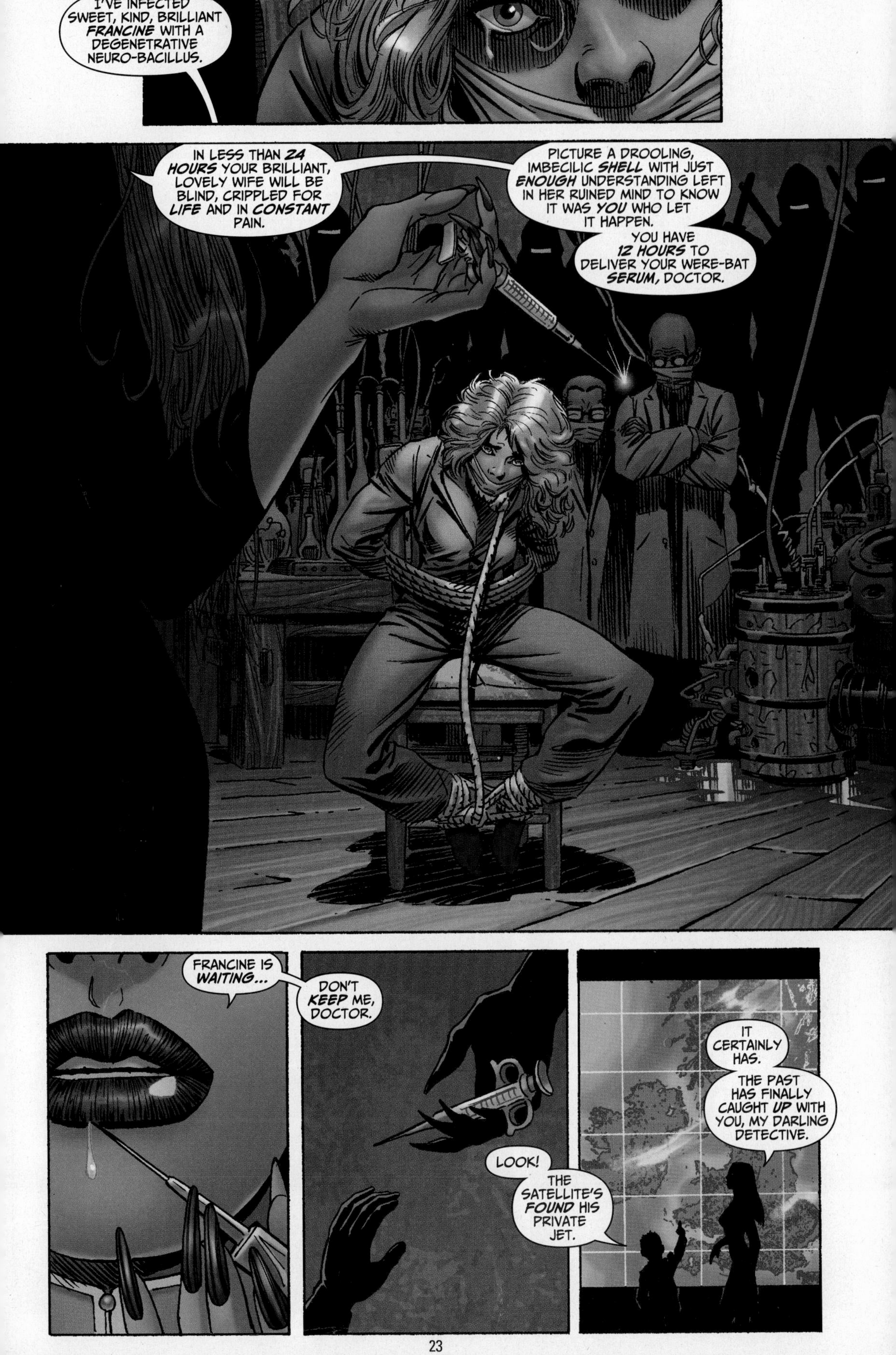
...ARE YOU LISTENING, DOCTOR? I KNOW YOU ARE.
I'VE INFECTED SWEET, KIND, BRILLIANT FRANCINE WITH A DEGENETRATIVE NEURO-BACILLUS.
IN LESS THAN 24 HOURS YOUR BRILLIANT, LOVELY WIFE WILL BE BLIND, CRIPPLED FOR LIFE AND IN CONSTANT PAIN.
PICTURE A DROOLING, IMBECILIC SHELL WITH JUST ENOUGH UNDERSTANDING LEFT IN HER RUINED MIND TO KNOW IT WAS YOU WHO LET IT HAPPEN.
YOU HAVE 12 HOURS TO DELIVER YOUR WERE-BAT SERUM, DOCTOR.
FRANCINE IS WAITING...
DON'T KEEP ME, DOCTOR.
LOOK! THE SATELLITE'S FOUND HIS PRIVATE JET.
IT CERTAINLY HAS.
THE PAST HAS FINALLY CAUGHT UP WITH YOU, MY DARLING DETECTIVE.

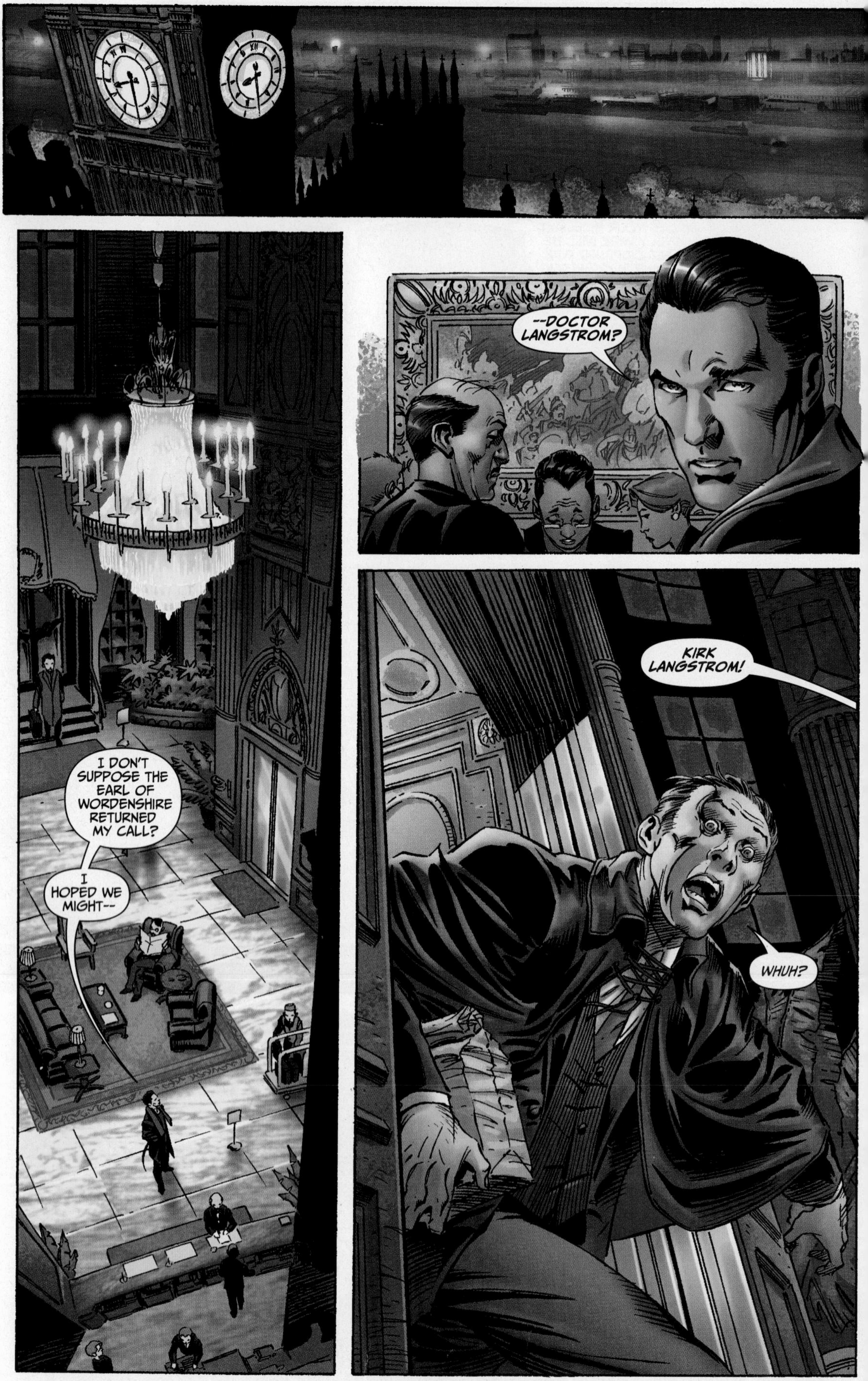
I DON'T SUPPOSE THE EARL OF WORDENSHIRE RETURNED MY CALL?
I HOPED WE MIGHT--
--DOCTOR LANGSTROM?
KIRK LANGSTROM!
WHUH?

KIRK. YOU'RE HERE WITH *ACTION FOR AFRICA*, RIGHT?

BRUCE... BRUCE WAYNE...

ERR...YES, YES... MY WIFE AND I ARE BOTH VERY ACTIVE IN THE... ERR...THE WHOLE *CHARITY* THING...

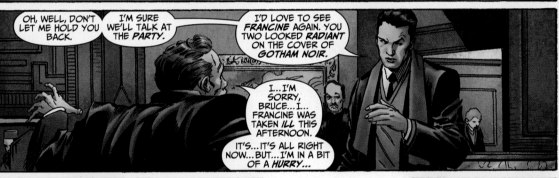

OH, WELL, DON'T LET ME HOLD YOU BACK.

I'M SURE WE'LL TALK AT THE *PARTY*.

I'D LOVE TO SEE *FRANCINE* AGAIN. YOU TWO LOOKED *RADIANT* ON THE COVER OF *GOTHAM NOIR*.

I...I'M SORRY, BRUCE...I... FRANCINE WAS TAKEN *ILL* THIS AFTERNOON.

IT'S...IT'S ALL RIGHT NOW...BUT...I'M IN A BIT OF A *HURRY*...

GINGER BEER. HER *FAVORITE*.

IF THERE'S ANYTHING WE CAN DO...

I'LL SEND *ALFRED*.

OH, NO, NO, NO.

THAT'S *SO* KIND OF YOU, BRUCE, BUT I KNOW YOU'LL BOTH BE *TIRED*, AND I....

I HAVE MY *OWN* TRANSPORTATION WORKED OUT.

ANY WAY...VISITING STARTS AT *SEVEN PM.*

MUST FLY.

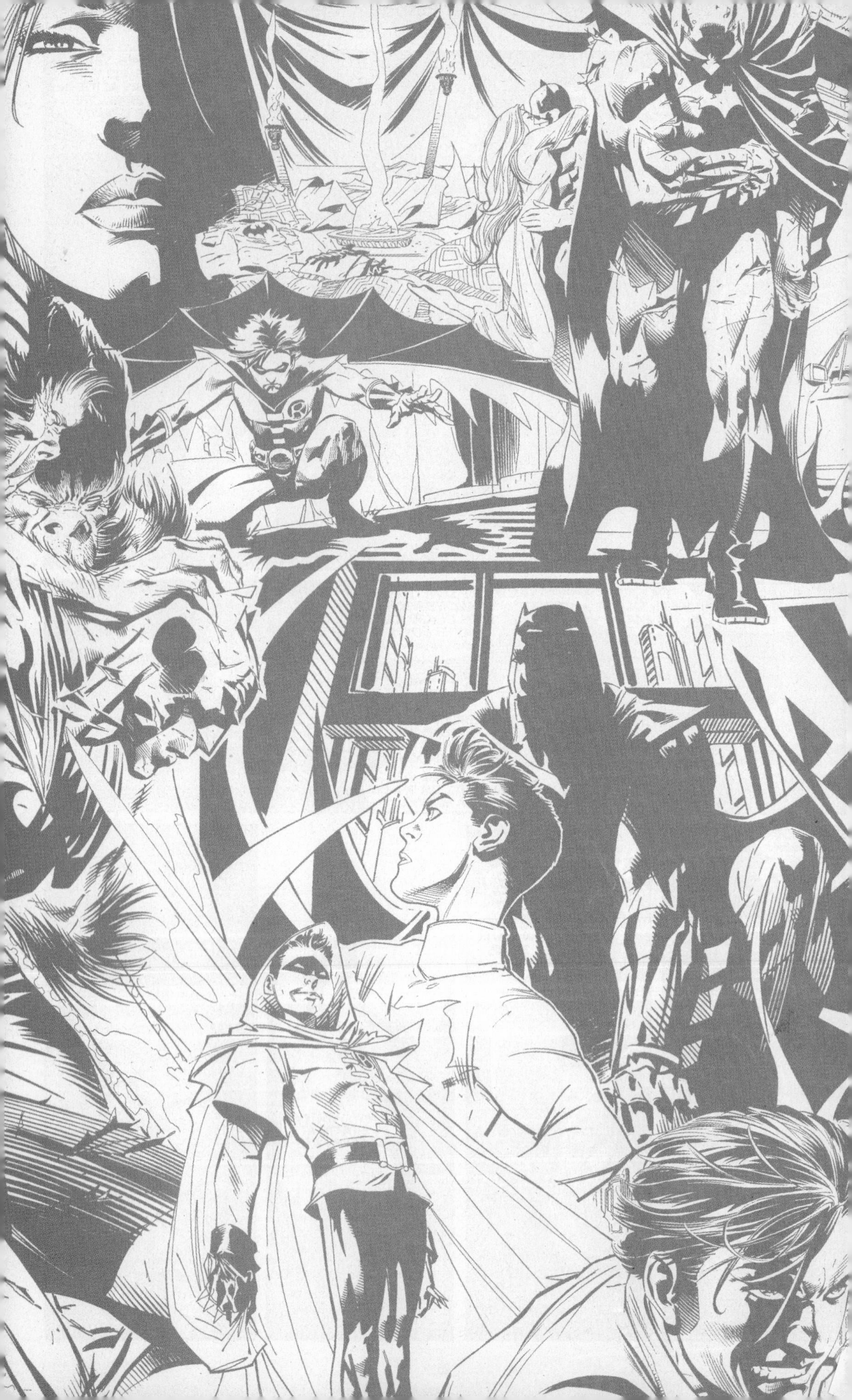

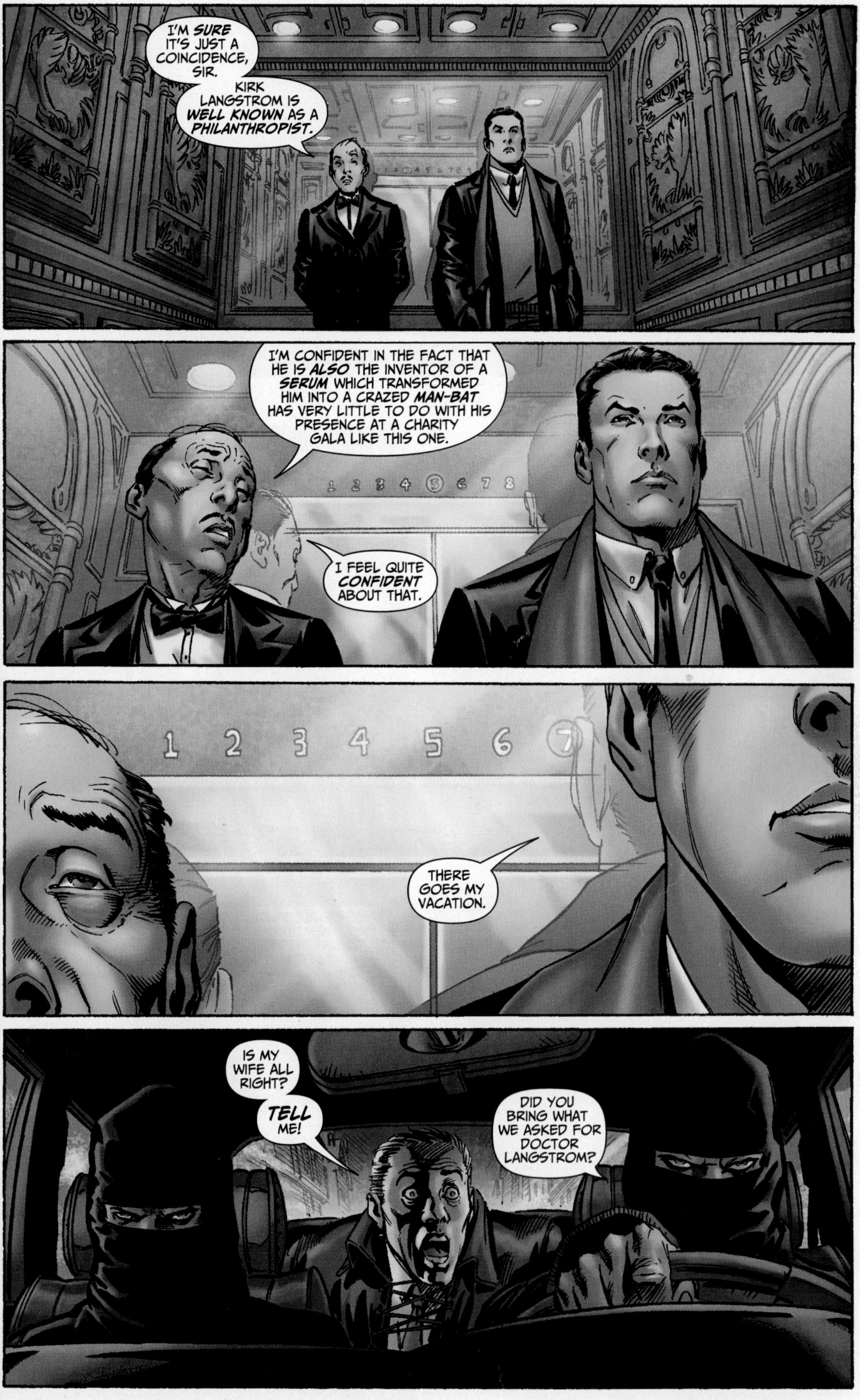
I'M SURE IT'S JUST A COINCIDENCE, SIR.
KIRK LANGSTROM IS WELL KNOWN AS A PHILANTHROPIST.
I'M CONFIDENT IN THE FACT THAT HE IS ALSO THE INVENTOR OF A SERUM WHICH TRANSFORMED HIM INTO A CRAZED MAN-BAT HAS VERY LITTLE TO DO WITH HIS PRESENCE AT A CHARITY GALA LIKE THIS ONE.
I FEEL QUITE CONFIDENT ABOUT THAT.
THERE GOES MY VACATION.
IS MY WIFE ALL RIGHT?
TELL ME!
DID YOU BRING WHAT WE ASKED FOR DOCTOR LANGSTROM?

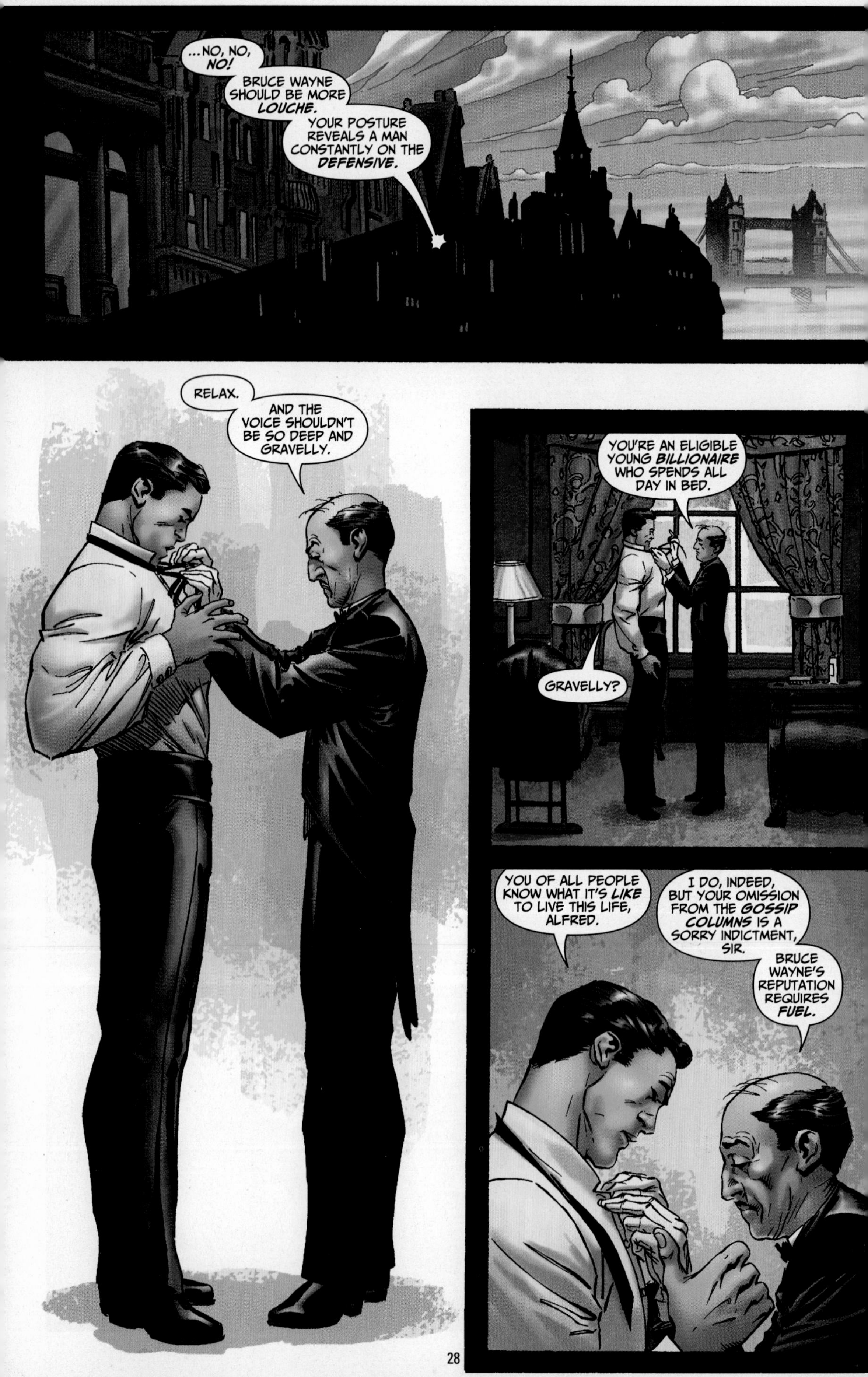

...NO, NO, NO!
BRUCE WAYNE SHOULD BE MORE LOUCHE.
YOUR POSTURE REVEALS A MAN CONSTANTLY ON THE DEFENSIVE.
RELAX.
AND THE VOICE SHOULDN'T BE SO DEEP AND GRAVELLY.
YOU'RE AN ELIGIBLE YOUNG BILLIONAIRE WHO SPENDS ALL DAY IN BED.
GRAVELLY?
YOU OF ALL PEOPLE KNOW WHAT IT'S LIKE TO LIVE THIS LIFE, ALFRED.
I DO, INDEED, BUT YOUR OMISSION FROM THE GOSSIP COLUMNS IS A SORRY INDICTMENT, SIR.
BRUCE WAYNE'S REPUTATION REQUIRES FUEL.

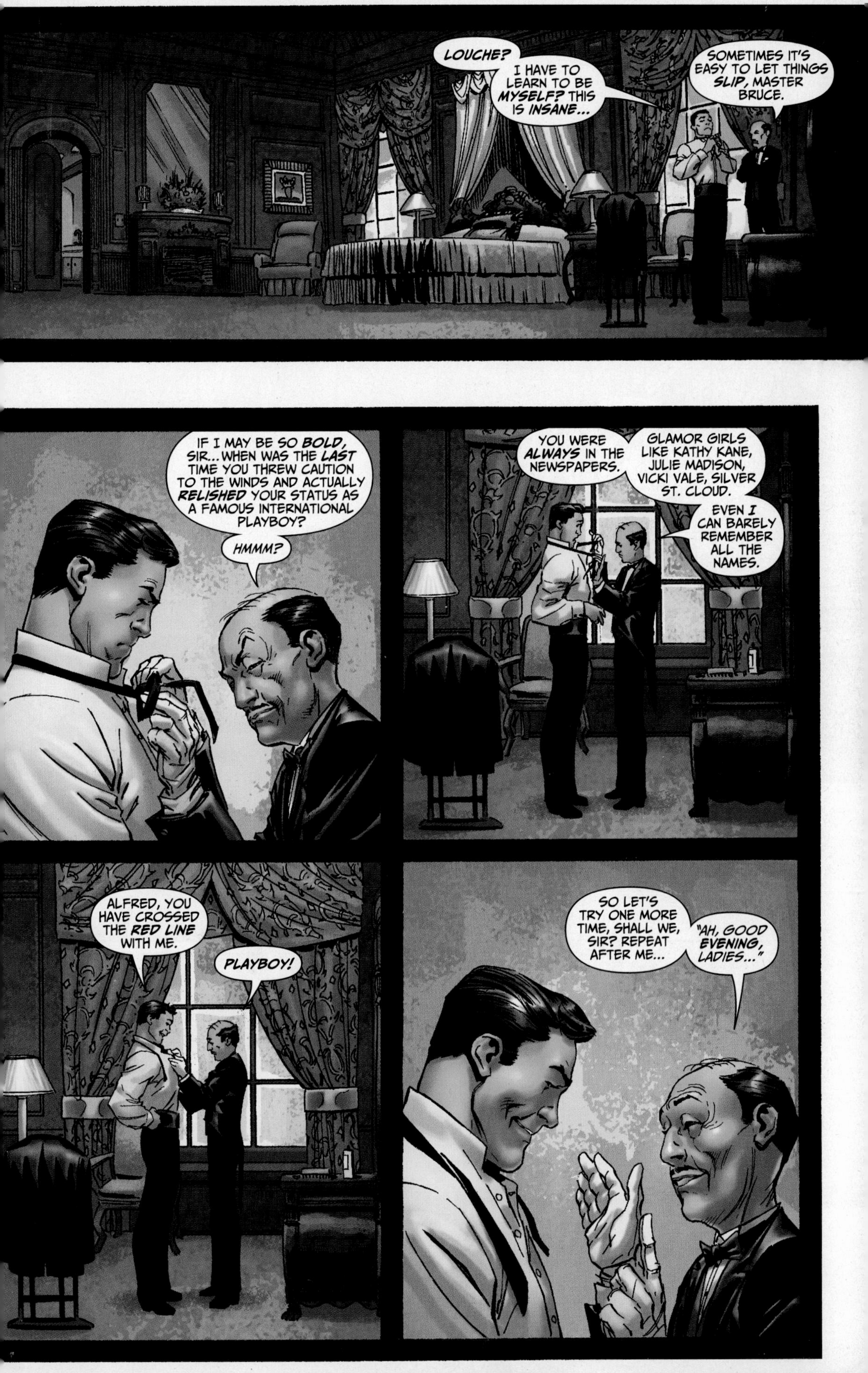

LOUCHE? I HAVE TO LEARN TO BE MYSELF? THIS IS INSANE...
SOMETIMES IT'S EASY TO LET THINGS SLIP, MASTER BRUCE.
IF I MAY BE SO BOLD, SIR...WHEN WAS THE LAST TIME YOU THREW CAUTION TO THE WINDS AND ACTUALLY RELISHED YOUR STATUS AS A FAMOUS INTERNATIONAL PLAYBOY?
HMMM?
YOU WERE ALWAYS IN THE NEWSPAPERS.
GLAMOR GIRLS LIKE KATHY KANE, JULIE MADISON, VICKI VALE, SILVER ST. CLOUD.
EVEN I CAN BARELY REMEMBER ALL THE NAMES.
ALFRED, YOU HAVE CROSSED THE RED LINE WITH ME.
PLAYBOY!
SO LET'S TRY ONE MORE TIME, SHALL WE, SIR? REPEAT AFTER ME...
"AH, GOOD EVENING, LADIES..."

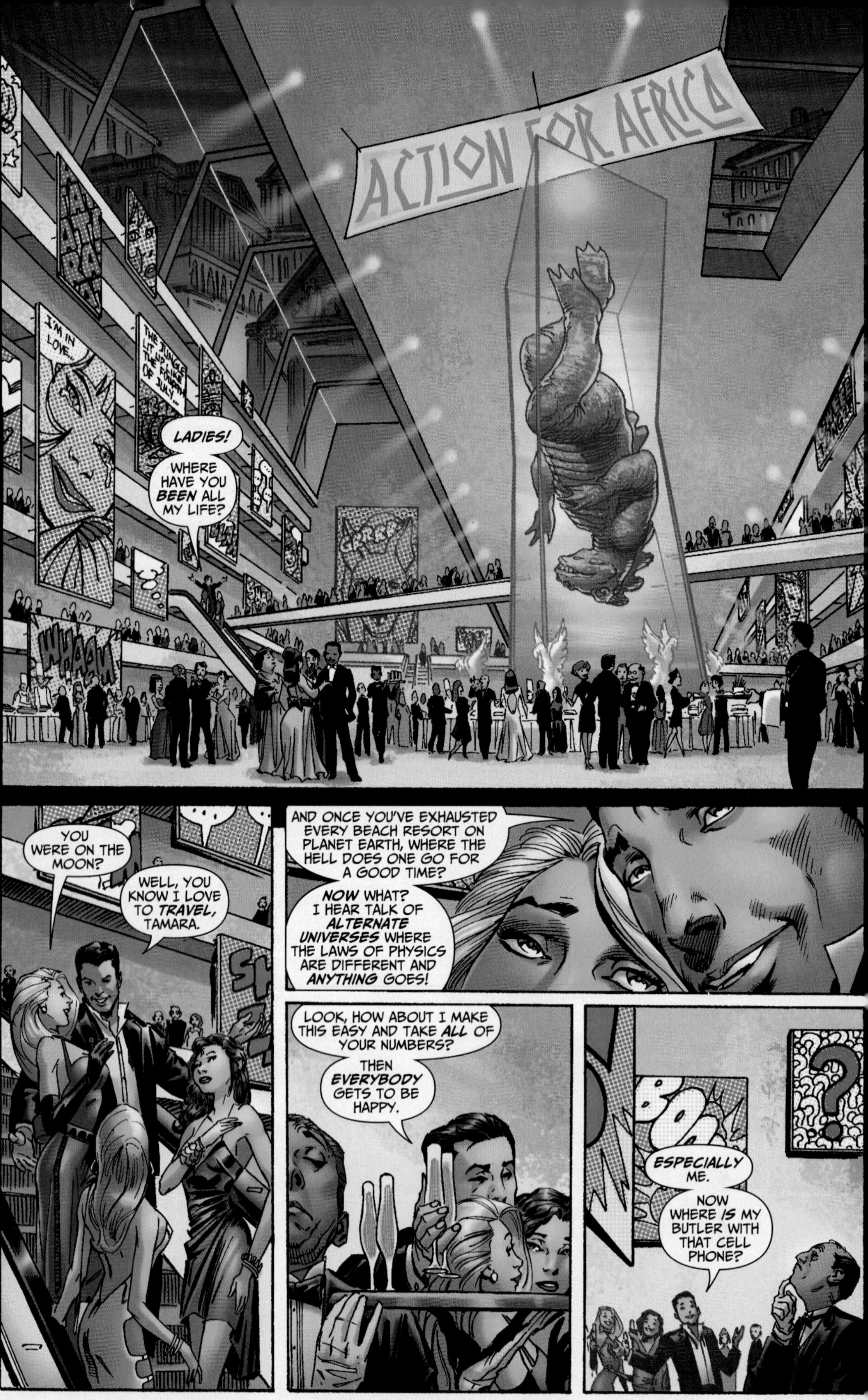
ACTION FOR AFRICA
I'M IN LOVE...
THE JUNGLE LIT UP LIKE THE FOURTH OF JULY...
LADIES!
WHERE HAVE YOU BEEN ALL MY LIFE?
YOU WERE ON THE MOON?
WELL, YOU KNOW I LOVE TO TRAVEL, TAMARA.
AND ONCE YOU'VE EXHAUSTED EVERY BEACH RESORT ON PLANET EARTH, WHERE THE HELL DOES ONE GO FOR A GOOD TIME?
NOW WHAT? I HEAR TALK OF ALTERNATE UNIVERSES WHERE THE LAWS OF PHYSICS ARE DIFFERENT AND ANYTHING GOES!
LOOK, HOW ABOUT I MAKE THIS EASY AND TAKE ALL OF YOUR NUMBERS?
THEN EVERYBODY GETS TO BE HAPPY.
ESPECIALLY ME.
NOW WHERE IS MY BUTLER WITH THAT CELL PHONE?

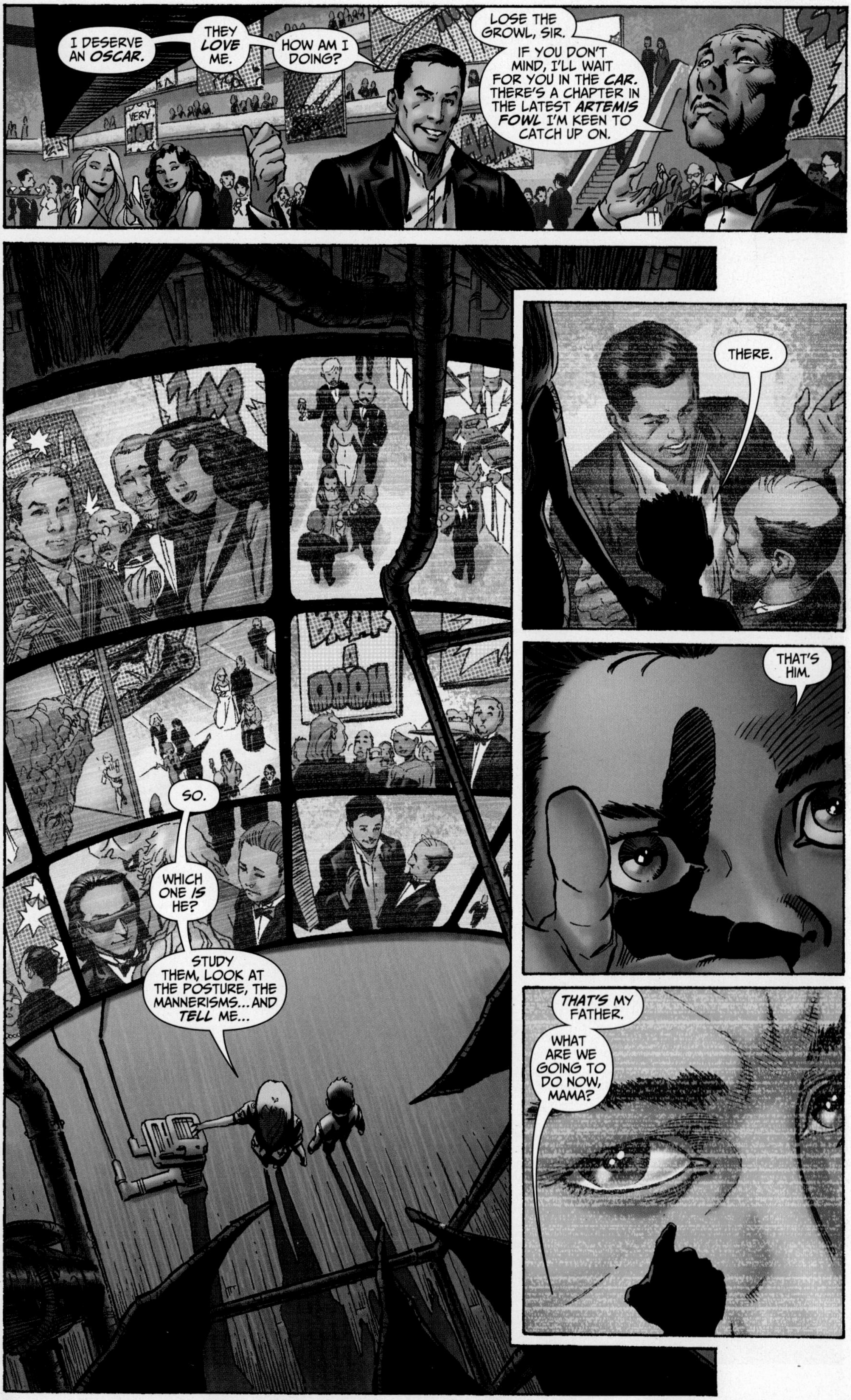
I DESERVE AN OSCAR.
THEY LOVE ME.
HOW AM I DOING?
LOSE THE GROWL, SIR.
IF YOU DON'T MIND, I'LL WAIT FOR YOU IN THE CAR. THERE'S A CHAPTER IN THE LATEST ARTEMIS FOWL I'M KEEN TO CATCH UP ON.
SO.
WHICH ONE IS HE?
STUDY THEM, LOOK AT THE POSTURE, THE MANNERISMS... AND TELL ME...
THERE.
THAT'S HIM.
THAT'S MY FATHER.
WHAT ARE WE GOING TO DO NOW, MAMA?

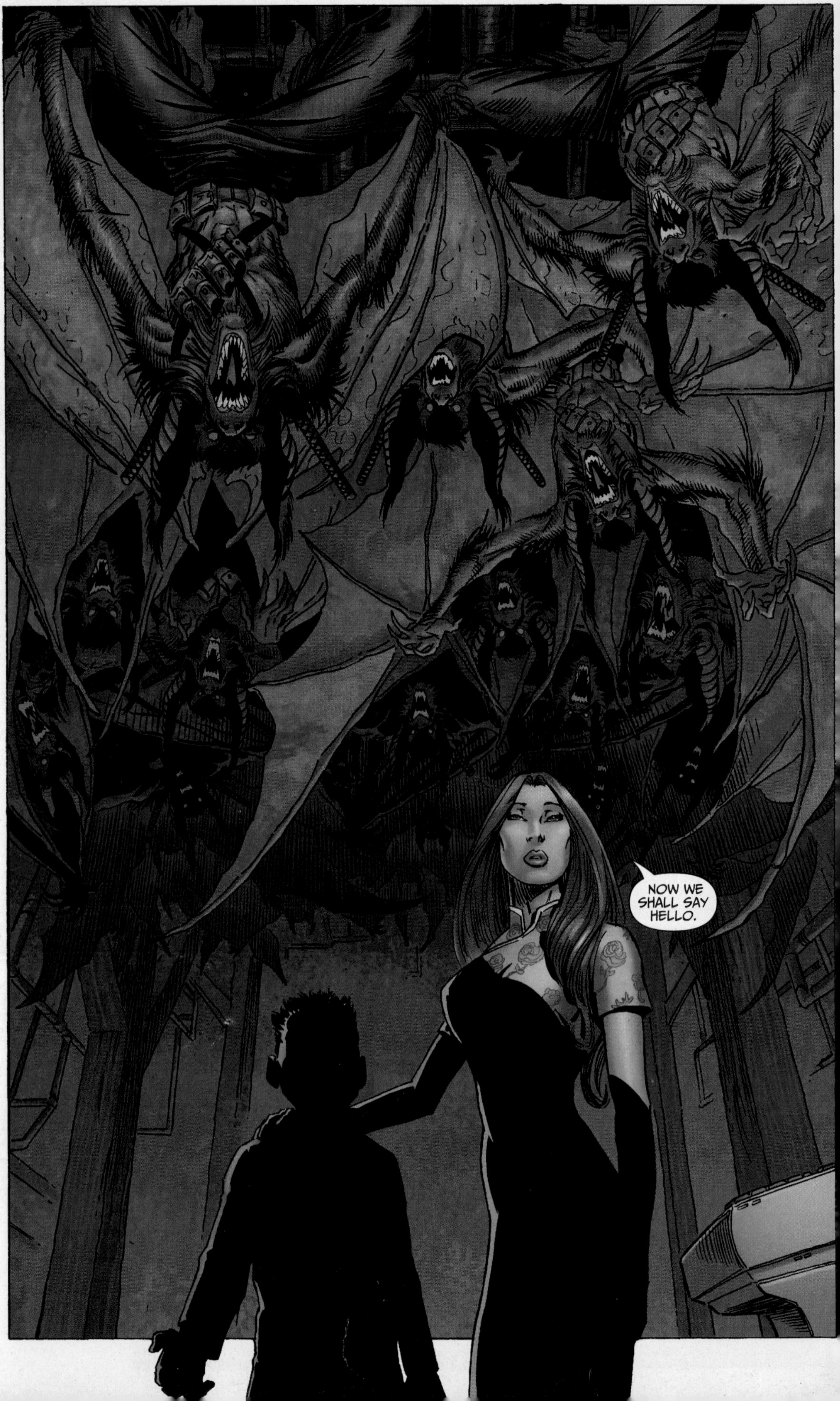
NOW WE SHALL SAY HELLO.

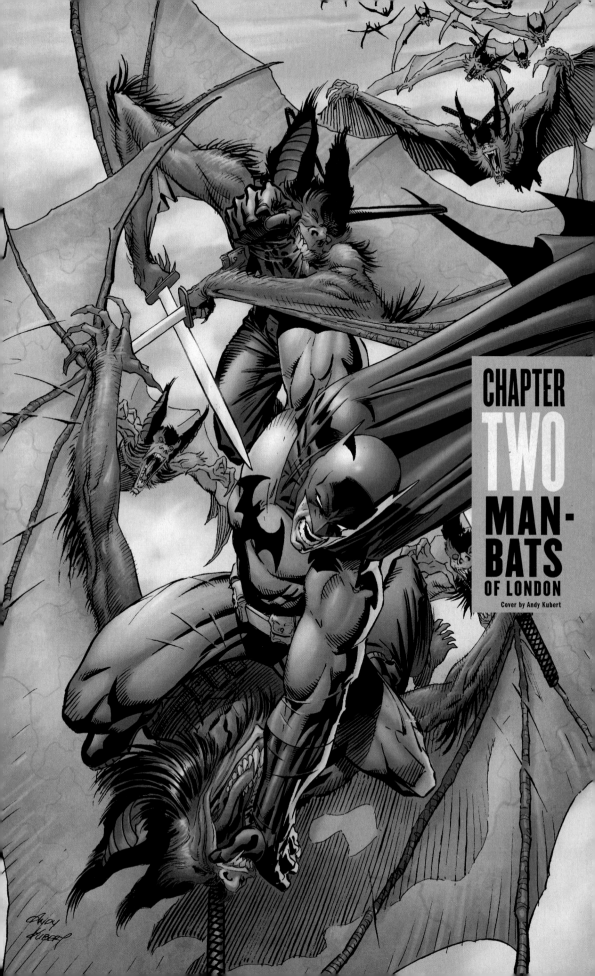

CHAPTER
TWO

MAN-
BATS
OF LONDON

Cover by Andy Kubert

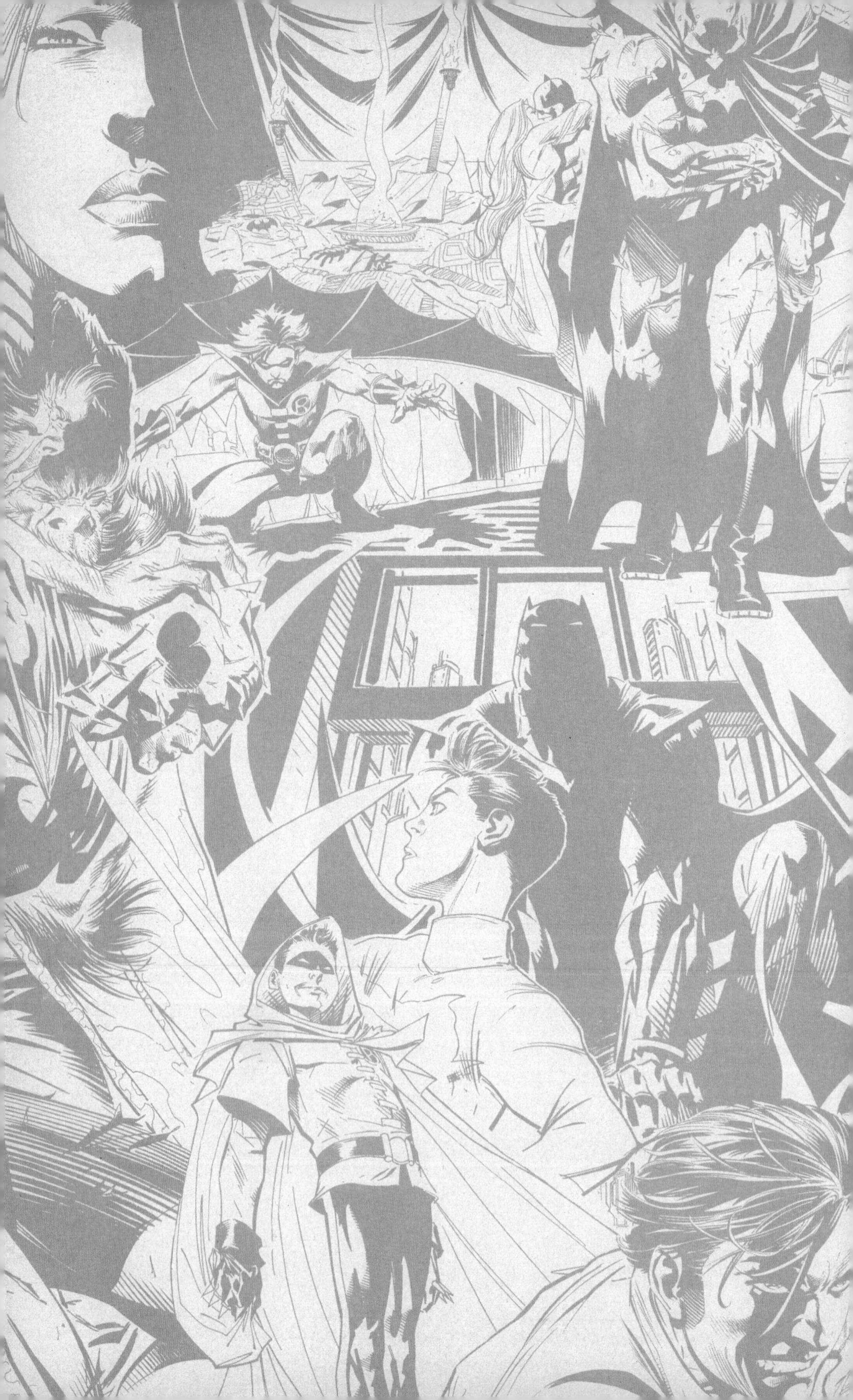

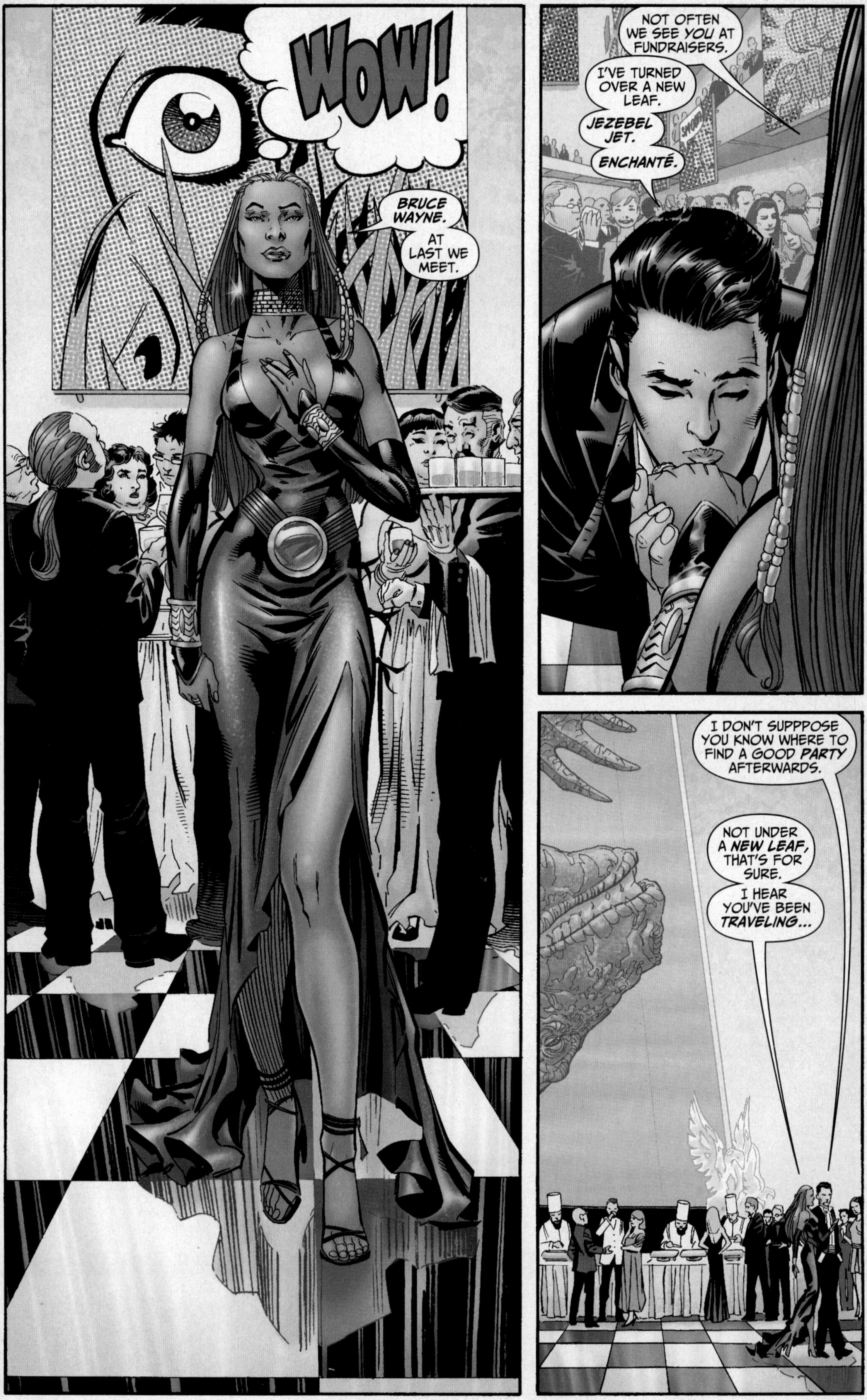
WOW!
BRUCE WAYNE.
AT LAST WE MEET.
NOT OFTEN WE SEE YOU AT FUNDRAISERS.
I'VE TURNED OVER A NEW LEAF.
JEZEBEL JET.
ENCHANTÉ.
I DON'T SUPPPOSE YOU KNOW WHERE TO FIND A GOOD PARTY AFTERWARDS.
NOT UNDER A NEW LEAF, THAT'S FOR SURE.
I HEAR YOU'VE BEEN TRAVELING...

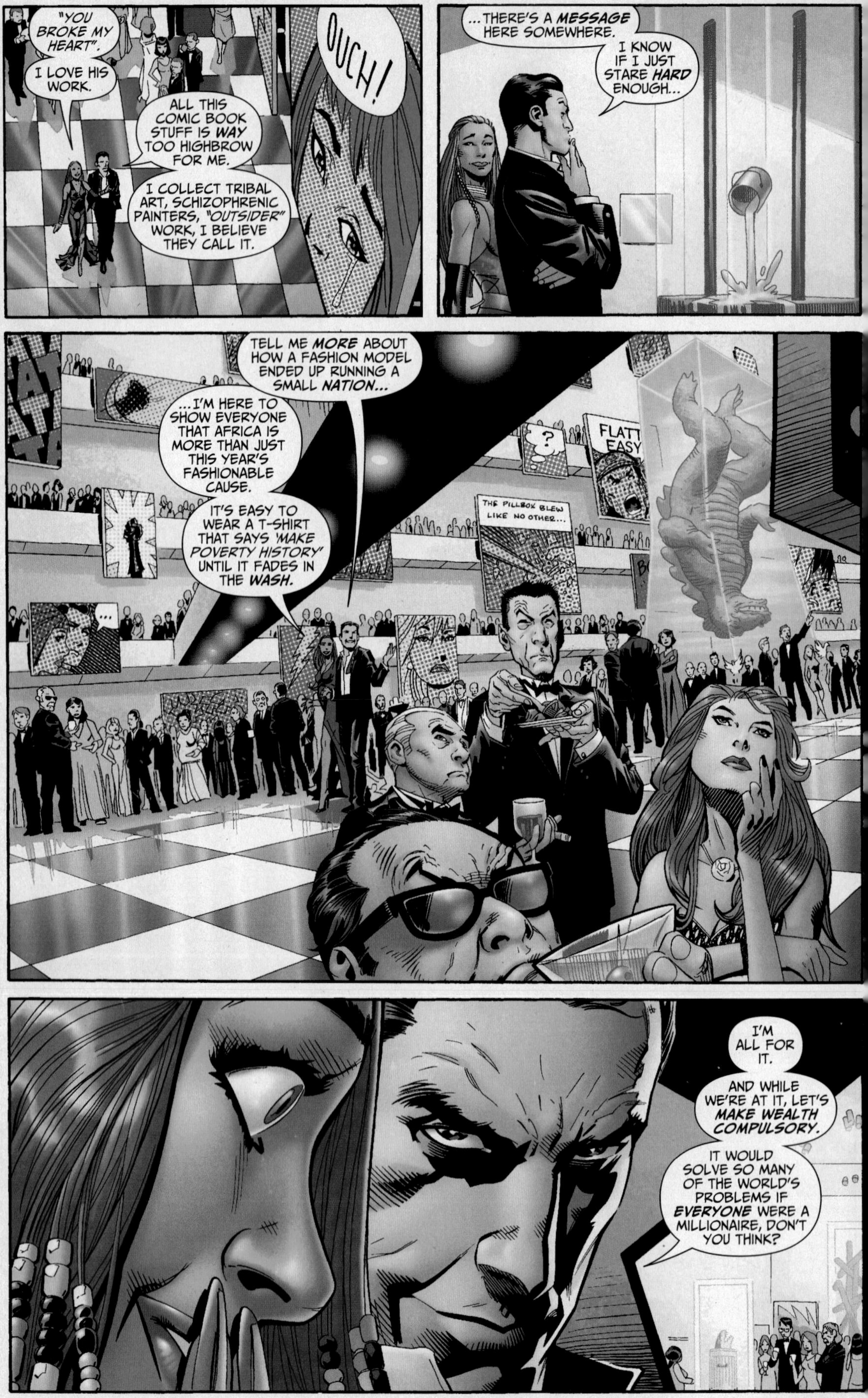
"YOU BROKE MY HEART".
I LOVE HIS WORK.
OUCH!
ALL THIS COMIC BOOK STUFF IS WAY TOO HIGHBROW FOR ME.
I COLLECT TRIBAL ART, SCHIZOPHRENIC PAINTERS, "OUTSIDER" WORK, I BELIEVE THEY CALL IT.
...THERE'S A MESSAGE HERE SOMEWHERE.
I KNOW IF I JUST STARE HARD ENOUGH...
TELL ME MORE ABOUT HOW A FASHION MODEL ENDED UP RUNNING A SMALL NATION...
...I'M HERE TO SHOW EVERYONE THAT AFRICA IS MORE THAN JUST THIS YEAR'S FASHIONABLE CAUSE.
IT'S EASY TO WEAR A T-SHIRT THAT SAYS 'MAKE POVERTY HISTORY' UNTIL IT FADES IN THE WASH.
THE PILLBOX BLEW LIKE NO OTHER...
I'M ALL FOR IT.
AND WHILE WE'RE AT IT, LET'S MAKE WEALTH COMPULSORY.
IT WOULD SOLVE SO MANY OF THE WORLD'S PROBLEMS IF EVERYONE WERE A MILLIONAIRE, DON'T YOU THINK?

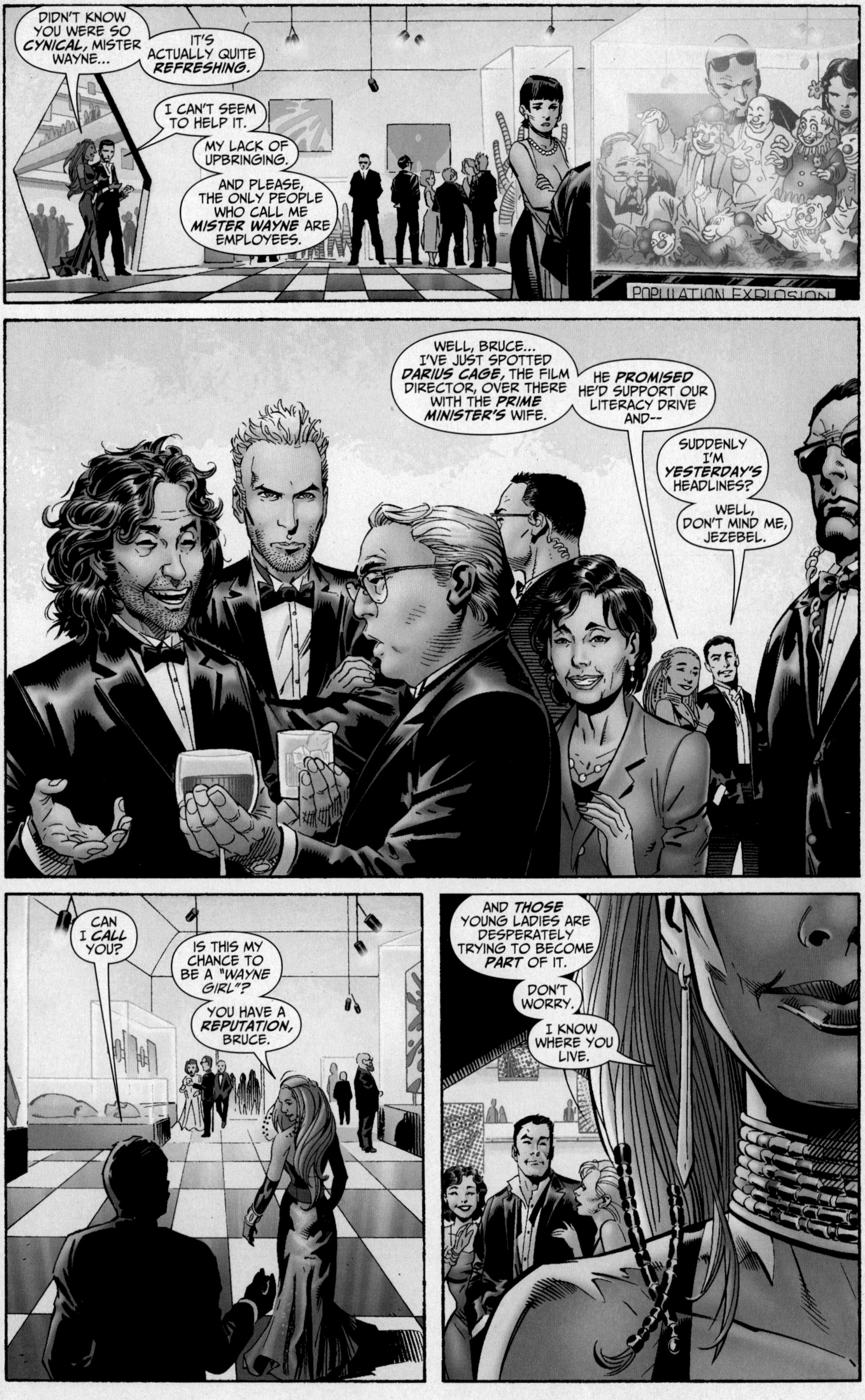
DIDN'T KNOW YOU WERE SO CYNICAL, MISTER WAYNE...
IT'S ACTUALLY QUITE REFRESHING.
I CAN'T SEEM TO HELP IT.
MY LACK OF UPBRINGING.
AND PLEASE, THE ONLY PEOPLE WHO CALL ME MISTER WAYNE ARE EMPLOYEES.
POPULATION EXPLOSION
WELL, BRUCE... I'VE JUST SPOTTED DARIUS CAGE, THE FILM DIRECTOR, OVER THERE WITH THE PRIME MINISTER'S WIFE.
HE PROMISED HE'D SUPPORT OUR LITERACY DRIVE AND--
SUDDENLY I'M YESTERDAY'S HEADLINES?
WELL, DON'T MIND ME, JEZEBEL.
CAN I CALL YOU?
IS THIS MY CHANCE TO BE A "WAYNE GIRL"?
YOU HAVE A REPUTATION, BRUCE.
AND THOSE YOUNG LADIES ARE DESPERATELY TRYING TO BECOME PART OF IT.
DON'T WORRY.
I KNOW WHERE YOU LIVE.

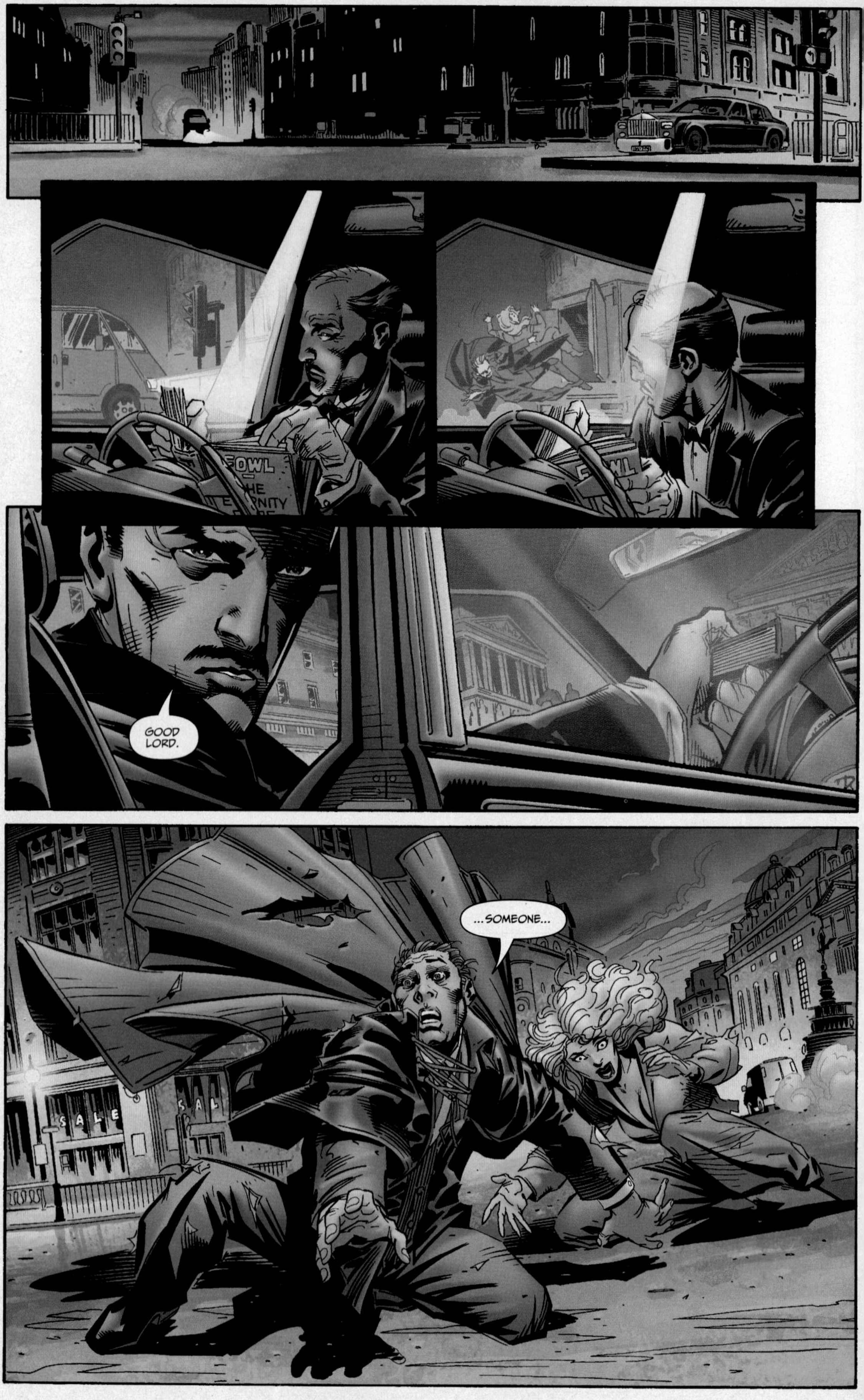
FOWL
THE ETERNITY
FOWL
GOOD LORD.
SALE
...SOMEONE...

PROFESSOR LANGSTROM?

LET ME *HELP* YOU.

YOU... YOU'RE BRUCE WAYNE'S *BUTLER,* AREN'T YOU?

YOU HAVE TO TELL THEM ALL TO *RUN!*

TELL THEM TO *HIDE!*

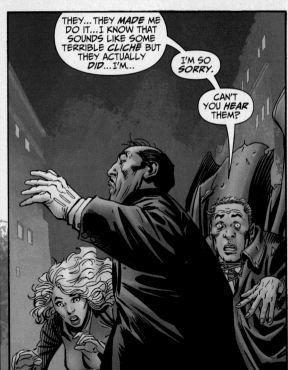

THEY...THEY *MADE* ME DO IT...I KNOW THAT SOUNDS LIKE SOME TERRIBLE *CLICHÉ* BUT THEY ACTUALLY *DID*...I'M...

I'M SO *SORRY.*

CAN'T YOU *HEAR* THEM?

FIT?

I DO *THREE HOURS* A DAY IN THE GYM, AS A MATTER OF FACT.

CAN YOU PLEASE *EXCUSE* ME FOR JUST *FIVE* MINUTES...MY BUTLER'S THE ONLY ONE WHO KNOWS HOW TO MAKE THE *CELLPHONE* WORK.

I GAVE THEM MY *MAN-BAT* SERUM!

I *HAD* TO!

GOD FORGIVE ME!

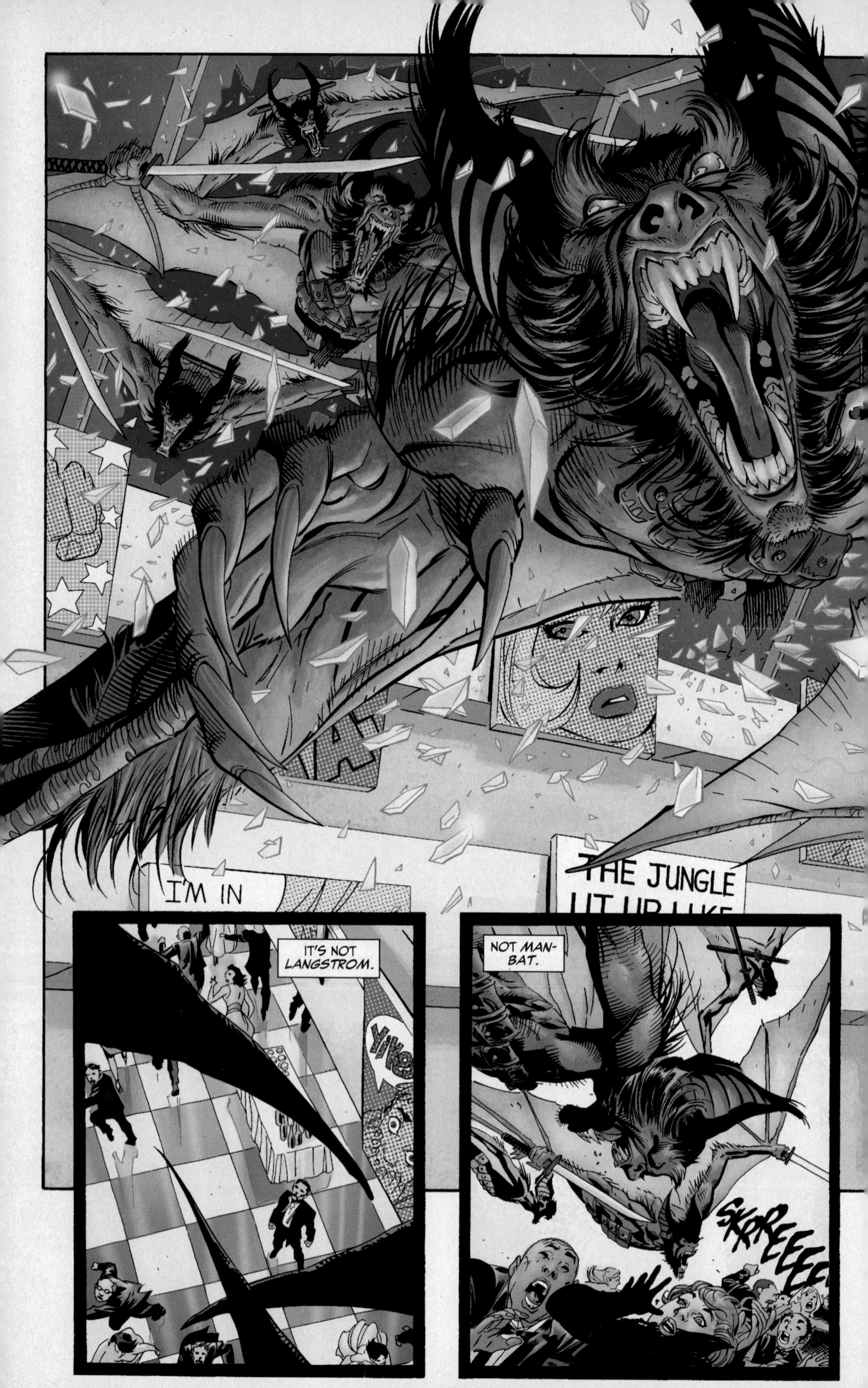
I'M IN
THE JUNGLE
IT'S NOT LANGSTROM.
NOT MAN-BAT.
SKREEEEE

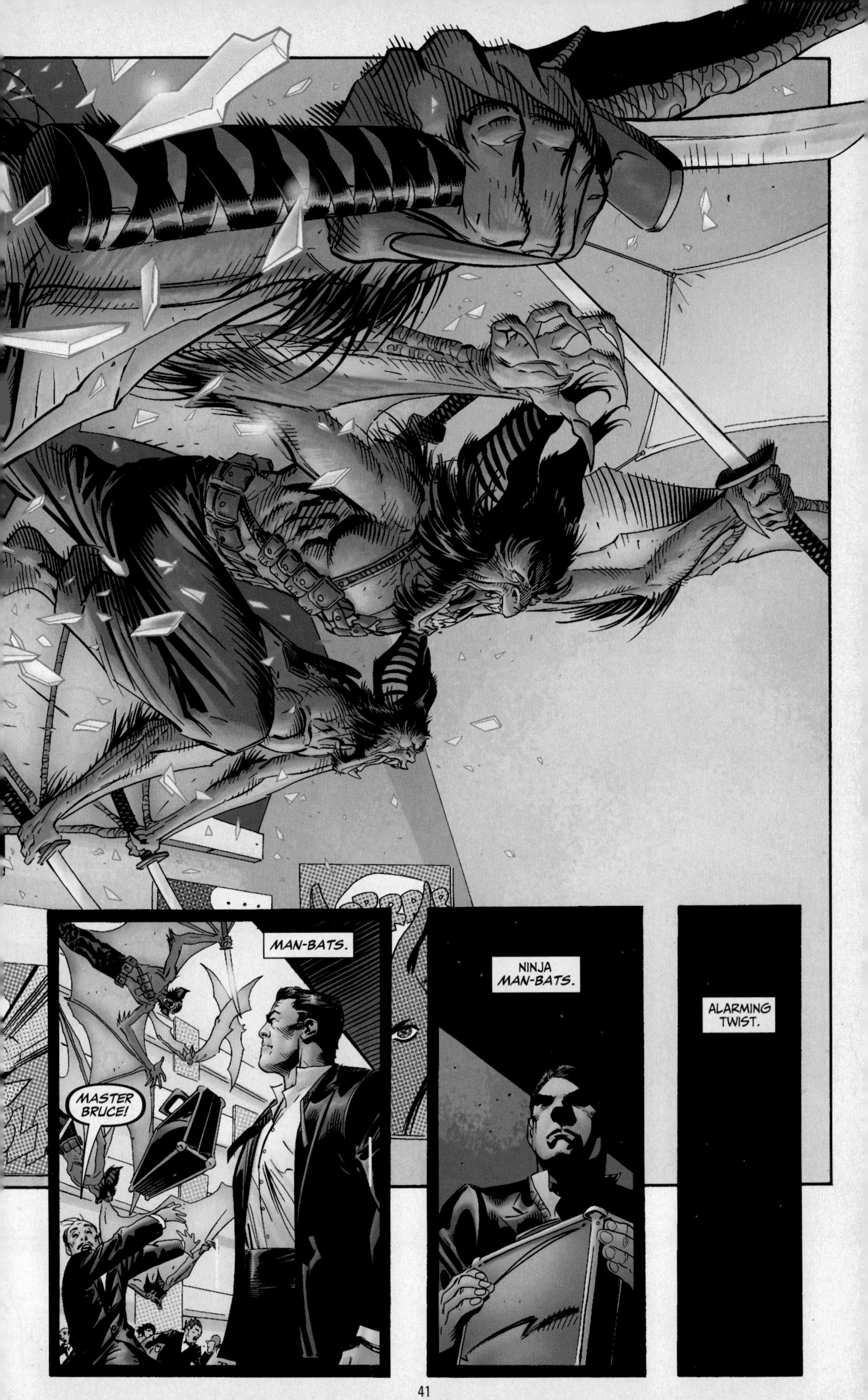
MAN-BATS.
MASTER BRUCE!
NINJA MAN-BATS.
ALARMING TWIST.

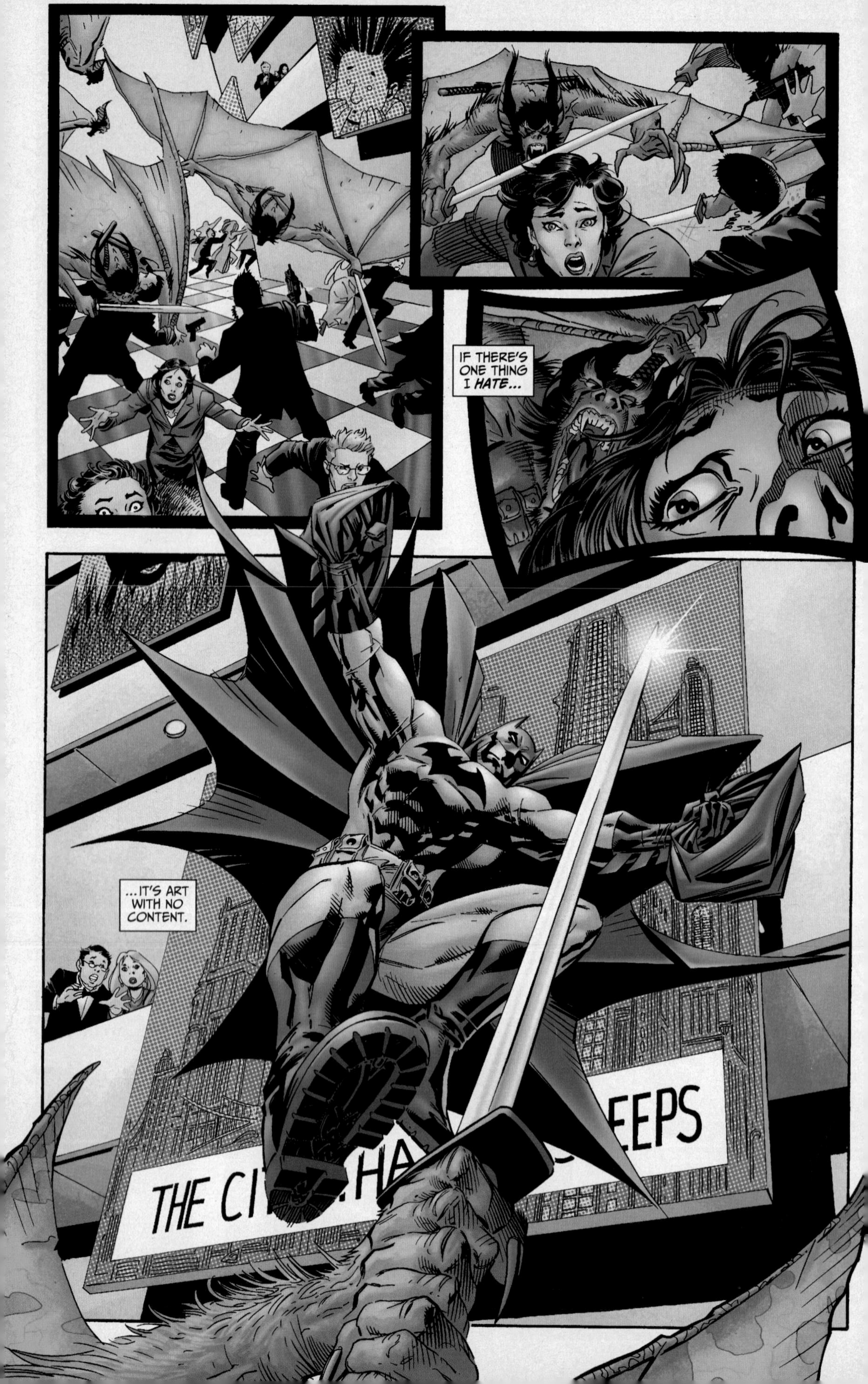
IF THERE'S ONE THING I *HATE*...
...IT'S ART WITH NO CONTENT.
THE CI HA EEPS

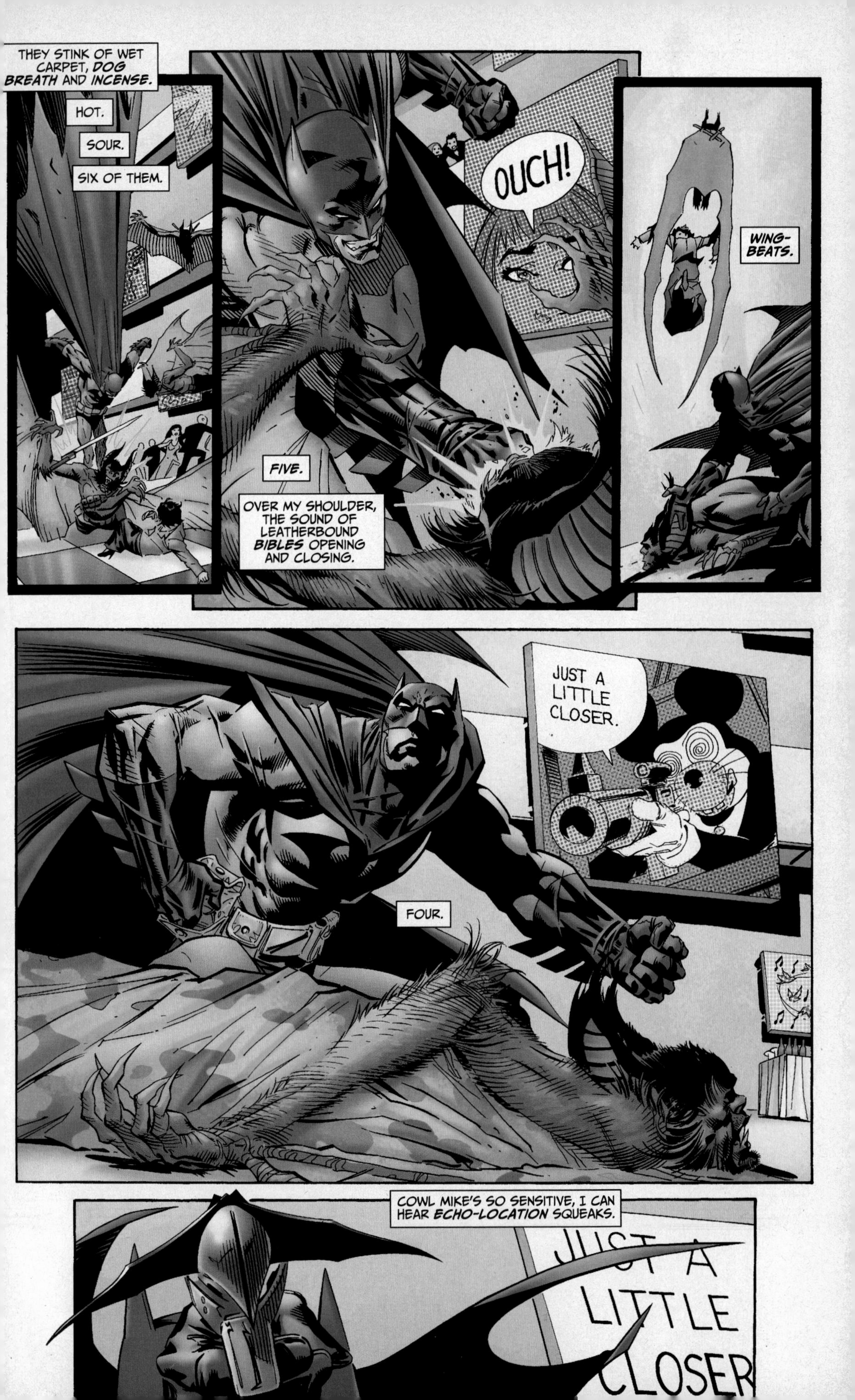
THEY STINK OF WET CARPET, DOG BREATH AND INCENSE.
HOT.
SOUR.
SIX OF THEM.
OUCH!
FIVE.
OVER MY SHOULDER, THE SOUND OF LEATHERBOUND BIBLES OPENING AND CLOSING.
WING-BEATS.
JUST A LITTLE CLOSER.
FOUR.
COWL MIKE'S SO SENSITIVE, I CAN HEAR ECHO-LOCATION SQUEAKS.
JUST A LITTLE CLOSER

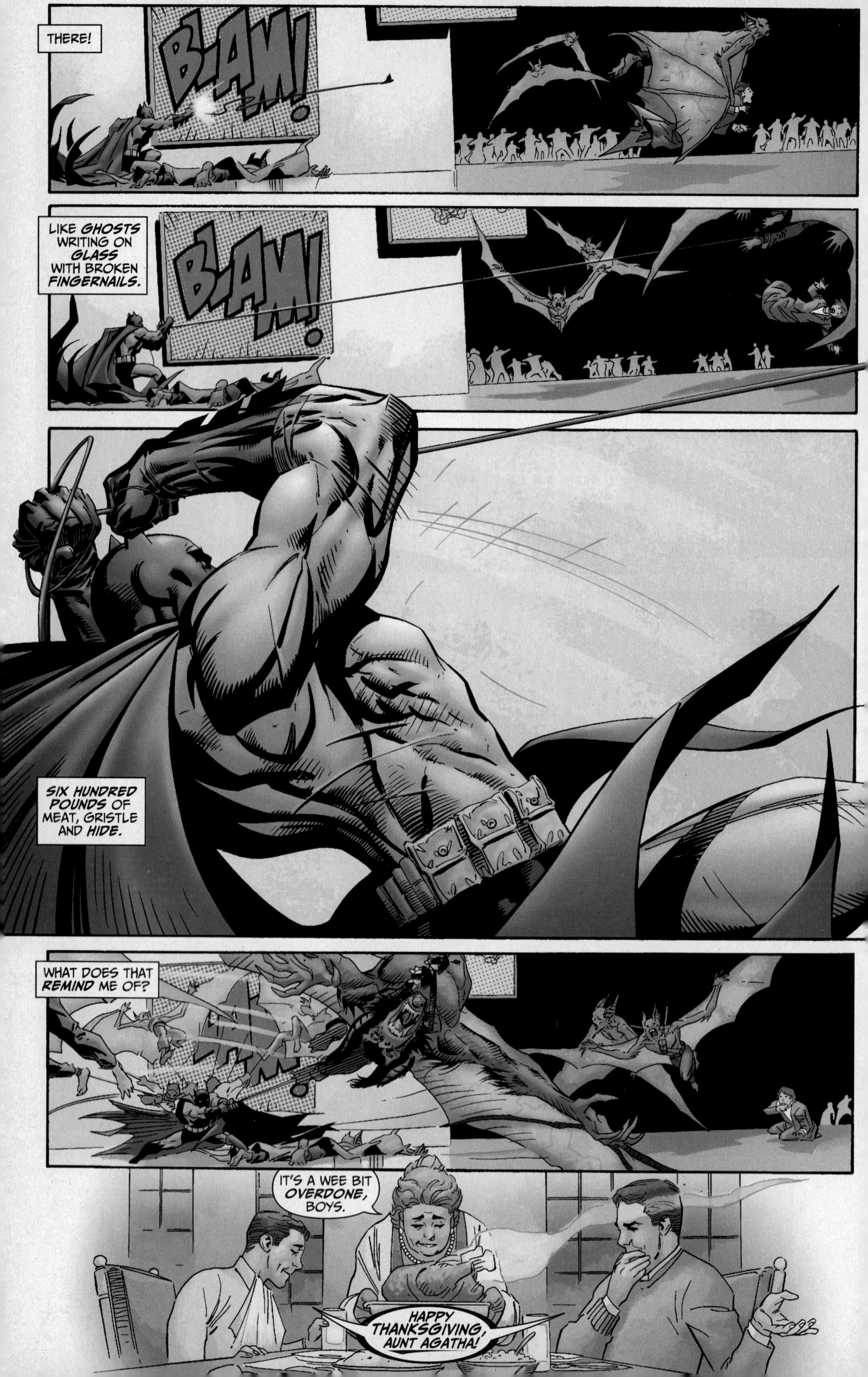
THERE!
BLAM!
LIKE GHOSTS WRITING ON GLASS WITH BROKEN FINGERNAILS.
BLAM!
SIX HUNDRED POUNDS OF MEAT, GRISTLE AND HIDE.
WHAT DOES THAT REMIND ME OF?
IT'S A WEE BIT OVERDONE, BOYS.
HAPPY THANKSGIVING, AUNT AGATHA!

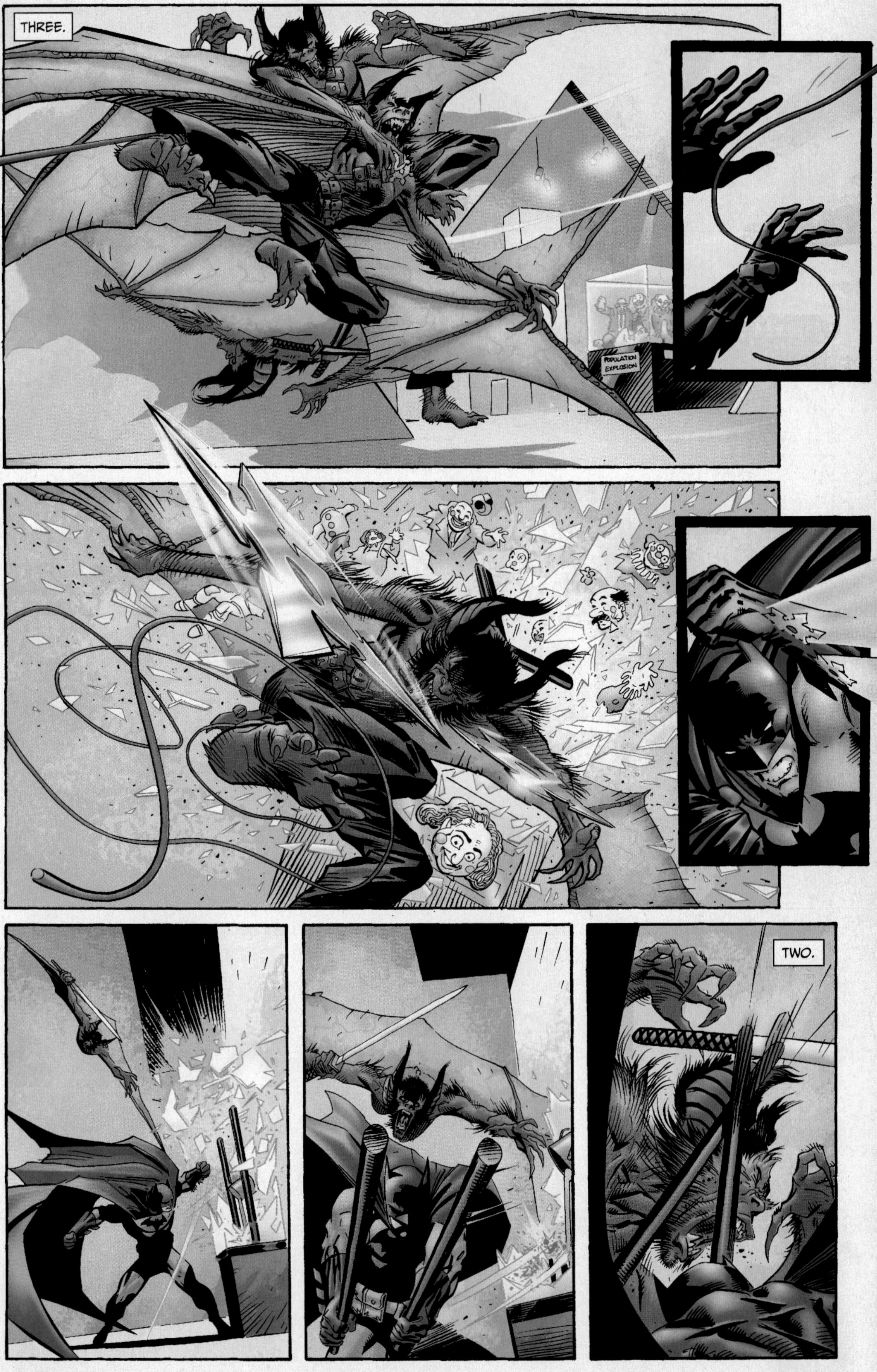
THREE.
POPULATION EXPLOSION
TWO.

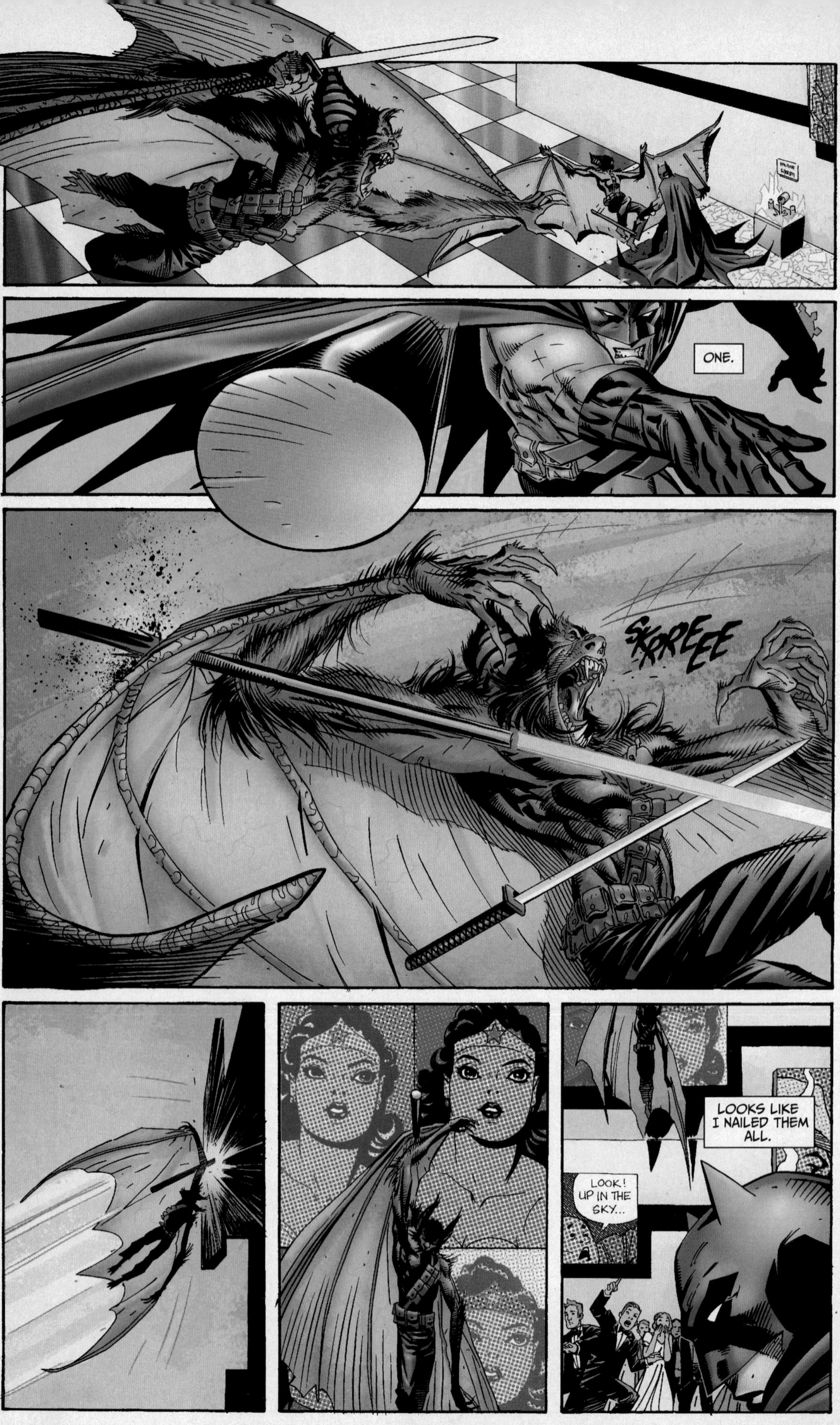
ONE.
SKREEE
LOOKS LIKE I NAILED THEM ALL.
LOOK! UP IN THE SKY...

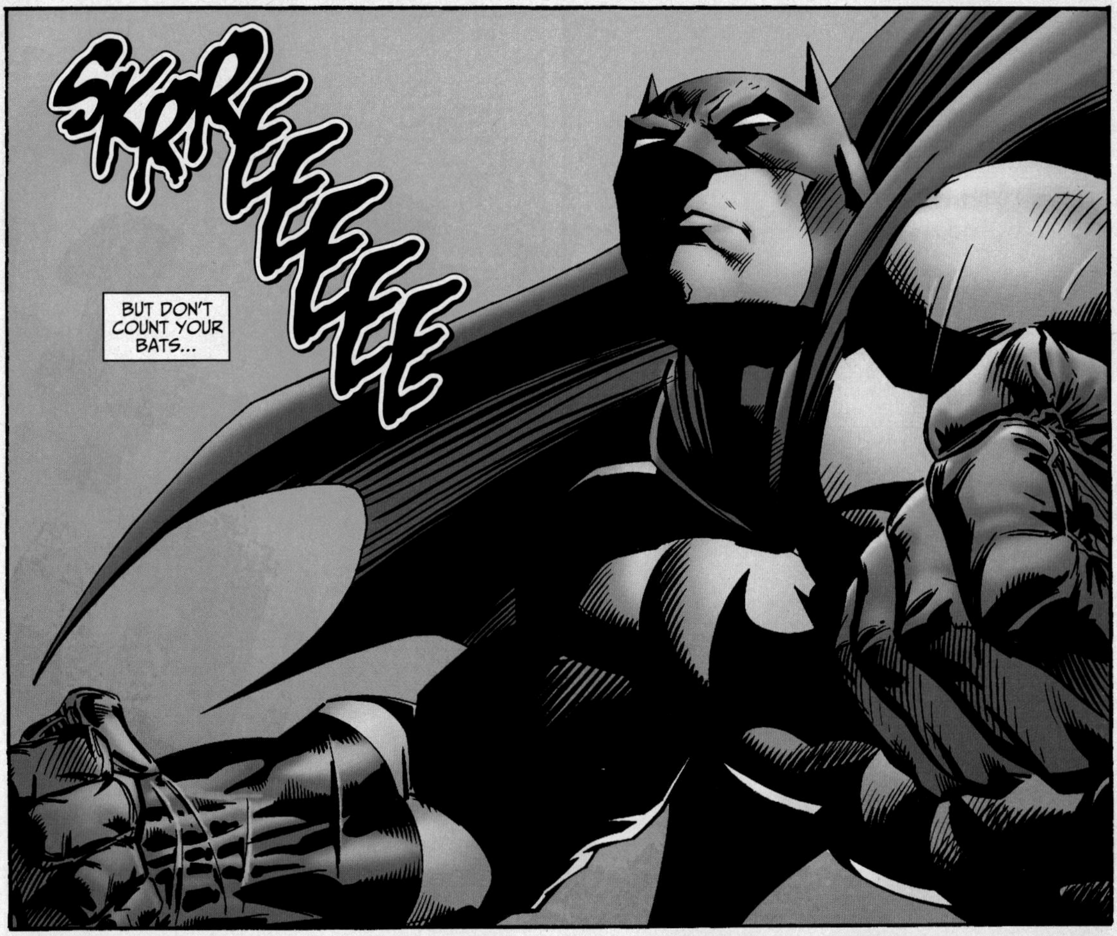
SKREEEEEEE
BUT DON'T COUNT YOUR BATS...

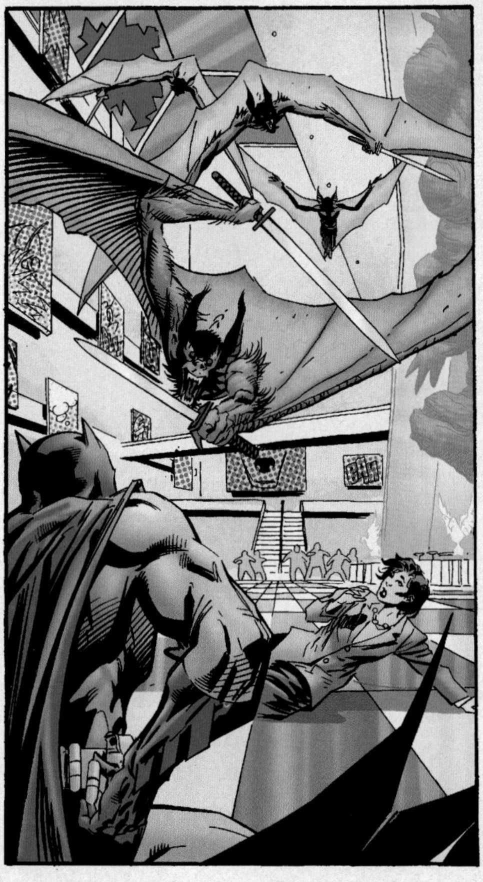

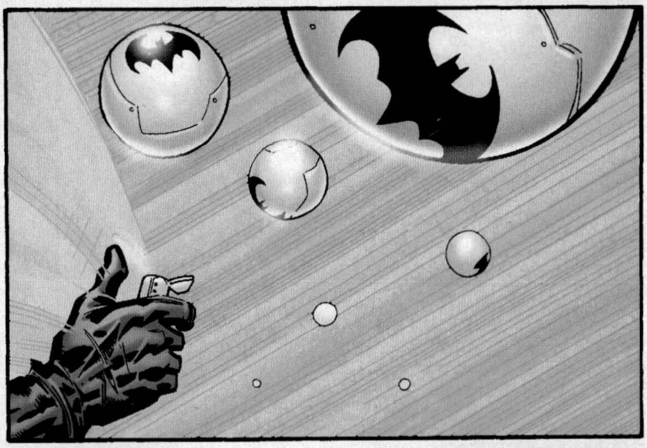

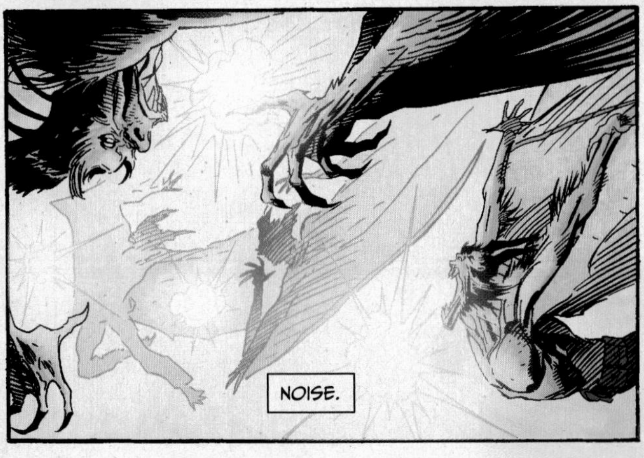
NOISE.

YOU OKAY?

DON'T HURT ME.

PLEASE DON'T.

EVERYONE OUT!

PLEASE.

CHASING US!

ONE OF THEM ATTACKING THE OTHERS!

PANDEMONIUM!

THIS WAY, MISS.

THE PRIME MINISTER'S WIFE...

...BRUCE WAYNE...

THEY'RE STILL IN THERE SOMEWHERE!

ALARM!

MORE NOISE.

LOTS OF IT.

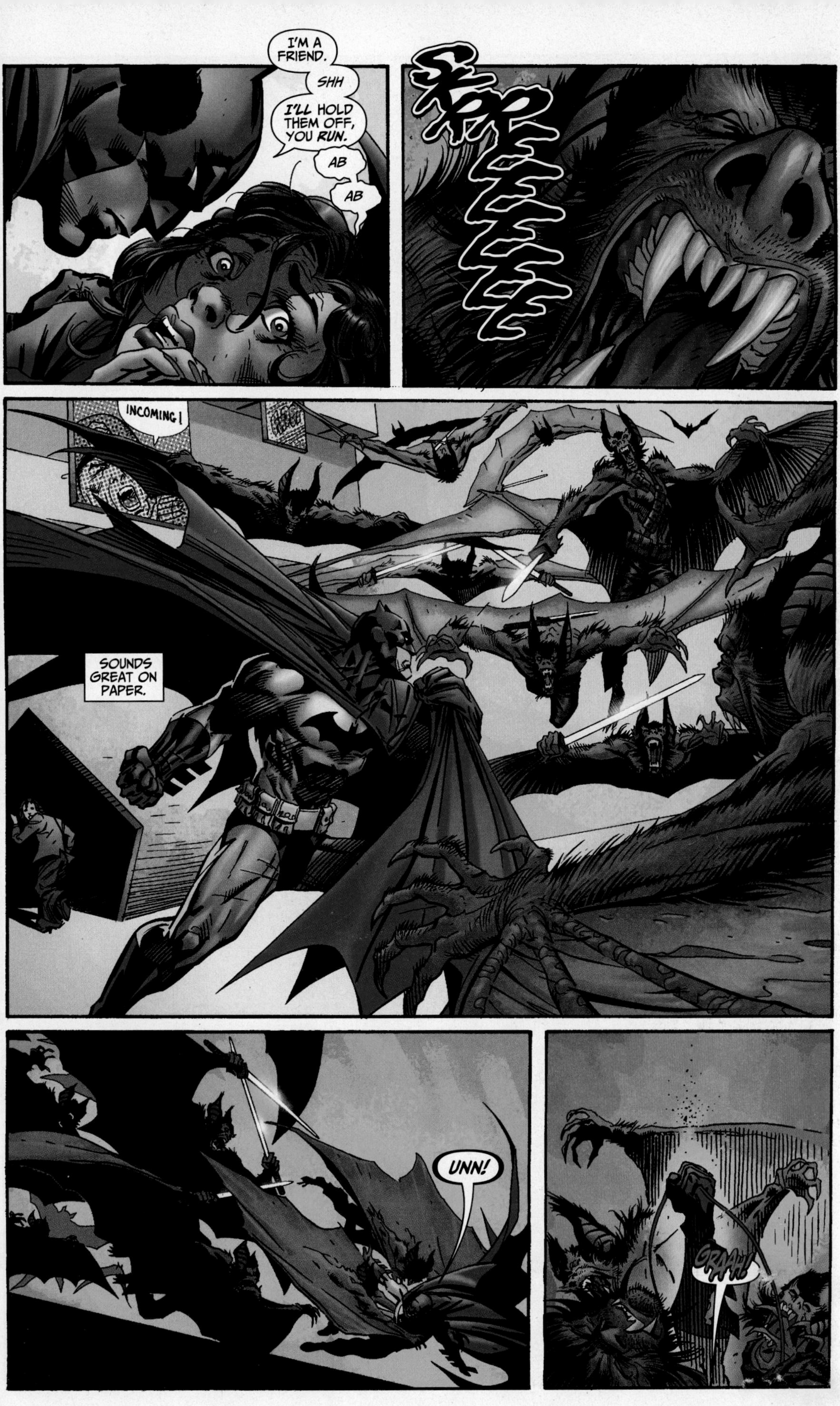
I'M A FRIEND.
SHH
I'LL HOLD THEM OFF, YOU RUN.
AB
AB
INCOMING!
SOUNDS GREAT ON PAPER.
UNN!
GRAAH!

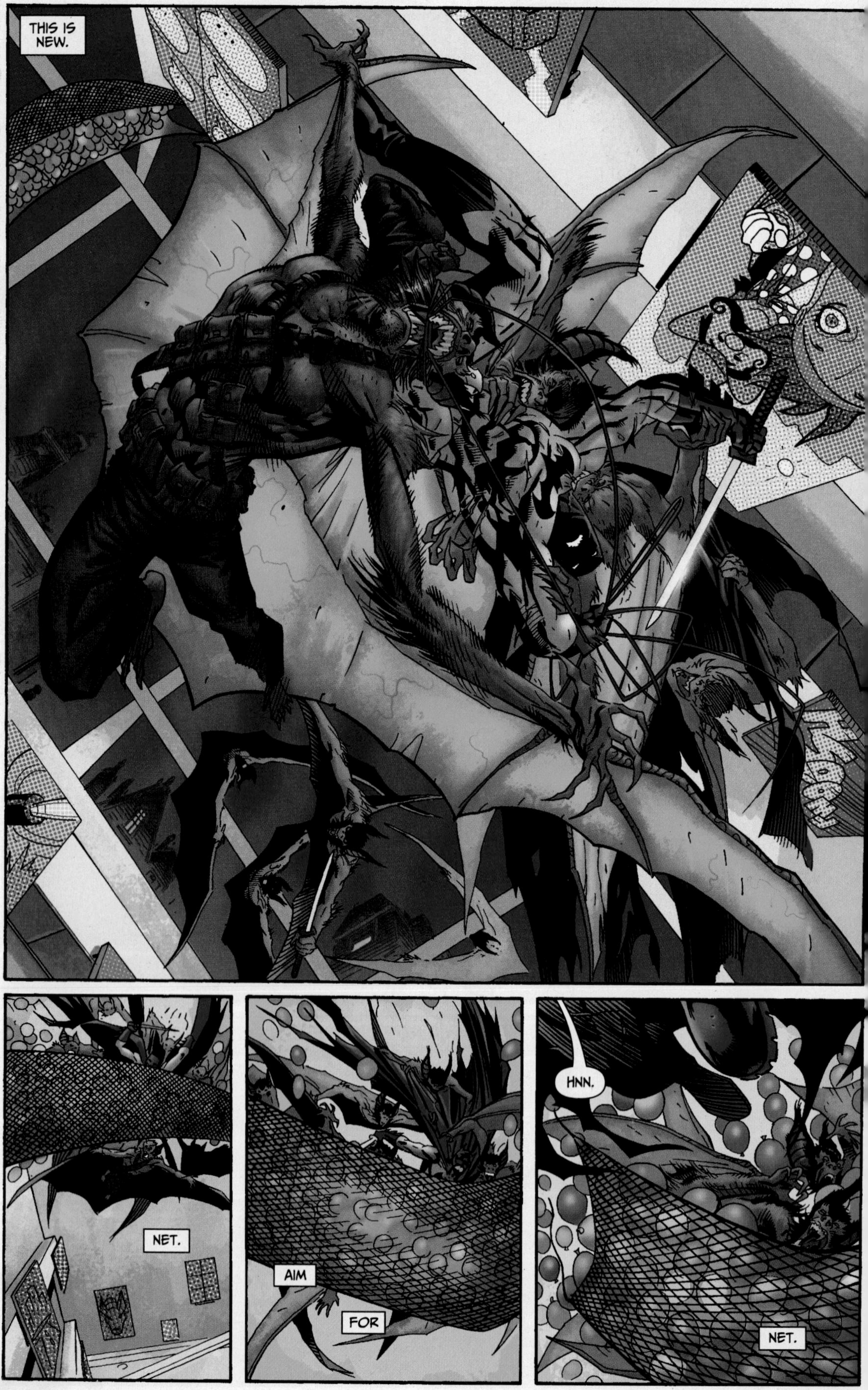
THIS IS NEW.
NET.
AIM
FOR
HNN.
NET.

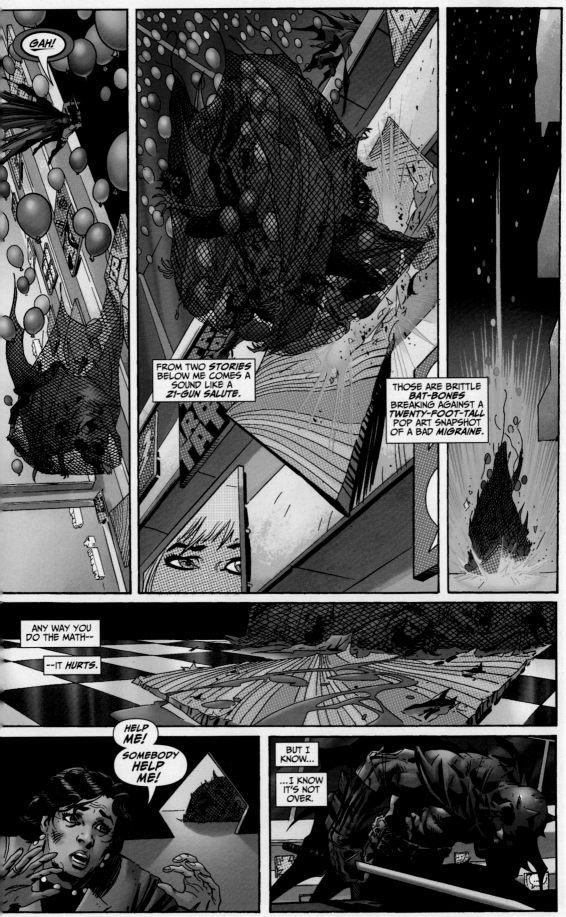

GAH!

FROM TWO *STORIES* BELOW ME COMES A SOUND LIKE A *21-GUN SALUTE*.

THOSE ARE BRITTLE *BAT-BONES* BREAKING AGAINST A *TWENTY-FOOT-TALL* POP ART SNAPSHOT OF A BAD *MIGRAINE*.

ANY WAY YOU DO THE MATH--

--IT *HURTS*.

HELP *ME!* SOMEBODY *HELP ME!*

BUT I KNOW...

...I KNOW IT'S NOT OVER.

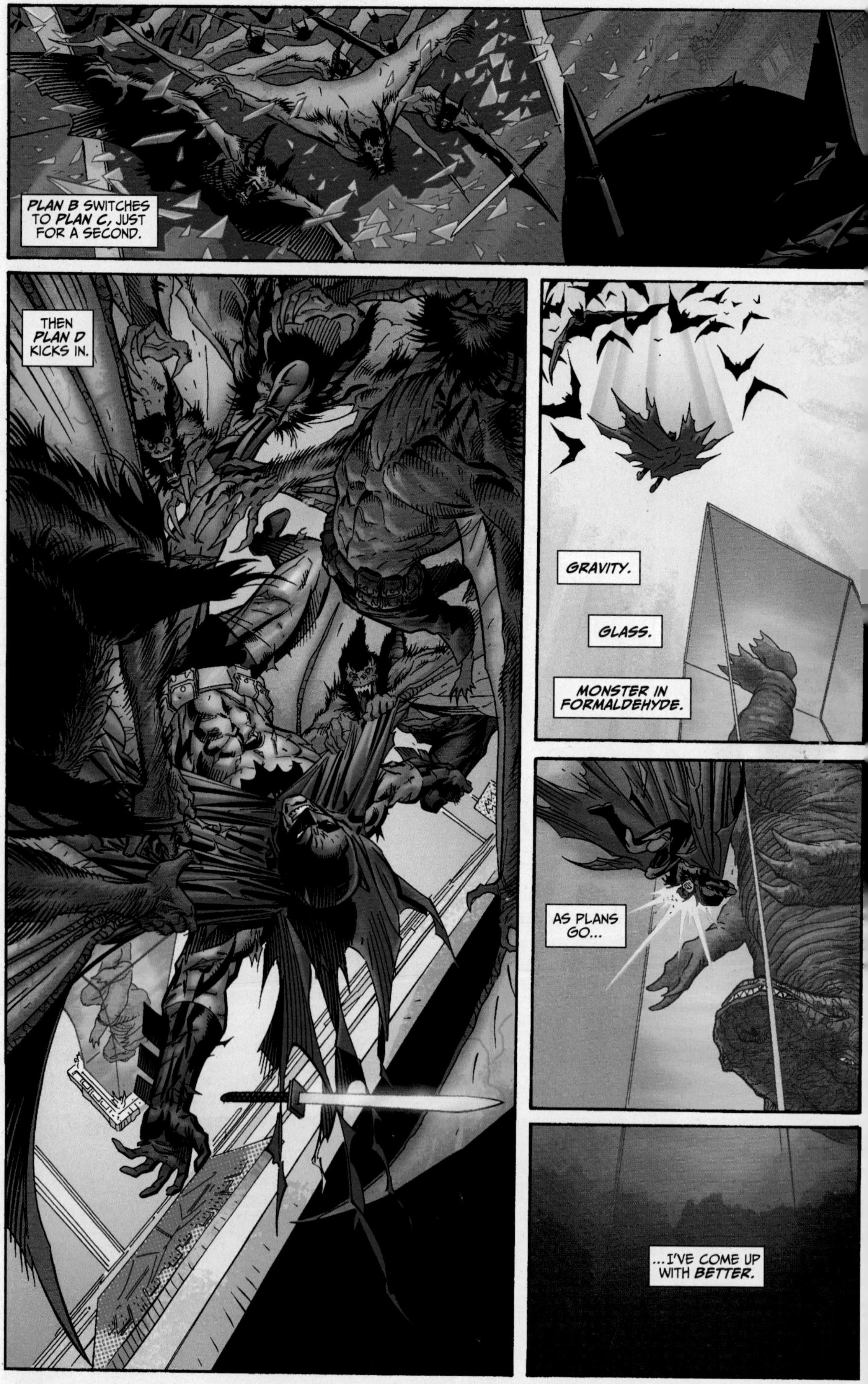
PLAN B SWITCHES TO PLAN C, JUST FOR A SECOND.
THEN PLAN D KICKS IN.
GRAVITY.
GLASS.
MONSTER IN FORMALDEHYDE.
AS PLANS GO...
...I'VE COME UP WITH BETTER.

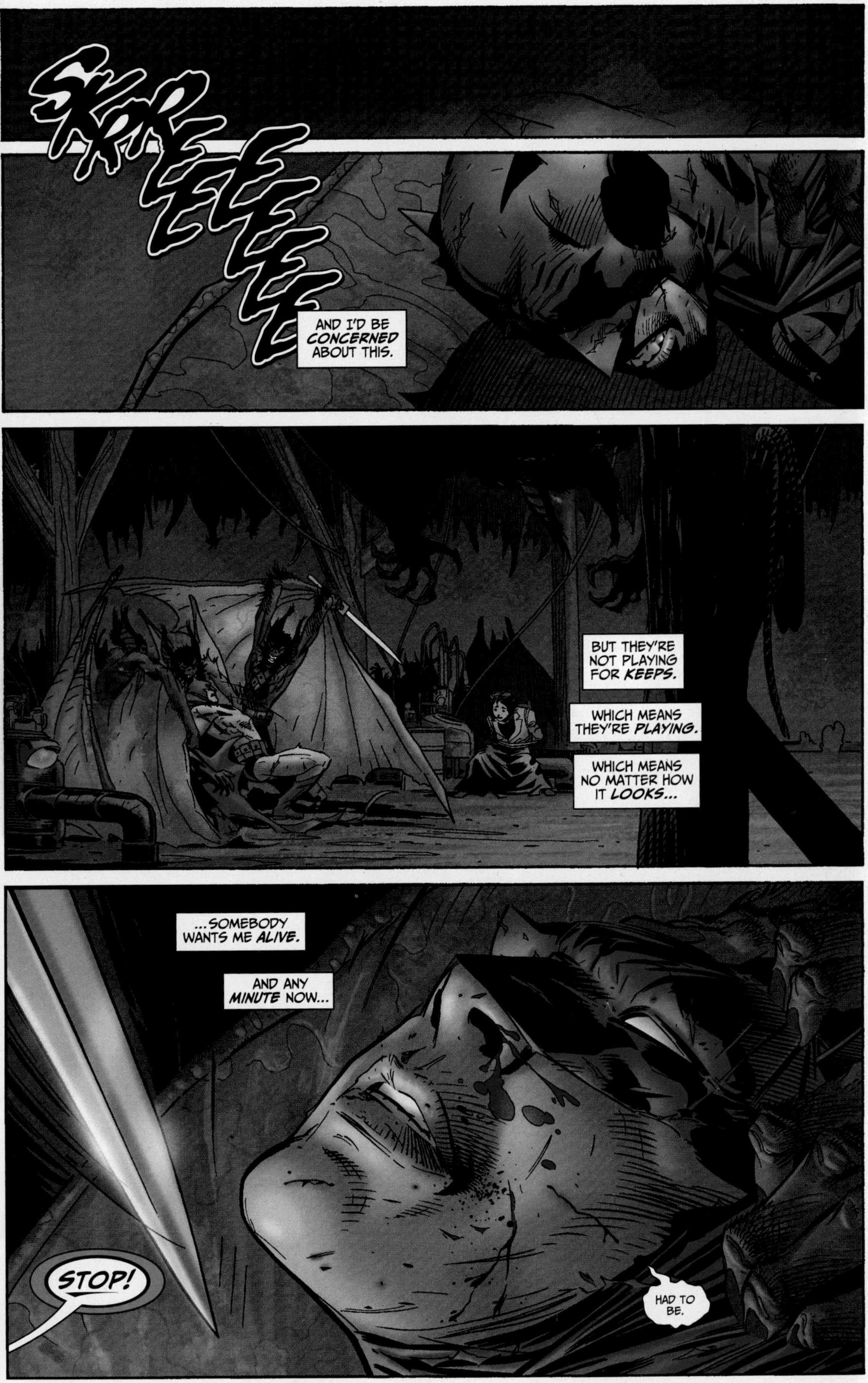
SKREEEEEEE
AND I'D BE CONCERNED ABOUT THIS.
BUT THEY'RE NOT PLAYING FOR KEEPS.
WHICH MEANS THEY'RE PLAYING.
WHICH MEANS NO MATTER HOW IT LOOKS...
...SOMEBODY WANTS ME ALIVE.
AND ANY MINUTE NOW...
STOP!
HAD TO BE.

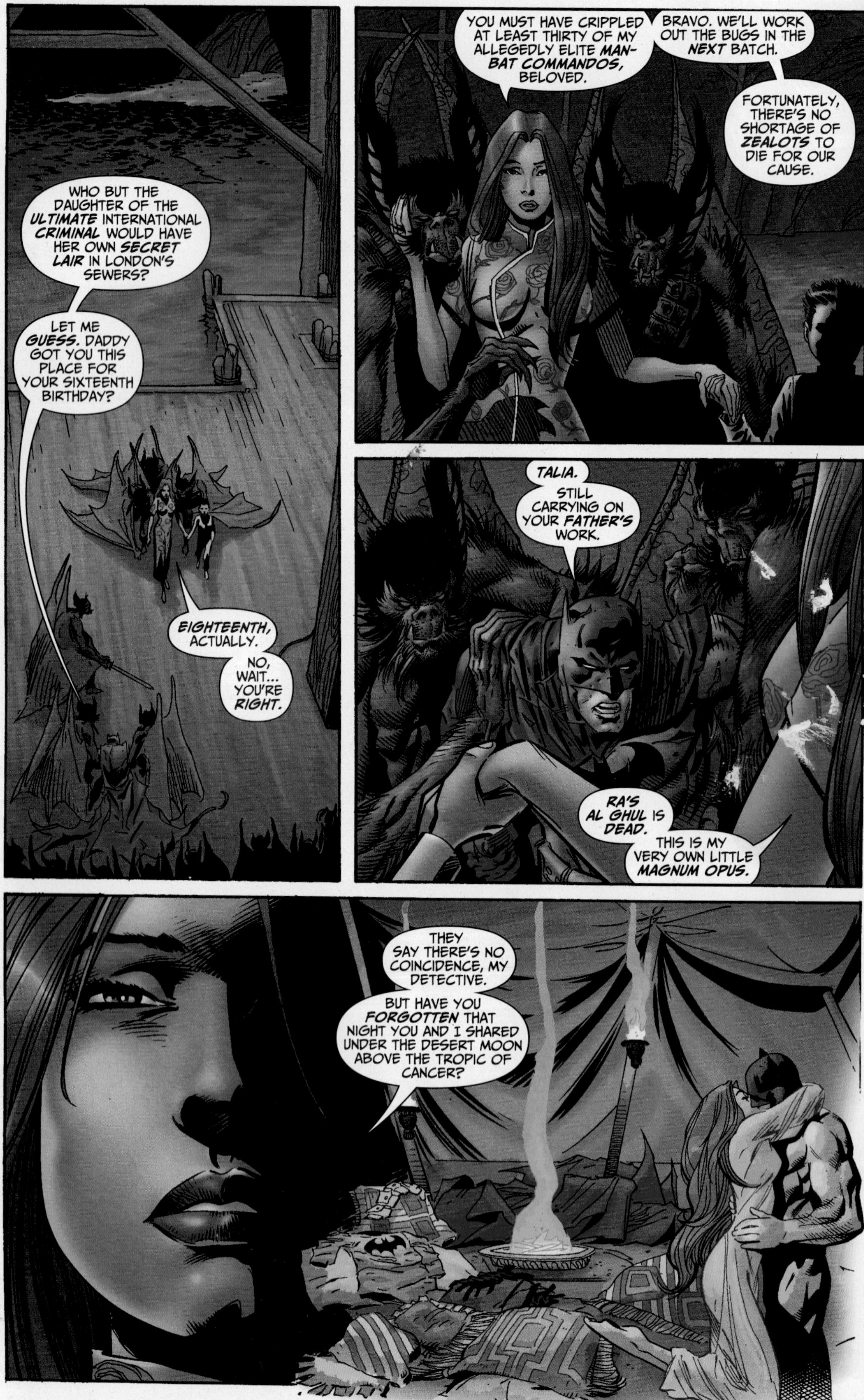
WHO BUT THE DAUGHTER OF THE ULTIMATE INTERNATIONAL CRIMINAL WOULD HAVE HER OWN SECRET LAIR IN LONDON'S SEWERS?
LET ME GUESS. DADDY GOT YOU THIS PLACE FOR YOUR SIXTEENTH BIRTHDAY?
EIGHTEENTH, ACTUALLY.
NO, WAIT... YOU'RE RIGHT.
YOU MUST HAVE CRIPPLED AT LEAST THIRTY OF MY ALLEGEDLY ELITE MAN-BAT COMMANDOS, BELOVED.
BRAVO. WE'LL WORK OUT THE BUGS IN THE NEXT BATCH.
FORTUNATELY, THERE'S NO SHORTAGE OF ZEALOTS TO DIE FOR OUR CAUSE.
TALIA.
STILL CARRYING ON YOUR FATHER'S WORK.
RA'S AL GHUL IS DEAD.
THIS IS MY VERY OWN LITTLE MAGNUM OPUS.
THEY SAY THERE'S NO COINCIDENCE, MY DETECTIVE.
BUT HAVE YOU FORGOTTEN THAT NIGHT YOU AND I SHARED UNDER THE DESERT MOON ABOVE THE TROPIC OF CANCER?

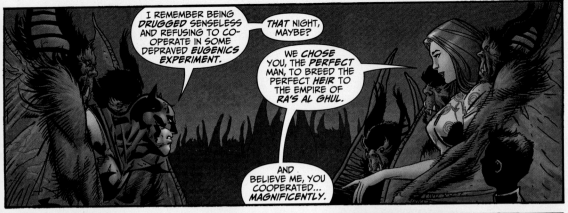

I REMEMBER BEING *DRUGGED* SENSELESS AND REFUSING TO CO-OPERATE IN SOME DEPRAVED *EUGENICS* EXPERIMENT.

THAT NIGHT, MAYBE?

WE *CHOSE* YOU, THE *PERFECT* MAN, TO BREED THE PERFECT *HEIR* TO THE EMPIRE OF *RA'S AL GHUL.*

AND BELIEVE ME, YOU COOPERATED... *MAGNIFICENTLY.*

BUT SINCE *THEN,* I'VE ALLOWED YOU TO EVADE YOUR... *RESPONSIBILITIES.*

HE'S BEEN TRAINED BY THE MASTERS OF THE *LEAGUE OF ASSASSINS,* BUT THE BOY IS GROWING BEYOND EVEN *MY* CONTROL NOW.

"BOY?"

HE LACKS *DISCIPLINE* AND THE GUIDING HAND OF A *GREAT* MAN.

I WILL RETURN TO THE *MOUNTAINS* WITH MY *CAPTIVE* AND THERE REBUILD MY *ARMY* OF MAN-BATS.

YOU'LL HEAR FROM ME AGAIN *SOON,* BELOVED, THOUGH I IMAGINE YOU MAY BE *BUSY.*

I INTEND TO HOLD THE *WHOLE WORLD* HOSTAGE TO A *NEW* KIND OF TERROR.

IN THE MEANTIME, I LEAVE THE TWO OF YOU TO GET *ACQUAINTED.*

DON'T ALLOW HIM TO CRAMP YOUR STYLE.

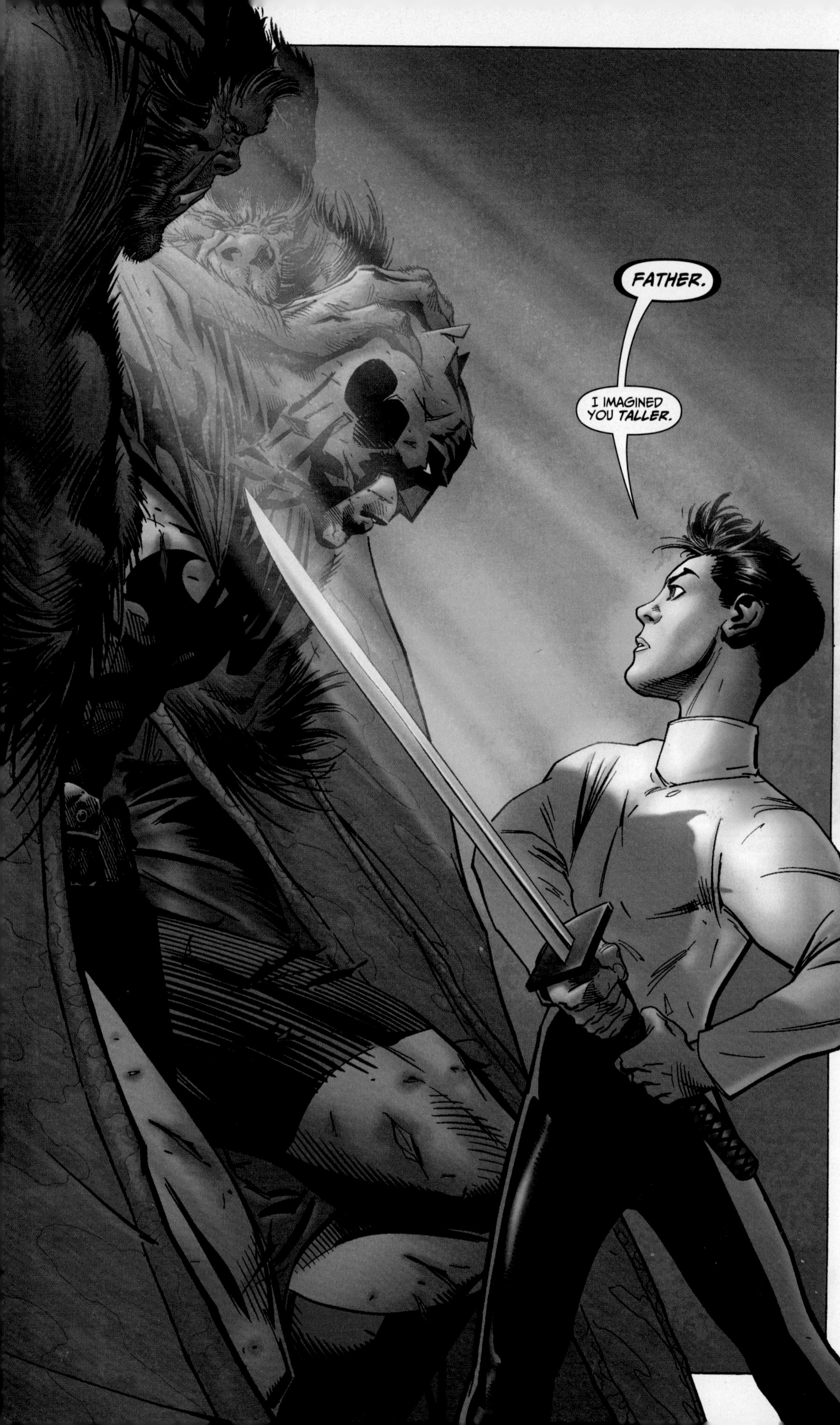
FATHER.
I IMAGINED YOU TALLER.

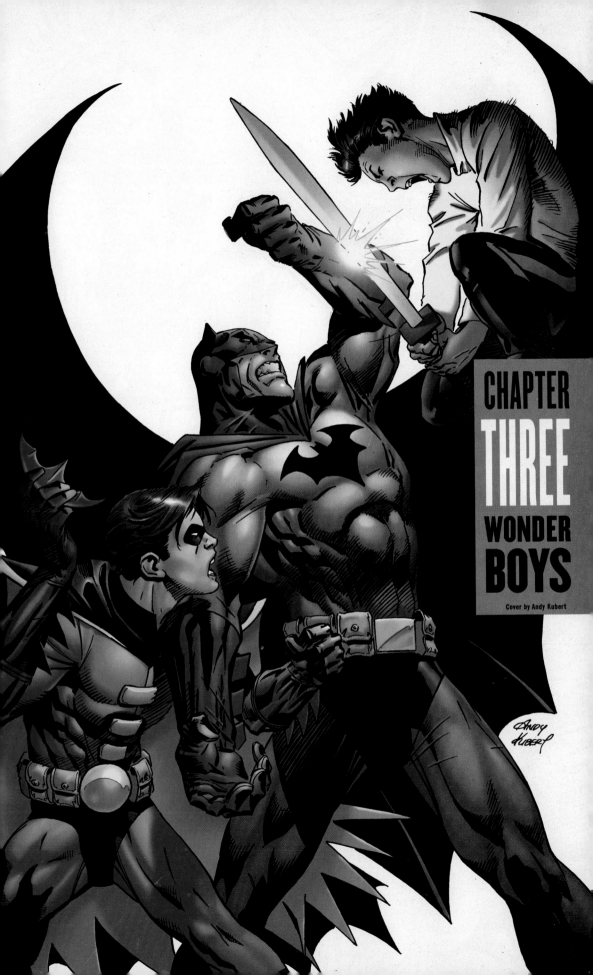

CHAPTER
THREE
WONDER
BOYS

Cover by Andy Kubert

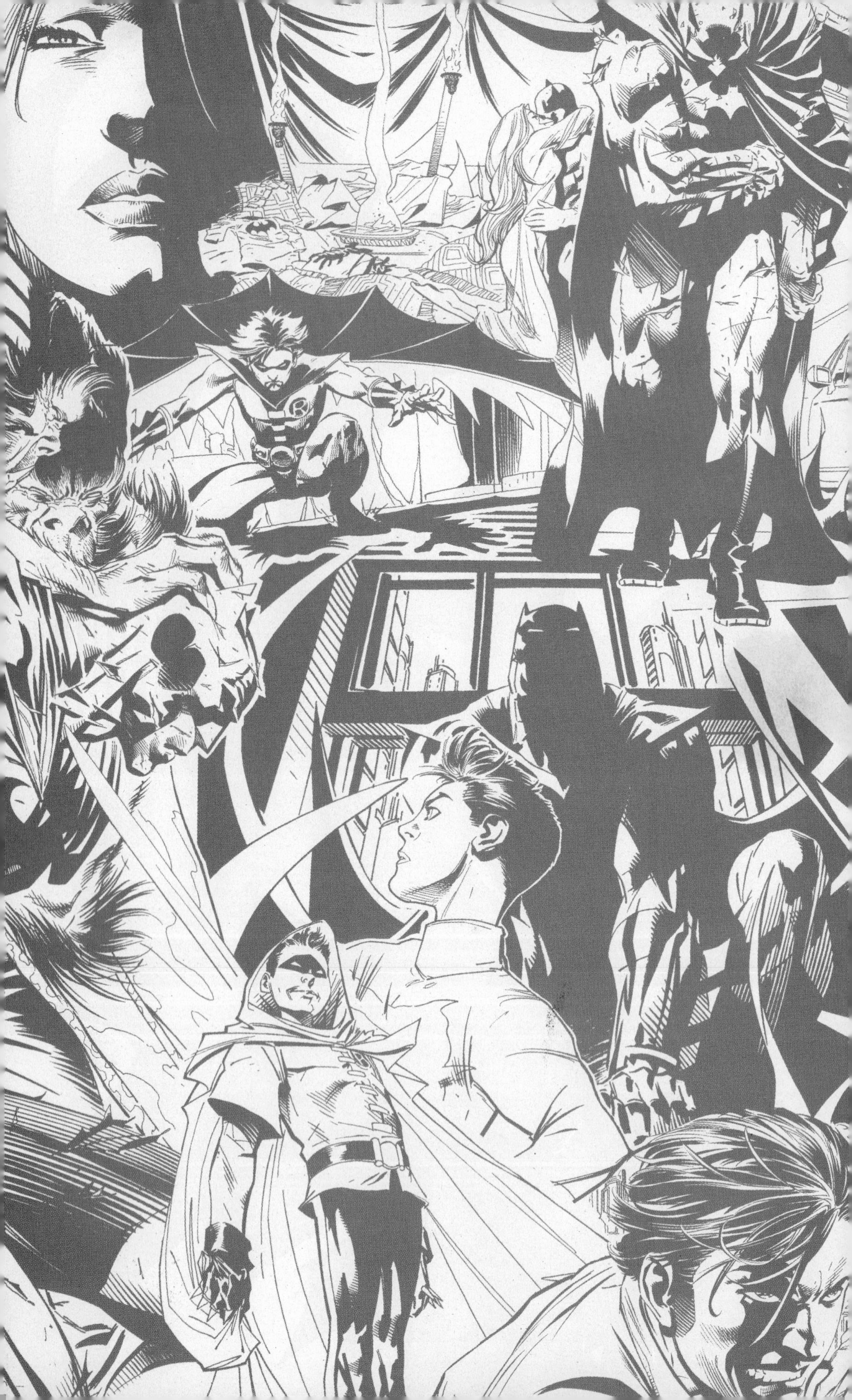

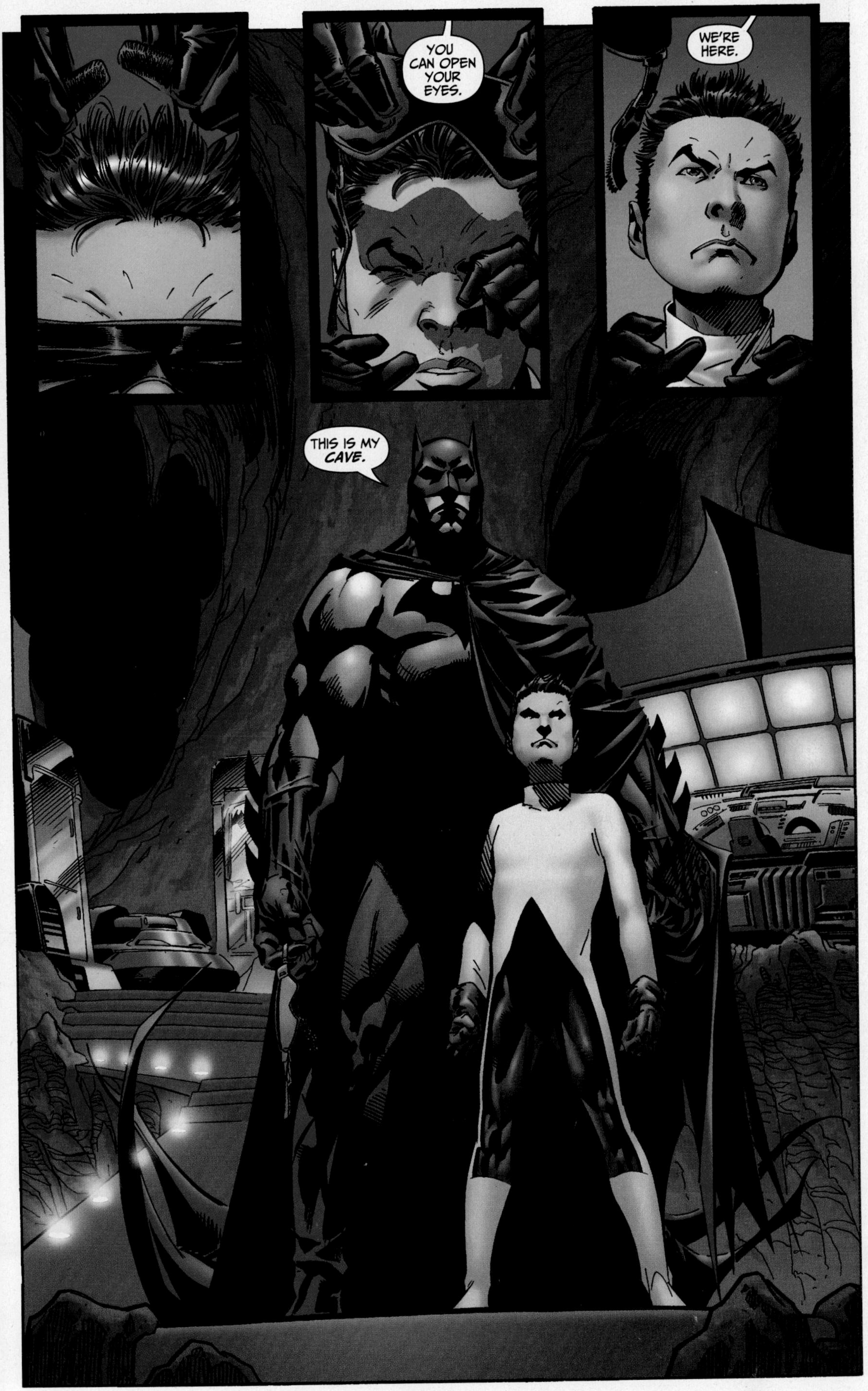
YOU CAN OPEN YOUR EYES.
WE'RE HERE.
THIS IS MY CAVE.

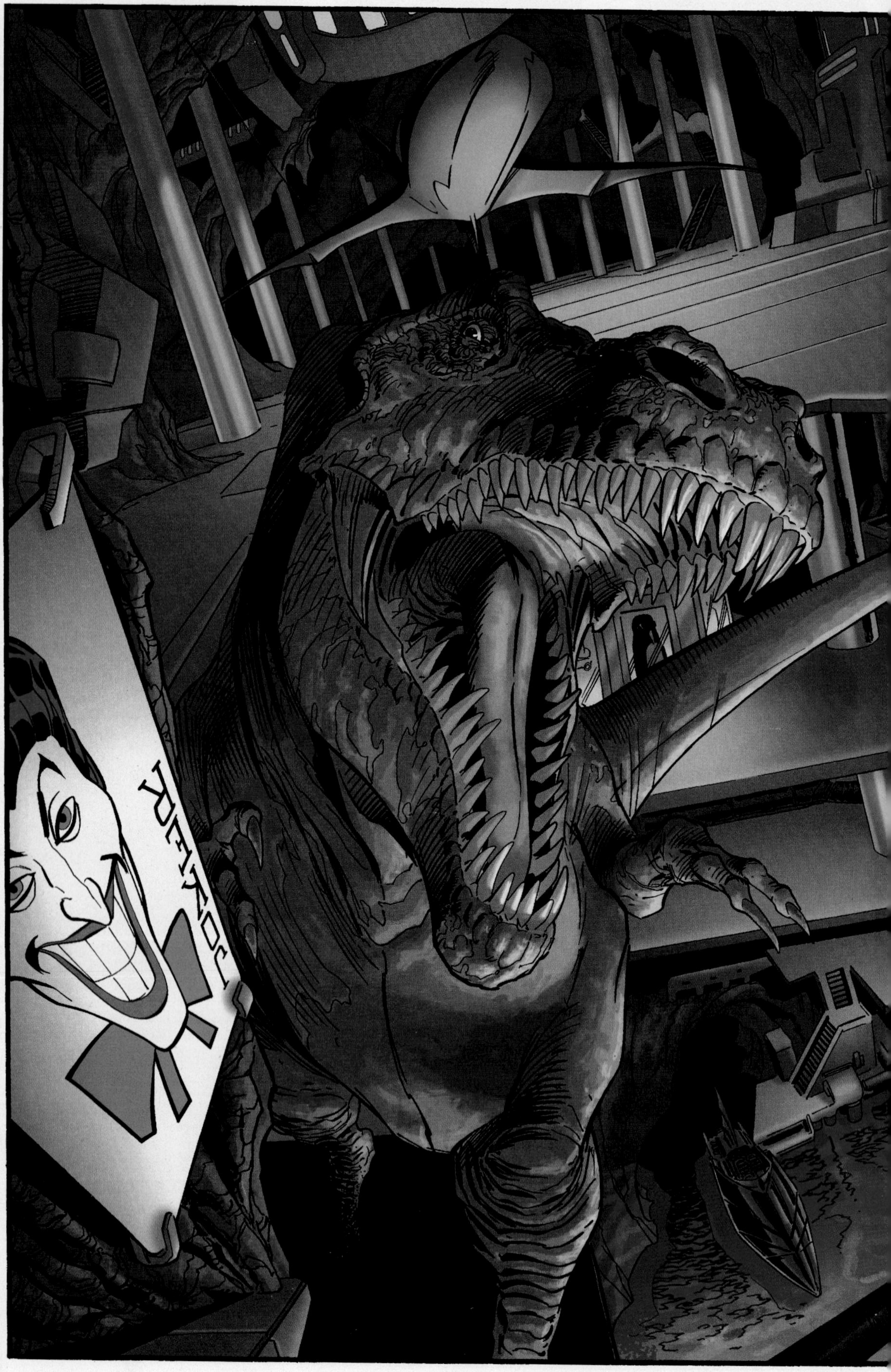
JOKER

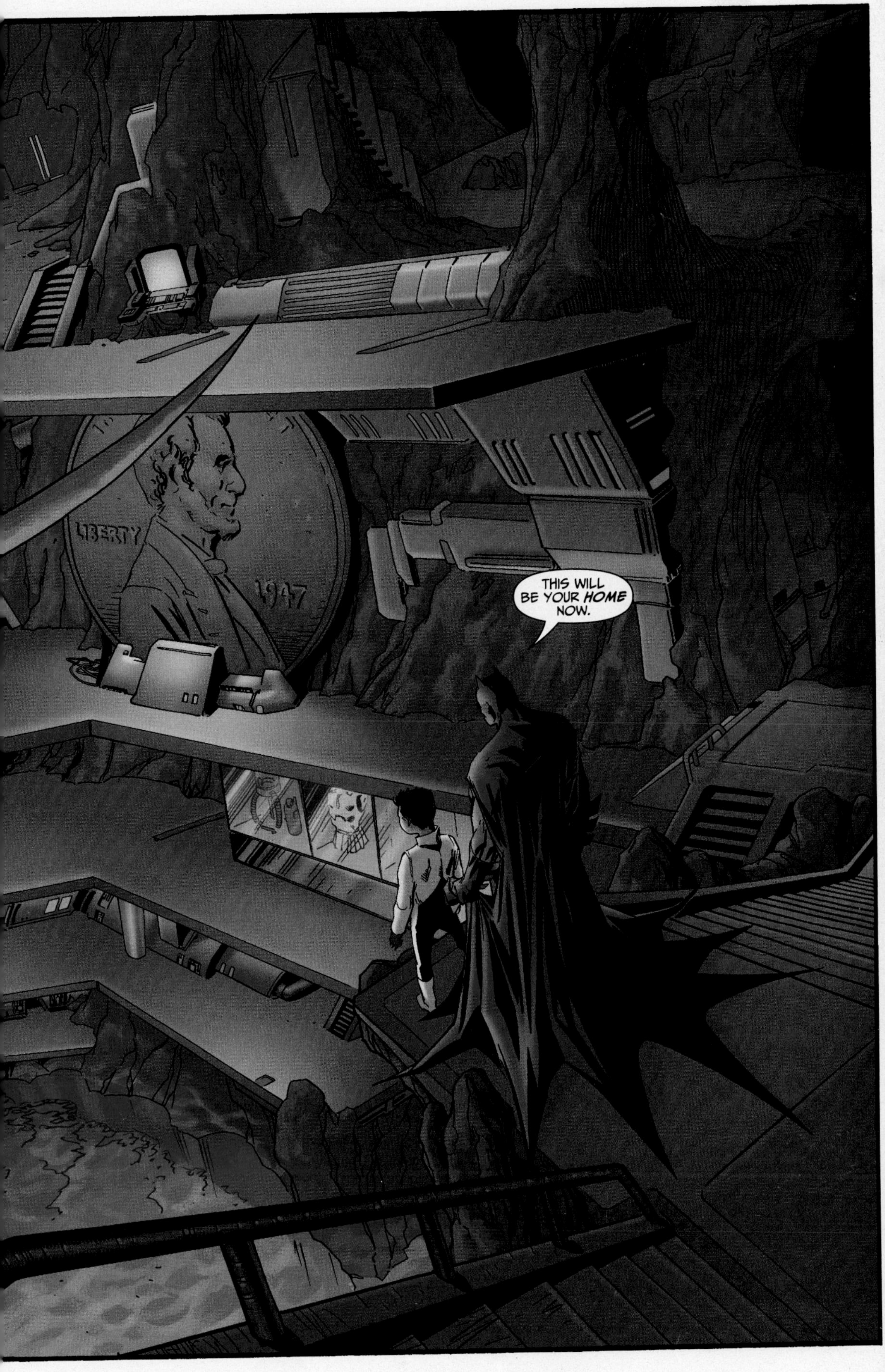
LIBERTY
1947
THIS WILL BE YOUR *HOME* NOW.

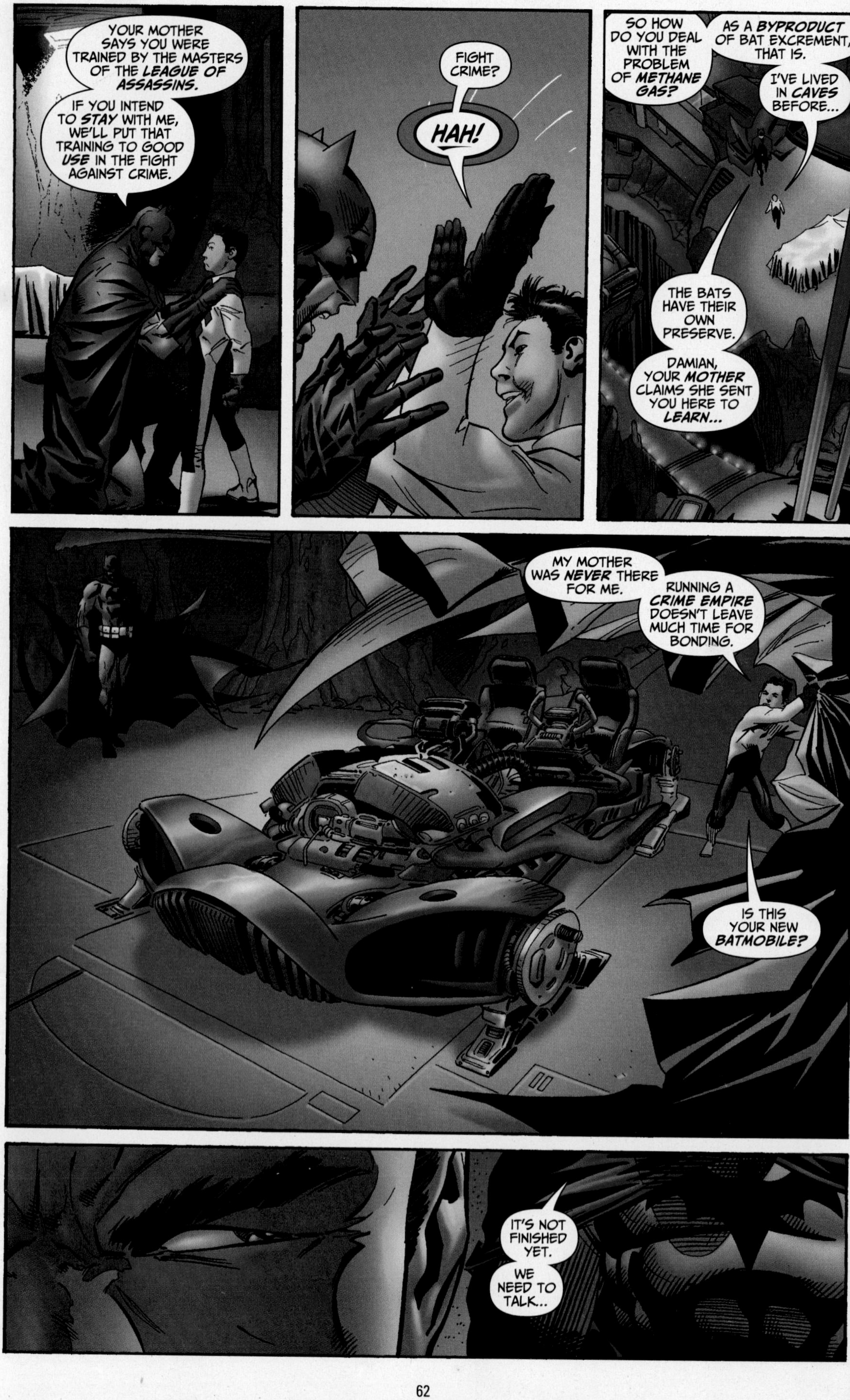
YOUR MOTHER SAYS YOU WERE TRAINED BY THE MASTERS OF THE LEAGUE OF ASSASSINS.
IF YOU INTEND TO STAY WITH ME, WE'LL PUT THAT TRAINING TO GOOD USE IN THE FIGHT AGAINST CRIME.
FIGHT CRIME?
HAH!
SO HOW DO YOU DEAL WITH THE PROBLEM OF METHANE GAS?
AS A BYPRODUCT OF BAT EXCREMENT, THAT IS.
I'VE LIVED IN CAVES BEFORE...
THE BATS HAVE THEIR OWN PRESERVE.
DAMIAN, YOUR MOTHER CLAIMS SHE SENT YOU HERE TO LEARN...
MY MOTHER WAS NEVER THERE FOR ME.
RUNNING A CRIME EMPIRE DOESN'T LEAVE MUCH TIME FOR BONDING.
IS THIS YOUR NEW BATMOBILE?
IT'S NOT FINISHED YET.
WE NEED TO TALK...

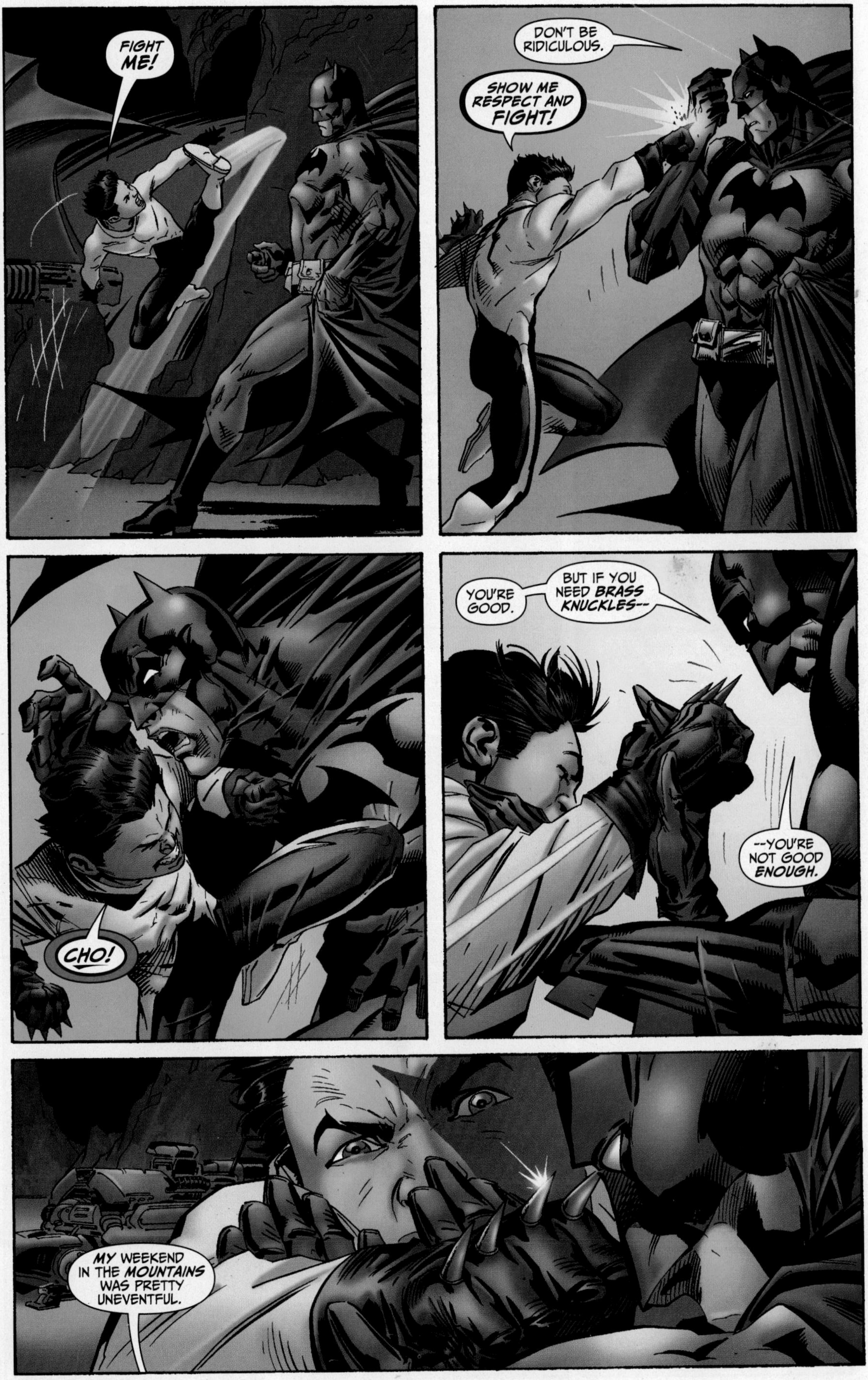

FIGHT ME!
DON'T BE RIDICULOUS.
SHOW ME RESPECT AND FIGHT!
CHO!
YOU'RE GOOD.
BUT IF YOU NEED BRASS KNUCKLES--
--YOU'RE NOT GOOD ENOUGH.
MY WEEKEND IN THE MOUNTAINS WAS PRETTY UNEVENTFUL.

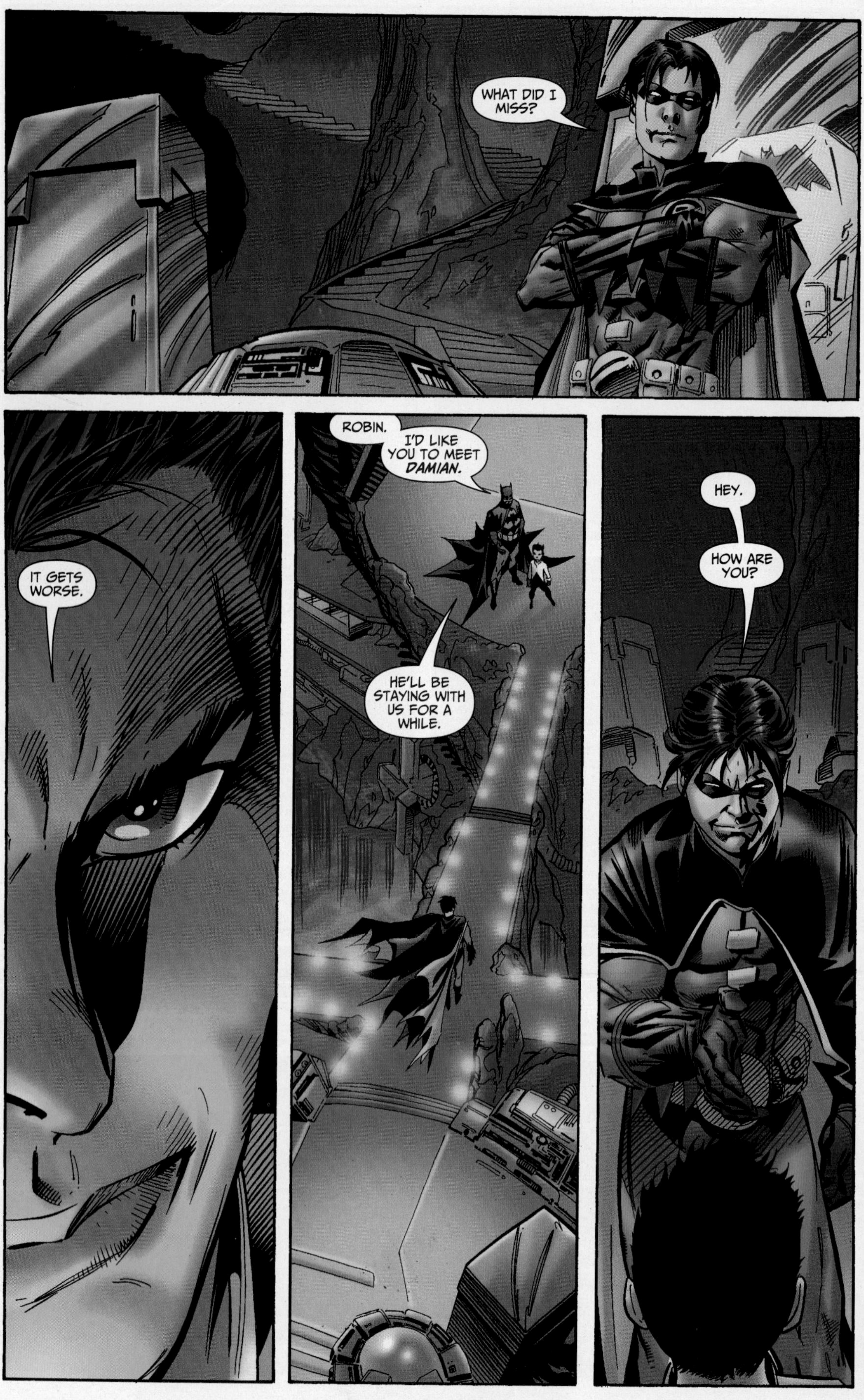
WHAT DID I MISS?
IT GETS WORSE.
ROBIN.
I'D LIKE YOU TO MEET DAMIAN.
HE'LL BE STAYING WITH US FOR A WHILE.
HEY.
HOW ARE YOU?

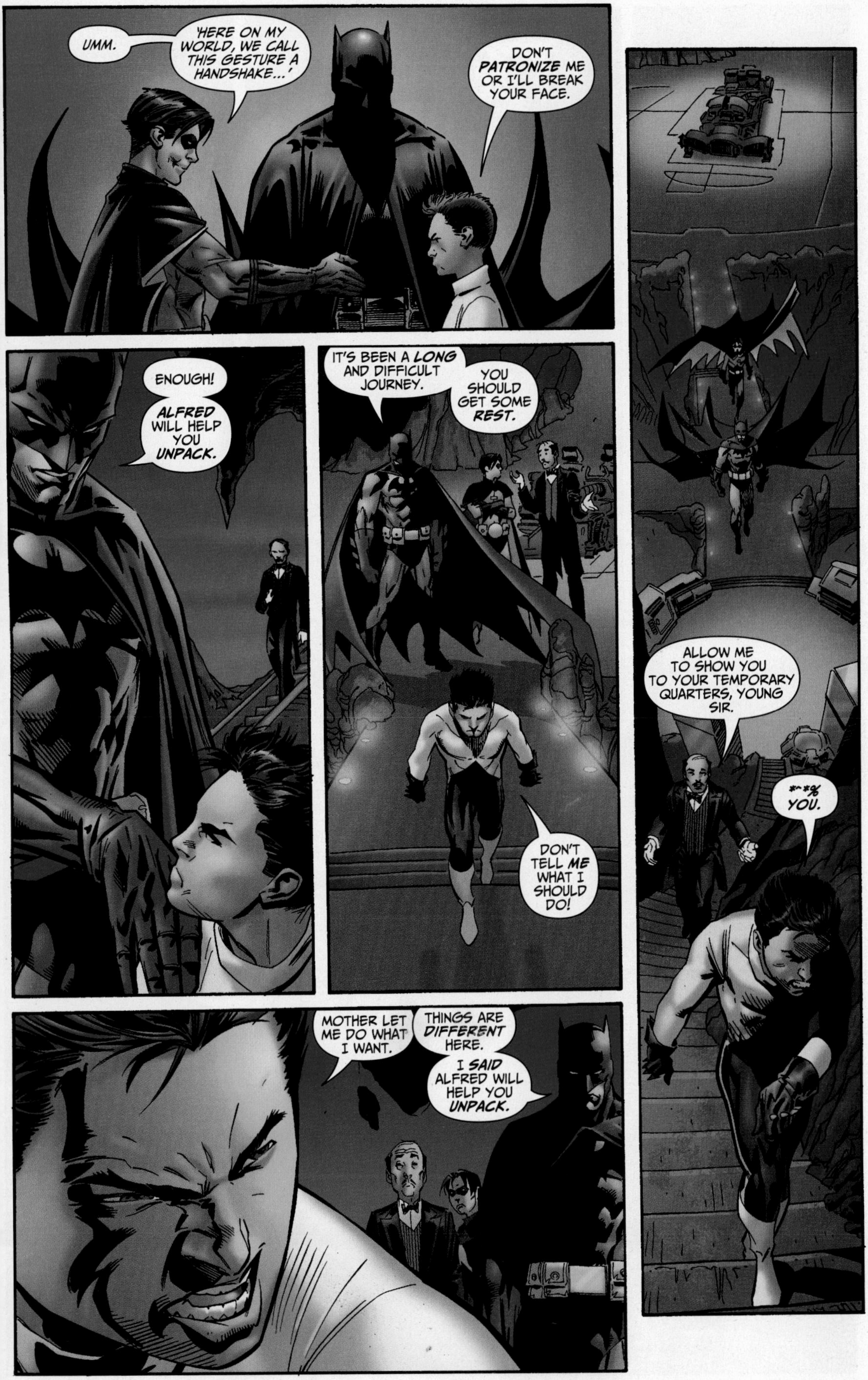
UMM.
'HERE ON MY WORLD, WE CALL THIS GESTURE A HANDSHAKE...'
DON'T PATRONIZE ME OR I'LL BREAK YOUR FACE.
ENOUGH!
ALFRED WILL HELP YOU UNPACK.
IT'S BEEN A LONG AND DIFFICULT JOURNEY.
YOU SHOULD GET SOME REST.
DON'T TELL ME WHAT I SHOULD DO!
MOTHER LET ME DO WHAT I WANT.
THINGS ARE DIFFERENT HERE.
I SAID ALFRED WILL HELP YOU UNPACK.
ALLOW ME TO SHOW YOU TO YOUR TEMPORARY QUARTERS, YOUNG SIR.
^% YOU.

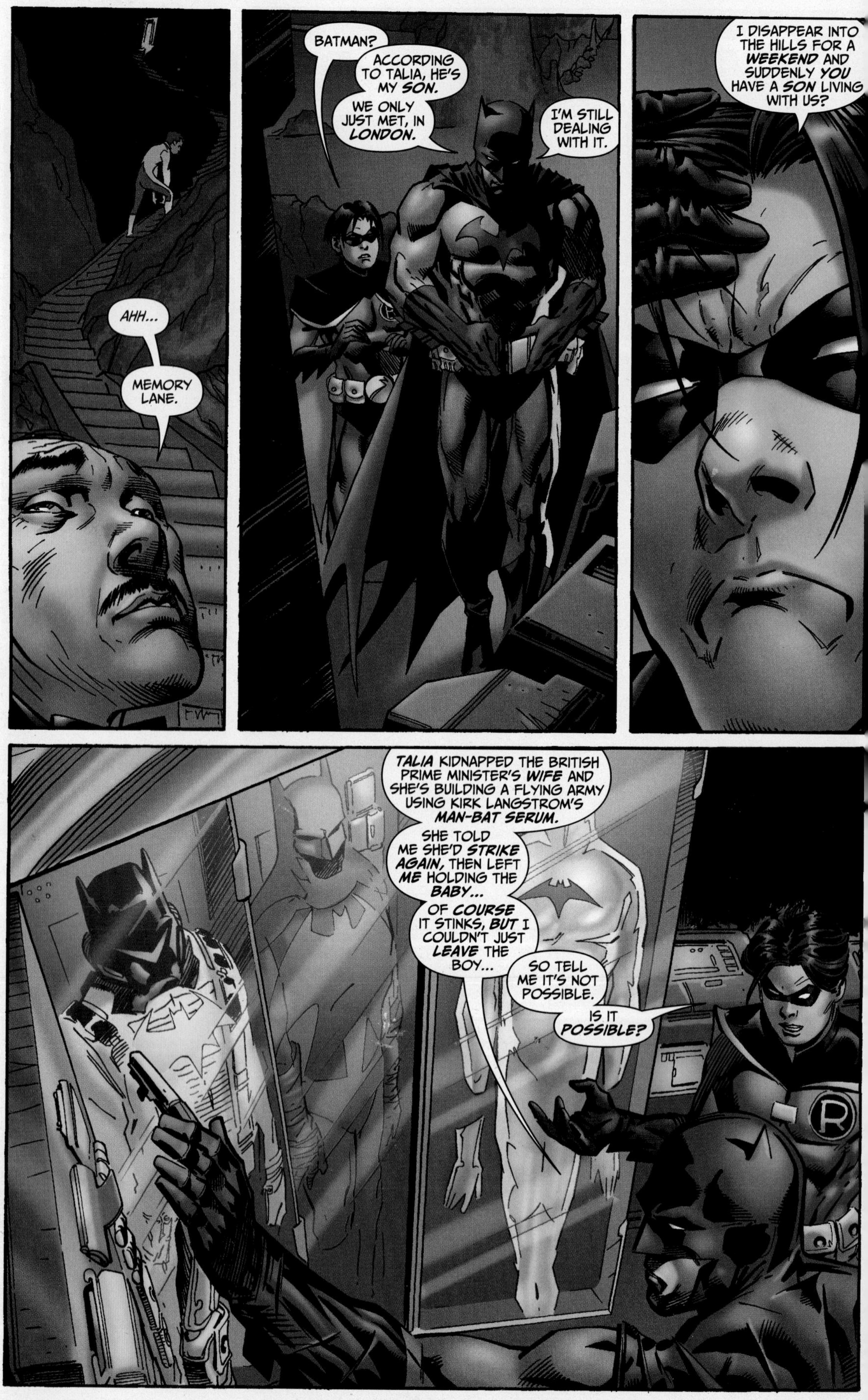
AHH...
MEMORY LANE.
BATMAN?
ACCORDING TO TALIA, HE'S MY SON.
WE ONLY JUST MET, IN LONDON.
I'M STILL DEALING WITH IT.
I DISAPPEAR INTO THE HILLS FOR A WEEKEND AND SUDDENLY YOU HAVE A SON LIVING WITH US?
TALIA KIDNAPPED THE BRITISH PRIME MINISTER'S WIFE AND SHE'S BUILDING A FLYING ARMY USING KIRK LANGSTROM'S MAN-BAT SERUM.
SHE TOLD ME SHE'D STRIKE AGAIN, THEN LEFT ME HOLDING THE BABY...
OF COURSE IT STINKS, BUT I COULDN'T JUST LEAVE THE BOY...
SO TELL ME IT'S NOT POSSIBLE.
IS IT POSSIBLE?

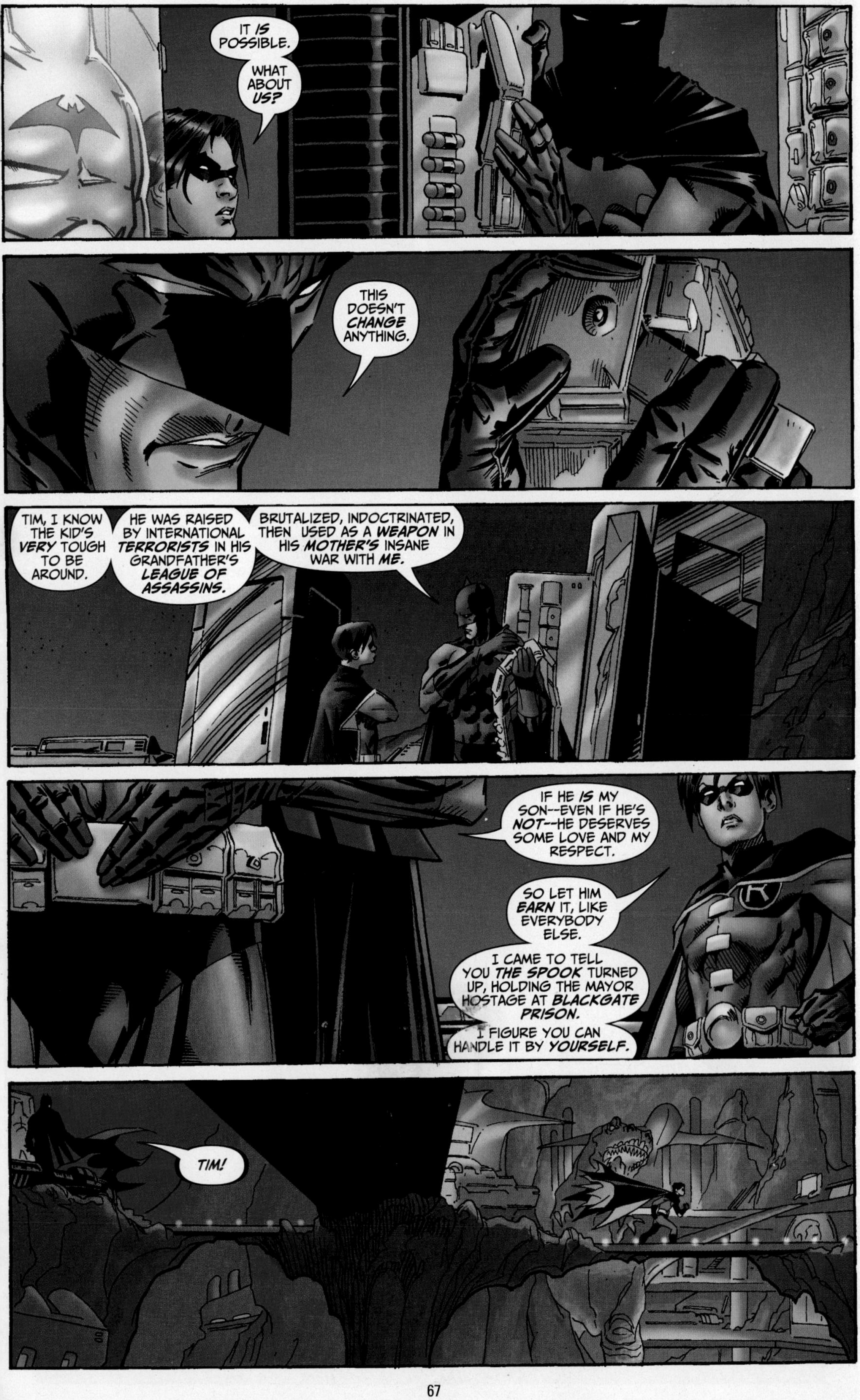
IT IS POSSIBLE.
WHAT ABOUT US?
THIS DOESN'T CHANGE ANYTHING.
TIM, I KNOW THE KID'S VERY TOUGH TO BE AROUND.
HE WAS RAISED BY INTERNATIONAL TERRORISTS IN HIS GRANDFATHER'S LEAGUE OF ASSASSINS.
BRUTALIZED, INDOCTRINATED, THEN USED AS A WEAPON IN HIS MOTHER'S INSANE WAR WITH ME.
IF HE IS MY SON--EVEN IF HE'S NOT--HE DESERVES SOME LOVE AND MY RESPECT.
SO LET HIM EARN IT, LIKE EVERYBODY ELSE.
I CAME TO TELL YOU THE SPOOK TURNED UP, HOLDING THE MAYOR HOSTAGE AT BLACKGATE PRISON.
I FIGURE YOU CAN HANDLE IT BY YOURSELF.
TIM!

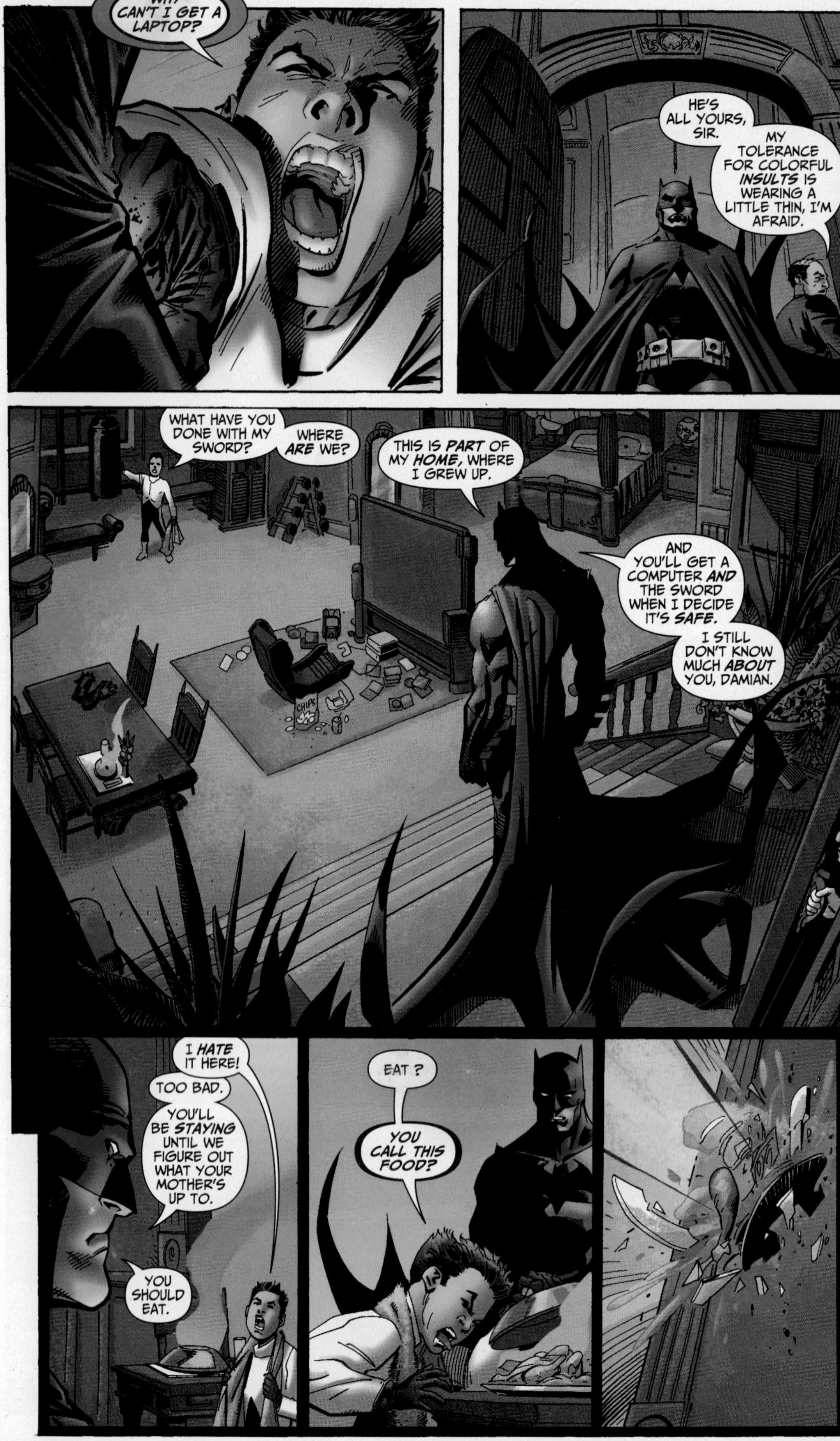
WHY CAN'T I GET A LAPTOP?
HE'S ALL YOURS, SIR.
MY TOLERANCE FOR COLORFUL INSULTS IS WEARING A LITTLE THIN, I'M AFRAID.
WHAT HAVE YOU DONE WITH MY SWORD?
WHERE ARE WE?
THIS IS PART OF MY HOME, WHERE I GREW UP.
AND YOU'LL GET A COMPUTER AND THE SWORD WHEN I DECIDE IT'S SAFE.
I STILL DON'T KNOW MUCH ABOUT YOU, DAMIAN.
CHIPS
I HATE IT HERE!
TOO BAD.
YOU'LL BE STAYING UNTIL WE FIGURE OUT WHAT YOUR MOTHER'S UP TO.
YOU SHOULD EAT.
EAT?
YOU CALL THIS FOOD?

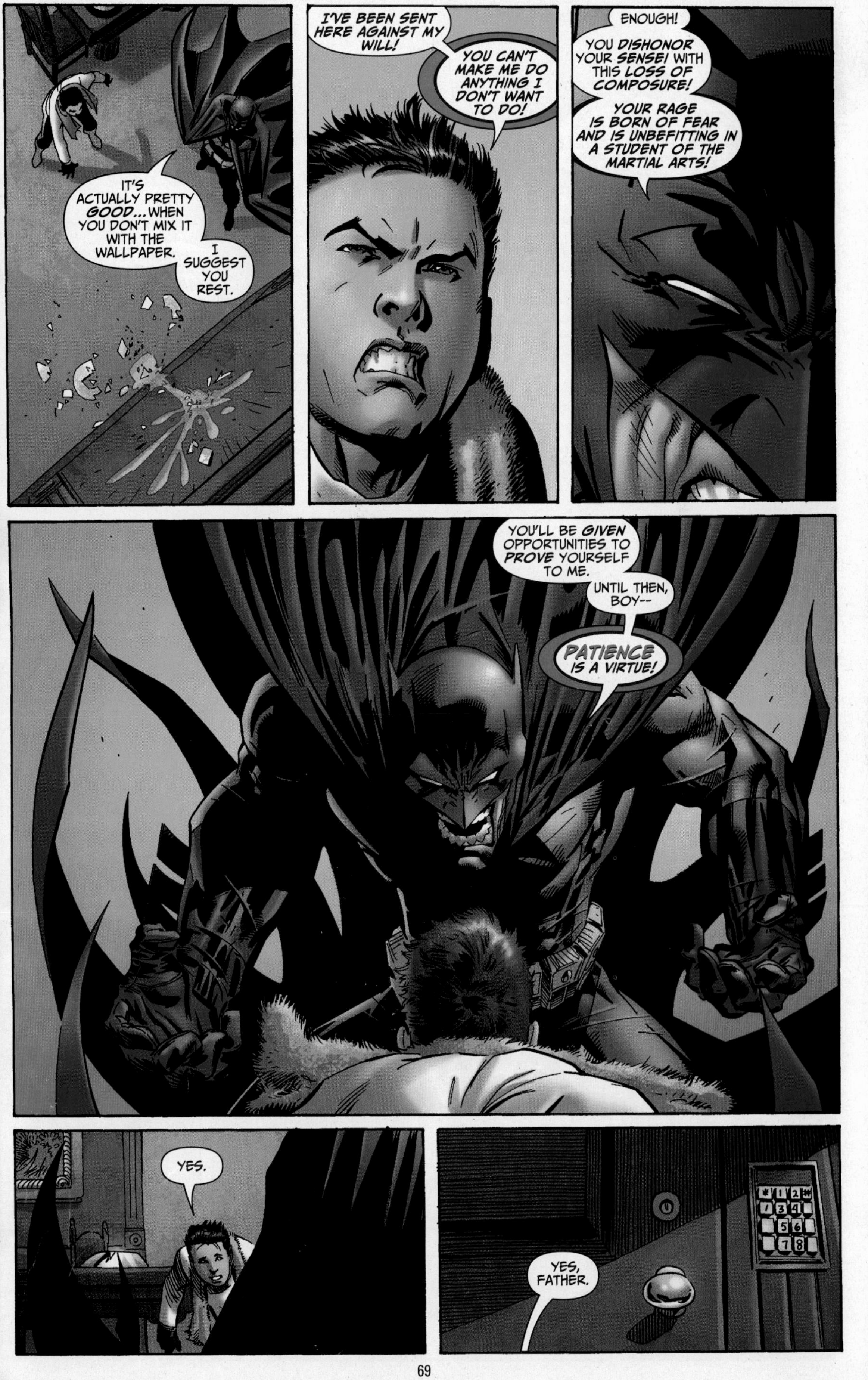

IT'S ACTUALLY PRETTY GOOD... WHEN YOU DON'T MIX IT WITH THE WALLPAPER.
I SUGGEST YOU REST.
I'VE BEEN SENT HERE AGAINST MY WILL!
YOU CAN'T MAKE ME DO ANYTHING I DON'T WANT TO DO!
ENOUGH!
YOU DISHONOR YOUR SENSEI WITH THIS LOSS OF COMPOSURE!
YOUR RAGE IS BORN OF FEAR AND IS UNBEFITTING IN A STUDENT OF THE MARTIAL ARTS!
YOU'LL BE GIVEN OPPORTUNITIES TO PROVE YOURSELF TO ME.
UNTIL THEN, BOY--
PATIENCE IS A VIRTUE!
YES.
YES, FATHER.

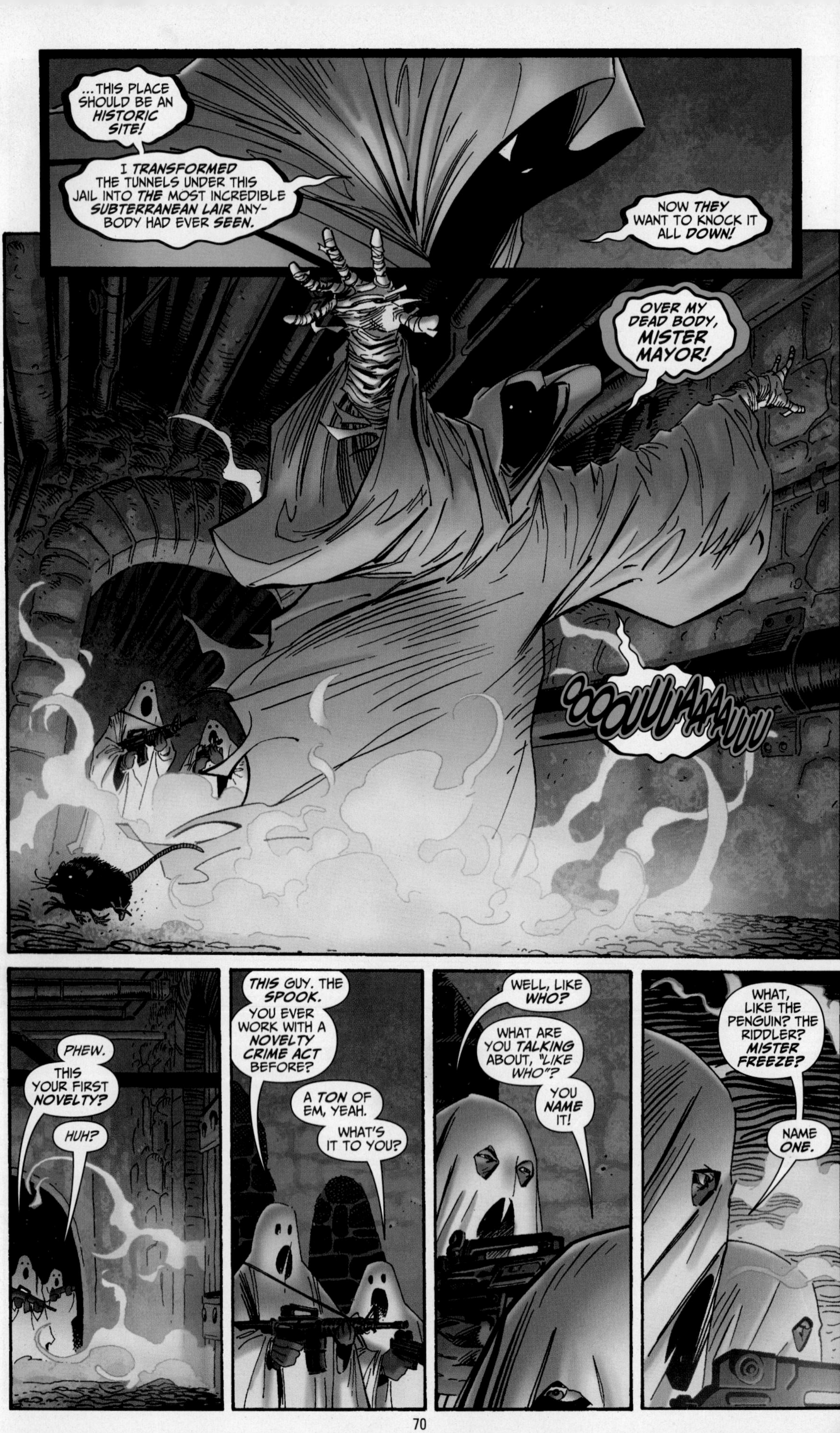

...THIS PLACE SHOULD BE AN HISTORIC SITE!
I TRANSFORMED THE TUNNELS UNDER THIS JAIL INTO THE MOST INCREDIBLE SUBTERRANEAN LAIR ANY-BODY HAD EVER SEEN.
NOW THEY WANT TO KNOCK IT ALL DOWN!
OVER MY DEAD BODY, MISTER MAYOR!
OOOOUUUUAAAAUUU
PHEW.
THIS YOUR FIRST NOVELTY?
HUH?
THIS GUY. THE SPOOK. YOU EVER WORK WITH A NOVELTY CRIME ACT BEFORE?
A TON OF EM, YEAH.
WHAT'S IT TO YOU?
WELL, LIKE WHO?
WHAT ARE YOU TALKING ABOUT, "LIKE WHO"?
YOU NAME IT!
WHAT, LIKE THE PENGUIN? THE RIDDLER? MISTER FREEZE?
NAME ONE.

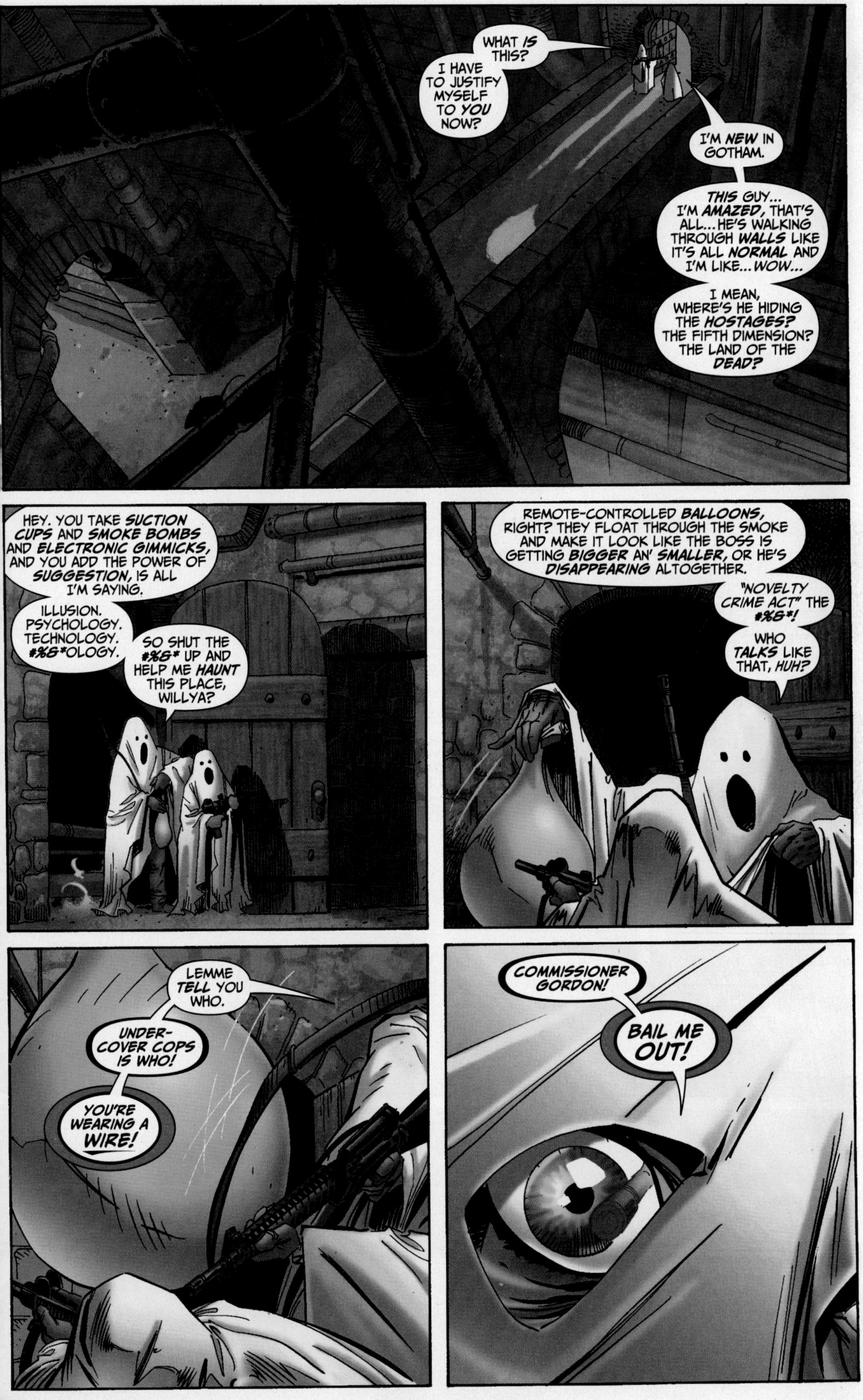
WHAT IS THIS? I HAVE TO JUSTIFY MYSELF TO YOU NOW?
I'M NEW IN GOTHAM.
THIS GUY... I'M AMAZED, THAT'S ALL... HE'S WALKING THROUGH WALLS LIKE IT'S ALL NORMAL AND I'M LIKE... WOW...
I MEAN, WHERE'S HE HIDING THE HOSTAGES? THE FIFTH DIMENSION? THE LAND OF THE DEAD?
HEY. YOU TAKE SUCTION CUPS AND SMOKE BOMBS AND ELECTRONIC GIMMICKS, AND YOU ADD THE POWER OF SUGGESTION, IS ALL I'M SAYING.
ILLUSION. PSYCHOLOGY. TECHNOLOGY. #%&*OLOGY.
SO SHUT THE #%&* UP AND HELP ME HAUNT THIS PLACE, WILLYA?
REMOTE-CONTROLLED BALLOONS, RIGHT? THEY FLOAT THROUGH THE SMOKE AND MAKE IT LOOK LIKE THE BOSS IS GETTING BIGGER AN' SMALLER, OR HE'S DISAPPEARING ALTOGETHER.
"NOVELTY CRIME ACT" THE #%&*!
WHO TALKS LIKE THAT, HUH?
LEMME TELL YOU WHO.
UNDER-COVER COPS IS WHO!
YOU'RE WEARING A WIRE!
COMMISSIONER GORDON!
BAIL ME OUT!

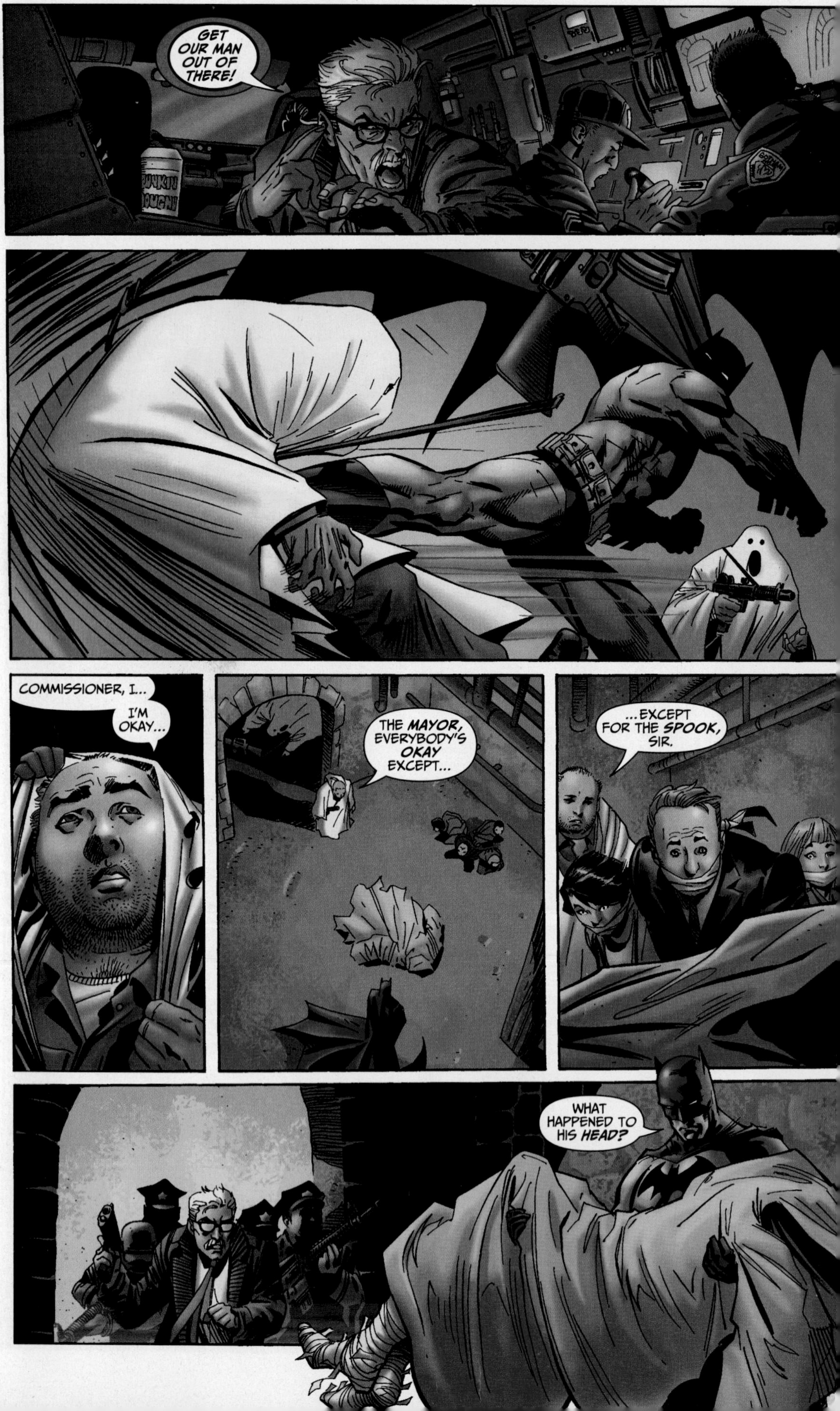
GET OUR MAN OUT OF THERE!
COMMISSIONER, I...
I'M OKAY...
THE MAYOR, EVERYBODY'S OKAY EXCEPT...
...EXCEPT FOR THE SPOOK, SIR.
WHAT HAPPENED TO HIS HEAD?

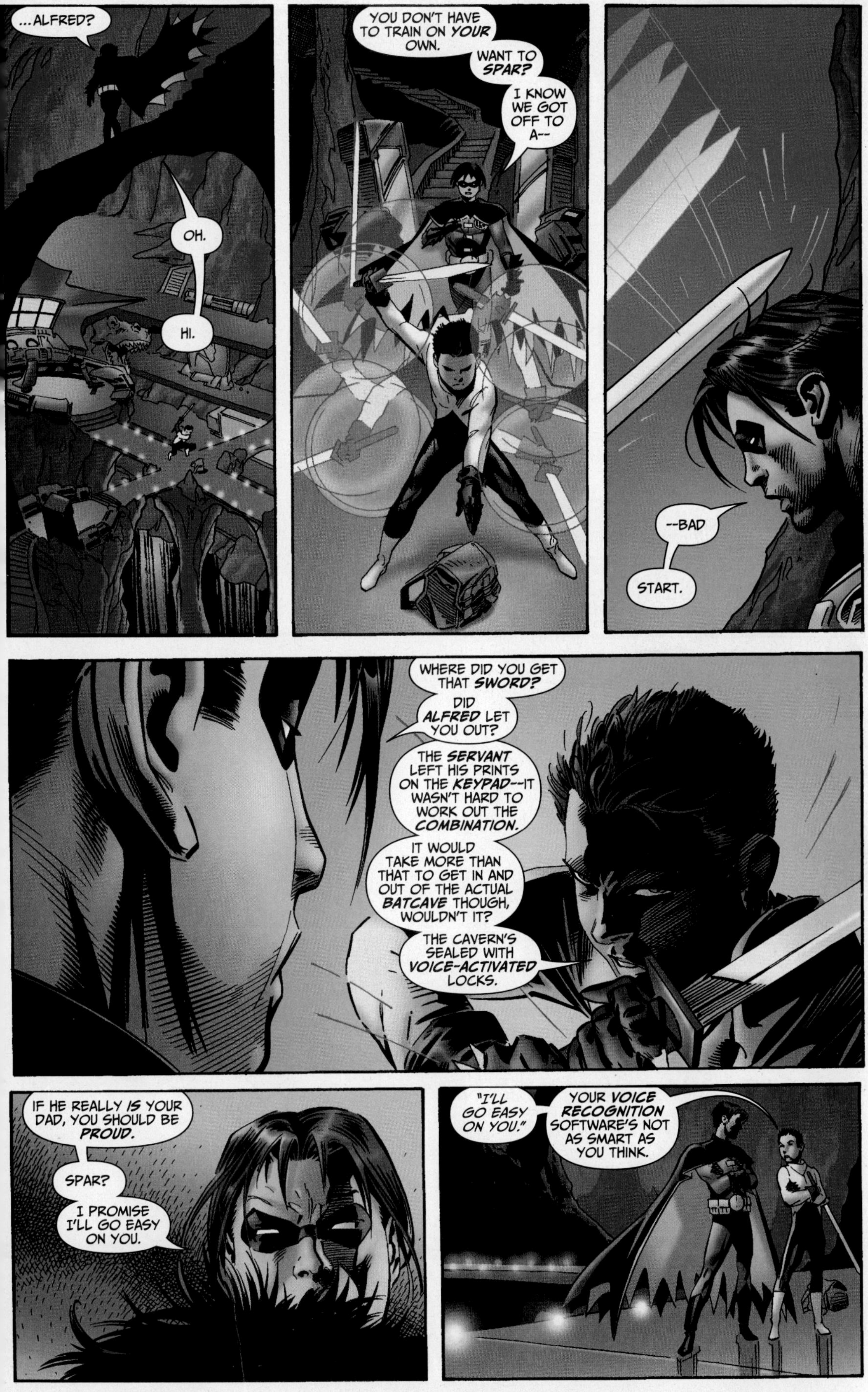
...ALFRED?
OH.
HI.
YOU DON'T HAVE TO TRAIN ON YOUR OWN.
WANT TO SPAR?
I KNOW WE GOT OFF TO A--
--BAD
START.
WHERE DID YOU GET THAT SWORD?
DID ALFRED LET YOU OUT?
THE SERVANT LEFT HIS PRINTS ON THE KEYPAD--IT WASN'T HARD TO WORK OUT THE COMBINATION.
IT WOULD TAKE MORE THAN THAT TO GET IN AND OUT OF THE ACTUAL BATCAVE THOUGH, WOULDN'T IT?
THE CAVERN'S SEALED WITH VOICE-ACTIVATED LOCKS.
IF HE REALLY IS YOUR DAD, YOU SHOULD BE PROUD.
SPAR?
I PROMISE I'LL GO EASY ON YOU.
"I'LL GO EASY ON YOU."
YOUR VOICE RECOGNITION SOFTWARE'S NOT AS SMART AS YOU THINK.

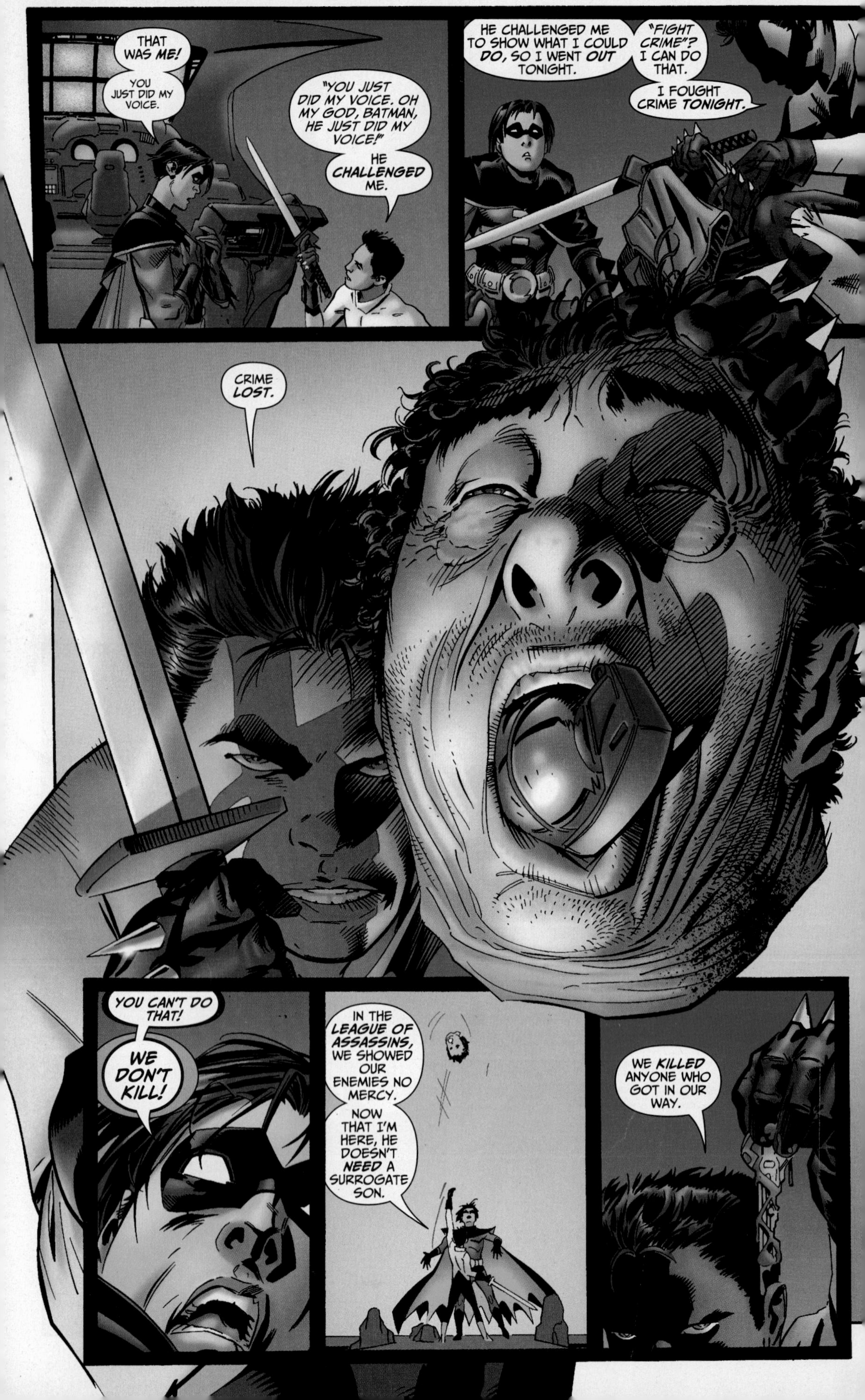
THAT WAS ME!
YOU JUST DID MY VOICE.
"YOU JUST DID MY VOICE. OH MY GOD, BATMAN, HE JUST DID MY VOICE!"
HE CHALLENGED ME.
HE CHALLENGED ME TO SHOW WHAT I COULD DO, SO I WENT OUT TONIGHT.
"FIGHT CRIME"? I CAN DO THAT.
I FOUGHT CRIME TONIGHT.
CRIME LOST.
YOU CAN'T DO THAT!
WE DON'T KILL!
IN THE LEAGUE OF ASSASSINS, WE SHOWED OUR ENEMIES NO MERCY.
NOW THAT I'M HERE, HE DOESN'T NEED A SURROGATE SON.
WE KILLED ANYONE WHO GOT IN OUR WAY.

HUH?

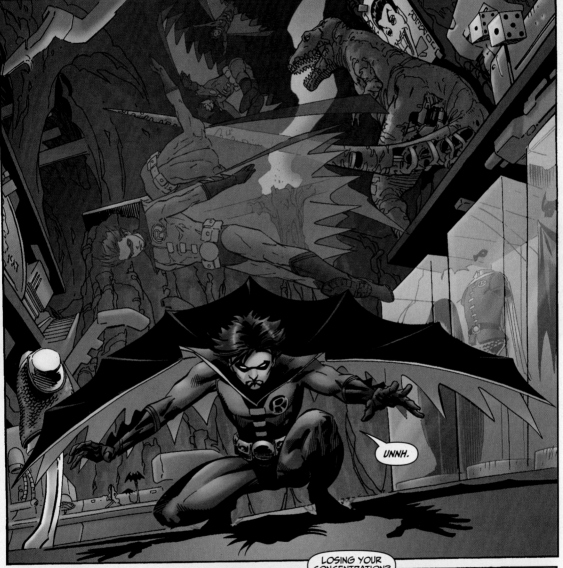

UNNH.

LOSING YOUR CONCENTRATION?

KLANG

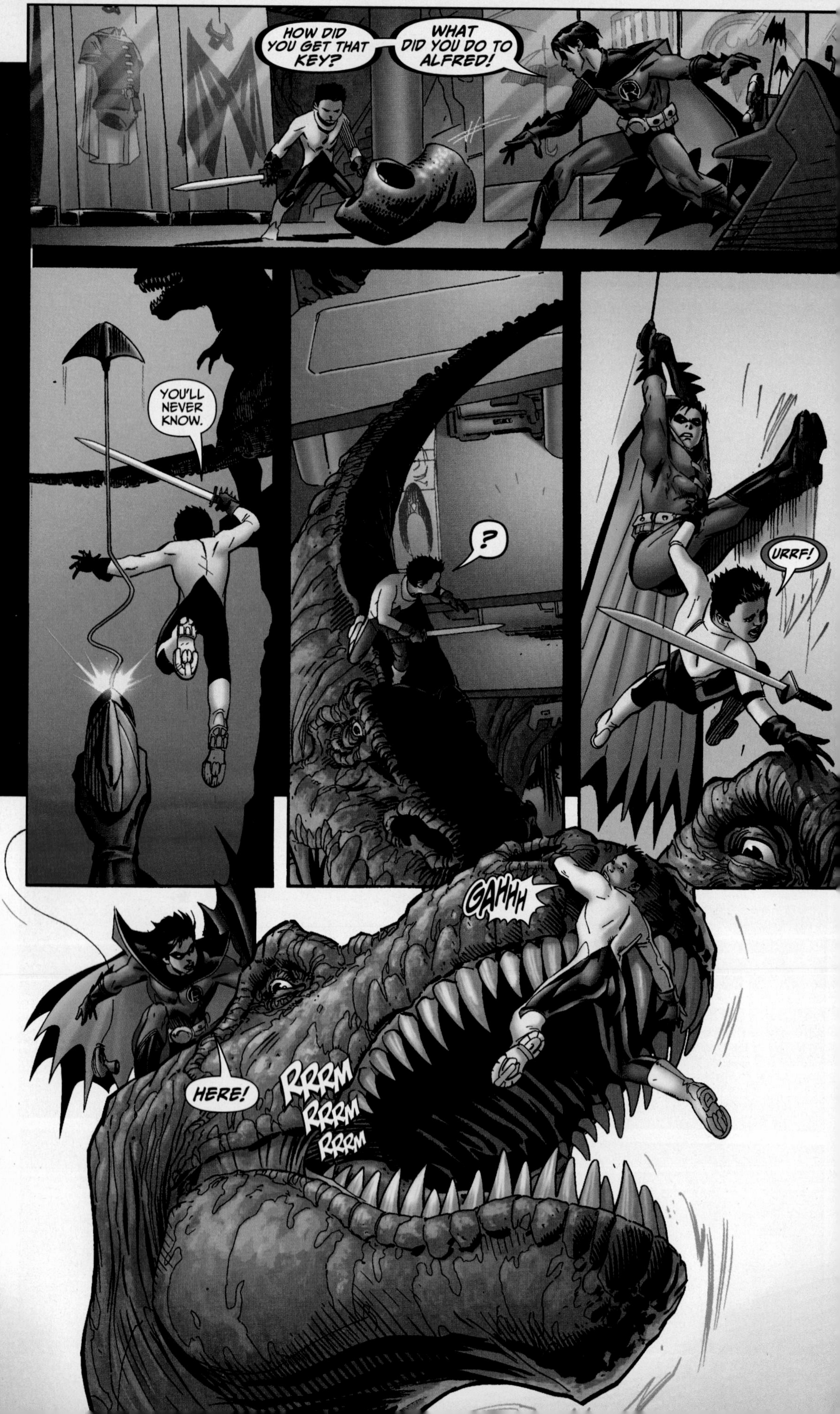
HOW DID YOU GET THAT KEY?
WHAT DID YOU DO TO ALFRED!
YOU'LL NEVER KNOW.
?
URRF!
GAHHH
HERE!
RRRM RRRM RRRM

GRAB HOLD BEFORE THE JAWS CLOSE!

GET A GRIP, WILL YOU?

WHY?

WHY ARE YOU ACTING LIKE SUCH A JERK?

BECAUSE YOU DON'T DESERVE ANY OF THIS.

YOU'RE ADOPTED!

BUT WHEN YOU'RE GONE, I'LL TAKE MY RIGHTFUL PLACE AT MY FATHER'S SIDE...

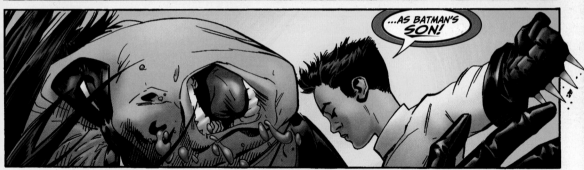

...AS BATMAN'S SON!

I'LL INHERIT EVERYTHING.

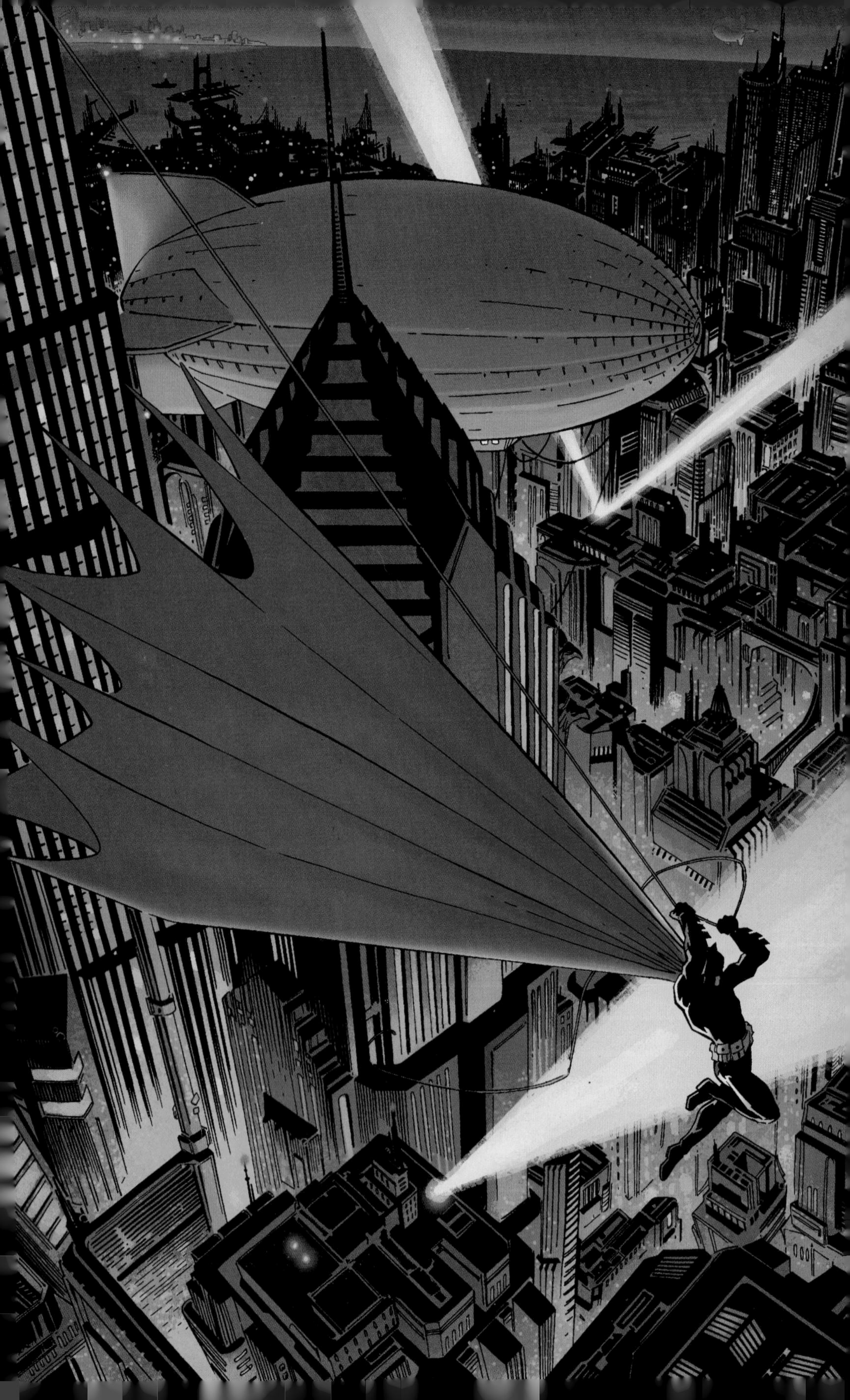

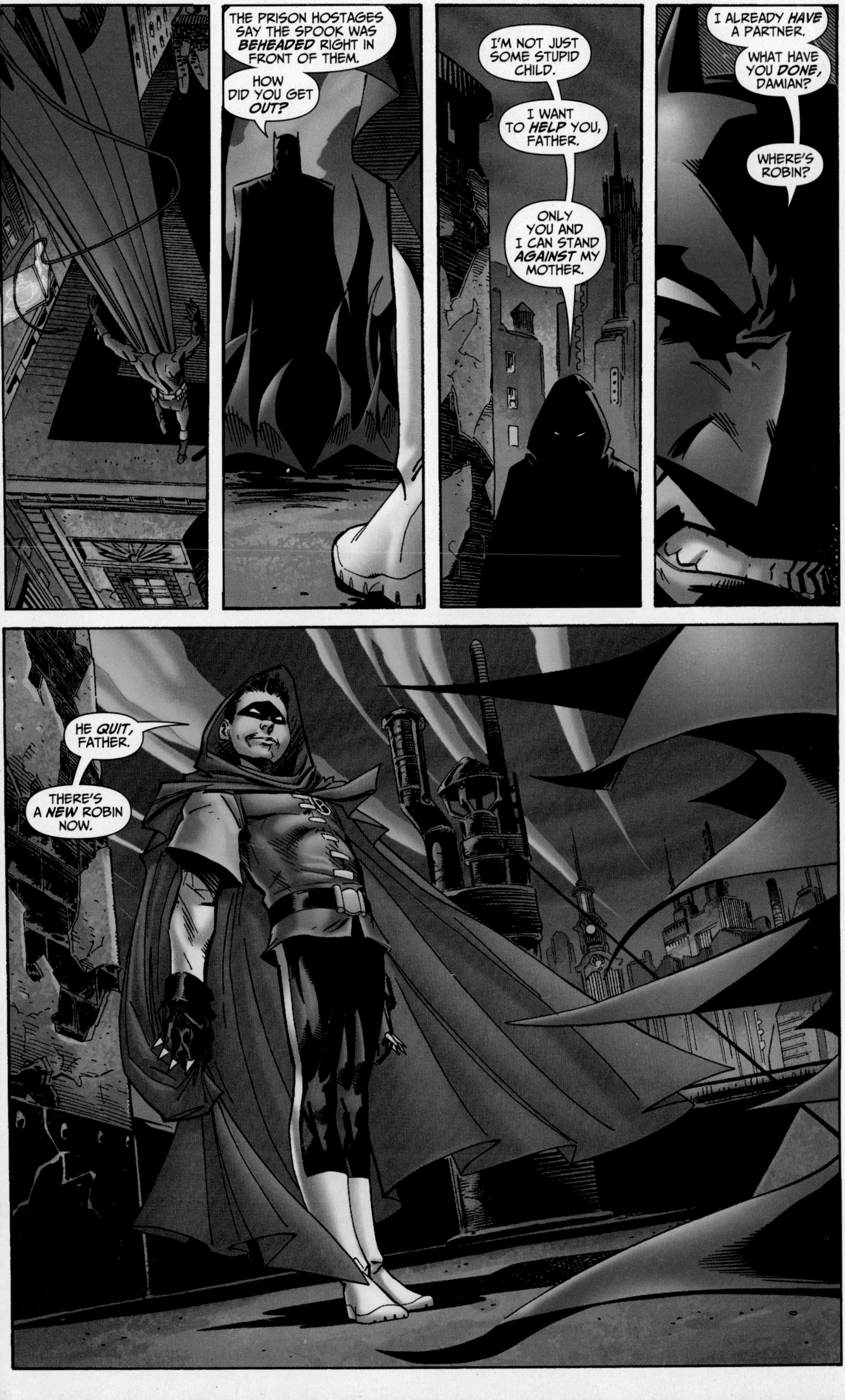
THE PRISON HOSTAGES SAY THE SPOOK WAS BEHEADED RIGHT IN FRONT OF THEM.
HOW DID YOU GET OUT?
I'M NOT JUST SOME STUPID CHILD.
I WANT TO HELP YOU, FATHER.
ONLY YOU AND I CAN STAND AGAINST MY MOTHER.
I ALREADY HAVE A PARTNER.
WHAT HAVE YOU DONE, DAMIAN?
WHERE'S ROBIN?
HE QUIT, FATHER.
THERE'S A NEW ROBIN NOW.

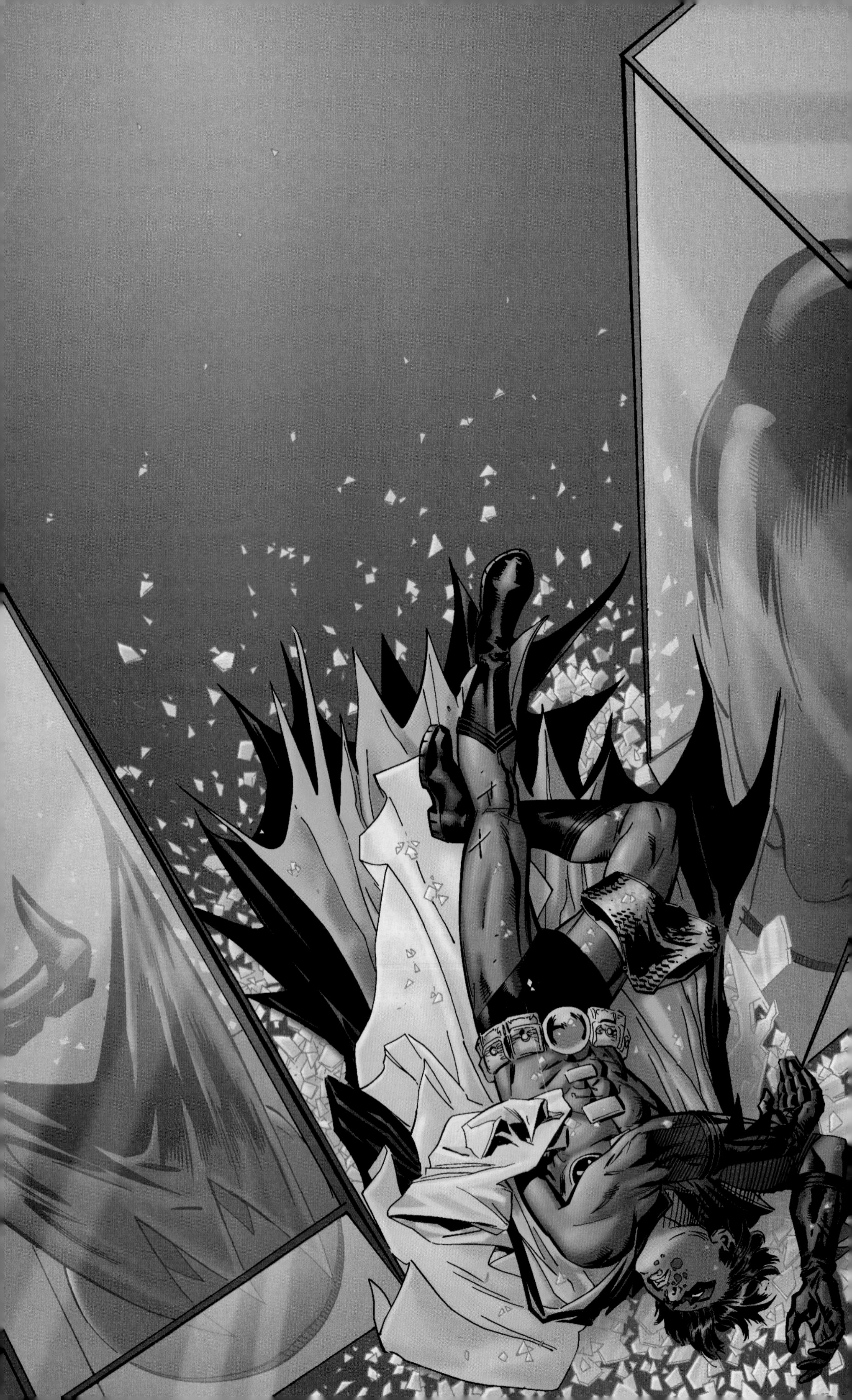

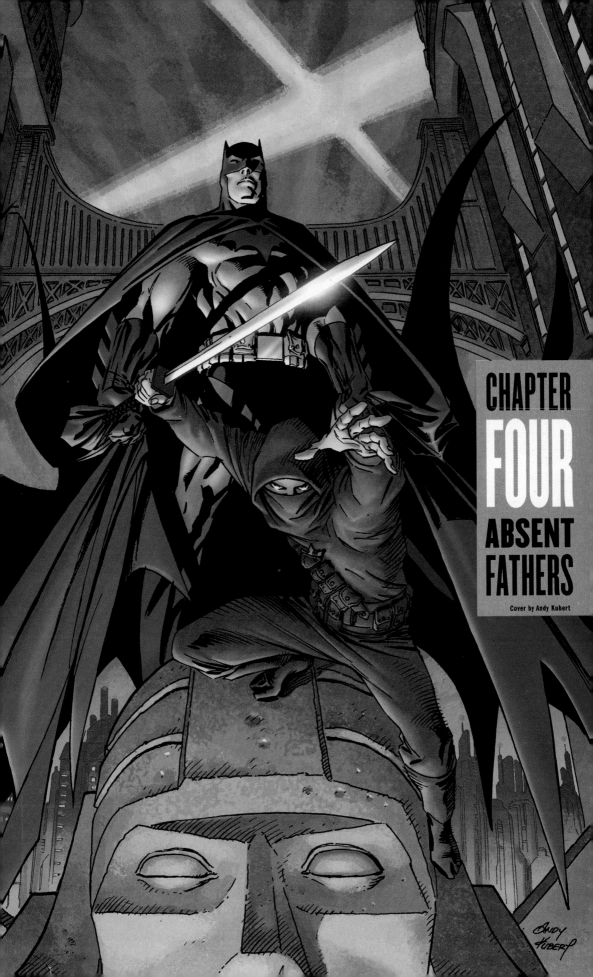

CHAPTER
FOUR
ABSENT
FATHERS

Cover by Andy Kubert

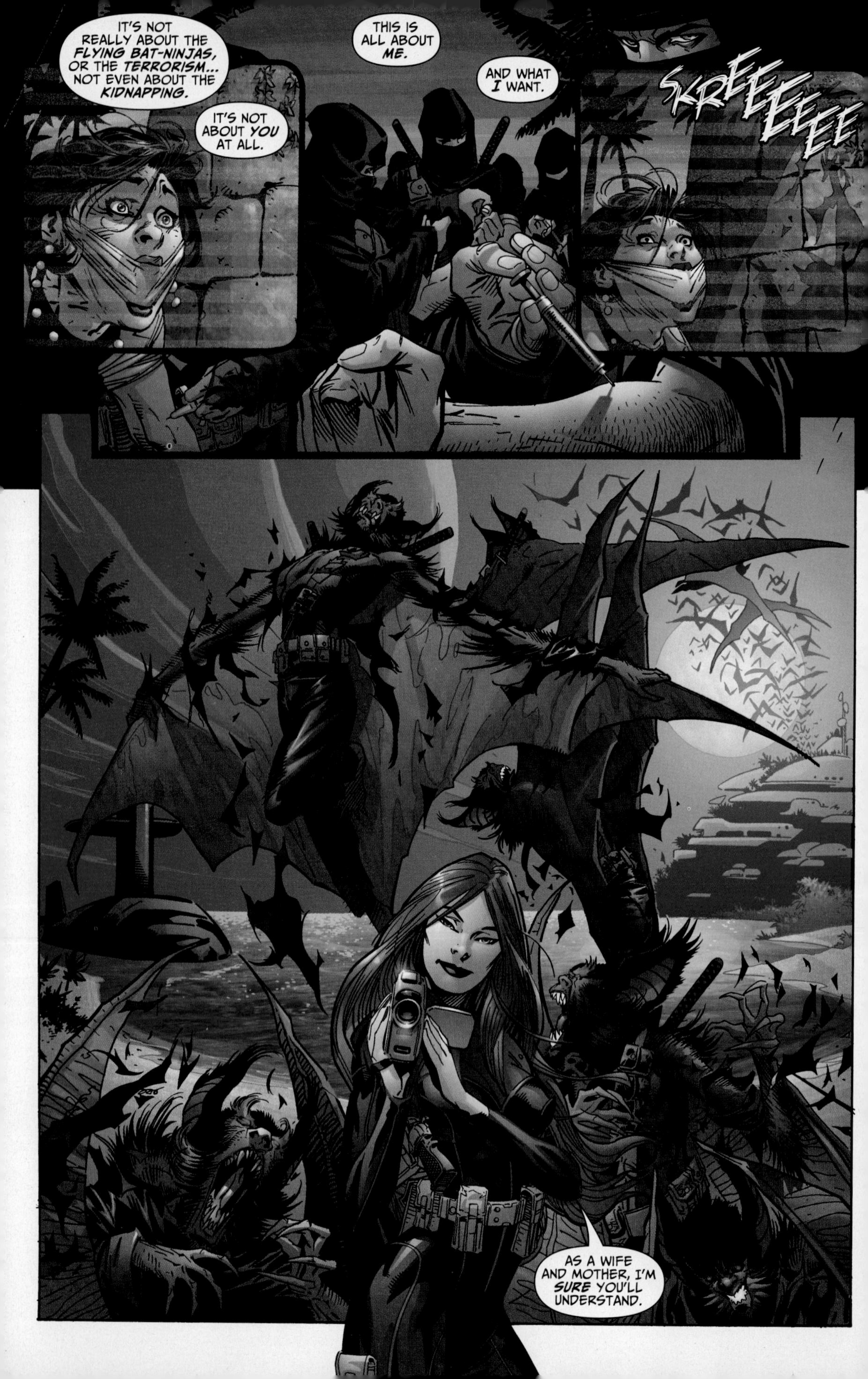
IT'S NOT REALLY ABOUT THE FLYING BAT-NINJAS, OR THE TERRORISM... NOT EVEN ABOUT THE KIDNAPPING.
IT'S NOT ABOUT YOU AT ALL.
THIS IS ALL ABOUT ME.
AND WHAT I WANT.
SKREEEEEEE
AS A WIFE AND MOTHER, I'M SURE YOU'LL UNDERSTAND.

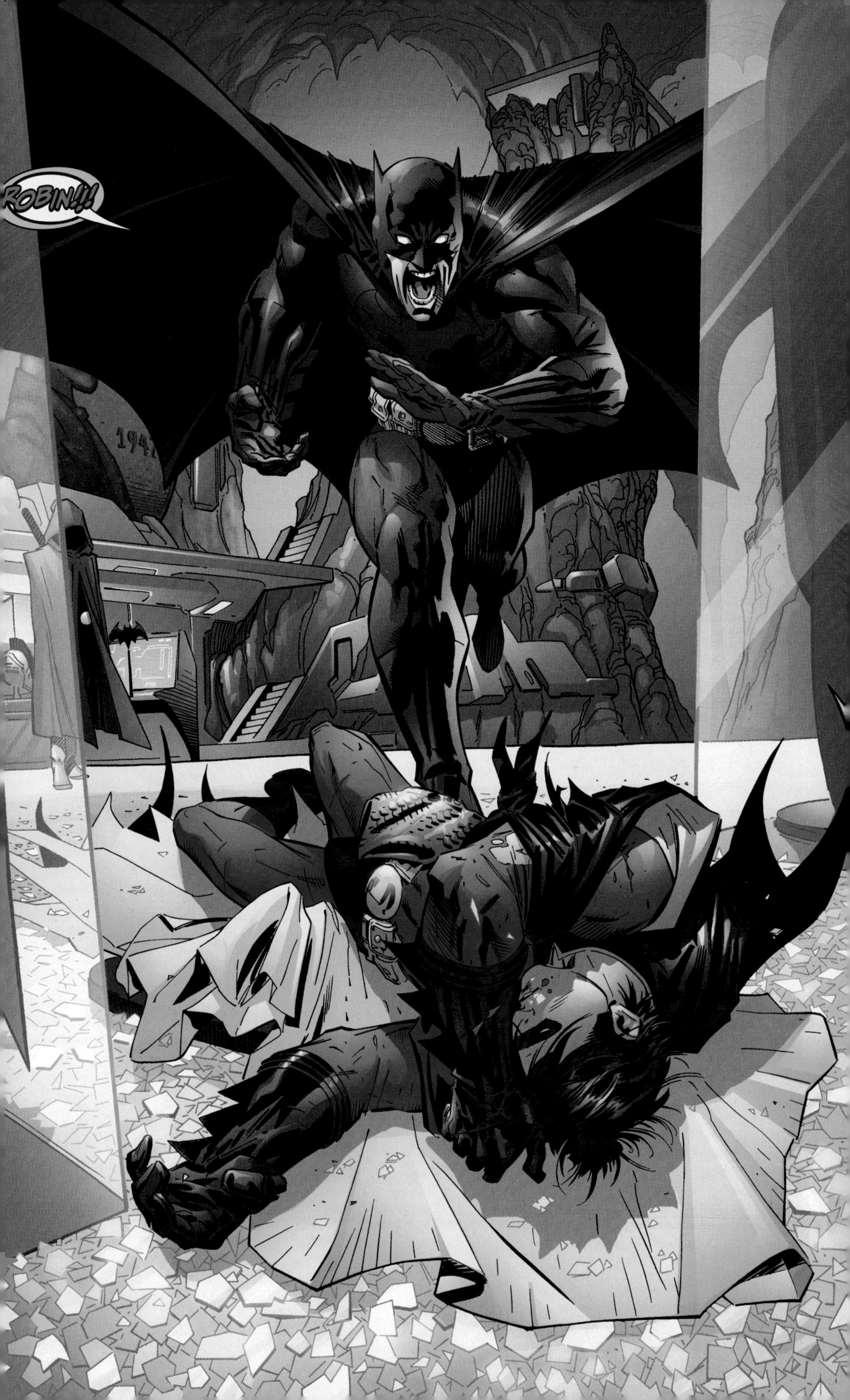
ROBIN!!!

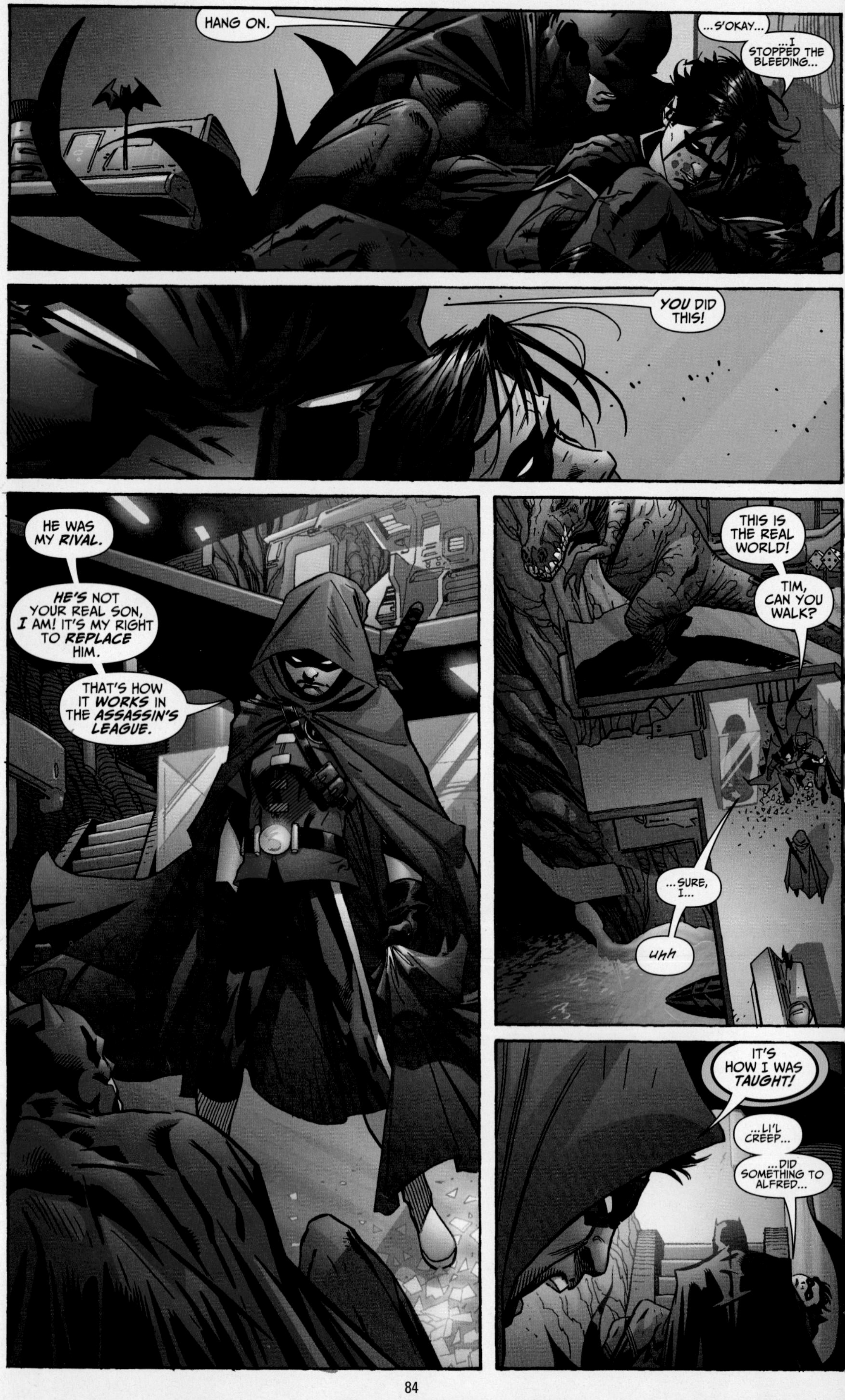
HANG ON.
...S'OKAY...
...I STOPPED THE BLEEDING...
YOU DID THIS!
HE WAS MY RIVAL.
HE'S NOT YOUR REAL SON, I AM! IT'S MY RIGHT TO REPLACE HIM.
THAT'S HOW IT WORKS IN THE ASSASSIN'S LEAGUE.
THIS IS THE REAL WORLD!
TIM, CAN YOU WALK?
...SURE, I...
uhh
IT'S HOW I WAS TAUGHT!
...LI'L CREEP...
...DID SOMETHING TO ALFRED...

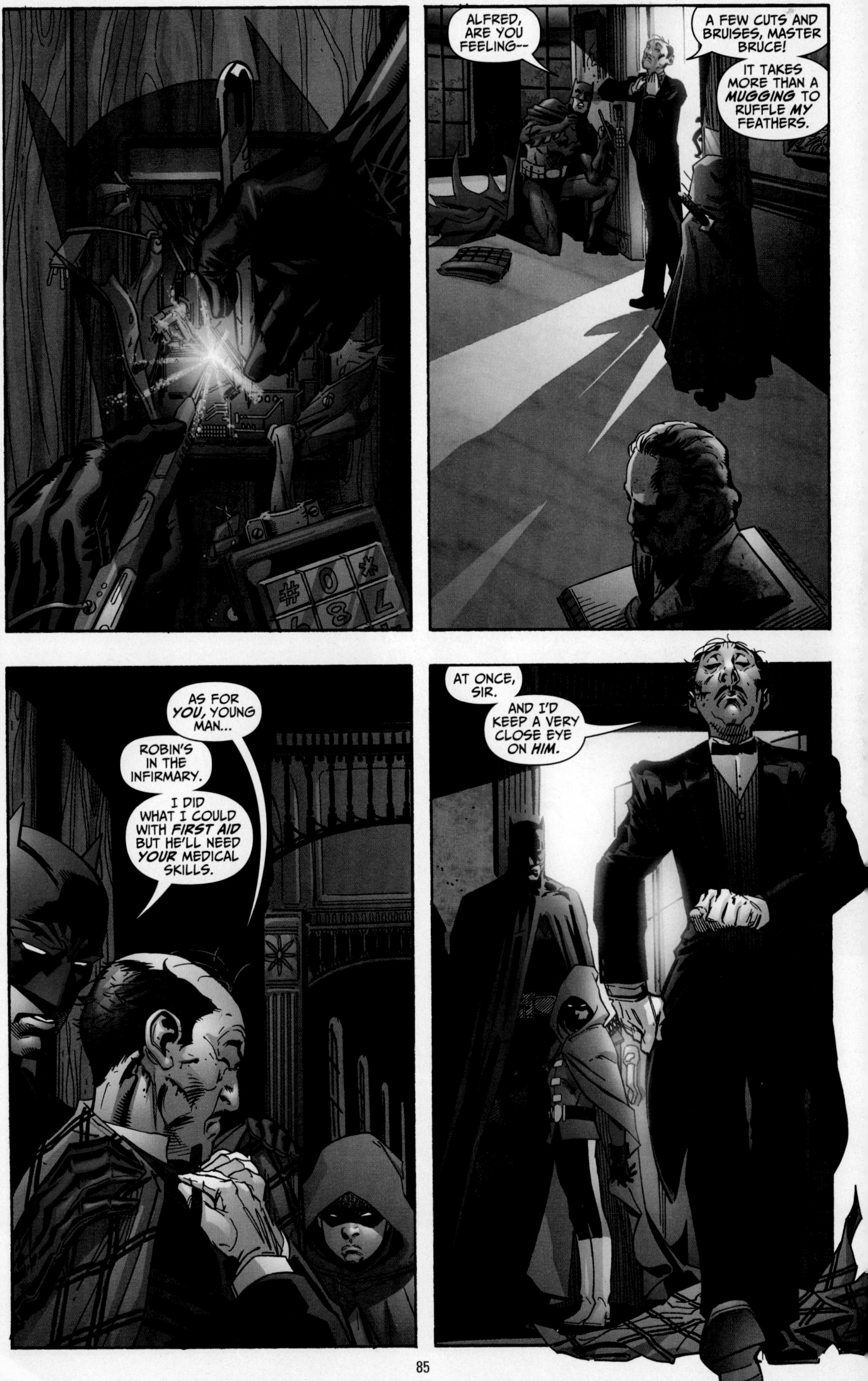
ALFRED, ARE YOU FEELING--
A FEW CUTS AND BRUISES, MASTER BRUCE!
IT TAKES MORE THAN A MUGGING TO RUFFLE MY FEATHERS.
AS FOR YOU, YOUNG MAN...
ROBIN'S IN THE INFIRMARY.
I DID WHAT I COULD WITH FIRST AID BUT HE'LL NEED YOUR MEDICAL SKILLS.
AT ONCE, SIR.
AND I'D KEEP A VERY CLOSE EYE ON HIM.

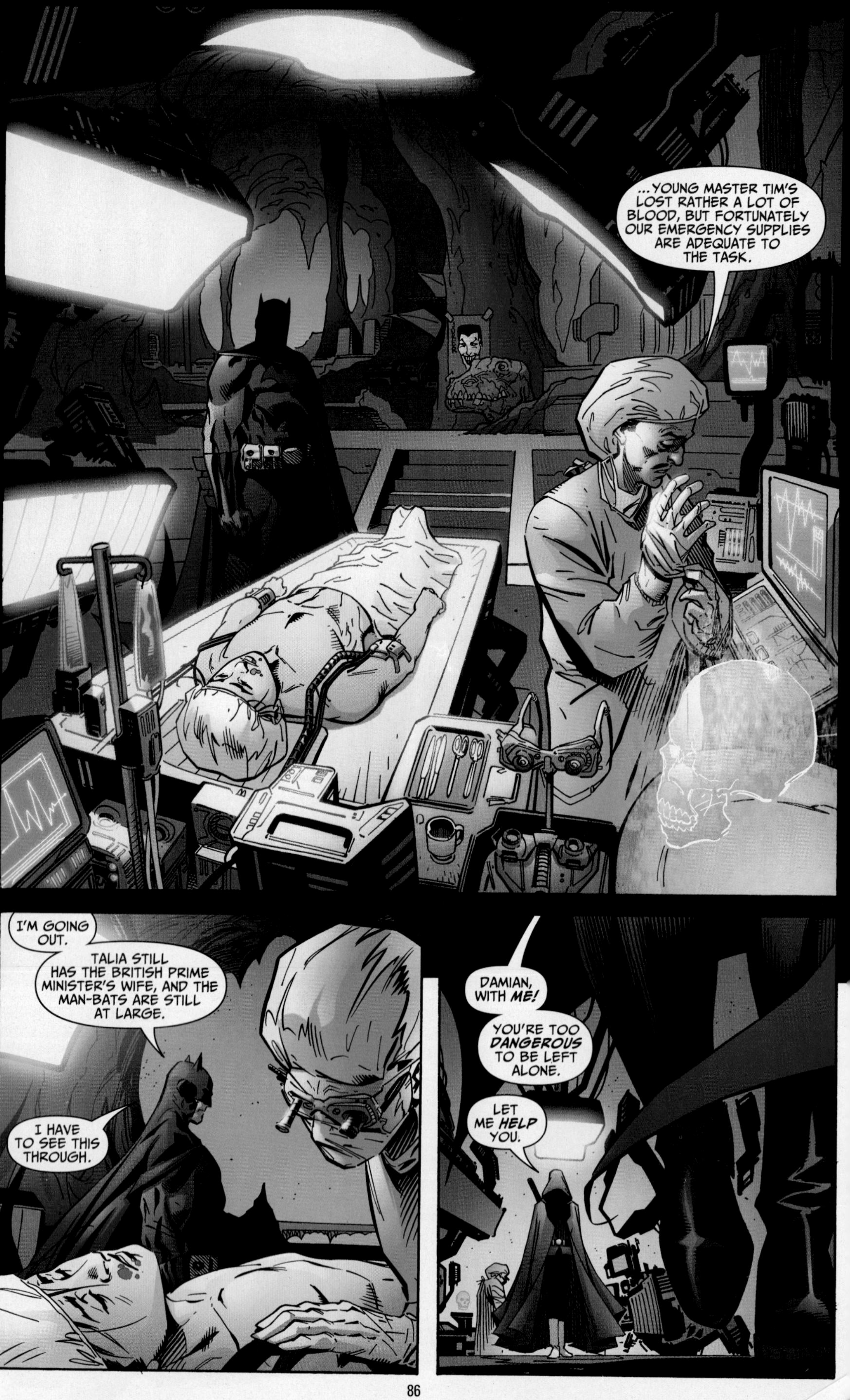
...YOUNG MASTER TIM'S LOST RATHER A LOT OF BLOOD, BUT FORTUNATELY OUR EMERGENCY SUPPLIES ARE ADEQUATE TO THE TASK.
I'M GOING OUT.
TALIA STILL HAS THE BRITISH PRIME MINISTER'S WIFE, AND THE MAN-BATS ARE STILL AT LARGE.
I HAVE TO SEE THIS THROUGH.
DAMIAN, WITH ***ME!***
YOU'RE TOO ***DANGEROUS*** TO BE LEFT ALONE.
LET ME ***HELP*** YOU.

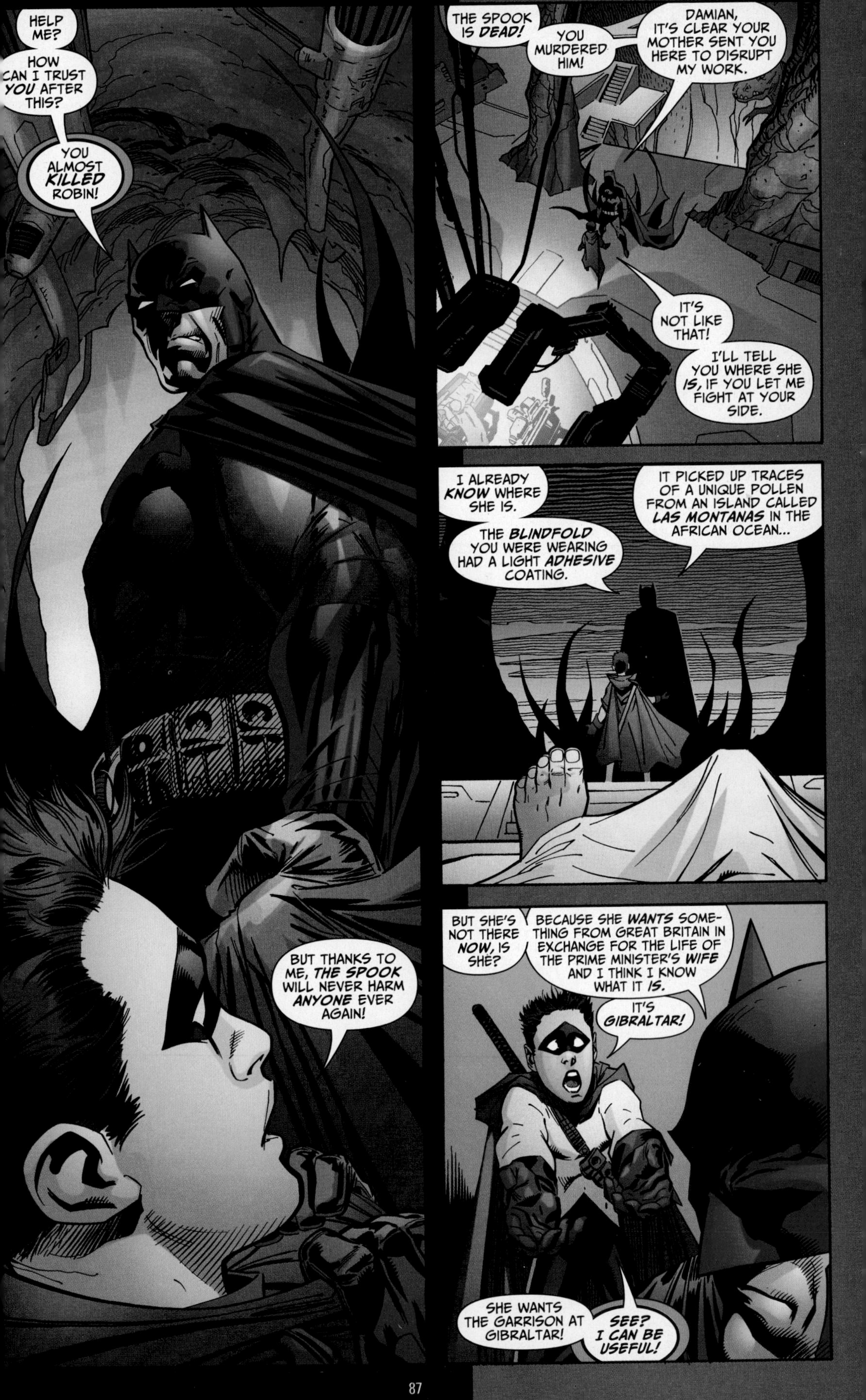
HELP ME?
HOW CAN I TRUST *YOU* AFTER THIS?
YOU ALMOST *KILLED* ROBIN!
BUT THANKS TO ME, *THE SPOOK* WILL NEVER HARM *ANYONE* EVER AGAIN!
THE SPOOK IS *DEAD!*
YOU MURDERED HIM!
DAMIAN, IT'S CLEAR YOUR MOTHER SENT YOU HERE TO DISRUPT MY WORK.
IT'S NOT LIKE THAT!
I'LL TELL YOU WHERE SHE *IS*, IF YOU LET ME FIGHT AT YOUR SIDE.
I ALREADY *KNOW* WHERE SHE IS.
THE *BLINDFOLD* YOU WERE WEARING HAD A LIGHT *ADHESIVE* COATING.
IT PICKED UP TRACES OF A UNIQUE POLLEN FROM AN ISLAND CALLED *LAS MONTANAS* IN THE AFRICAN OCEAN...
BUT SHE'S NOT THERE *NOW*, IS SHE?
BECAUSE SHE *WANTS* SOMETHING FROM GREAT BRITAIN IN EXCHANGE FOR THE LIFE OF THE PRIME MINISTER'S *WIFE* AND I THINK I KNOW WHAT IT *IS*.
IT'S *GIBRALTAR!*
SHE WANTS THE GARRISON AT GIBRALTAR!
SEE? I CAN BE USEFUL!

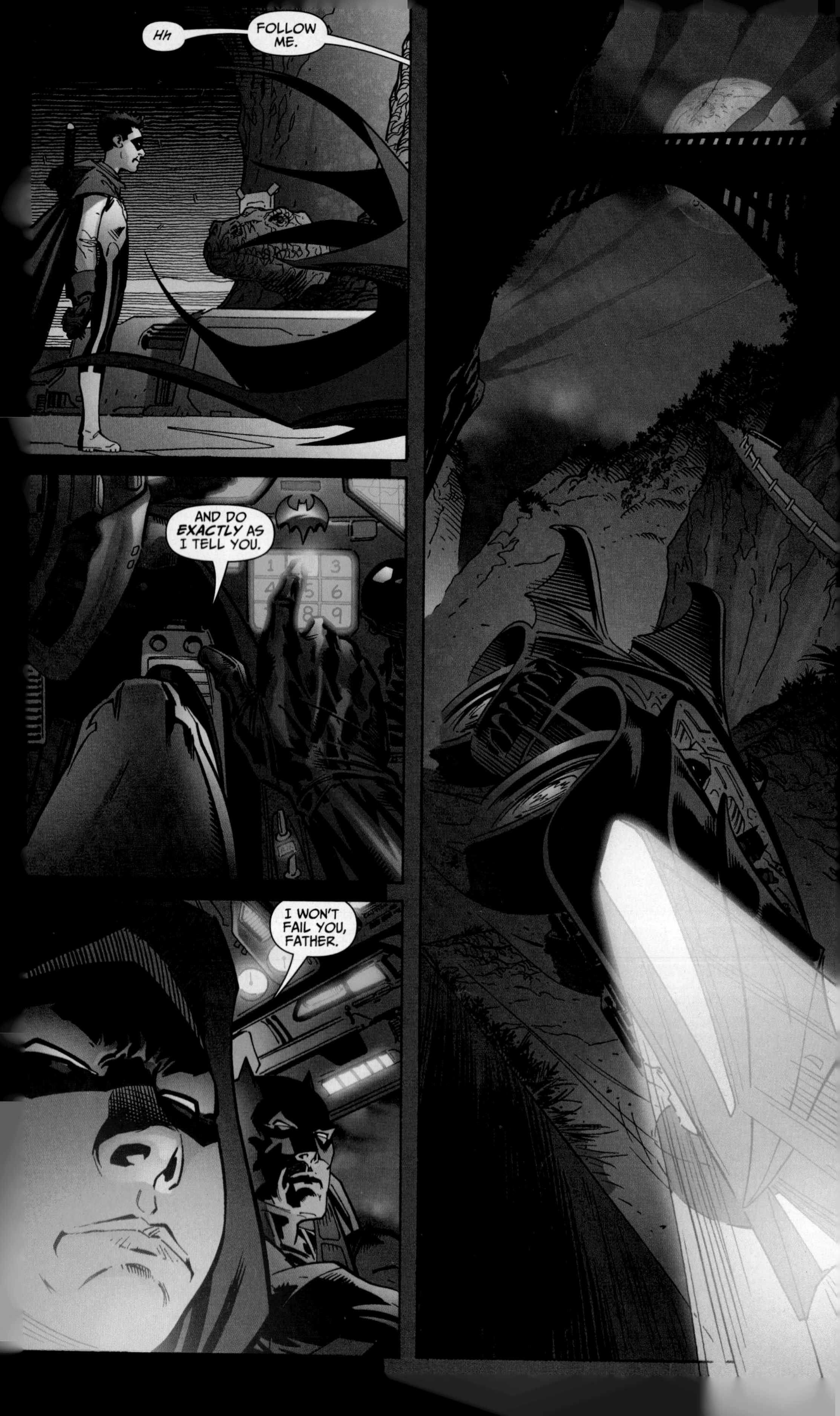

Hh
FOLLOW ME.
AND DO EXACTLY AS I TELL YOU.
I WON'T FAIL YOU, FATHER.

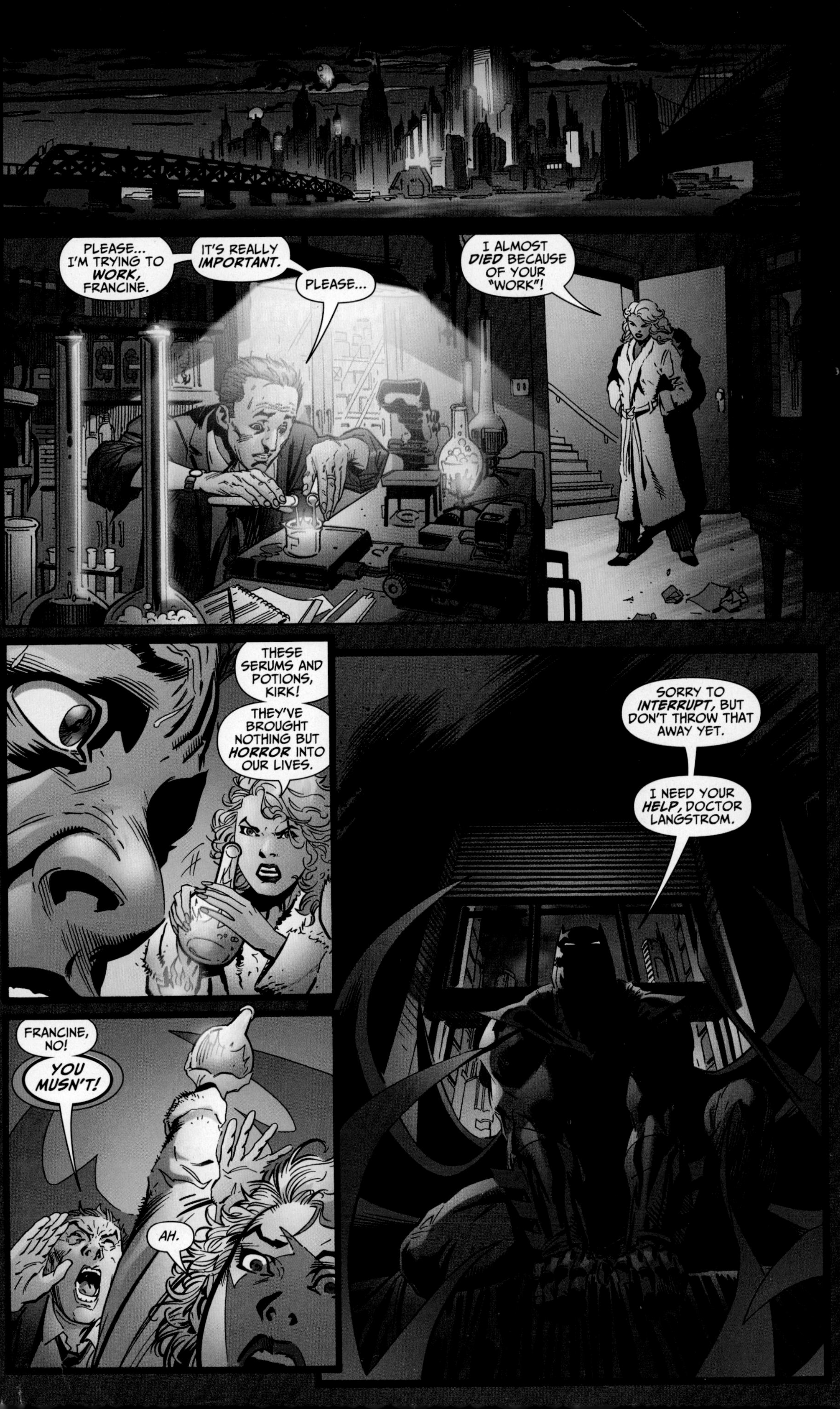

PLEASE... I'M TRYING TO WORK, FRANCINE.
IT'S REALLY IMPORTANT.
PLEASE...
I ALMOST DIED BECAUSE OF YOUR "WORK"!
THESE SERUMS AND POTIONS, KIRK!
THEY'VE BROUGHT NOTHING BUT HORROR INTO OUR LIVES.
FRANCINE, NO! YOU MUSN'T!
AH.
SORRY TO INTERRUPT, BUT DON'T THROW THAT AWAY YET.
I NEED YOUR HELP, DOCTOR LANGSTROM.

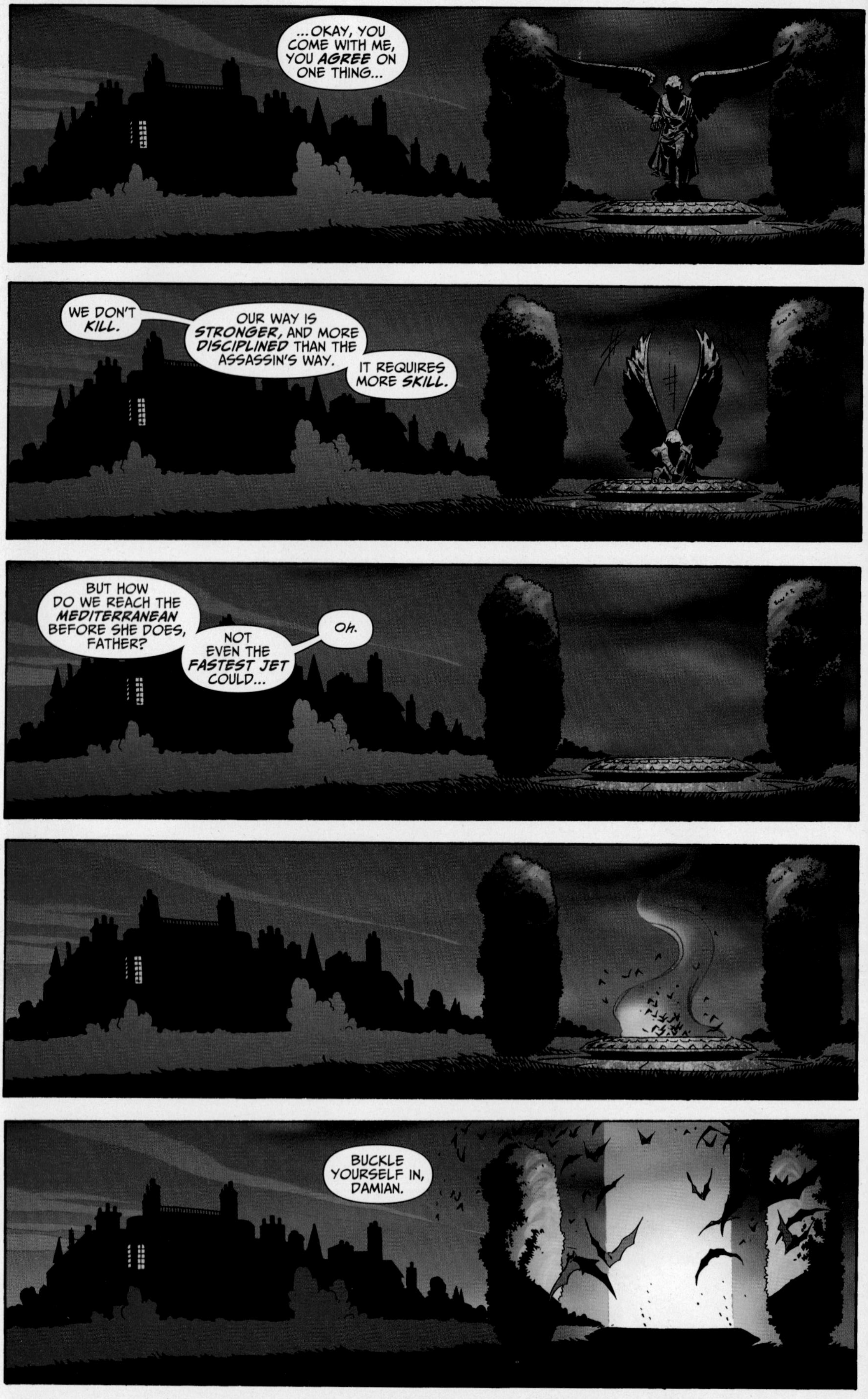
...OKAY, YOU COME WITH ME, YOU AGREE ON ONE THING...
WE DON'T KILL.
OUR WAY IS STRONGER, AND MORE DISCIPLINED THAN THE ASSASSIN'S WAY.
IT REQUIRES MORE SKILL.
BUT HOW DO WE REACH THE MEDITERRANEAN BEFORE SHE DOES, FATHER?
NOT EVEN THE FASTEST JET COULD...
Oh.
BUCKLE YOURSELF IN, DAMIAN.

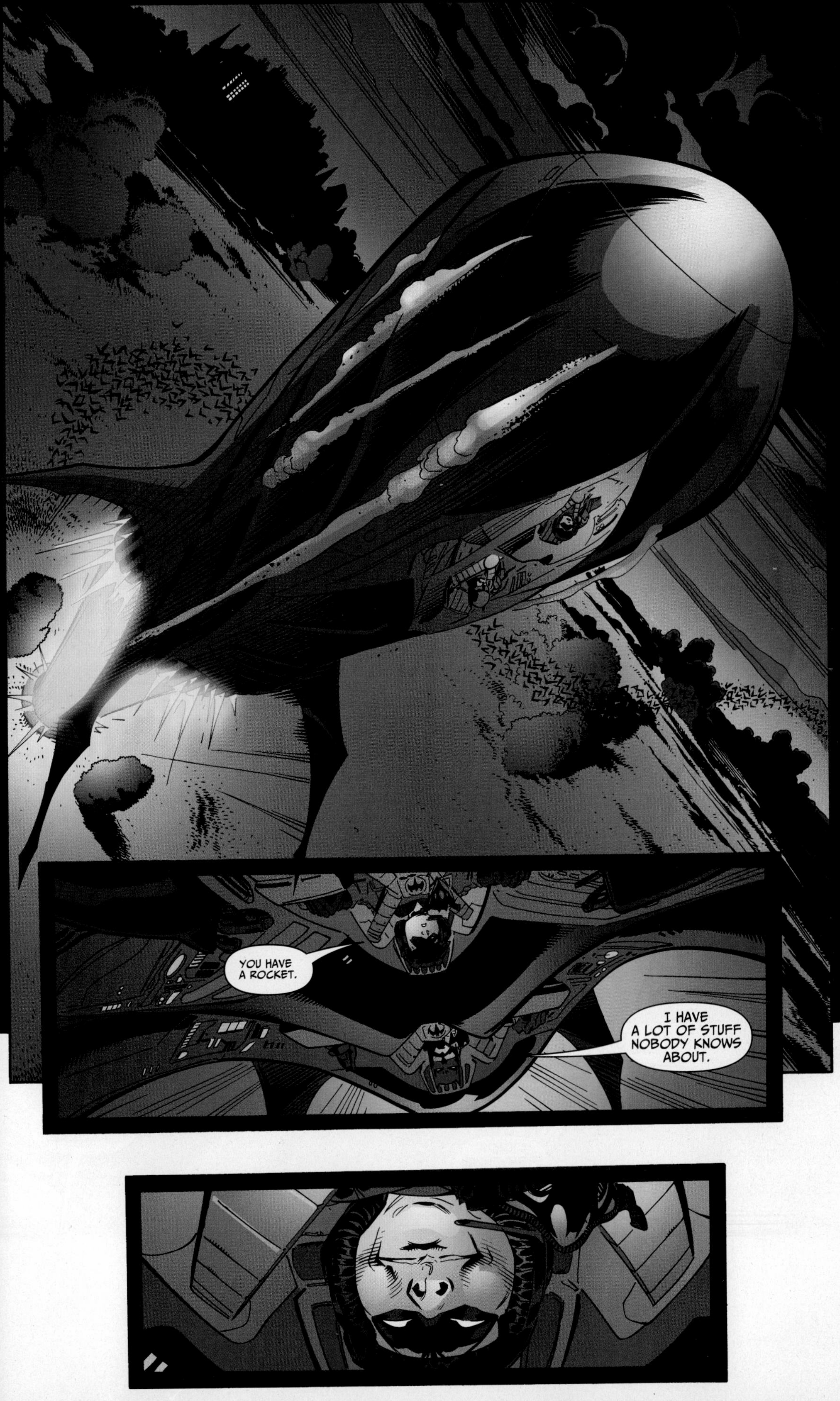
YOU HAVE A ROCKET.
I HAVE A LOT OF STUFF NOBODY KNOWS ABOUT.

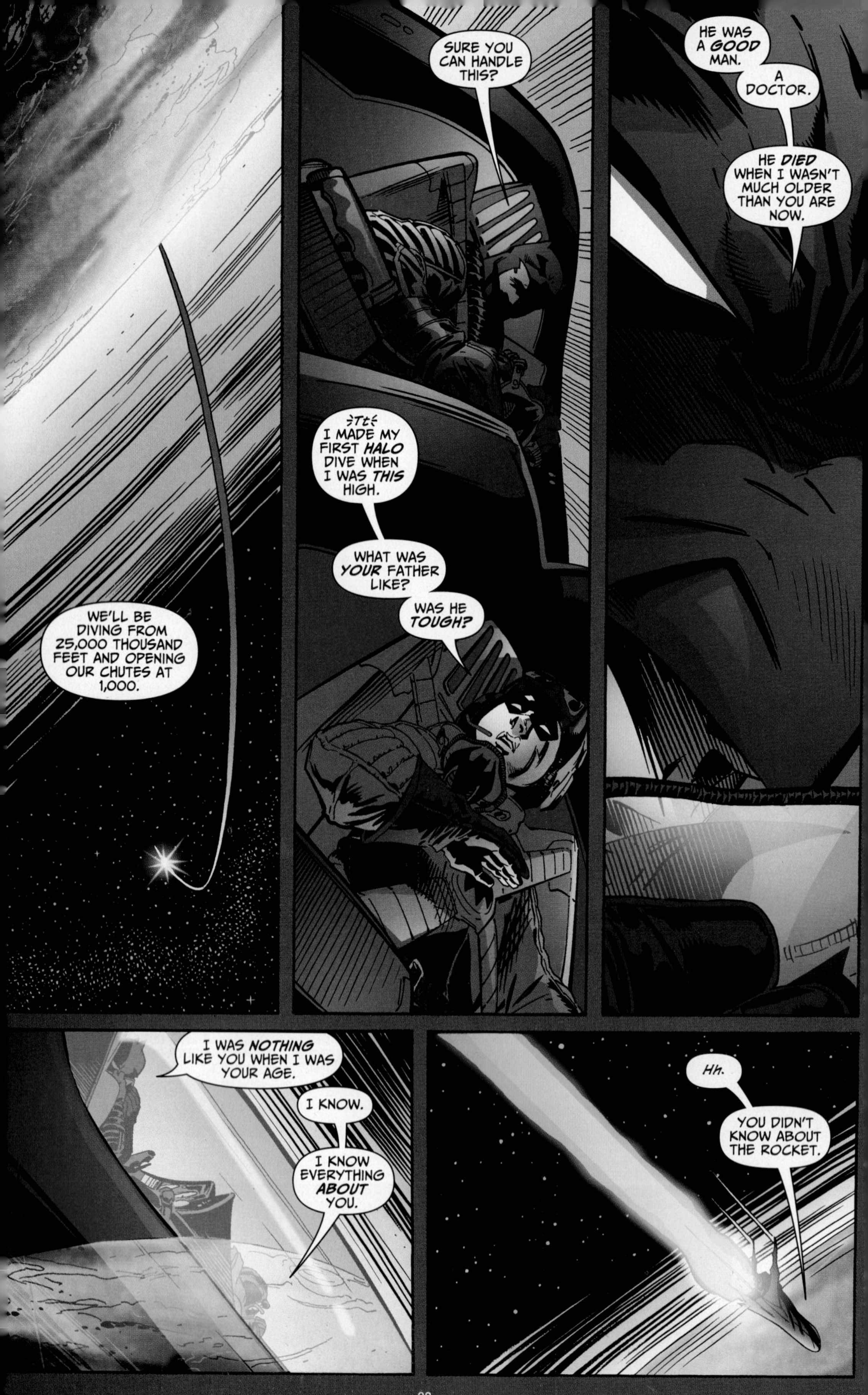
WE'LL BE DIVING FROM 25,000 THOUSAND FEET AND OPENING OUR CHUTES AT 1,000.
SURE YOU CAN HANDLE THIS?
TT
I MADE MY FIRST HALO DIVE WHEN I WAS THIS HIGH.
WHAT WAS YOUR FATHER LIKE?
WAS HE TOUGH?
HE WAS A GOOD MAN.
A DOCTOR.
HE DIED WHEN I WASN'T MUCH OLDER THAN YOU ARE NOW.
I WAS NOTHING LIKE YOU WHEN I WAS YOUR AGE.
I KNOW.
I KNOW EVERYTHING ABOUT YOU.
Hh.
YOU DIDN'T KNOW ABOUT THE ROCKET.

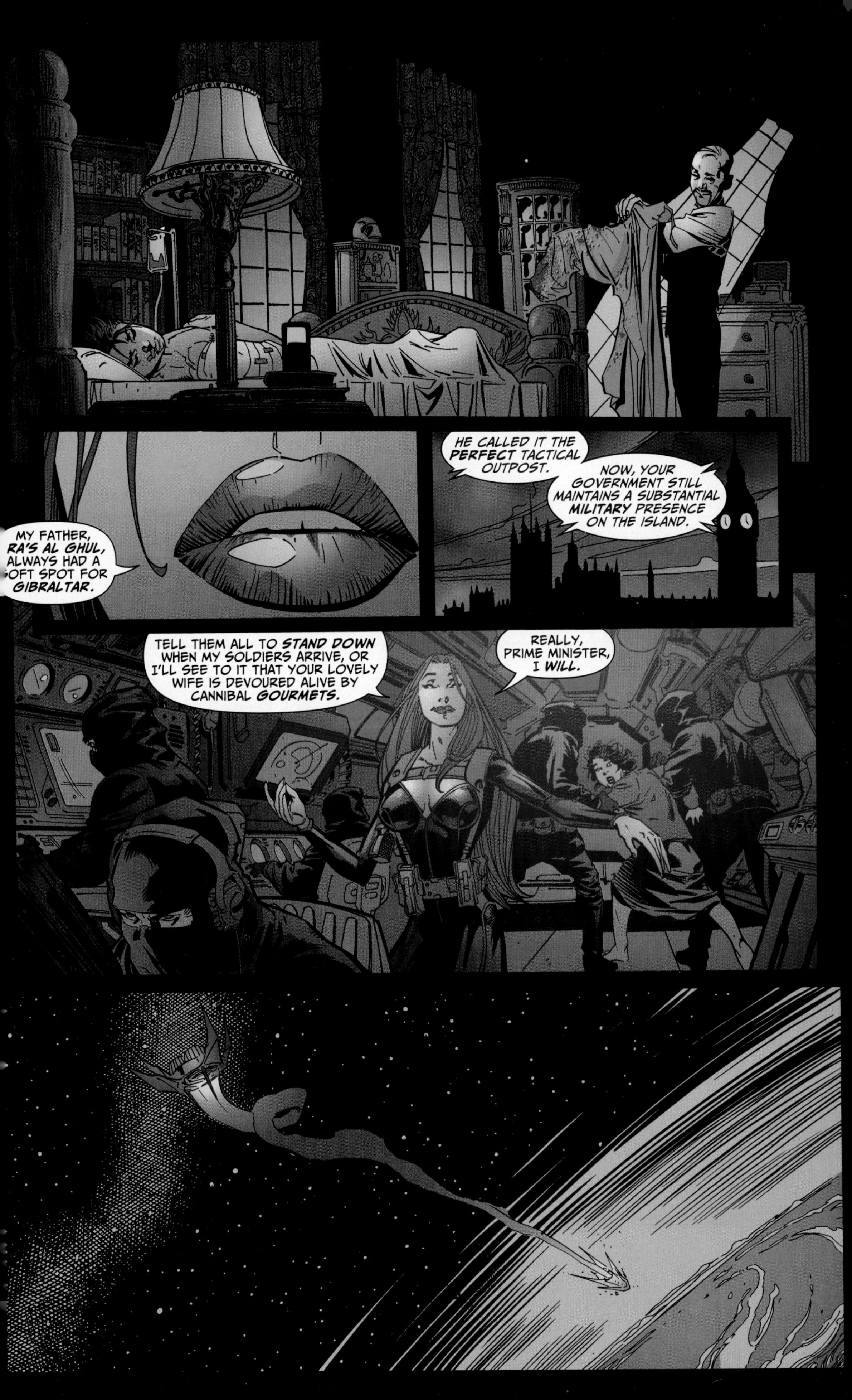
MY FATHER, RA'S AL GHUL, ALWAYS HAD A SOFT SPOT FOR GIBRALTAR.
HE CALLED IT THE PERFECT TACTICAL OUTPOST.
NOW, YOUR GOVERNMENT STILL MAINTAINS A SUBSTANTIAL MILITARY PRESENCE ON THE ISLAND.
TELL THEM ALL TO STAND DOWN WHEN MY SOLDIERS ARRIVE, OR I'LL SEE TO IT THAT YOUR LOVELY WIFE IS DEVOURED ALIVE BY CANNIBAL GOURMETS.
REALLY, PRIME MINISTER, I WILL.

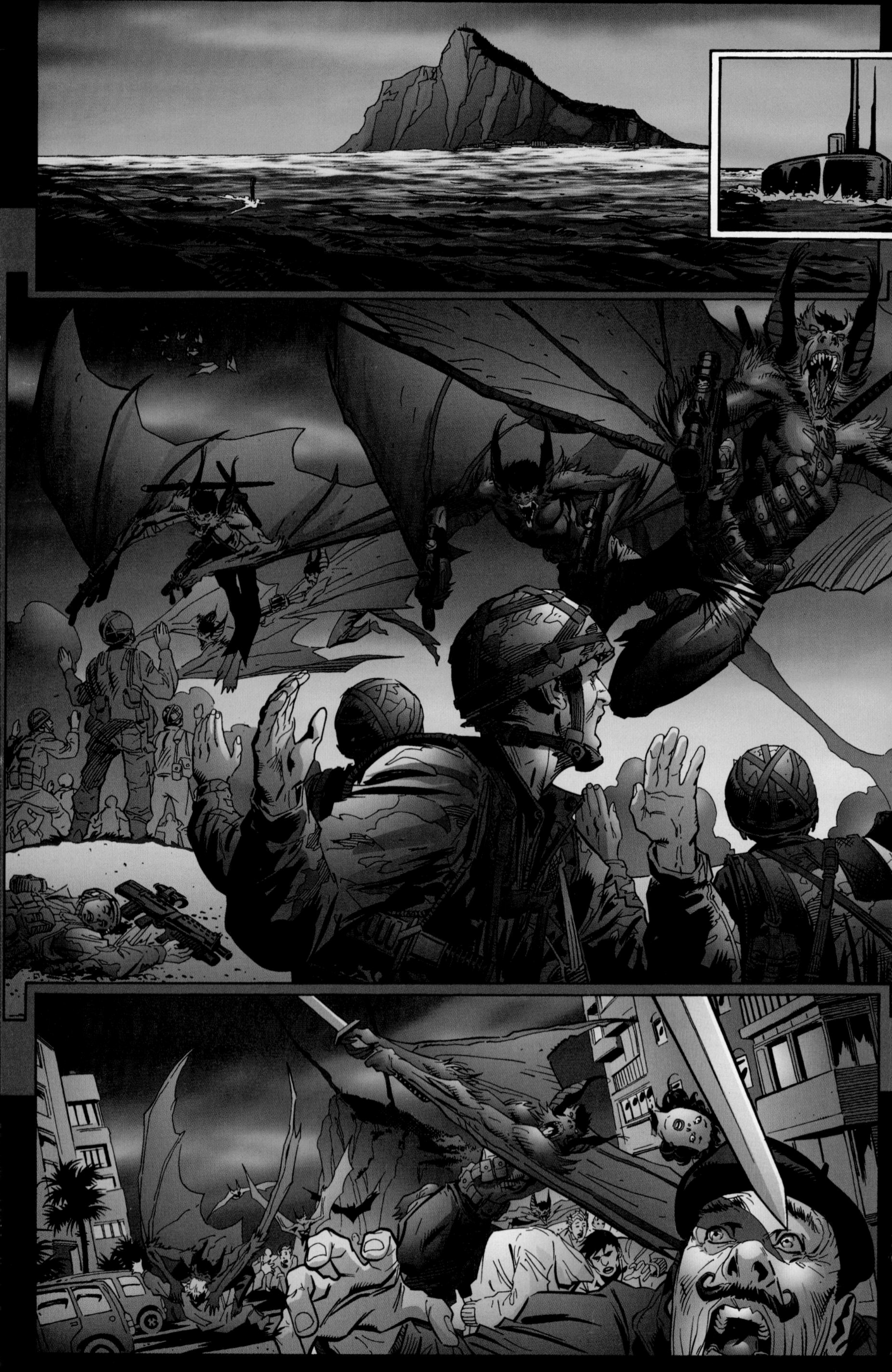

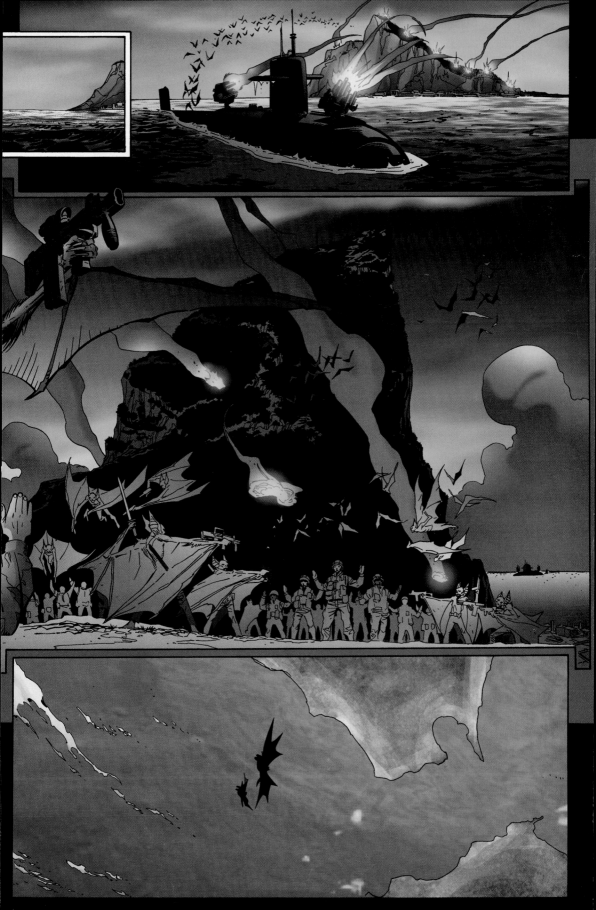

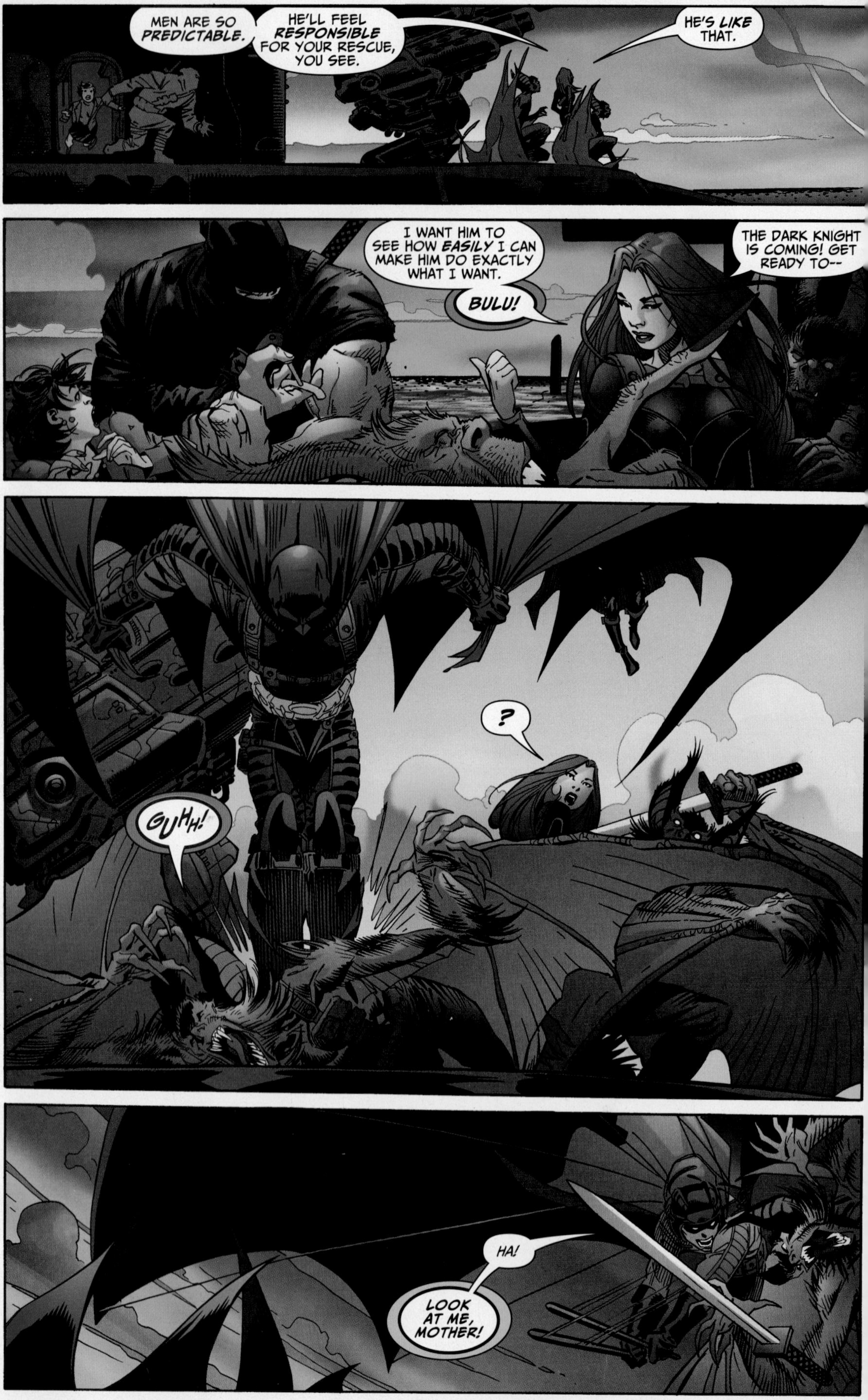
MEN ARE SO PREDICTABLE.
HE'LL FEEL RESPONSIBLE FOR YOUR RESCUE, YOU SEE.
HE'S LIKE THAT.
I WANT HIM TO SEE HOW EASILY I CAN MAKE HIM DO EXACTLY WHAT I WANT.
BULU!
THE DARK KNIGHT IS COMING! GET READY TO--
?
GUHH!
HA!
LOOK AT ME, MOTHER!

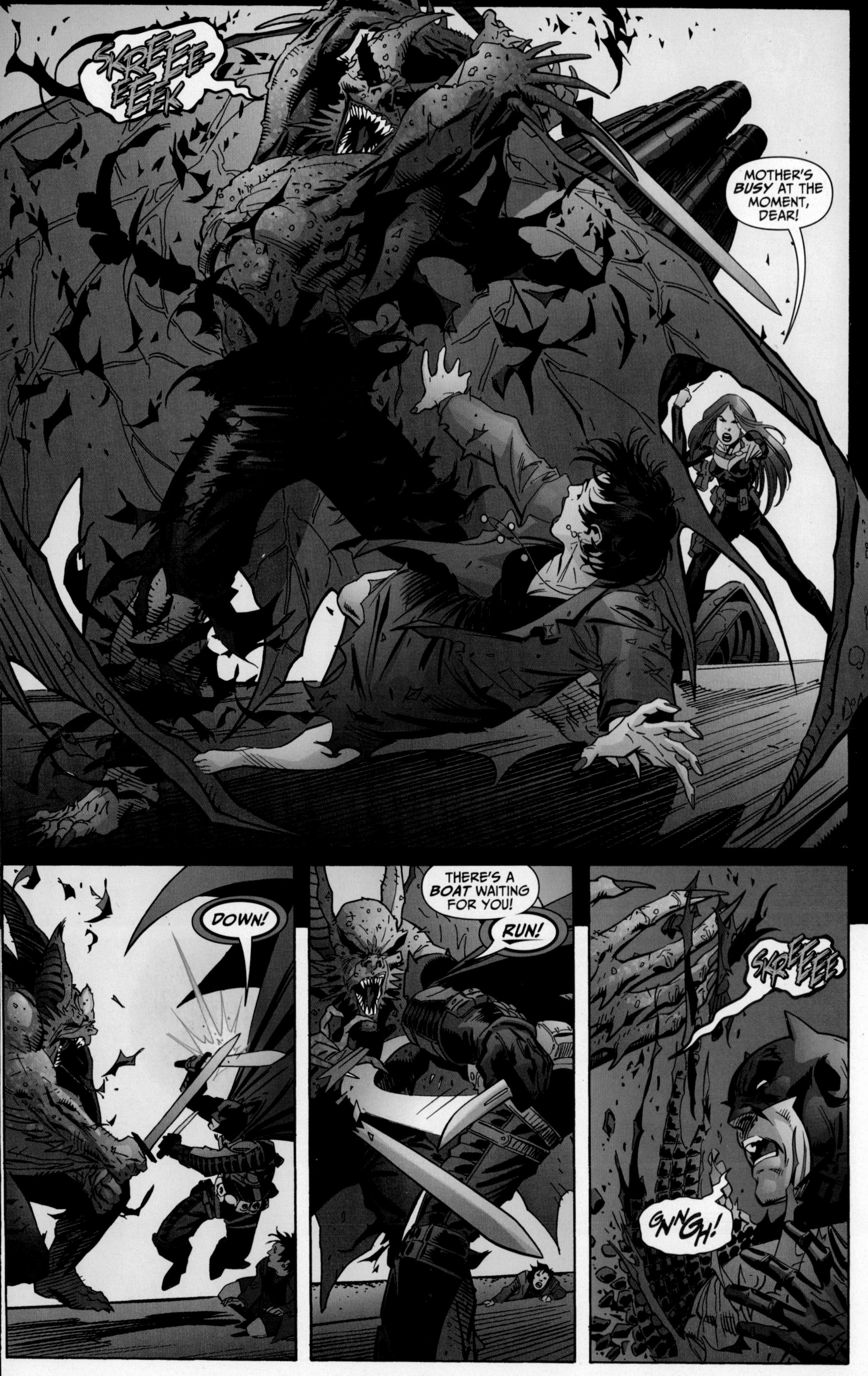
SKREEEE EEEK
MOTHER'S BUSY AT THE MOMENT, DEAR!
DOWN!
THERE'S A BOAT WAITING FOR YOU!
RUN!
SKREEEEE
GNNGH!

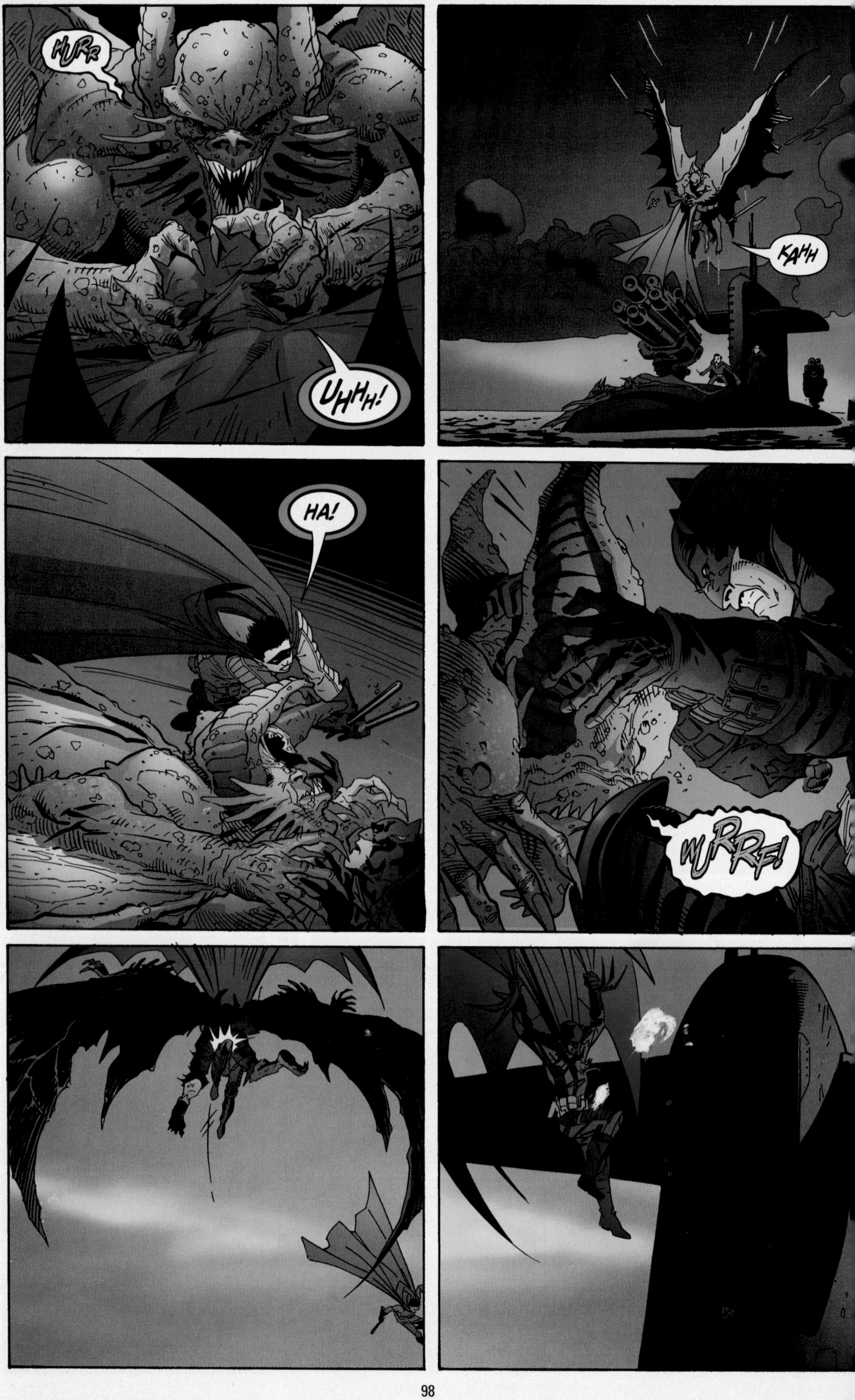
HURRR
UHHH!
KAHH
HA!
WURRF!

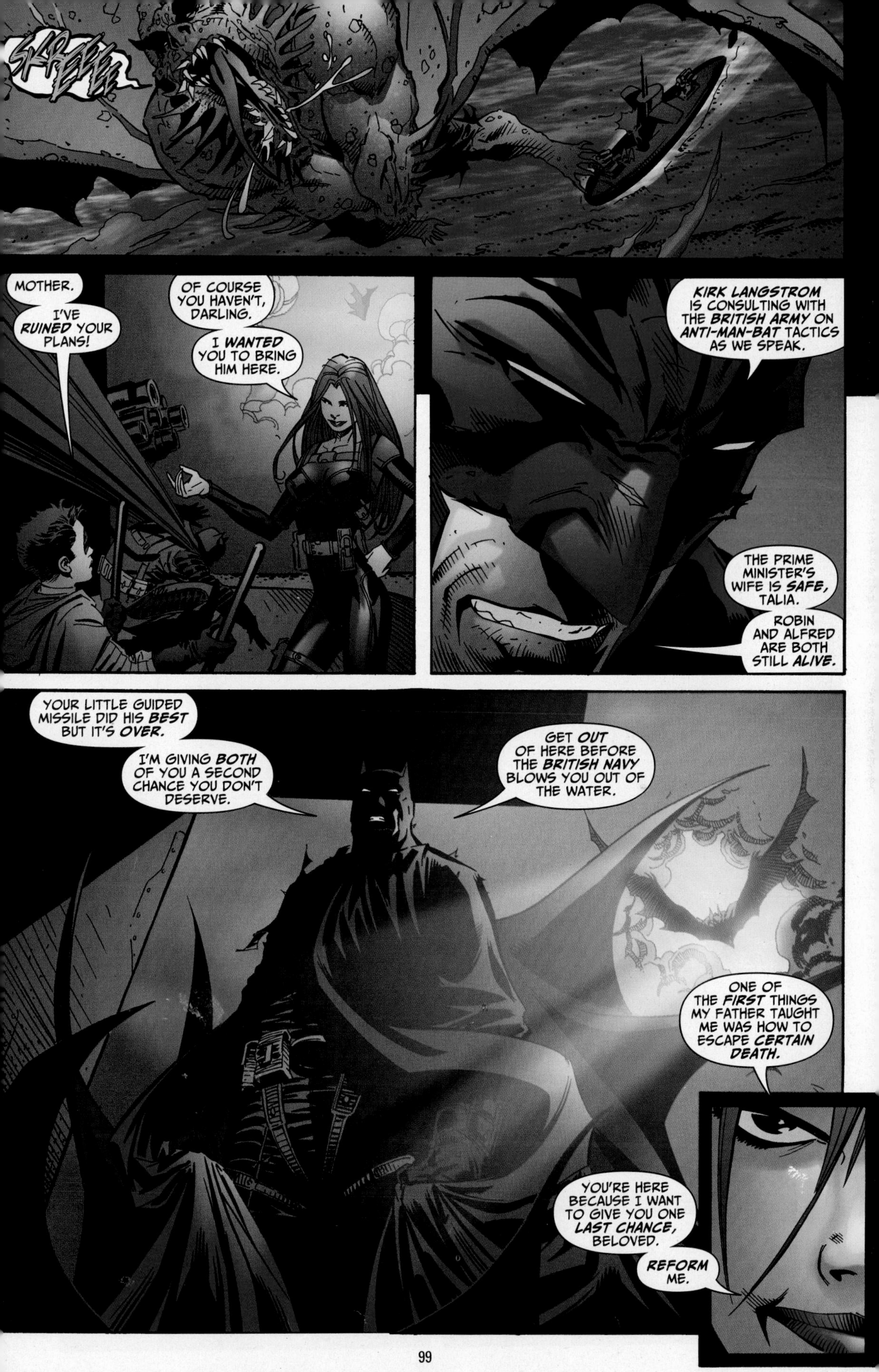
SKREEEE
MOTHER.
I'VE RUINED YOUR PLANS!
OF COURSE YOU HAVEN'T, DARLING.
I WANTED YOU TO BRING HIM HERE.
KIRK LANGSTROM IS CONSULTING WITH THE BRITISH ARMY ON ANTI-MAN-BAT TACTICS AS WE SPEAK.
THE PRIME MINISTER'S WIFE IS SAFE, TALIA.
ROBIN AND ALFRED ARE BOTH STILL ALIVE.
YOUR LITTLE GUIDED MISSILE DID HIS BEST BUT IT'S OVER.
I'M GIVING BOTH OF YOU A SECOND CHANCE YOU DON'T DESERVE.
GET OUT OF HERE BEFORE THE BRITISH NAVY BLOWS YOU OUT OF THE WATER.
ONE OF THE FIRST THINGS MY FATHER TAUGHT ME WAS HOW TO ESCAPE CERTAIN DEATH.
YOU'RE HERE BECAUSE I WANT TO GIVE YOU ONE LAST CHANCE, BELOVED.
REFORM ME.

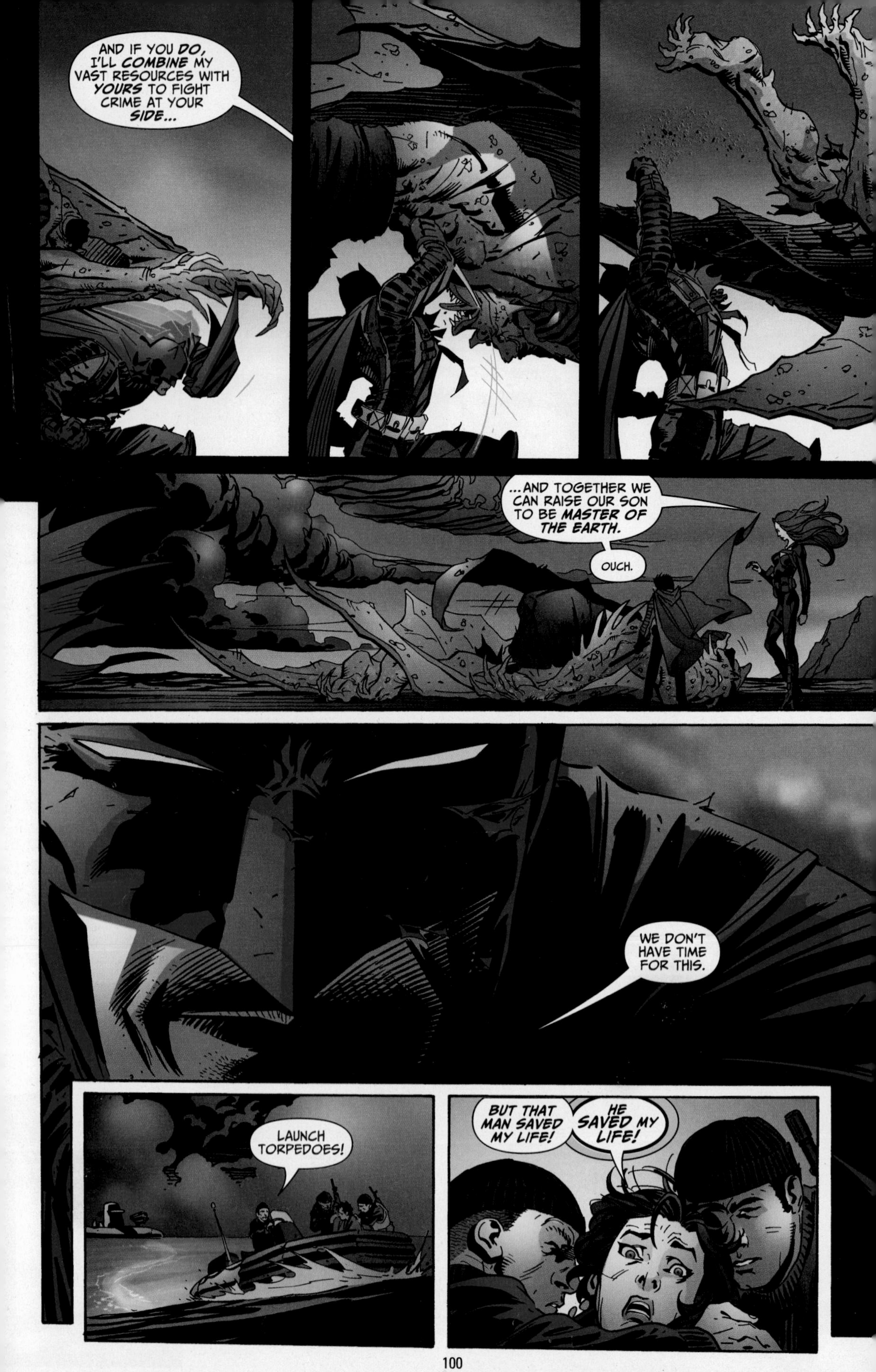
AND IF YOU DO, I'LL COMBINE MY VAST RESOURCES WITH YOURS TO FIGHT CRIME AT YOUR SIDE...
...AND TOGETHER WE CAN RAISE OUR SON TO BE MASTER OF THE EARTH.
OUCH.
WE DON'T HAVE TIME FOR THIS.
LAUNCH TORPEDOES!
BUT THAT MAN SAVED MY LIFE!
HE SAVED MY LIFE!

YOU KNOW I *ALWAYS* GET WHAT I *WANT,* BELOVED.

AND WHAT I WANT IS *YOU.*

I WANT US TO FULFILL MY FATHER'S WISHES AND BE A *FAMILY.*

WHO ELSE IN THIS WORLD IS *LIKE US,* BRUCE WAYNE?

THE CENTURY'S *GREATEST* CRIMEFIGHTER, THE *DAUGHTER* OF ITS GREATEST *CRIMELORD.*

AND THEIR *GENETICALLY PERFECT CHILD.*

JOIN ME AND I PROMISE I'LL *NEVER* THREATEN CIVILIZATION AGAIN.

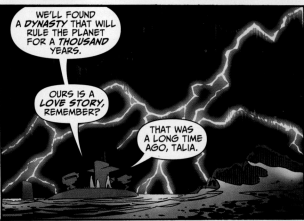

WE'LL FOUND A *DYNASTY* THAT WILL RULE THE PLANET FOR A *THOUSAND* YEARS.

OURS IS A *LOVE STORY,* REMEMBER?

THAT WAS A LONG TIME AGO, TALIA.

THEN IT'S *WAR.*

AND YOU'RE *RESPONSIBLE.*

MY DEAR *DETECTIVE,* MY MAD, BILLIONAIRE, BRILLIANT *GENIUS* WITH YOUR SECRET HIDEOUTS, YOUR DOUBLE LIFE AND YOUR *JUSTICE LEAGUE* MEMBERSHIP...

...IT'S NOT *OVER.*

FOR PEOPLE LIKE *US,* THE WORLD IS THE GAMEBOARD, AND *NATIONS* ARE PAWNS.

DAMIAN! WOULD YOU RATHER STAY WITH *ME* OR GO WITH YOUR *FATHER?*

DO I HAVE TO CHOOSE?

I WOULD MUCH RATHER WE WERE ALL *TOGETHER.*

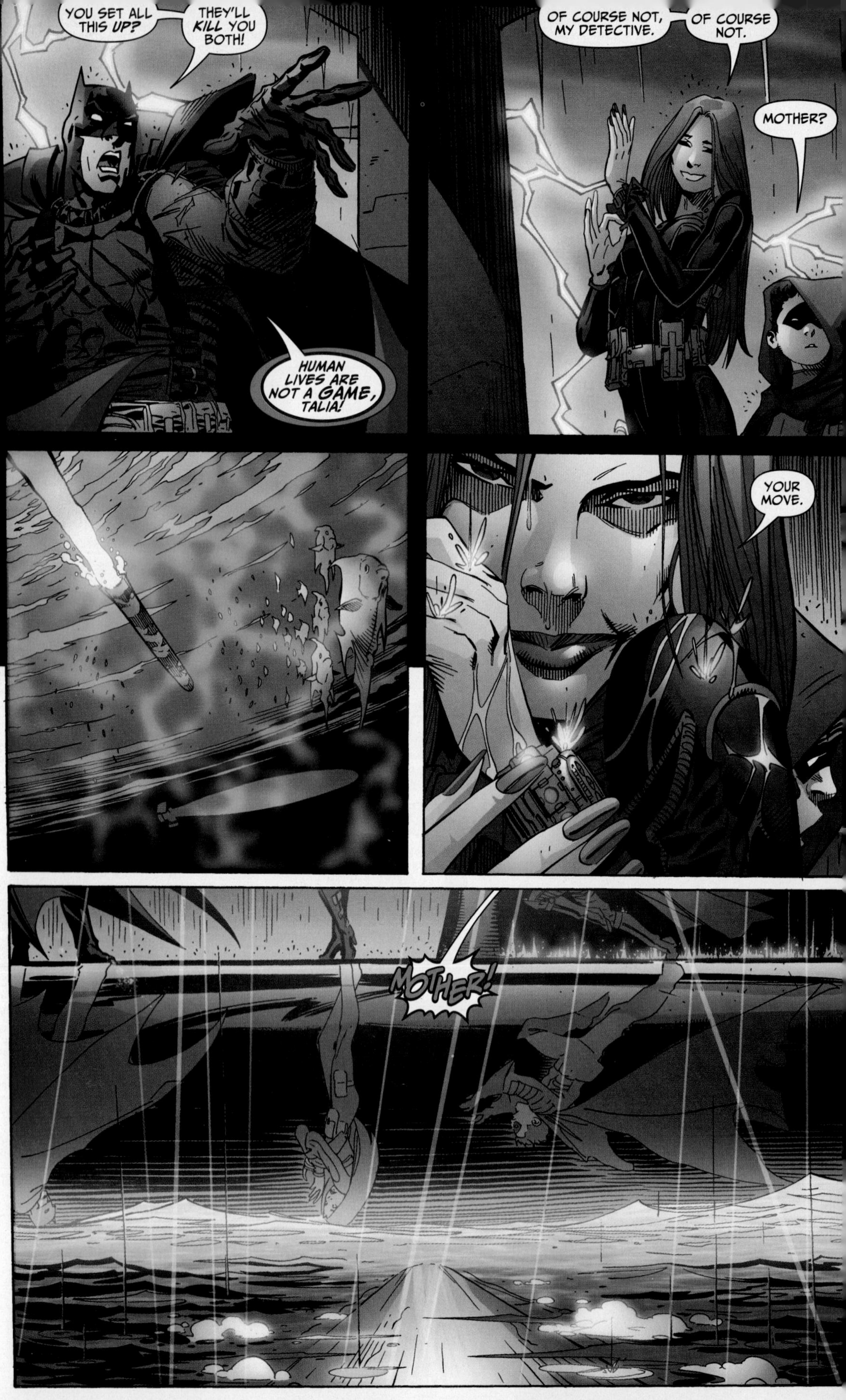
YOU SET ALL THIS UP?
THEY'LL KILL YOU BOTH!
HUMAN LIVES ARE NOT A GAME, TALIA!
OF COURSE NOT, MY DETECTIVE.
OF COURSE NOT.
MOTHER?
YOUR MOVE.
MOTHER!

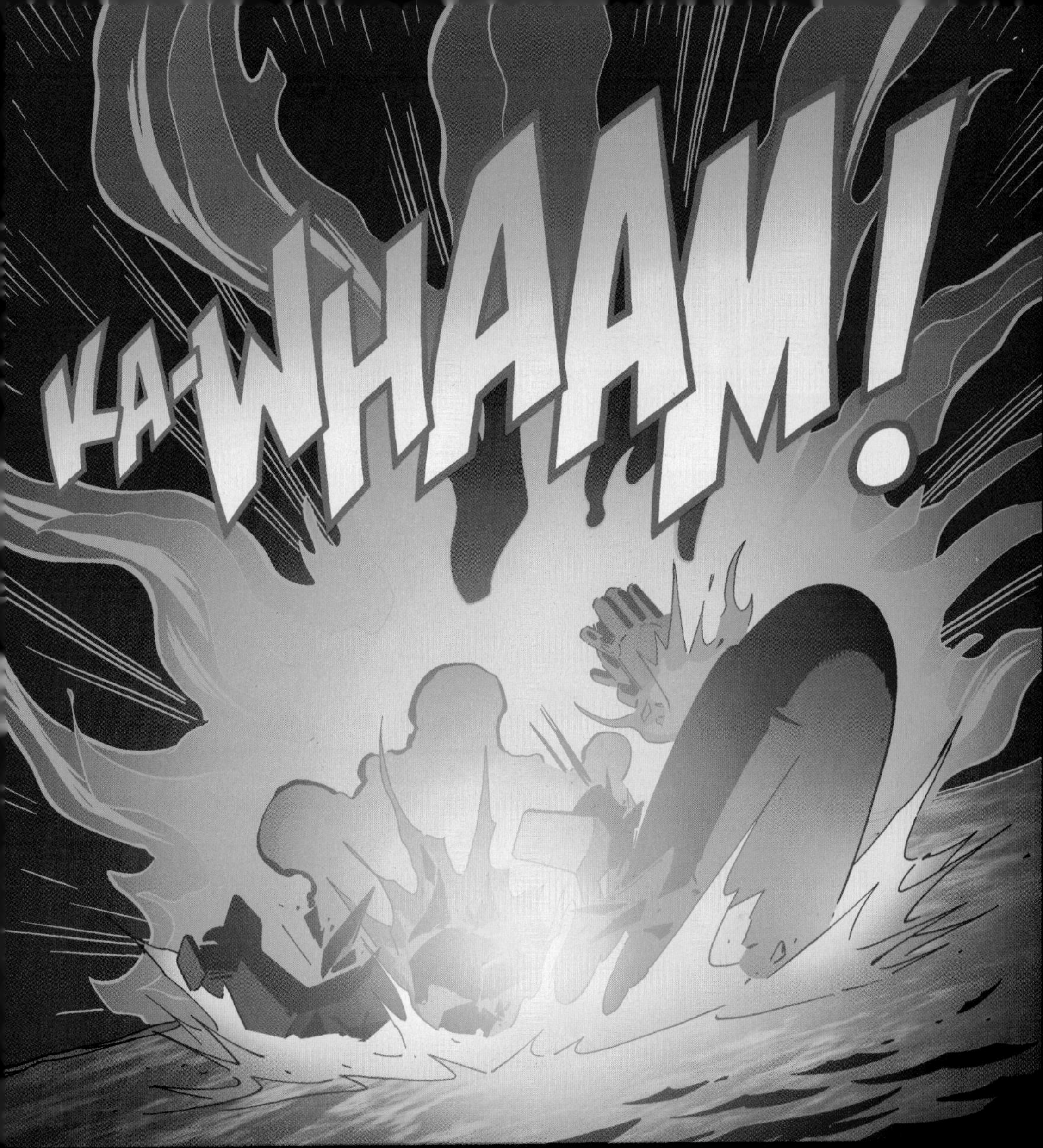
KA-WHAAM!

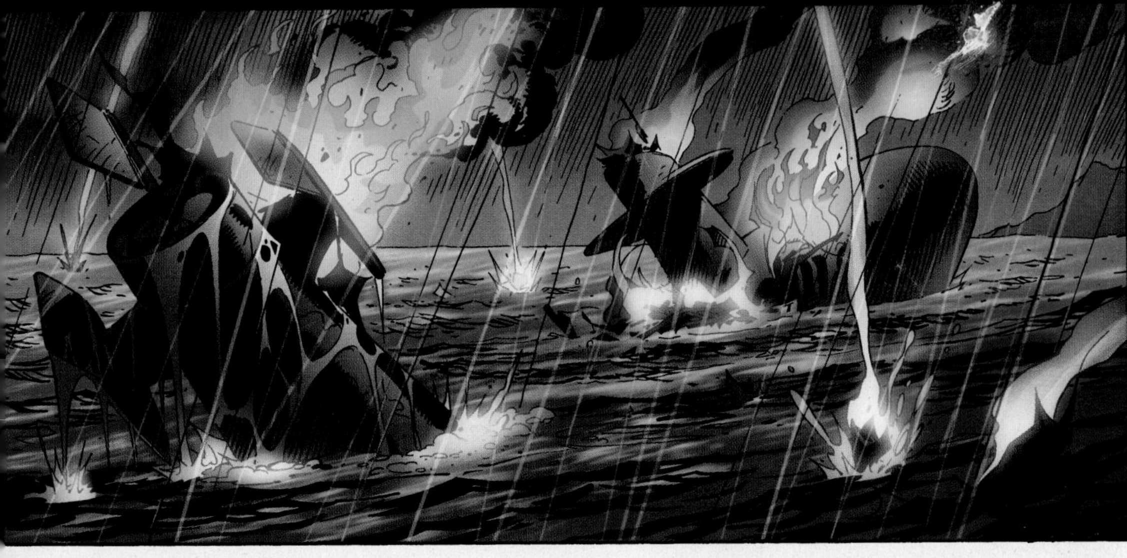

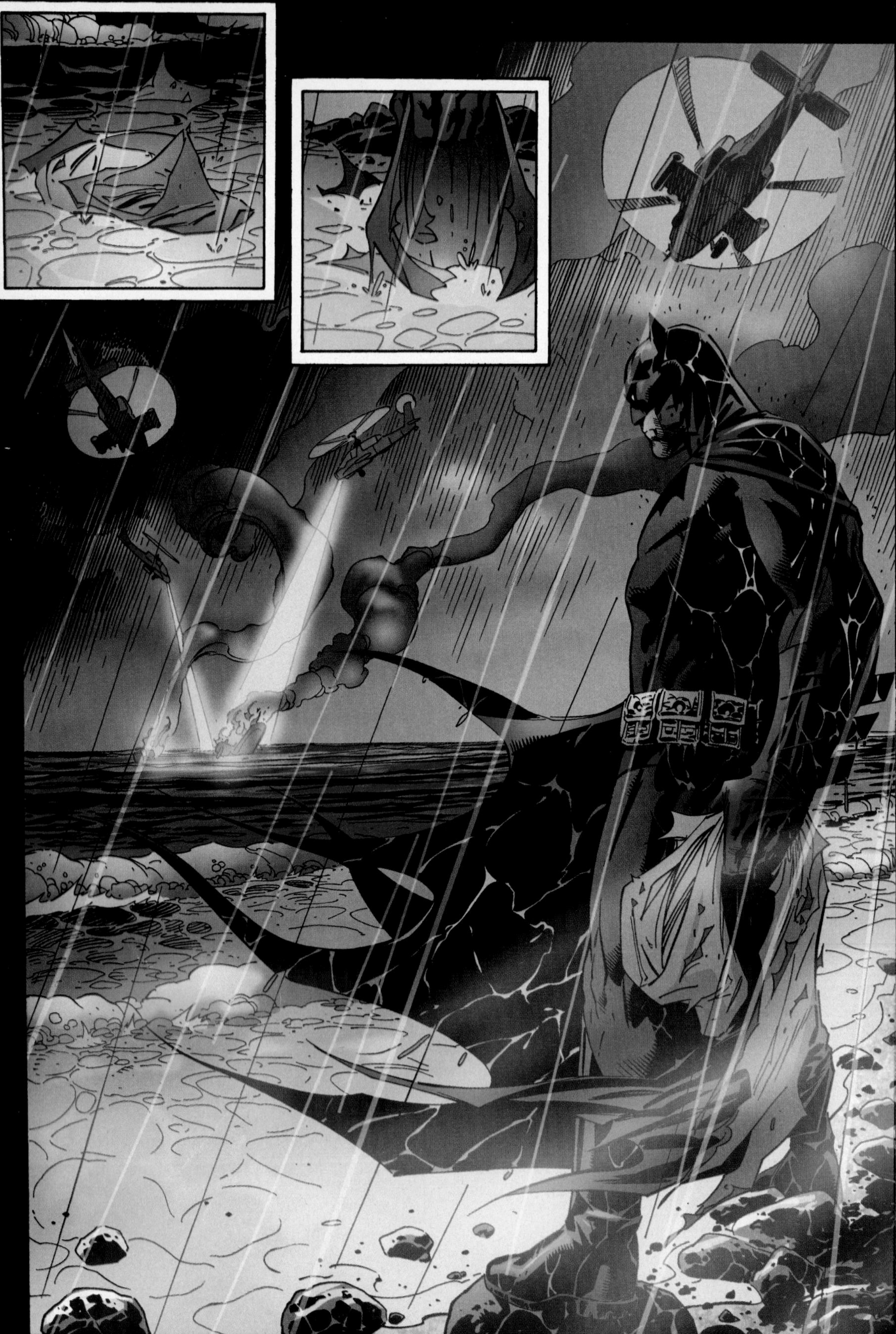

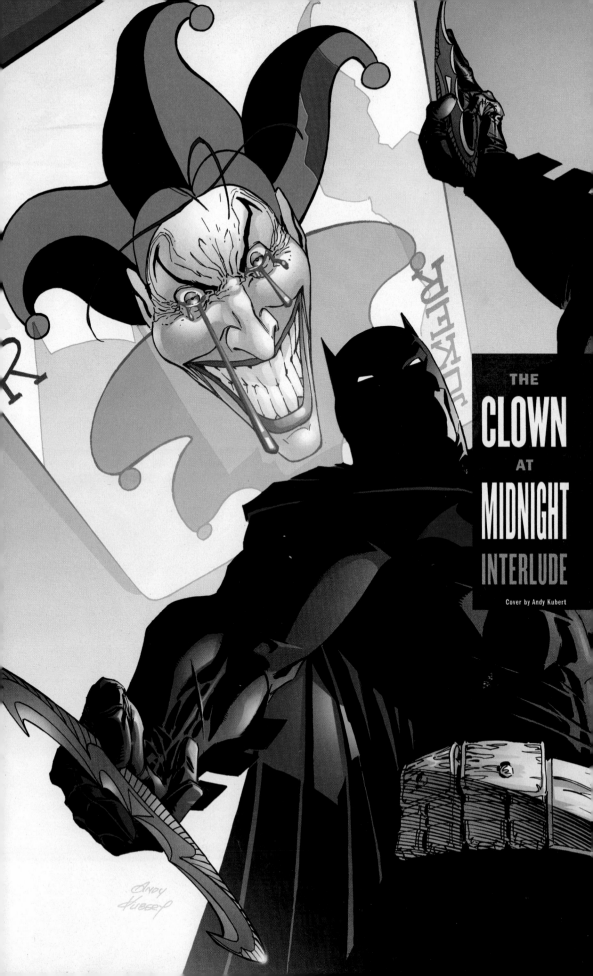

THE
CLOWN
AT
MIDNIGHT
INTERLUDE

Cover by Andy Kubert

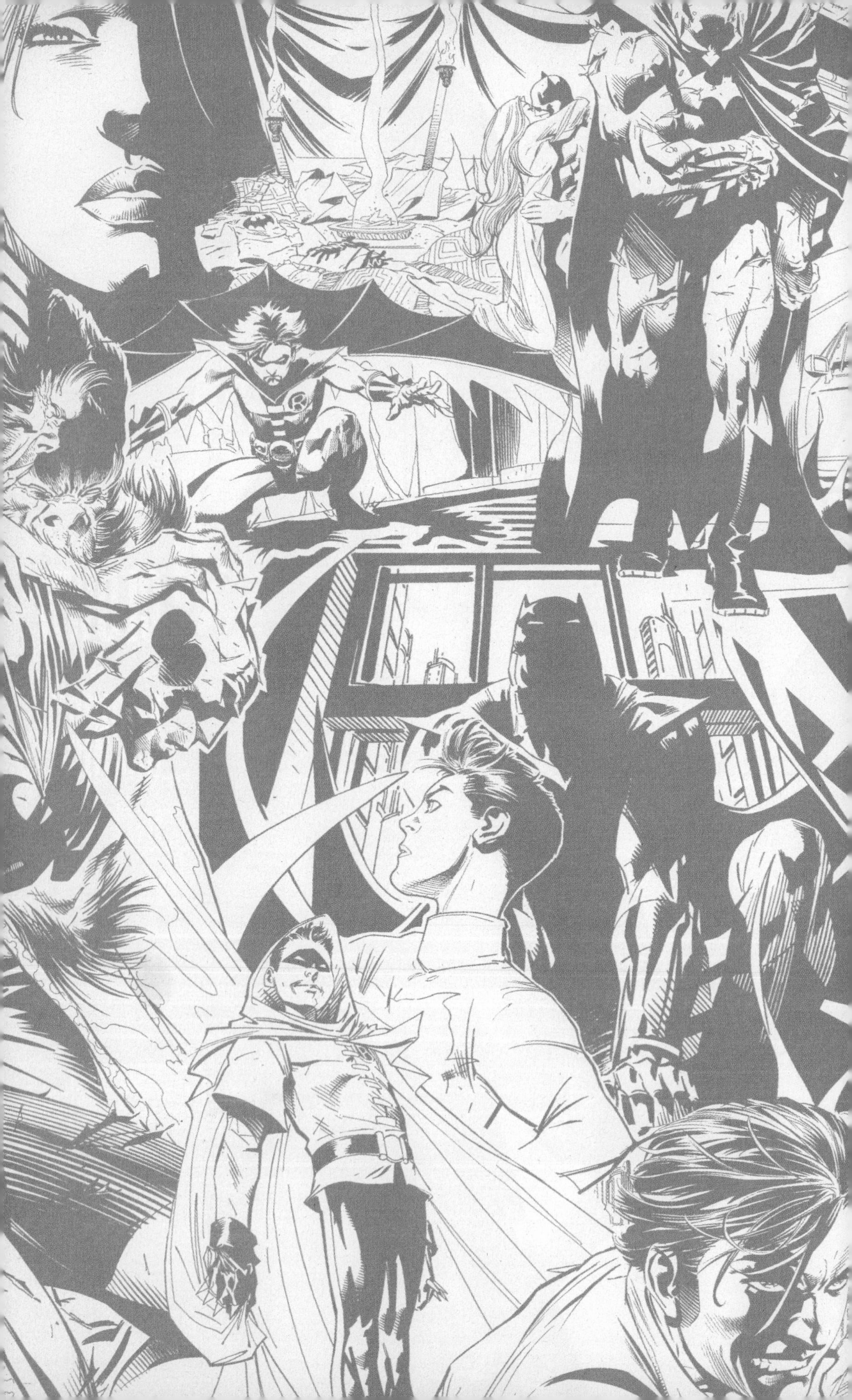

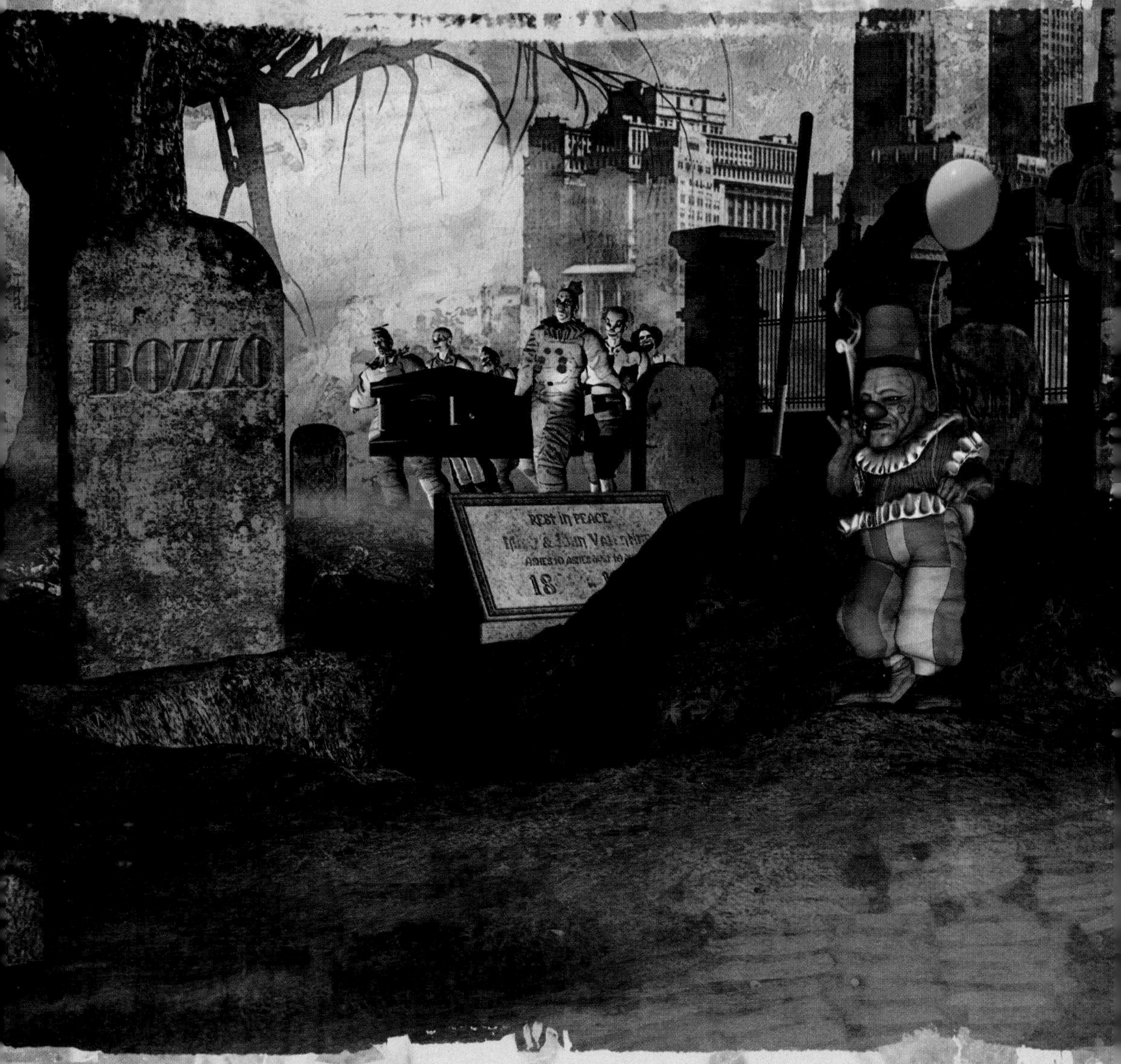
BOZZO
REST IN PEACE

There's something about clowns at a funeral and it's hard to say if it's sad or if it's funny.

The CLOWN at MIDNIGHT

Chapter 1 – PUTTING BOZZO TO BED

Rain goes clickety-clack-tack through the sticks and branches of bare, bony graveyard elms, the kind that stand as if ashamed, like strippers past their best – danced out to a standstill in the naked lights, all down to nothing but fretwork and scaffolding, jutting hips, nicotine-stained fingers, and summer gone south for the winter.

"Deeply beloved blah blah blah…" the priest intones with all the ecumenical fire and conviction of an "I Speak Your Weight" machine. *"Stop me if you've heard this one before…"*

What could be sadder and funnier than clowns at the cemetery, in the sniveling Gotham rain by the Red Hook dockyards, laying to rest their finest, their best, their golden boy?

Of all the henchmen, all the hoods, the fat man in the supersize-me coffin had led the pack. It's thanks to Bozzo the Bandit most of these comedians are still alive to bury him, when so many underlings of The Boss have met with abrupt and untimely terminations of contract down the years at the pale, cold hands of their infamous ringleader.

It's always been the same, Bozzo used to say: the smirking gift of a fat and smoldering Cuban cigar, followed by a hasty exit, a loud, flat bang, and what sounded like a drum of slurry hitting a ceiling fan. Or electricity would be used in some amusing and ultimately fatal way. Or there'd be champagne mixed with hydrochloric acid. Or rats. The Boss could transform anyone or anything into an agent of Death when he tired of you, or when you stopped making him laugh, or sometimes it was for no real reason except that he felt like doing something random and you just happened to be there, in the right place at the wrong time.

The traditional payback for loyalty was death and madness. That was the rule around The Boss.

But somehow these eight men survived and made their jump from the joyride just before it derailed, all thanks to Bozzo the Bandit's dictum – *"Y'all gotta keep him laughin', boys, 'cause when the laughin' stops the genocide starts, and the genocide starts with you…"*

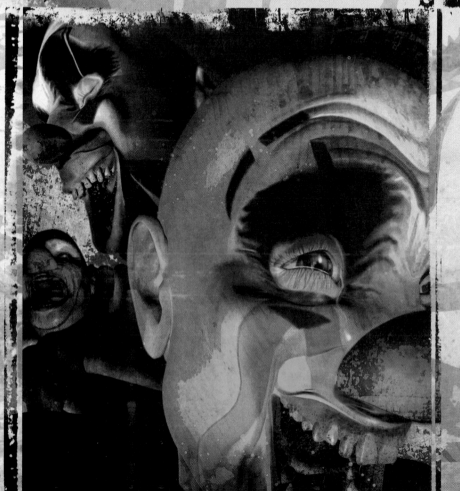

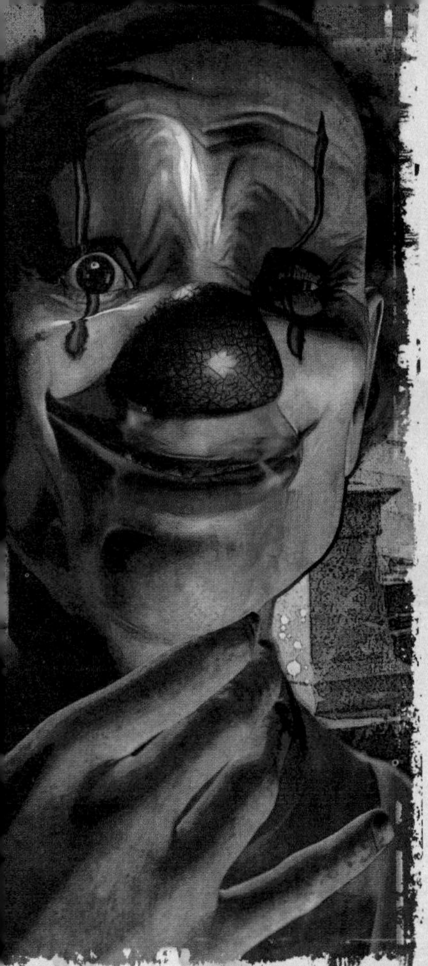

So it's maybe something like that on Peanuts Parker's mind that makes him want to snigger a little. Maybe it's the solemnity of this big hungry hole in the ground, and this stumbling train of has-beens with painted-on smiles to hide their "secret identities" from the authorities. Maybe it's the cloying stench of black and red flowers coiled in a dirty wreath for a dead king. Or maybe it's just the bitter wine of dumb luck dying on the vine that tastes so scary and so ridiculous.

His fingers, oozing sweat and cold, slide on the polished pine (only the best for Bozzo!) and the thought that he could easily lose control of the hefty cabinet is laugh-out-loud funny and disturbing at the same time.

He can hear snorting, hysterical bull grunts from the other pallbearers too, moving in a ring, the way you'd pass a yawn or a precious secret around. Peanuts swallows hard to ease the clench of nausea's greasy glove in his gut, but he knows something's wrong and he knows what it is. He can smell it.

There's a huge and twisted ugliness inside him that has to get out or he'll go mad holding it in. He wants to tell the other clowns how cruddy and broken and uncomfortable he feels inside, but their garish faces are stretching, leering, and opening up like colorful envelopes all around him, in a way that's so awful and funny to look at he decides to face the dirt and deal with that instead.

Peanuts wonders if he too looks like a tattooed death's head, knowing that he does, as the juddering, jangling needle buzz in his spine screws his nerve cables tighter and tighter, until he's sure the rotten ladder of vertebrae must snap. He's swallowed battery acid, is how it feels, with every part of him clenching into a rictus. A premature rigor mortis is stiffening his numb fingers, spreading like an itch only the Reaper can scratch. No one can deny he's the worst sort of clown, all teeth and bleeding gums, as he cracks his head back on its hing stalk of bone and gristle to cackle out a black and red voltage, as if by roaring and spitting the shocking pain ose into the sky in the form of thick wet streamers he'll be free of it.

Everyone he's ever known, he's let down, and now he's about to spoil Bozzo's big day too. If there's a special Hell for sers he's on the guest list, VIP, plus none. It's so funny, it hurts. It hurts so much, it's funny.

The coffin slips from Peanuts' grasp like he knows it has to, a massive dead weight shearing off its axis into the ute fist of gravity. Everything is going wrong all at once. Casually, the coffin crushes Charlie Cheesemold's sternum splinters and splits the man's head open the way you'd smack an egg on the rim of an iron pan. Like an overstuffed itcase, the box pops its locks and tips Bozzo's immense mortal remains into the arms of his grieving friends and lleagues. Four hundred pounds of flesh and bone and pine comes rolling in like an avalanche across a vivid tangle of reaming rags and smeared greasepaint, unstoppable.

Everybody's laughing now, in the bloody chaos and mortuary stink of the aftermath. It's like a day at the circus in ell. Racked with spasms, and all writhing together in the grip of the same atrocity, the funeral party sprays stomach ning through laced fingers and makeup in its mad scramble to join the deceased in comedy Valhalla. The retching, uckling screeches pitch higher and higher, tuning themselves to a glassy, operatic crescendo only bats can hear. aniacal and shrill with terror until the very last gasp, one by one the funnymen stop laughing and die.

A damp shroud of edgy quiet settles discreetly. The rain falls clickety-clack-tack, counting time, while the crows range themselves along branches, evil notes on a skeleton scale, scoring the sheet music for a funeral march in aggy pants and banana shoes.

What can be funnier or more sad than eight murderous clowns mining the mother lode itself? The ultimate unchline, the terminal gag, the killer finish…

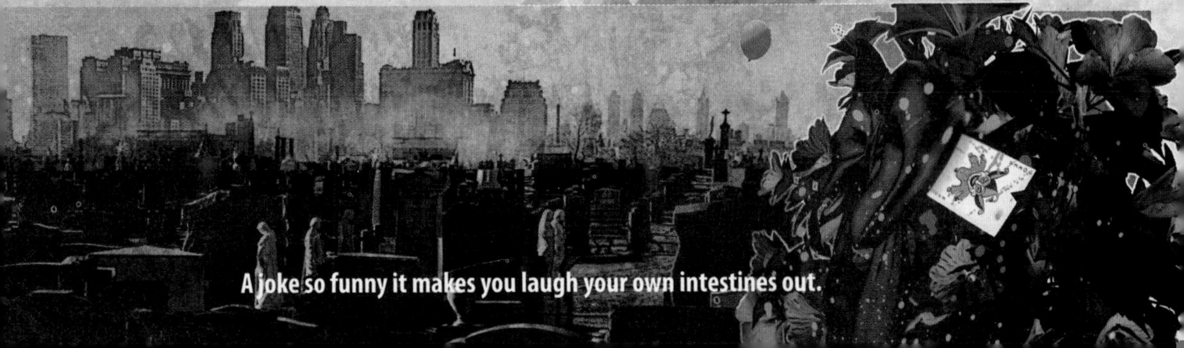
A joke so funny it makes you laugh your own intestines out.

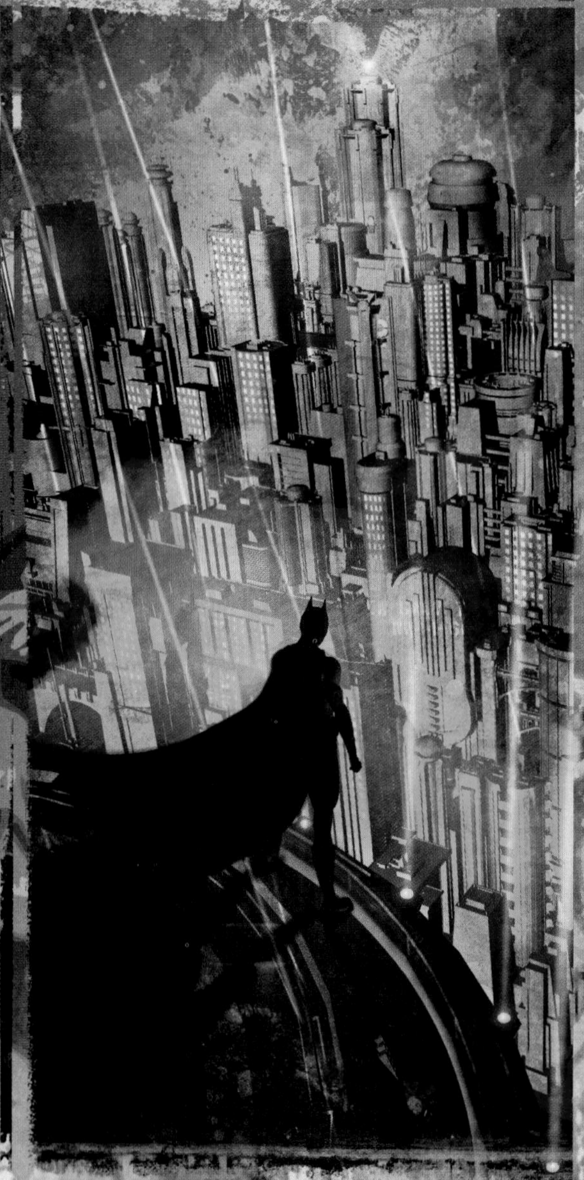

Chapter 2 – THE KNIGHT AND THE CITY

Welcome to Gotham City, a party ten miles long and six miles wide. From The Hill to Cathedral Square, from Amusement Mile to Blackgate Penitentiary, a 21st-century American Babylon has shouldered its way up from the mudflats and sauntered into the spotlights, eager to dazzle and seduce the world.

Gotham City, where the greasy electromagnetics of human need, hope, and fear radiate into a new January night so rank you can taste it like tinfoil on your fillings. Where crime swaps spit with high society and everything's for sale. Where grimy clouds snag and burst on the vicious needle points of world-famous Deco-Industrial superscrapers on Wall Street and Levi and spill out more, and more, and more of the burning, glamorous downpour Gothamites call rain and know so well. It's the kind of town that whispers "baby" while it's picking your pockets, that promises the world and delivers the gutter, or vice versa, and puts out your lights with a kiss, or a bullet, then forgets your name before dawn.

Deep in the dense architectural reefs of midtown, primary reds and yellows and the hot purples of gigantic moving advertising hoardings are turning the rain to something that might as well be liquid stained glass, braiding it through the wound-tight sinews of the Aparo Bridge, scything across the docks and railway sidings, then crowding into the narrow floodlit canyons of 8th Avenue, Finger and Crescent, to rinse the lowlifes and the high rollers off the bustling streets and back into the bars, the theaters, the crack houses, restaurants and clip joints, as if the sky itself, in some spontaneous creative frenzy, has chosen to empty an ocean of raw printer's ink on the gaudy, just and unjust citizens of Gotham alike.

Gotham City. 10:23 p.m. One more night in the self-proclaimed most incredible city in the world.

Where people go who love the floodlit intensity of its teeming, restless avenues. Where human lives are bought and sold and innocence is up for trade. Where dreams turn solid and bleed. Where ghosts are real and monsters leave their footprints in the dust.

Where lives the man who has no price, the man who cannot be bought or sold or swayed from his singular path.

Black against the foundry glare of corporate signatures written large as houses, a jet figurehead, mounted on a marble and iron plinth 250 feet high at the top of Gotham Center, he wraps himself in crackling shadows and reads the fumes and divines the luminous car-headlight entrails that spill from the belly of the Beast. He smells the night and its nine million lives, soaks in its pheromones, its chemistry, its individual emotions carried as scent molecules on the breath of the city. He immerses himself in its perspiration, its animal dynamics, tastes its moods, its metals.

The Batman smells fear above all. Fear is rising from the streets the way carnival balloons rise on the hot thermals. Overwhelming fear. Like antelope on the veldt, the citizens of Gotham can sense a predator waking up hungry, prowling on the perimeter where the wild things are…

"I got there too late, Alfred," he explains. "They called themselves the Boys of St. Genesius. The usual small-time crime clowns with one thing in common; all of them, at one time or another, worked with the same man." He pauses, lets the echo underline his words. "I found a card with the wreath. The flowers are genetically engineered to release a short-acting toxic venom in aerosol form. One drop of the stuff is enough to kill an elephant."

"There's only one conclusion I can draw..."

He turns it over in his hand once again, as if in a magic trick, but the face on the Card With No Number refuses to disappear.

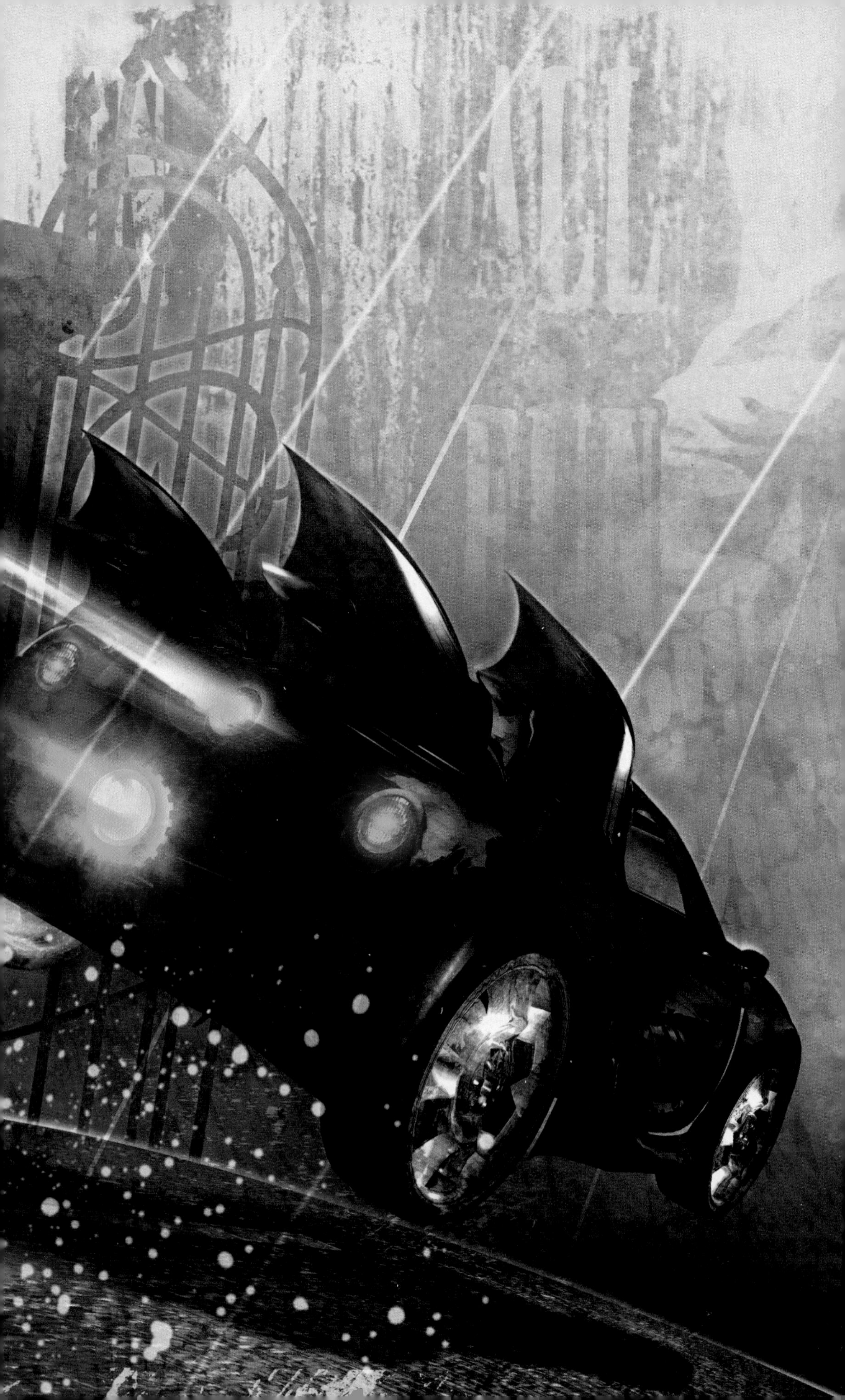

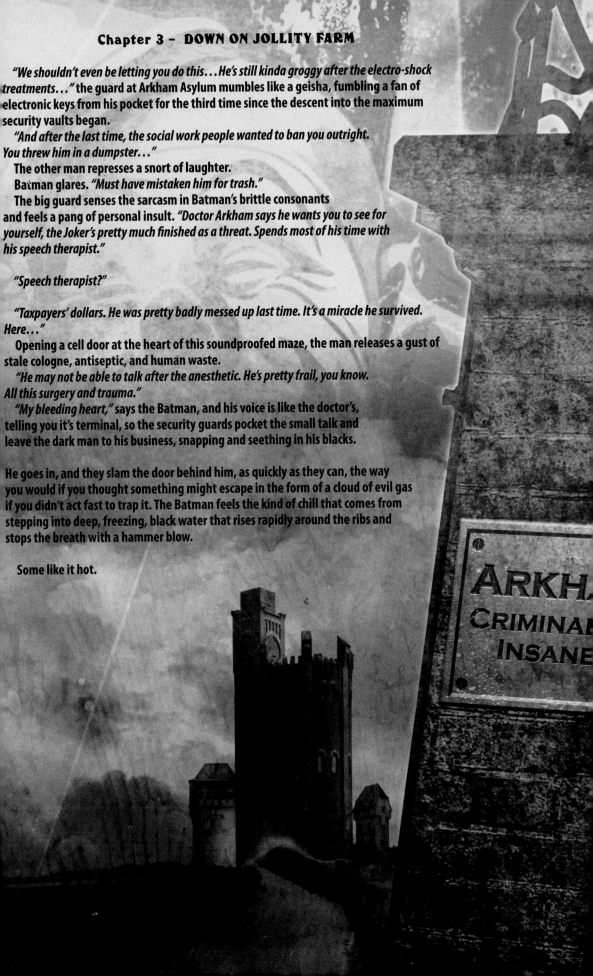

Chapter 3 – DOWN ON JOLLITY FARM

"We shouldn't even be letting you do this…He's still kinda groggy after the electro-shock treatments…" the guard at Arkham Asylum mumbles like a geisha, fumbling a fan of electronic keys from his pocket for the third time since the descent into the maximum security vaults began.

"And after the last time, the social work people wanted to ban you outright. You threw him in a dumpster…"

The other man represses a snort of laughter.

Batman glares. *"Must have mistaken him for trash."*

The big guard senses the sarcasm in Batman's brittle consonants and feels a pang of personal insult. *"Doctor Arkham says he wants you to see for yourself, the Joker's pretty much finished as a threat. Spends most of his time with his speech therapist."*

"Speech therapist?"

"Taxpayers' dollars. He was pretty badly messed up last time. It's a miracle he survived. Here…"

Opening a cell door at the heart of this soundproofed maze, the man releases a gust of stale cologne, antiseptic, and human waste.

"He may not be able to talk after the anesthetic. He's pretty frail, you know. All this surgery and trauma."

"My bleeding heart," says the Batman, and his voice is like the doctor's, telling you it's terminal, so the security guards pocket the small talk and leave the dark man to his business, snapping and seething in his blacks.

He goes in, and they slam the door behind him, as quickly as they can, the way you would if you thought something might escape in the form of a cloud of evil gas if you didn't act fast to trap it. The Batman feels the kind of chill that comes from stepping into deep, freezing, black water that rises rapidly around the ribs and stops the breath with a hammer blow.

Some like it hot.

ARKHA

CRIMINAL

INSANE

The Joker's different.

"I got your calling card," the Batman says.

Eyes flit like birds on fire beneath the stained bandages, flickering with the tiny lightning strikes of his derangement, his chemical sickness. The bony chest rises and waits to fall, as if he's onstage, catching his breath in the hush before the applause.

"Who's working with you?" the Batman says again.

The archnemesis sticks to the Fifth but the jaws work, champing gently, insistently, behind grubby gauze wrap, and the bird-eyes glitter with a sickness that never sleeps. Still, no sound emerges from the blunt, erased head. Instead, he blinks repeatedly, the same pattern over and over again, winking a chant in Morse that Batman first detects then spells out beneath his breath.

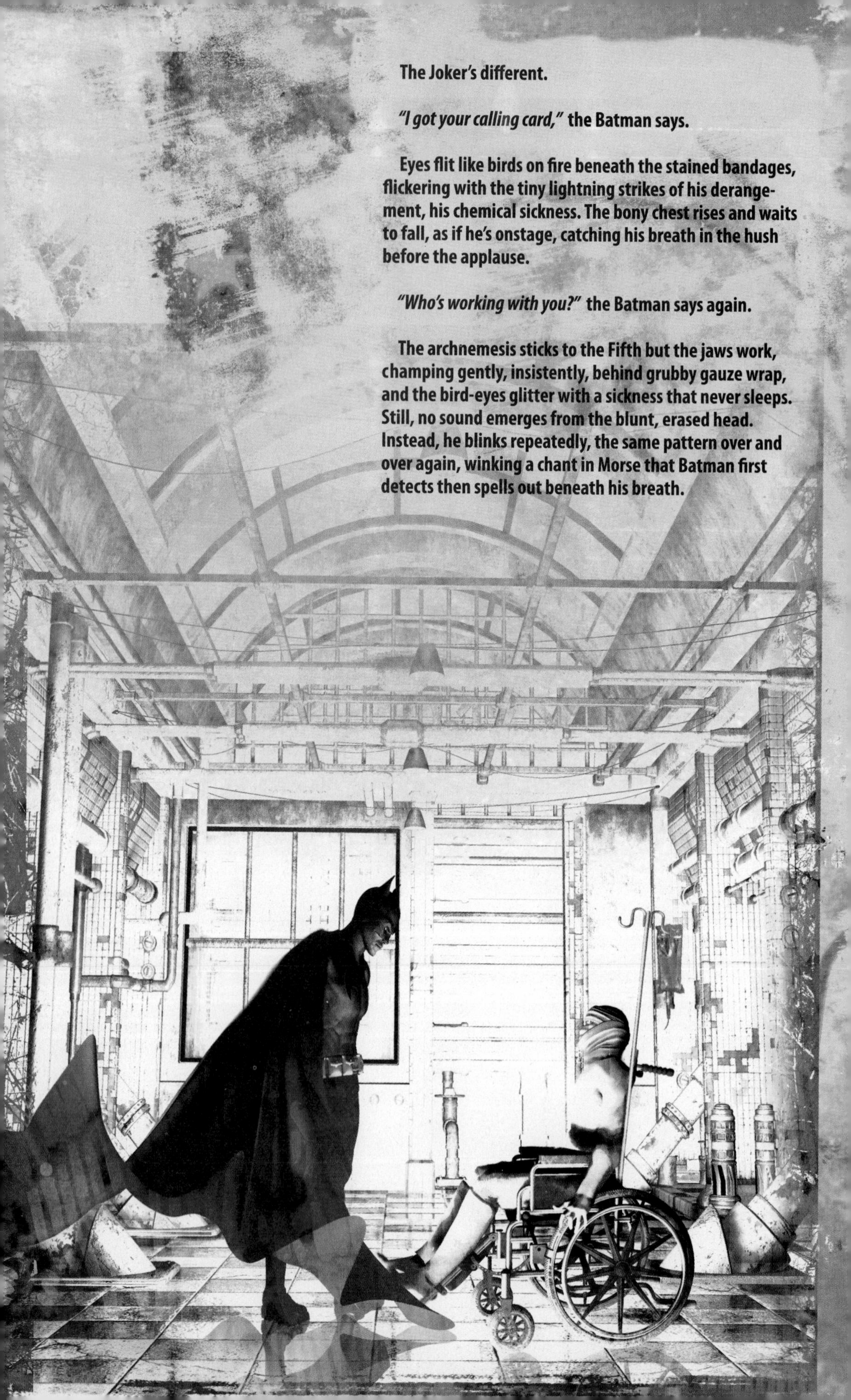

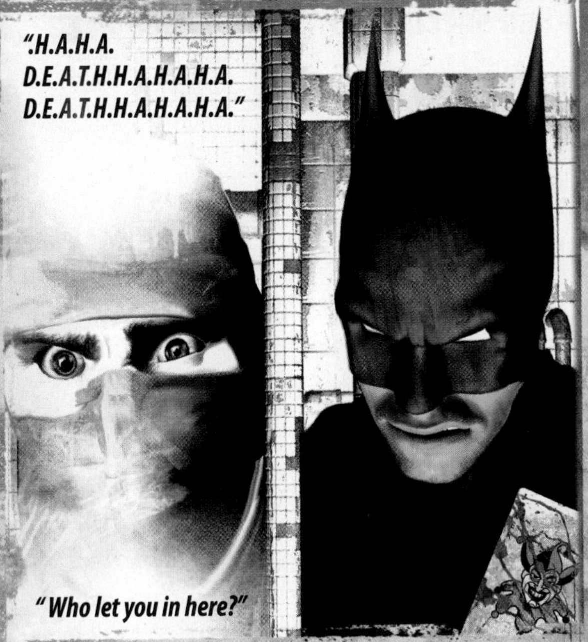
".H.A.H.A.
D.E.A.T.H.H.A.H.A.H.A.
D.E.A.T.H.H.A.H.A.H.A."
"Who let you in here?"

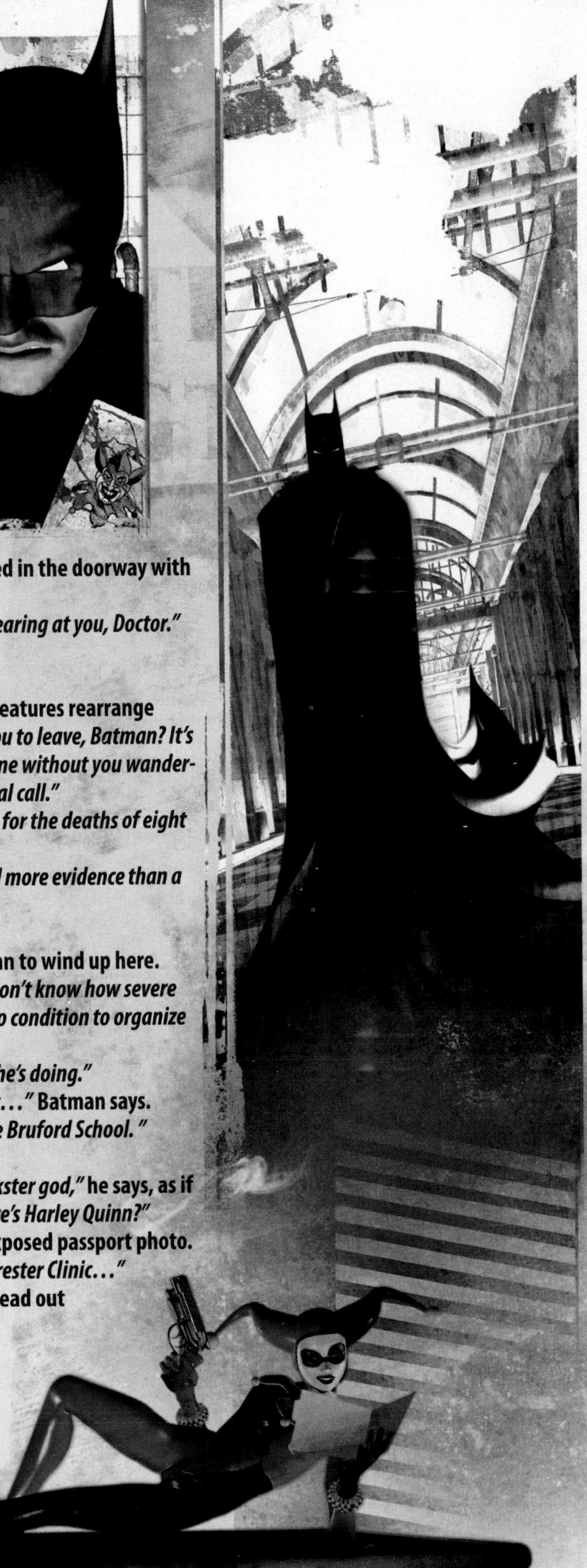

Batman turns to face Jeremiah Arkham, framed in the doorway with a spiky halo of uncombed hair.

"See how he's blinking?" Batman says. *"He's swearing at you, Doctor."*

"What?"

"Morse code."

"Blinking? In Morse code?" Arkham's haunted features rearrange themselves into a mask of derision. *"May I ask you to leave, Batman? It's a hard enough job here among the criminally insane without you wandering through the halls whenever you feel like a social call."*

"Your star patient has already been responsible for the deaths of eight men today."

"That could have been anybody, Batman! I need more evidence than a twitching eyelid."

"You'll get it. This is only the start."

Arkham suppresses a smirk. He expects Batman to wind up here.

"He's recovering from a near fatal trauma. We don't know how severe the brain damage could be, and he's certainly in no condition to organize gangland hits."

"Don't let him fool you. He knows exactly what he's doing."

They pause at the doors. *"This speech therapist..."* Batman says.

"Miss Wisakedjak. She graduated from The Rose Bruford School."

Batman's lip curls.

"Wisakedjak is the name of the Cree Indian trickster god," he says, as if it's something only idiots wouldn't know. *"Where's Harley Quinn?"*

Arkham's face bleaches to resemble an overexposed passport photo.

"She's receiving corrective treatment at the Forrester Clinic..." he tries to say confidently, but the words drop dead out of his mouth.

"Better make sure," says Batman.

Chapter 4 – HER SPECIAL DAY

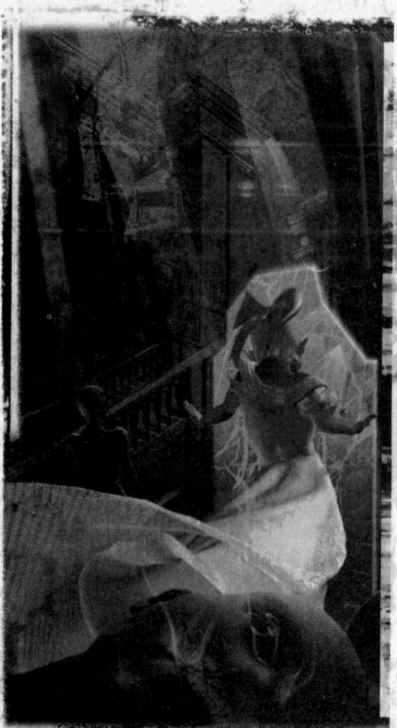

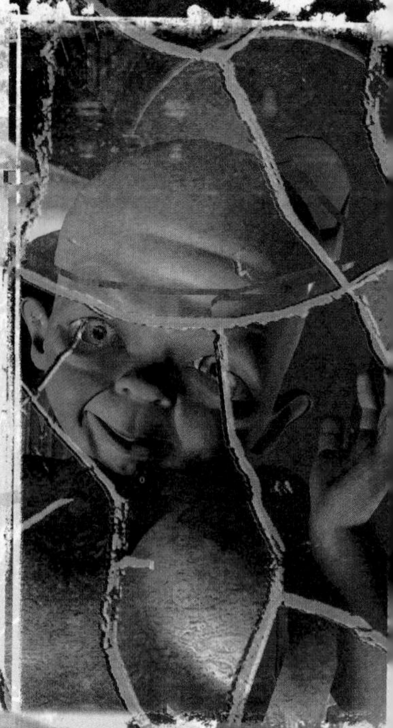

Four miles south, in the charred and broken-down shadows of Black Brothers Department Store, or at least what's left of it after the big insurance fire, it might at first glance appear that a strange child is trying on a wedding dress in front of a cracked mirror, but there's more to this scene than meets the eye. The little figure sways lightly from side to side on stained satin ballet pumps, humming a mindless, one-note melody, as though it's waiting for its cue and the inevitable moment in the movie where the kiddie turns around to reveal the face of a leering, wizened dwarf with an axe and the operating system of a shark where a mind should be.

Sheba gets that movie star double-take often. She was born with microcephaly and sees things with a plain, high-contrast clarity that many Zen masters might envy.

During the Joker's short-lived ringmaster-from-Hell phase, the craze for creepy dwarfs and henchmen with odd congenital conditions reached fever pitch and drew to the City many otherwise unemployable characters from the margins – it was an equal opportunity era when the ambitious pinhead could fast-track to the top and score steady gigs at the swankiest clubs in town. All you had to do was look all starey-eyed in fetish diapers and break a few things while the Boss threatened his victims. So it was for Solomon and Sheba.

Scored with a soundtrack of wheezing calliopes and Wurlitzer steam organs played backwards, their little lives unfolded, while grinding, blind horses went around and around and around on their rusty poles, making the Boss laugh all the more wildly in the swamp-black Southern Gothic twilights they all loved so much. Those were days and nights of cattle prods, of fishnet and ultraviolet light, of porno candyfloss spiked with strychnine. She filed her teeth by mistake one night, then Solomon did the same to prove his love for her. The Boss treated them well and seemed genuinely amused by their cartoonish perspectives. You might be forgiven, like Sheba, for thinking that the good times would last forever although no times ever do.

Even when He was caught and put away again, leaving his tiny, imbecilic henchmen to fend for themselves like Hansel and Gretel in Hell, luck continued to smile on Solomon and Sheba. They were discovered by policemen, hiding in the engine of the carnival ghost train, and embraced by the Bohemian demimonde of East Gotham Village. Soon the pair were everywhere, on catwalks and fashion shoots, lending color to metal videos and artpunk happenings.

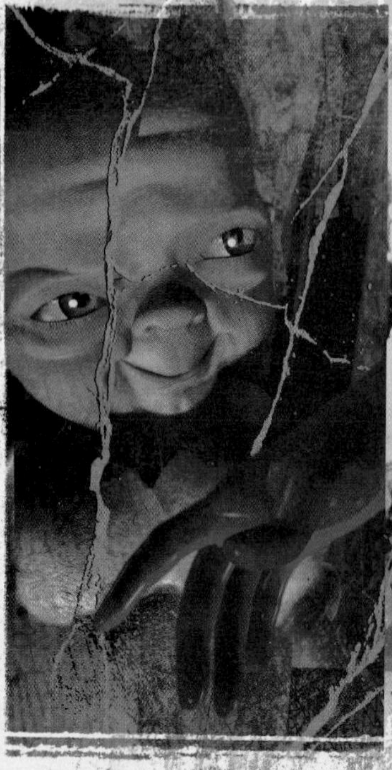

So she dances in front of the mirror, the perfect bride-to-be, endlessly unable to comprehend a world where the Boss could ever be cruel. In her head it is always sunrise and everything is always on the verge of making complete sense.

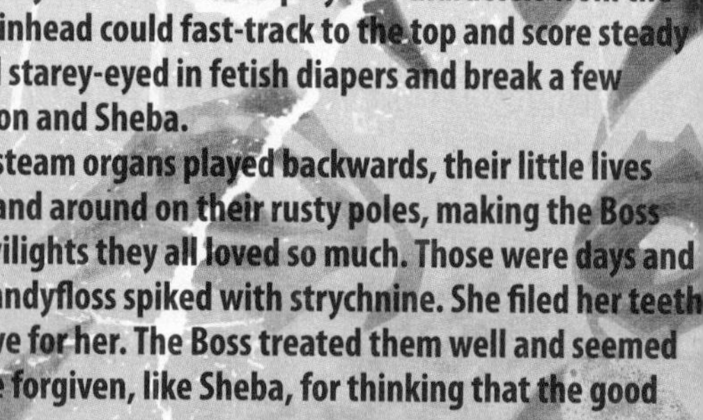

Sheba knows her lovely Solomon is dead before everyone else does because, when she looks in the mirror for the first time ever it seems somehow empty.

But before she can do anything else, the nice lady with the head full of Christmas bells comes back to lead Sheba up the grand skeleton staircase to collect her wedding bouquet from the Boss. Sheba remembers the Boss – his vague, archaic, playing-card face bobs like a balloon in her low-res memory – and smiles a toothy grin. The flowers are roses.

Red and black roses piled like cake.

Chapter 5 - NIRVIKALPA SAMADHI

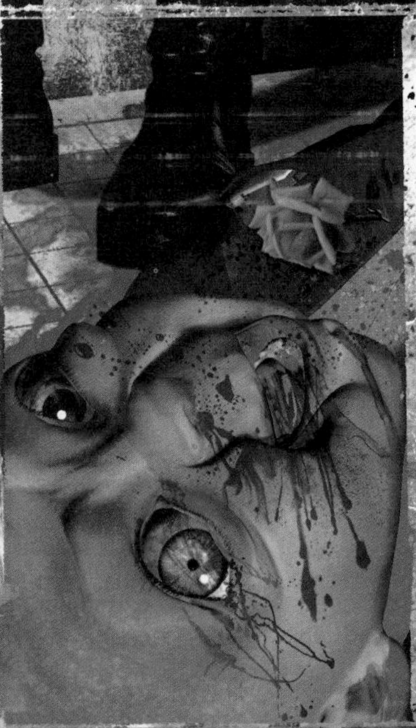

"We know what killed him. We're talking about a new airborne strain of the Joker poison. You all heard Batman — the flowers are carrying a death pollen. The aerosol nerve agent activates when the red and the black flowers are brought together and remains effective for ten minutes."

Police Commissioner Gordon makes his explanations brief, like text messages. His men are uneasy around the Batman. They say he brings bad luck.

The pathologist steps back to give the Dark Knight access to the tiny corpse in its tiny, stupid tuxedo. Uttering a prayer for the dead he learned from the Lamas in Nanda Parbat, Batman extracts a sample of blood into a clear ampule, then clips it back into his utility belt. The rest he hands to Gordon. Uniformed cops in gas masks and a dead dwarf; it's like a fetish club in here. Even the walls are sweating.

"We need an antidote. Fast," Gordon barks.

"It won't happen again," the Batman vows.

"So the Joker's wiping out his old henchmen. Good riddance. Maybe when he gets done, he'll kill himself."

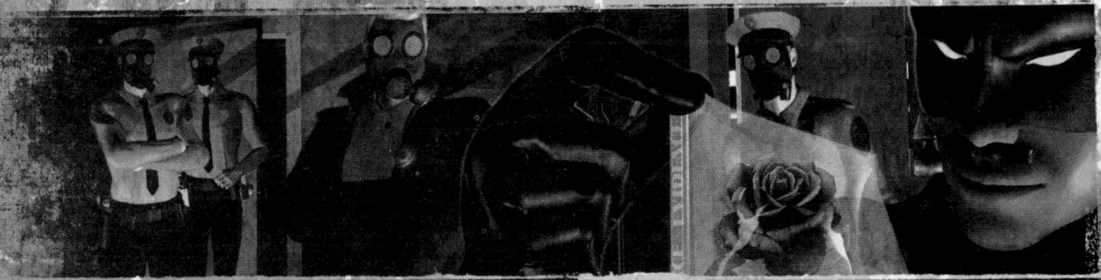

Gordon nods at Solomon's grinning corpse.

"You remember what this little creep did to me?" He shudders. *"The Joker and his whole circus can go to hell as far as I'm concerned!"*

"There's something more to this," the Batman says.

"You think? Since when did killing the hired help stop being one of his favorite pastimes?"

"If it's him, there has to be more. He always leaves a clue. A pattern. You know that," the Batman says, slowing his breathing to trigger Delta-wave activity before entering Nirvikalpa Samadhi, the supreme meditative state.

"Are you listening to me at all?" Gordon says. Batman nods curtly, very still and silent, scanning for the pattern he knows is there. When he finds it, the corners of his mouth twitch upwards. The Joker always plays to his theme.

Rebirth. Snake scales, red and black. Blood on the tuxedo. Red Hook and Black Brothers and the Red House. And red, and black. The big game is there in plain sight, as always. Life and death transformed into one more ugly, unfunny gag.

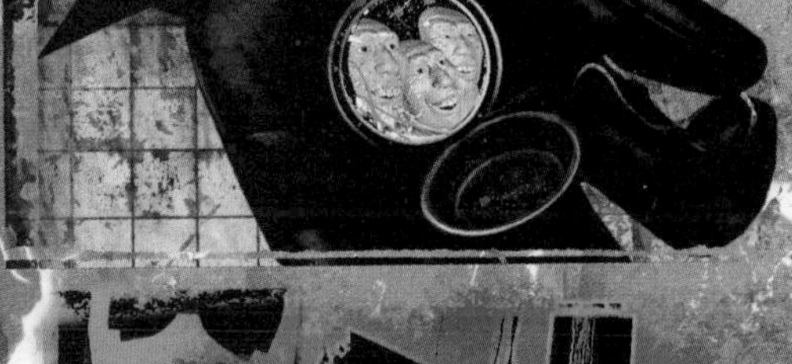

The Joker, as ever, can't help giving it all away.

"No one else is going to die," Batman says and is gone, leaving Gordon alone in a room with an open window.

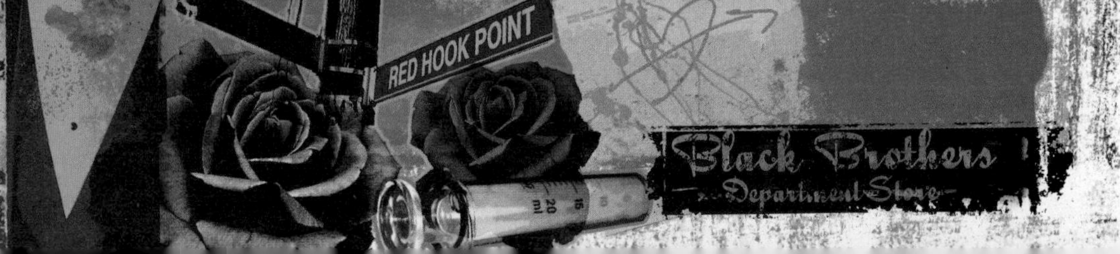
LA MAISON ROUGE
RED HOOK POINT
Black Brothers
Department Store

Chapter 6 - JOKER MAGGOT

In the white, empty cell, the flat, pressurized silence is relieved by these three things only - the crawling ticks of fluorescent lighting, the slow crackle of breathing – if breathing sounded like paper being torn and torn again and torn again, obsessively, into tiny scraps – and the pin-thin whine of a mosquito that rode in on Batman's cape and now finds itself locked in a madhouse with something bad for company.

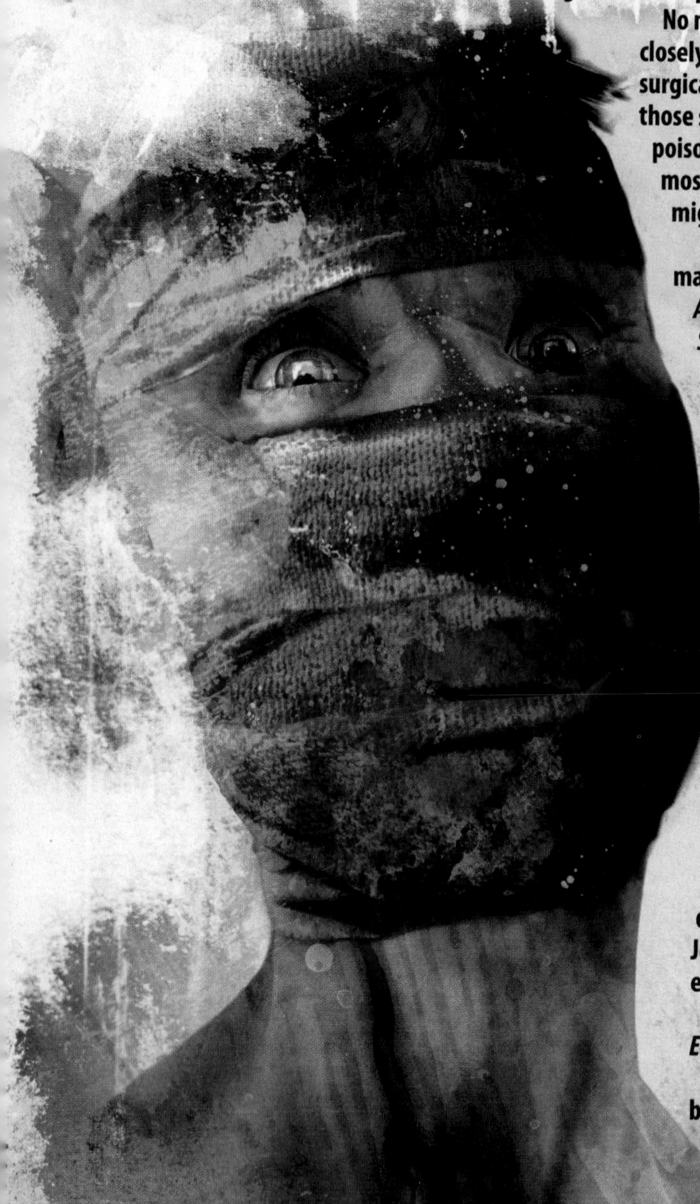

No movement registers either until you look very closely to see the jaws working in stealth beneath surgical gauze and pins. Don't even think about those sly mandibles chewing down on some poison mantra as the dreadful eyes track the poor mosquito's lazy flight-path, the way a spider's might, triangulating its victim.

He's scrolling through a list of things that make him laugh. *Blind babies. Landmines. AIDS. Beloved pets in bad road accidents. Statistics. Pencilcases. BRUNCH! The Periodic Table of the Elements.*

The insect selects a moon-white hand, the left, and settles there like a NASA landing module. It folds its little wings back neatly, takes air in through its tracheae, then eases its hypodermic tool face into the weave of the Joker's papery skin and begins to pulse, gorging on blood flow.

Geniuses suffering irreversible brain damage. REAL bad news. Shattered faith. Sombreros. Politics. Fish being gutted. Fish being gutted. Fish being gutted.

Like a grub growing all wrong in a tiled cocoon, like a caterpillar liquefying to filth in its own nightmares, or a fetus dissolving in sewage and sour milk, the Joker dreams, awake. His is the *mal ojo,* the evil eye. He wills Death upon the world.

Bowel cancer. Fish being gutted. Mister Ed. Guns in schools. Cripples. Racism.

Breathing slowly in his bright and boundless Hell, the Clown Prince of Cruelty dreams a new face, a new world, a Year Zero. An unforgettable golden age of blood-red comedy and crime!

Alzheimer's.

The mosquito, meanwhile, gets the message, shudders and falls from the Joker's hand. Blind and crippled, it spins in circles on the radiant floor, choking on tainted blood.

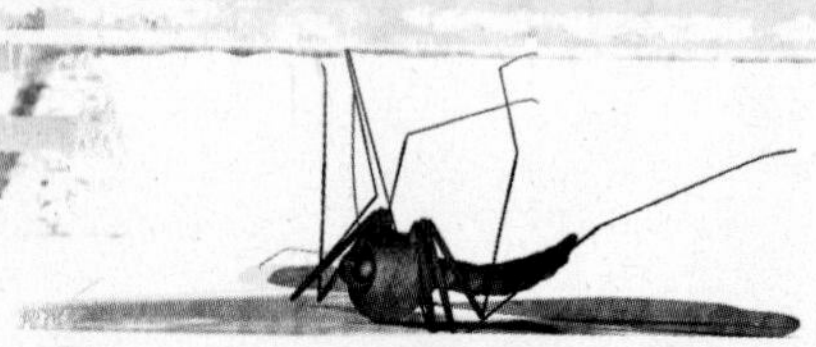

Batman.

He watches the tiny life go out, listens to the fading whine as it slowly curls up, like a hand becoming a fist, and dies.

Batman.

Eager to be born, he counts backward to midnight.

Chapter 7 – THE CHECKERBOARD DOLL

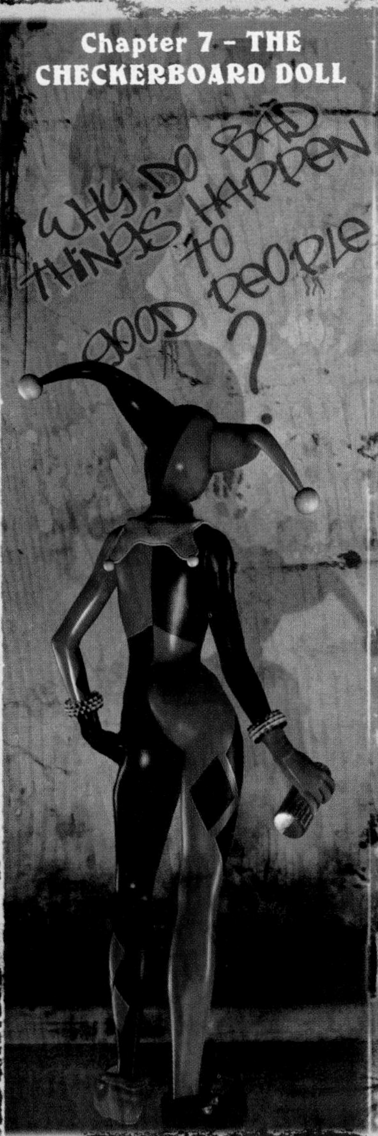
WHY DO BAD THINGS HAPPEN TO GOOD PEOPLE ?

Harley Quinn's been busy since she blew the kook farm, trailing her EEG cables like Medusa locks. It was fun to be free, fun to have a purpose again. It was something to keep the spooks away.

The flowers are only dangerous when they're brought together, of course. Combine the red and the black and *voilà!* The perfect Romantic murder weapon is born – a death rosary. She loves the way his corkscrew mind works. Her obsession, her puddin, her Joker. She goes gooey when she thinks of his ghastly mask of hate. She loves his shattered thoughts, imagining them in all their labyrinthine, jewelled disarray as unknown cities on a distant planet and she, the girl explorer, lost among sinister wonders.

She's all hearts and flowers since he surfaced from his coma. Every week she'd slip away from her cell and bounce all the way to Arkham. As Jane Wisakedjak she's been playing the role of the Joker's quiet Bostonian speech therapist for the last three months. As for the real Jane, who never danced naked or watched the sun rise over the peaks of Bora Bora or took a chance on the classified ads section, what remains of her lies gently rotting beneath the lonely floorboards of her ground floor apartment. Harley's heart beats happily as she dots the question mark she's sprayed on the wall, then skips a beat as a deadly voice splits the gloom.

"He's changed, Harley Quinn," it says.

Her eyes roll, fractured semi-precious stones set like charms in a frightened little Halloween-cake face. She's cute like a Chihuahua pup with rabies, or a baby swinging an open razor.

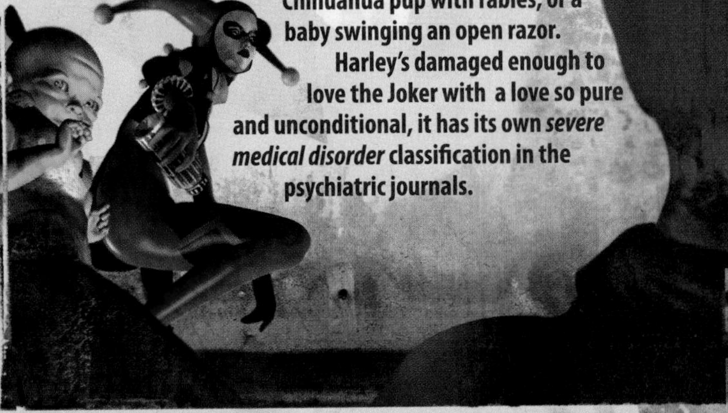

Harley's damaged enough to love the Joker with a love so pure and unconditional, it has its own *severe medical disorder* classification in the psychiatric journals.

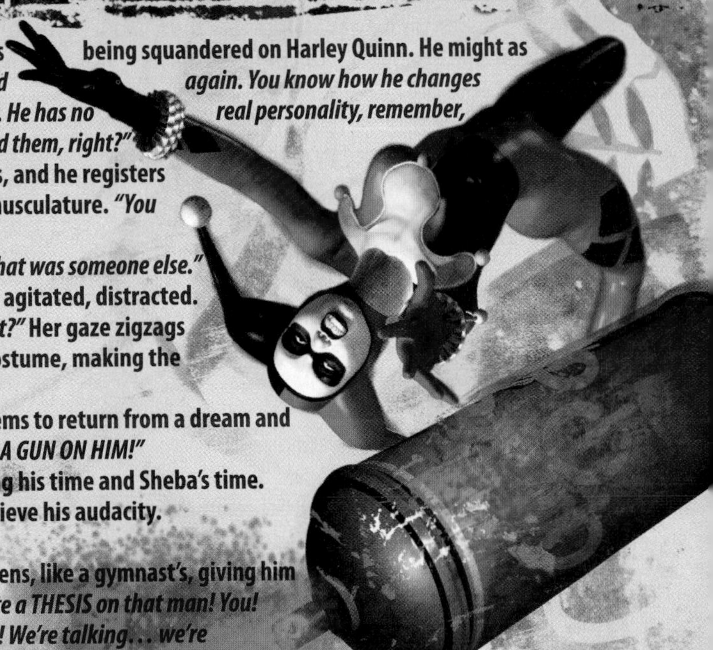

"Harley, you have to stop killing for him. He's sick," the Batman ventures, well aware that reason's being squandered on Harley Quinn. He might as well debate ethics with a tiger kitten. *"He's changed again. You know how he changes every few years. You wrote the book, Doctor Quinzel. He has no real personality, remember, only a series of 'superpersonas.' That's what you called them, right?"*

Her brow furrows. *"What do you know?"* she says, and he registers the flex of tension that snakes through her taut musculature. *"You tried to kill him! You shot him,"* she works out.

"I didn't shoot him," the Batman is telling her. *"That was someone else."*

"Batman shot him!" her voice is becoming shrill, agitated, distracted. *"And you're Batman, aren't you? Dressed up like that?"* Her gaze zigzags around the room as her muscles shift under her costume, making the checkerboard ripple.

"I don't use a gun, Harley," Batman says. She seems to return from a dream and focuses on him with a bellowing snarl. *"YOU USED A GUN ON HIM!"*

"That wasn't me," he says again, but he's wasting his time and Sheba's time.

"So now you're NOT Batman?" She can hardly believe his audacity.

"Of course I am."

"ARE YOU TRYING TO SAY I'M MAD?" Her body tightens, like a gymnast's, giving him less than a fraction of a second to prepare. *"I wrote a THESIS on that man! You! You will NEVER NEVER EVER comprehend that artist! We're talking... we're talking the PICASSO of Crime! The Great Modernist in a postmodern tradition! The. The. The. HIM! He will spawn SCHOOLS OF THOUGHT!! I know this, Batman... I have a doctorate and I can KICK YOUR ASS!"*

Harley goes into action like her special effects budget is limitless and becomes a boneless whirl of red and black gymnastics that is suddenly whipping overhead, suddenly aiming, cocking, and firing her dainty little revolver in one movement so fluid, so economical, and so improbable that the Batman, astonished, almost forgets to react.

Almost. The bullet chops a silver-gray furrow out of the Kevlar shielding of his cowl, pulverizing chunks of protective fabric in hard slo-mo. He wants to applaud and award marks out of ten. Instead, he calculates her speed and momentum, spinning on his heel to be ready for her next attack.

Harley lands behind him, soundless, a deadly human chessboard that unfolds to be everywhere at once and knots her arm around Sheba's neck, pulling it back to expose the plush white skin to the edge of her blade.

"Jokerday begins at midnight," she cackles with the creepy, wasted, little girl voice that she can make sound as if it's coming from all the shadows in all the corners of the room. *"Mistah Jay says he's putting his past to rest!"*

Batman tries to speak, to warn her, but she shouts him down and presses the blade closer to Sheba's throat. *"We'r celebratin' the resurrection with the ultimate sacrifice!"* As she drags the squealing underground superstar backward to a funereal flower display, Harley and her captive seem to transform into an absurdist performance troupe, dying death in front of an audience of one.

"But first. . . time to smell the roses, Sheba! Mistah Jay says a big new world is coming over the hill, like the circus!" Harley squeals, and draws blood from the wailing, pop-eyed Sheba. *"What do YOU got to offer?"*

"Fireworks," Batman answers.

First he torches the murder blossoms with incendiary pellets from his utility belt. It takes two seconds.

Then he rescues the squalling, hysterical Sheba, who's spinning in her wedding dress like the shuttlecock in a badminton game. Three seconds.

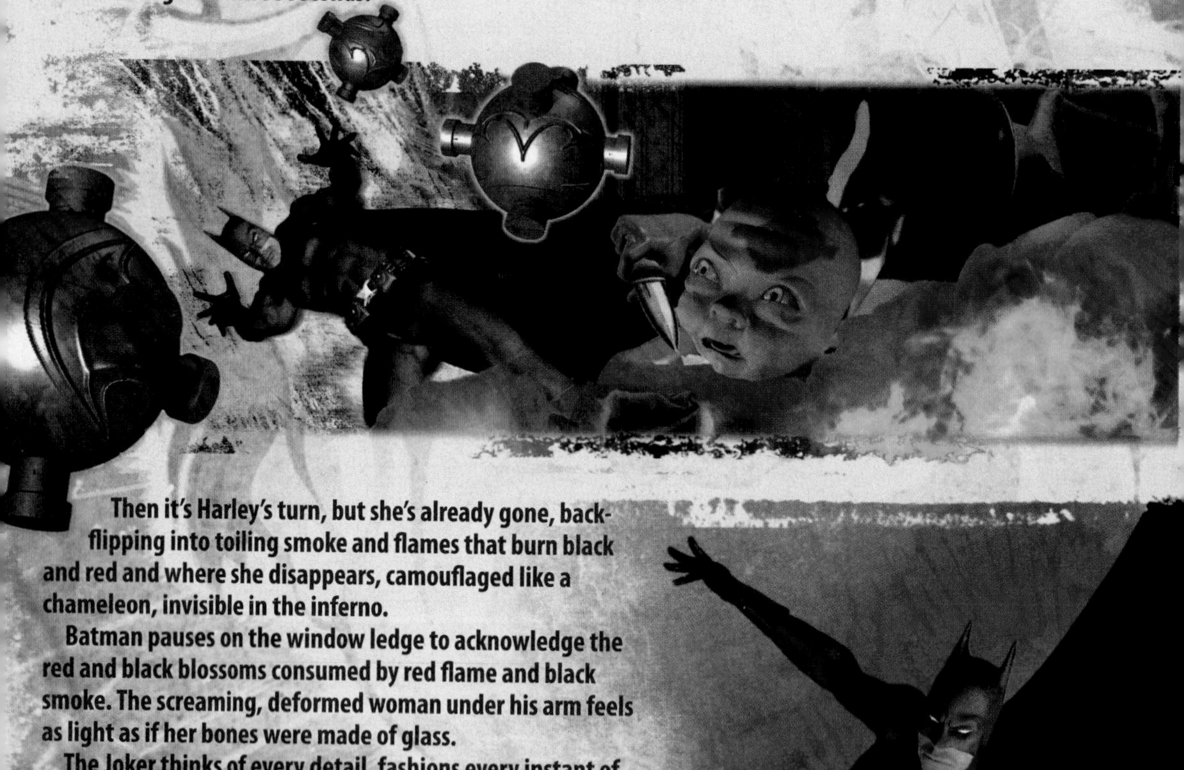

Then it's Harley's turn, but she's already gone, back-flipping into toiling smoke and flames that burn black and red and where she disappears, camouflaged like a chameleon, invisible in the inferno.

Batman pauses on the window ledge to acknowledge the red and black blossoms consumed by red flame and black smoke. The screaming, deformed woman under his arm feels as light as if her bones were made of glass.

The Joker thinks of every detail, fashions every instant of every event into a work of gross and evil artistry.

He leaves Sheba with her friends at *Gotham Noir,* the scandal sheet, and awaits the inevitable escalation of hostilities.

It's 11:40 p.m.

The radio mike inside Batman's cowl crackles to life. Alfred's voice, as clipped and regimental as a retired Sergeant Major's lawn, brings the expected news. *"Sir. The alarms just went off at Arkham Asylum."*

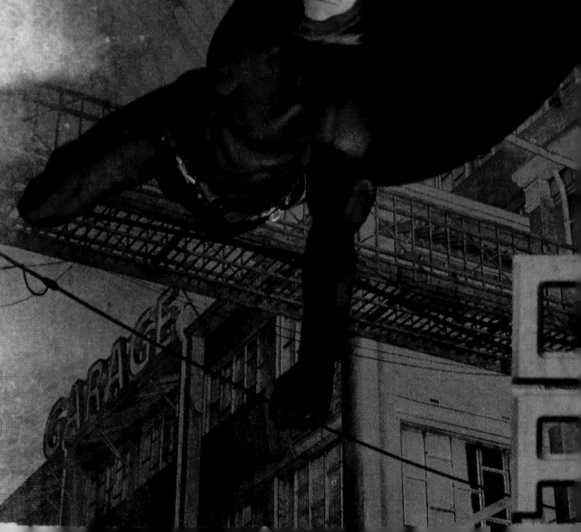
GARAGE

Chapter 8 – JOKER UNBOUND

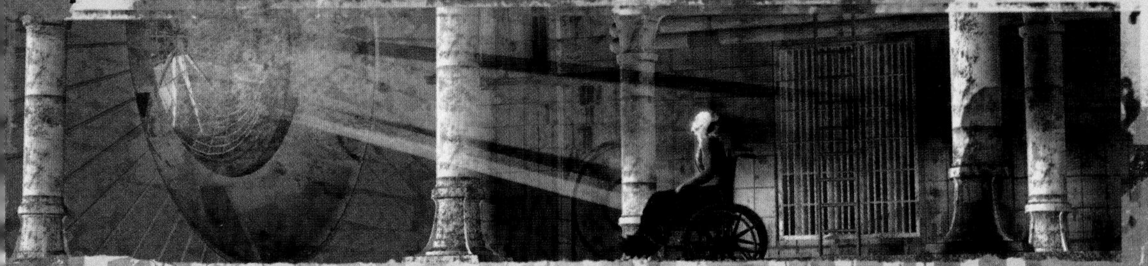

The fiend stops chewing, mouth filled with a swill of black bile. As an avid consumer of his own chemical experiments, the Joker's immunity to poison concoctions that might kill another man in an instant has been developed over years of dedicated abuse. The capsule of venom that his "speech-therapist" passed him on a spatula before the electro-therapy sessions is where it belongs beneath his tongue, dissolving in his mouth, releasing its contents slowly in the form of an acrid black liqueur that burns as it melts across his tongue and the roof of his reconstructed palate.

He savors the stinging hallucinogenic heat and, like the god Shiva, holds the poison mix in place, thickening it with more and more saliva. *"UMMM,"* he gobbles in a fearful, quavering voice, *"UMMMMMMM! UMMMM!,"* rattling his chair wildly until the cell door unlocks and the curious Screw is drawn closer to see what's up.

In less time than it takes for this second to become the next, Lou Perroni (37, a bodybuilder and collector of Ramones memorabilia, GSOH) is pedalling backward, making the noises cattle make at the slaughterhouse gate, clawing at his face where the adhesive spit burns black holes in his skin. It doesn't take much longer for the contaminants to go to work in his bloodstream and for Lou's shocking, inhuman lowing to contort into the biggest, most awful howl of laughter you ever heard. The skin splits at the corners of Lou's lips but he just can't stop the churning carnival

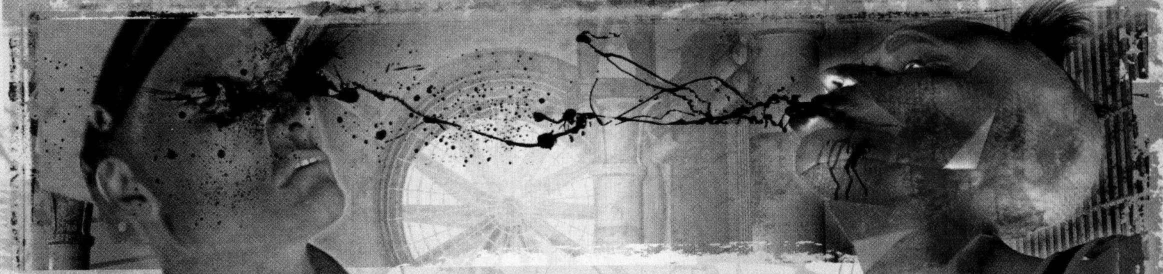

inside. He's laughing red and black and red and black till there's nothing left to laugh. Until, almost tenderly, he turns inside out through his mouth.

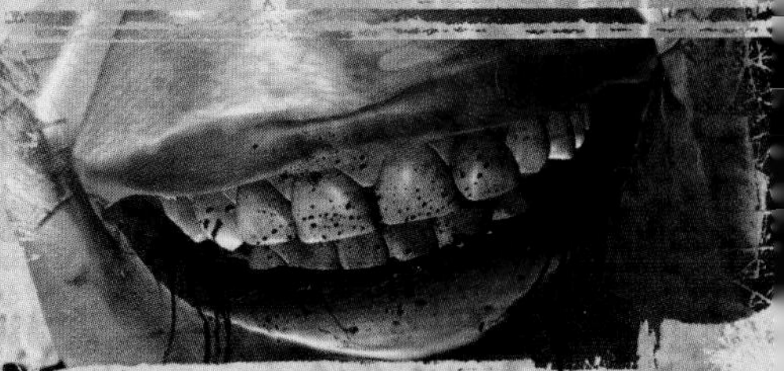

Sliding in the rubbery red chaos that was lately a drinking buddy, Cassius Collins (26, fond of violence, karaoke, conflicted) performs a spectacular, impromptu pratfall, then, astonished, watches the Joker rising from his wheelchair, the way a rabbit watches car headlights bearing down, unable to move a single, spotlit muscle. The madman's limbs appear to unlatch as though some psychotic god has chosen to give life to a complicated Swiss Army knife. The Joker's head rotates, with black contagion drizzling off his chin onto his chest in slow, syrupy drips. The green lasers of his eyes target the keys at the big man's belt, and he shakes his head.

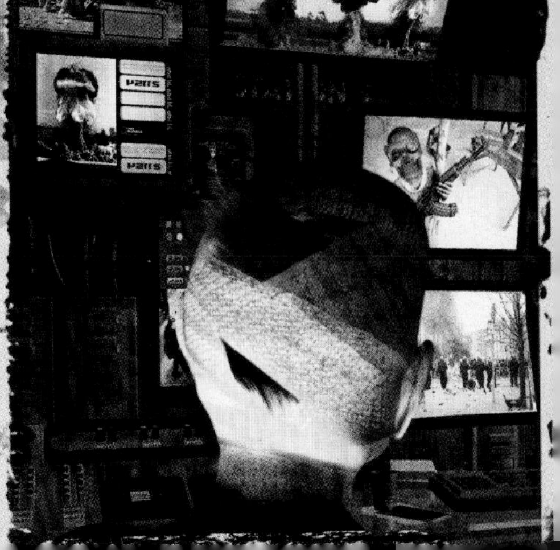

In the silence that follows Cassius Collins' seedy, humiliating death at the hands of the Master of Mirth, the lights crackle and fizz like children suppressing giggles behind the teacher's back. Blood puddles thickly around his specially soft hospital slippers as the Joker pads down the soundproofed halls, leaving sticky red prints on the tiles, killing everyone he meets, effortlessly.

It's not quite twelve and he has a little time to spare before the climactic debut of The Clown At Midnight, his latest reinvention.

Dazed, hyperventilating, and stinking of blood, he finds himself exhilarated, in a room where they keep all the TV screens and decides to watch the news for a few seconds, to see what's been happening while he's been tucked away in his coma.

What face, he wonders, will the bogeyman of this dark century wear?

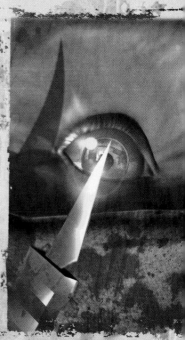

In the tidy little operating theater, he selects a pair of sharp scissors, carefully opening and closing several of them until he finds the one with the perfect creak. It's time to peel himself from his dead skin like a snake, and only the finest tools will do. He clips the bandages away in a stately, ritual procession that lets them fall in dirty ribbons to the floor.

It's time to meet the man in the mirror.

He hears himself gasp as the final layers are shed, feels the jolt of shock.

A screaming schizophrenic, tripping on LSD, might grab a pack of crayons and scrawl this face before digging out his own eyes with teaspoons. The face in the glass looks like a stopped clock, flash-frozen at some desperate eternal midnight of the soul, and no matter how hard he tries the smile is stuck there, as if on hooks.

His remarkable coping mechanism, which saw him transform a personal nightmare of disfigurement into baleful comedy and criminal infamy all those years ago — happily chuckling to himself in the garage as he constructed outlandish Joker-Mobiles which gently mocked the young Batman's pretensions in the Satire Years before Camp, and New Homicidal, and all the other Jokers he's been — now struggles to process the raw, expressionistic art brutal of his latest surgical makeover.

He tries to remember how the doctors in Arkham say he has no Self, and maybe they're right, or maybe just guessing. Maybe he is a new human mutation, bred of slimy industrial waters, spawned in a world of bright carcinogens and acid rains. Maybe he is the model for 21st-century big-time multiplex man, shuffling selves like a croupier deals cards, to buffer the shocks and work some alchemy that might just turn the lead of tragedy and horror into the fierce, chaotic gold of the laughter of the damned. Maybe he is special, and not just a gruesomely scarred, mentally-ill man addicted to an endless cycle of self-annihilating violence. Stranger things have happened.

His body goes into spasm. His gut cramps down as if gravitational forces have conspired and shifted to bring him to his knees. From there he rolls onto his side, whining horribly. The whine is the signal, the radio, the new sound of his self coming through like a frequency.

"I'm a cockroach!" he squeals, and kicks first one leg, and then the other, acting out a disturbing can-can of contraction, labor, and birth as the Asylum alarm bells ring wildly. "La Cucaracha! La Cucaracha! The pain is terrible! I want morphine! I'm having a baby!" he wheezes, then cackles, then coughs, jazzing like a showgirl delivering a donkey onstage. "La Cucaracha-hahahahaha!" Multiple Joker voices vie for control as he prepares to give blasphemous birth to himself like the Word of God in reverse. His only regret is that Batman isn't here to witness his obscene display, his rampant pathology in full flower. Batman.

"They can't keep me here I know a way out…You see I hold the winning card…" he says, before the voice changes to a throaty theatrical chuckle. "You're in my power Batman Ho Ho! I could pull off your mask now — and end your reign! I could even kill you but I won't! HAHAHAHA Let him live!" Then a nasal, aristocratic whine. "He's so amusing when he tries to match wits with me… hehehehehe" Batman.

"Take a look! We resemble each other!" The chorus of voices fades out one by one, strangled into silence, diminishing into whispers and ghosts of threats and disgusting boasts. He begins to croon like a frightened mother to a sick child she's doomed to lose.

"And I'm looony, like a lightbulb-battered bug. Aren't…aren't I just good enough to EAT! Stop…stop…stop me…if you've heard this one…" Until there is only a single Joker voice smacking its lips in the huge echoing emptiness of a place, let's call it his soul, of such utter dereliction there are no words broken enough to describe it.

"Stop." The Joker from Hell lives here, The Deathly Dandy, The Laughing Leper — he loves all the weird old nicknames the papers used to give him — The Clown Prince of Pain. Bringing death to his victims, with a smile. He gets to his feet, confronting the mirror's awful image once more. Now he can see exactly where it's all gone wrong. He reaches up to smooth back a lock of oily green hair that feels as brittle, metallic, and unnatural as it did on the day he crawled from the oozing waste pipes at the Monarch Playing Card Company and was born a second time, slick with multicolored metals and unfiltered madness. "There," he says, setting the unruly strand in place…

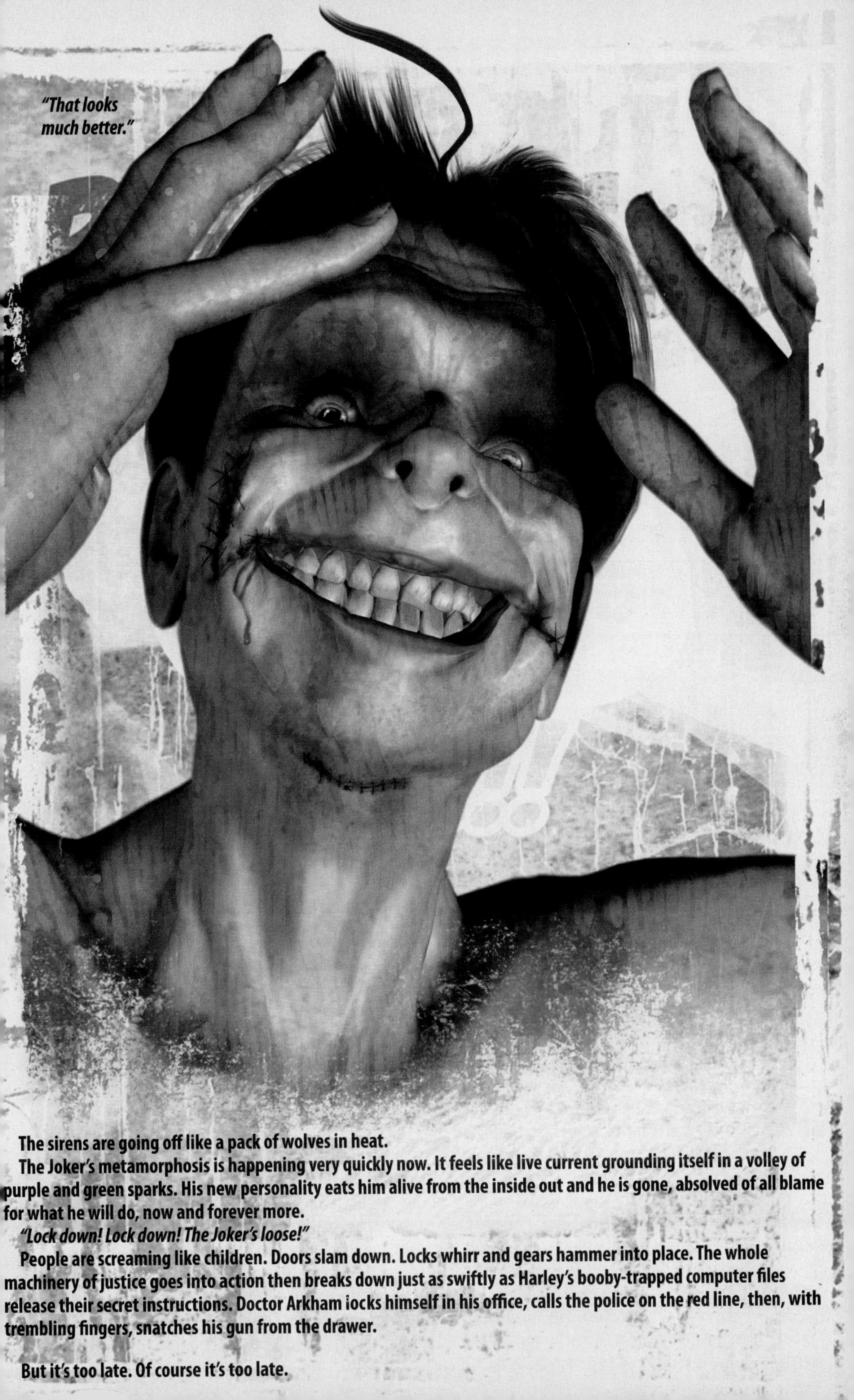
"That looks much better."

The sirens are going off like a pack of wolves in heat.

The Joker's metamorphosis is happening very quickly now. It feels like live current grounding itself in a volley of purple and green sparks. His new personality eats him alive from the inside out and he is gone, absolved of all blame for what he will do, now and forever more.

"Lock down! Lock down! The Joker's loose!"

People are screaming like children. Doors slam down. Locks whirr and gears hammer into place. The whole machinery of justice goes into action then breaks down just as swiftly as Harley's booby-trapped computer files release their secret instructions. Doctor Arkham locks himself in his office, calls the police on the red line, then, with trembling fingers, snatches his gun from the drawer.

But it's too late. Of course it's too late.

Chapter 9 – HARLEQUIN OF HELL

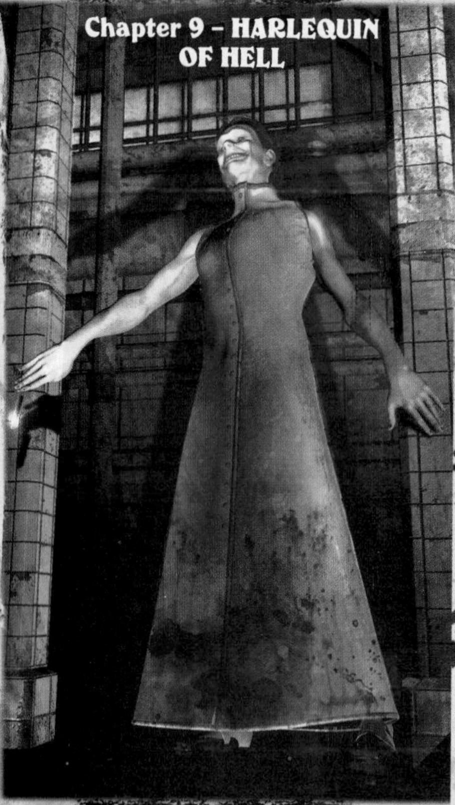

He thinks of Batman, smiling because he cannot stop.

The Joker walks stiffly, growing accustomed to a new skeleton, new gravity, new rules. He feels like a god again – th Thin White Duke of Death with his graveyard grin and his eternal promise of humiliation and pain. Jack of All Crimes, the Knave of Razors. The surgeons have invoked a bony ghoul into being, a diseased demon jester from a negative world beyond all human laws, tuned to frequencies so fast and so hot that th skin of his brain feels like it's 8:15 a.m. at ground zero in Hiroshima. They have only themselves to blame.

The Joker wipes blood flecks from his cheek and dreams of hi throne beneath a handicapped sun. He dreams of giving birth from his mouth to pestilence and desolation, soiling the world with flowers of death. He dreams of creeping through a million shattered windows where ten million terrified, vulnerable children hide behind couches and wait for night to fall and for him to find them. He dreams awake. His leprous skin crawling, his brittle ghost fingers twitching, as he reaches out to explore his new limits and finds there are none. There is only the horizon going on forever and a door that just opens and opens and opens. He's almost free again.

Then something is in his way, spoiling his big, fat visionary moment like that tall guy with the hairdo who sits down right in front of you at the cinema just when the movie's all set to start.

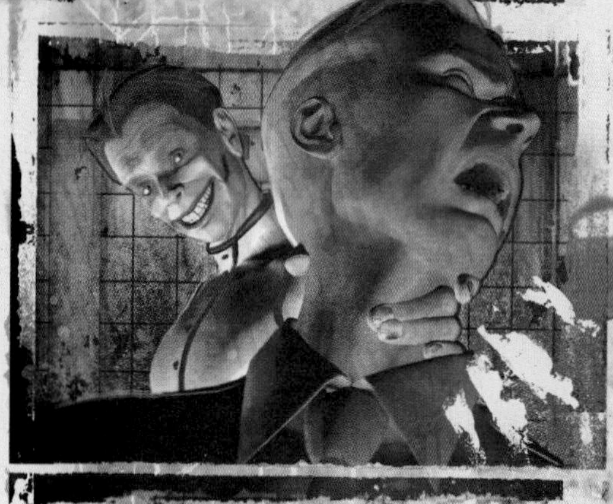

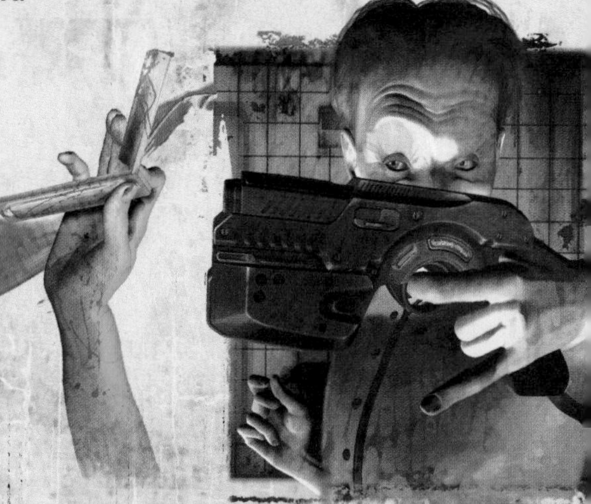

It's something that looks like the most boring board game ever invented, with pleady, needy blue eyes just made for gently slitting with razors, Andalusian Dog-style.

It's a dinner gone cold. It reminds him of something he once gorged on but never, ever wants to eat again.

"Puddin," it says.

The Harlequin of Hell cocks his head, the grin fixed, the bone and gum exposed as if in a biology demonstration.

"Puddin," he repeats. He hates board games. They're his least favorite dessert.

She runs to him across the tiles, suddenly uncoordinated and awkward, flushed with hormones and neurological seizures. Her little bells jingle like it's Christmas Morning in the madhouse.

"Puddin," she sobs helplessly. He looks so mean. Harley's almost scared to approach him. Everything she once recognized is gone now, seared, vivisected, or electro-shocked into extinction. The man she loved has been evicted from his own face, leaving these unfinished smudges of skin and bone and rouge, this radical grafting of tissue that passes for an expression. He has gone beyond her understanding into a religious agony of perfection. Harley Quinn imagines she can see radioactive light spilling from her Saint, her Joker, from his ears and eyes. The pure angelic rapture of his transformation strikes his motley disciple as a rattling concussion of black and red slates behind her eyelids, making her stammer like her tongue's caught on a nail in the wind.

"Suh-suh-sorry I was almuh-most late, Mistah Jay. He's coming... the Batman's coming. I brung him for ya, puddin! Right on the stroke of midnight like ya wanted!" Dazzled by revelation, she gets this feeling that she's no longer worthy of him and can't seem to do anything but stutter in the phosgene flashbacks of his presence.

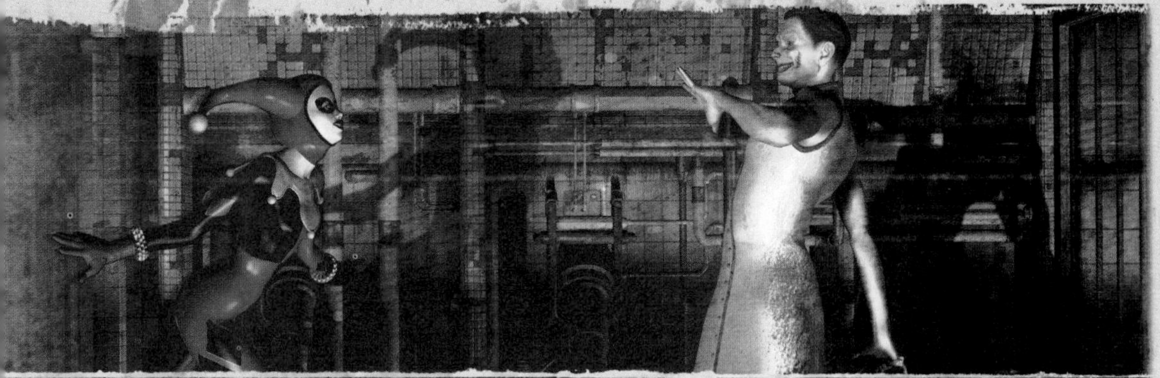

"Puddin," he agrees. He takes the last black death rose from her and pins it to his lapel. Then he grips her wrist and vists her arm up her back as he leans in close. Her eyes are bright.

"Batman dead at midnight on the steps of Arkham Asylum," she whispers. *"Right?"*

She can smell the lovely, rancid chemicals on his breath. She can feel his clammy fever heat and see his insanity urging like serum from every open pore. The pain in her arm intensifies.

"Batman?" he says. The Joker grins on and draws back his blade sharply, savoring the moment, as he prepares to ut the last and best of his lackeys like a playing card on the stroke of midnight.

"Harley!" The voice is like steel striking rock. She can feel the Joker jump and sees the sheet lightning of sheer error flash in his eyes for just a second. *"Red Hook. Black Brothers. La Maison Rouge,"* the Batman growls. *"It's a picture f a checkerboard."* Understanding knits itself across her brow – a little "H" under the domino mask. *"Like you."*

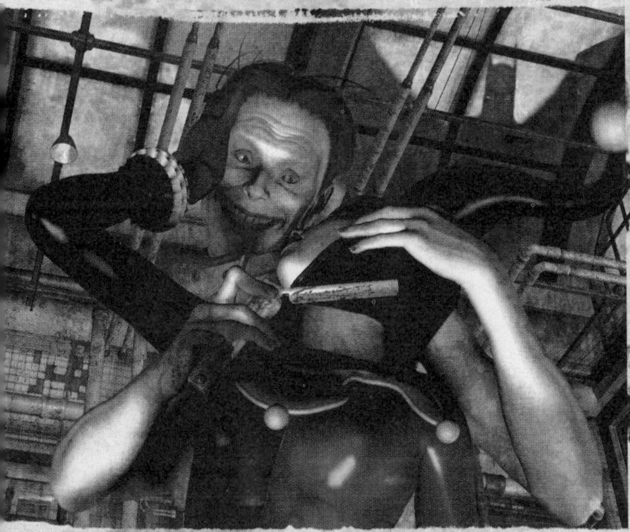

"That's not true," she stutters. Her arm is being stressed to breaking point.

"It's you, Harley, not me. He cared for you. Killing you will prove he's more than human. I'm only here because he wants me to watch."

She shakes her head, jingling, a court jester in denial. *"He wouldn't..."* she faces the Joker again.

"It's not like that, puddin! BATMAN dies at midnight, remember?"

His chest rises and falls. His face almost creaks as he tries to smile some more. And he shakes his head left to right, with a look that curdles the lymph in her glands.

"Don't make me hurt you..." she sobs, catching sight of the razor's stealthy movement. *"You still love me, don't you?"* He simply grins.

"I still love you," she whimpers. *"I always will."*

He whips his arm back and the blade draws a silver arc, a trajectory that can only end in her throat. But Harley Quinn, cornered, puts rats to shame and moves so much faster than even her beloved Joker can recall. It takes him completely by surprise when she punches her knee upwards. With the kind of splintering crack a bullwhip makes, the Joker's left forearm folds up like a blind man's cane and the razor flies from his dead fingers to clink across the tiles. Harley wriggles free of the flapping, smashed limb leaving the Joker a quiet moment to contemplate the splintered bone shards projecting at a fifty-degree angle from his skinny wrist. The grin never leaves his face and never will, despite the flaring up of agony that registers as a sharp constriction of his jet black pupils.

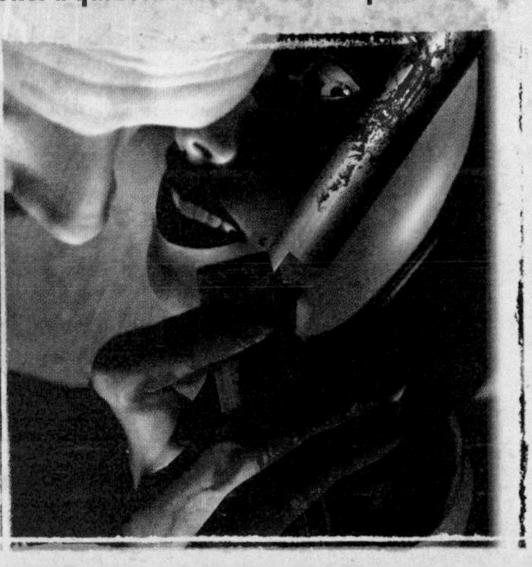

"I'm so sorry! I'm so sorry," she sobs. Her world is falling apart. Harley turns her panicked eyes to Batman, as if for advice, then back to the Joker.

"I'll let you live, but it would be better if you looked more like me," the Joker says, only it sounds like *"Uffleff yoofla buf bef beffer lukked um lik me."* So much for speech therapy.

"Harley, no..." the Batman whispers, as she makes the only choice her heart allows and tiptoes towards the Boss with her head lowered like a nun's. He tilts her chin up and gently trails a bloody razor's edge down the soft, fuzzy peach skin of her cheek. Harley closes her eyes and bites her trembling lip as it turns to jelly.

"Do it," she whispers *"If that's what you want..."*

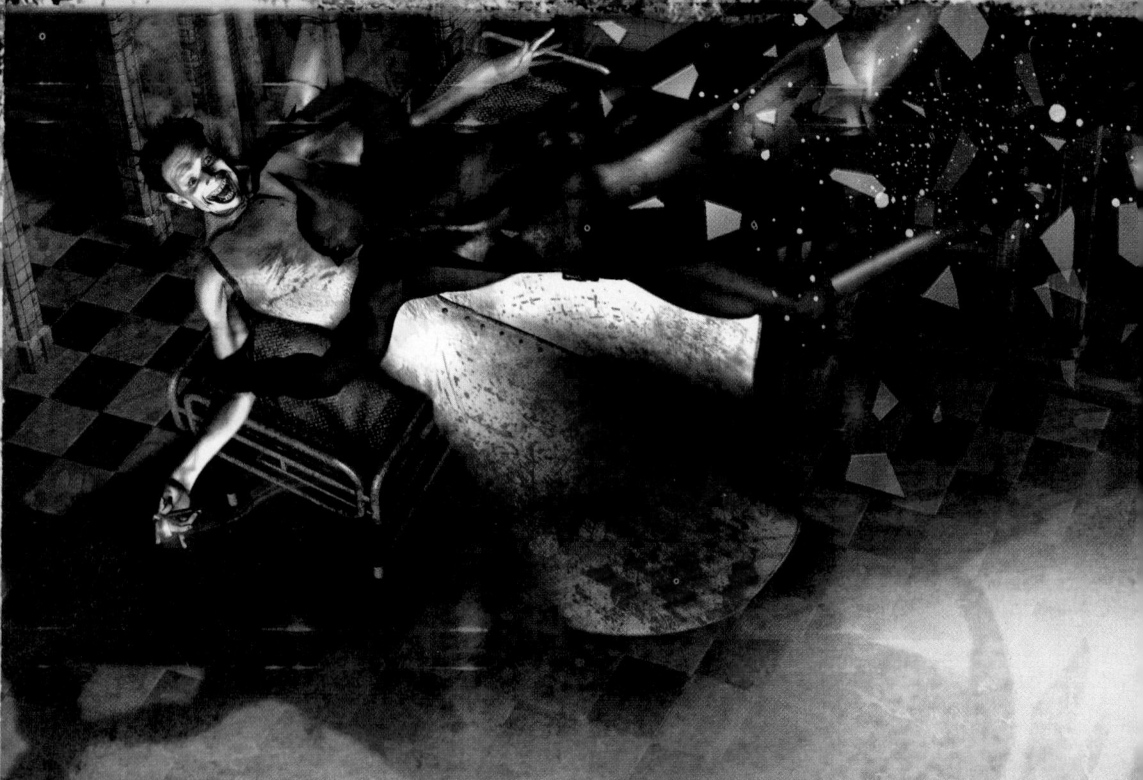

The Joker hits a hospital gurney in a tangle of bones, then collects himself together the way a mantis might and springs at Batman, who drops flat on the floor as the maniac whips his arms in broad figures-of-eight that make the razors whicker overhead like propellers. Calculating, Batman spins on his shoulder, tangles the Joker's legs in a *silat* move, and levers him onto his back with a painful crack.

"I didn't shoot you," Batman says, as if talking will make a difference. As if anything will but violence. They pause for a moment, breathing rapidly, sharing oxygen.

The Joker strikes. The razor embeds in Batman's forearm then gets dragged down across the palm of his glove. Ignoring the chewing pain and the gash that gapes like a consumptive mouth in the flat of his hand, he grips the blade, snaps it, and drives his elbow into the Joker's chin.

The lunatic is still grinning, biting and snapping at Batman's face. His red-rimmed eyes are juicing, his florid lips dribbling and spitting a spray of liquid sparks that makes Batman's skin sizzle and raises tiny blisters. When he glances up, the corridors are empty, except for Harley Quinn sobbing in the corner like a rag doll some kid dropped behind her when she discovered ponies or boys.

The Joker doesn't care anymore. He's picking up speed, casting distorted shadows on the tiled walls, as he drags his foot like Asmodeus, the lame demon, the tempter and destroyer. Limping, he heads for the Asylum's wide-open doors, the shimmering wall of rain, and the city stretched out like a glittering necklace around a naked throat.

"They all used to ask me, 'What makes the Joker laugh?' and I'd point to YOU. We'd all laugh at you and your stupid bat-toys behind your back.

"Both of us trying to find meaning in a meaningless world! Why be a disfigured outcast when I can be a notorious Crime God? Why be an orphaned boy when you can be a superhero?

"You can't kill me without becoming like me. I can't kill you without losing the only human being who can keep up with me. Isn't it IRONIC?!"

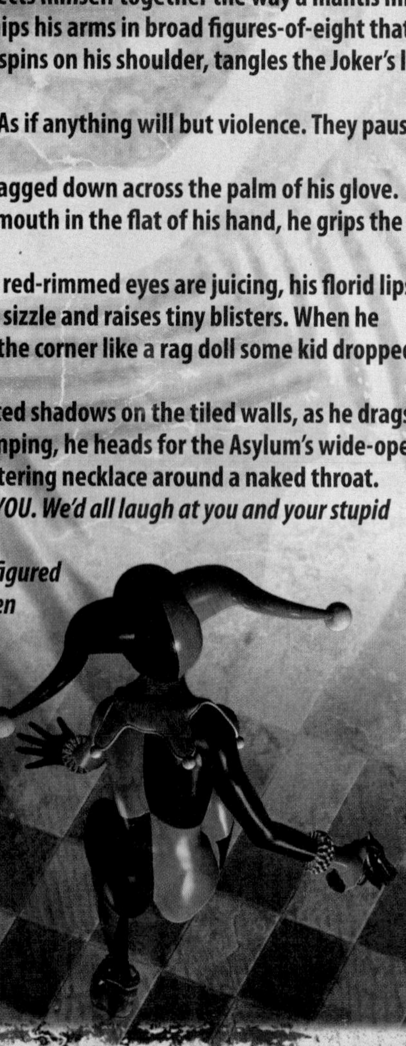

He thinks about trying to say all these things, but words seem so tasteless somehow. They fail to explain his feelings or to plumb the pure white depths of his loathing, his ecstasy.

He simply wants to maim Batman. He simply wants Batman to lose his dignity in the dirt. He simply wants Batman to give in to chaos.

He simply wants the goddamn Batman to finally get the goddamn joke.

Chapter 10 – THE UNBEARABLE INEVITABILITY OF BATMAN AND THE JOKER

"When I get out of here," he begins boldly, but his reconstructed jaw and palate can only struggle with the demands he's acing on them as he mashes the words into a subhuman paste of slobbery vowels and clicking consonants, so that, *"I'll ipple and blind you! I'll cut out your frontal lobes! I'll castrate you and turn your precious city into a cesspit while you drool in ur cave!"* becomes mangled phonetics and toxic intent.

"You're going nowhere," Batman says. It's the sort of all-purpose, semi-hypnotic phrase he often uses to draw fetish-mpulsive criminals like the Joker into familiar patterns of interaction, to elicit familiar chains of response. It's not work-g this time; the lurching silhouette advances under the sparking overheads like a bad dream waking up to find it's real.

The Batman knows he has no choice: if the Joker takes one step past this threshold into the world beyond, it's red and ack carnage all the way home. The threat in those sour green eyes is unmistakable. If he ever gets loose again, Gotham ill face a one-man holocaust and witness the descent of an angel of snickering, mirthless death without mercy or eaning or restraint. No matter what else happens, the Joker must be contained here, tonight, as the second hand esitantly, steadily approaches midnight's full stop.

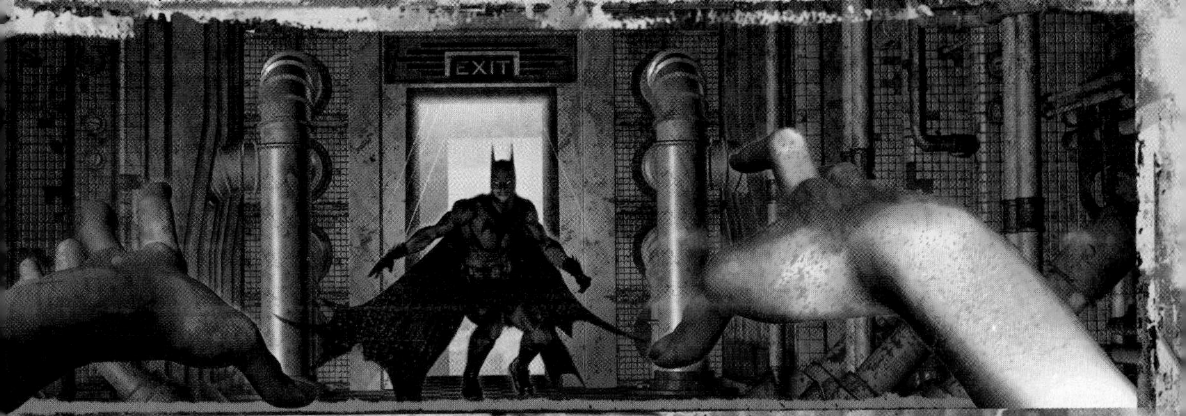
EXIT

The eyes of the two men lock into place like dancers in a ango. It's as dangerous to look the Joker in the eye as it is o train a telescope on the sun, they say, but Batman has aced down this blue-hot blinding lunacy before.

"If you don't turn around and walk back to your padded ell, I'll put you down like a dog," Batman says. *"I promise."*

Unflinching, he nails his stare in place until it's the Joker vho blinks and glances away, troubled by what he sees. His nsanity is like an ocean he can barely stay afloat in; Batman's is like a searchlight.

"It's the oldest, bestest gag in the book," the Joker spits nd slurs, eager for the last laugh. *"Red and Black. Like a at. In a dream. In a window.*

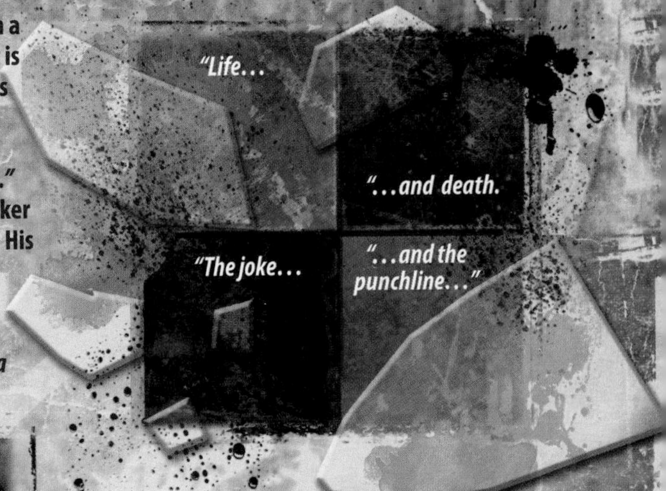
"Life...
"...and death.
"The joke...
"...and the punchline..."

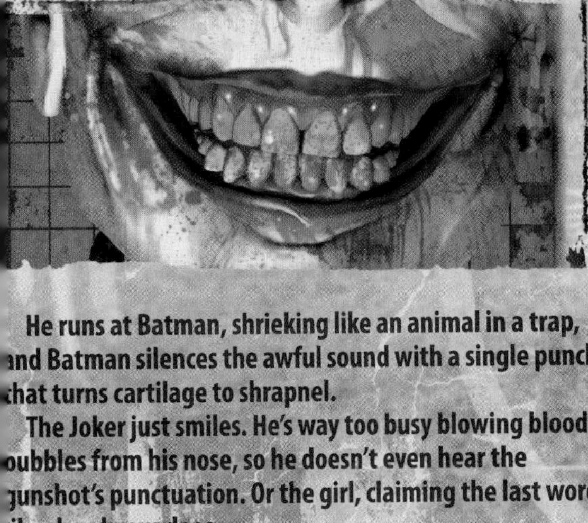

Batman shakes his head. *"I don't know what you're talking about."*

"That's why it could never be you," the Joker slobbers on, incoherently. *"I could never kill you... ...Where would the act be without my straight man?"*

He runs at Batman, shrieking like an animal in a trap, and Batman silences the awful sound with a single punch that turns cartilage to shrapnel.

The Joker just smiles. He's way too busy blowing blood bubbles from his nose, so he doesn't even hear the gunshot's punctuation. Or the girl, claiming the last word like she always does.

"You gotta stop ignoring me, Mistah Jay," says Harley Quinn in a quavery voice that seems to taste of bitter cordite and cauterized flesh.

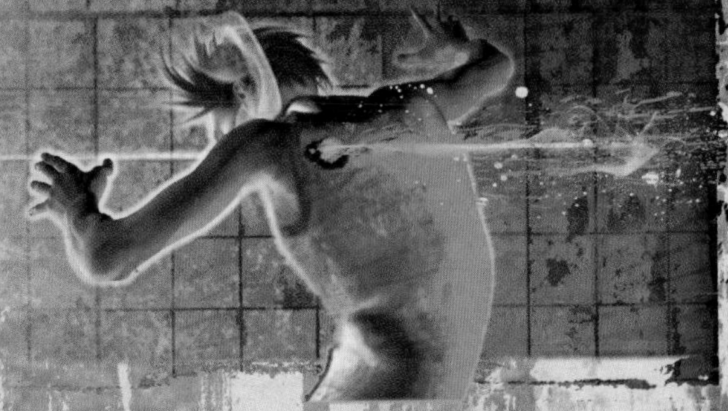

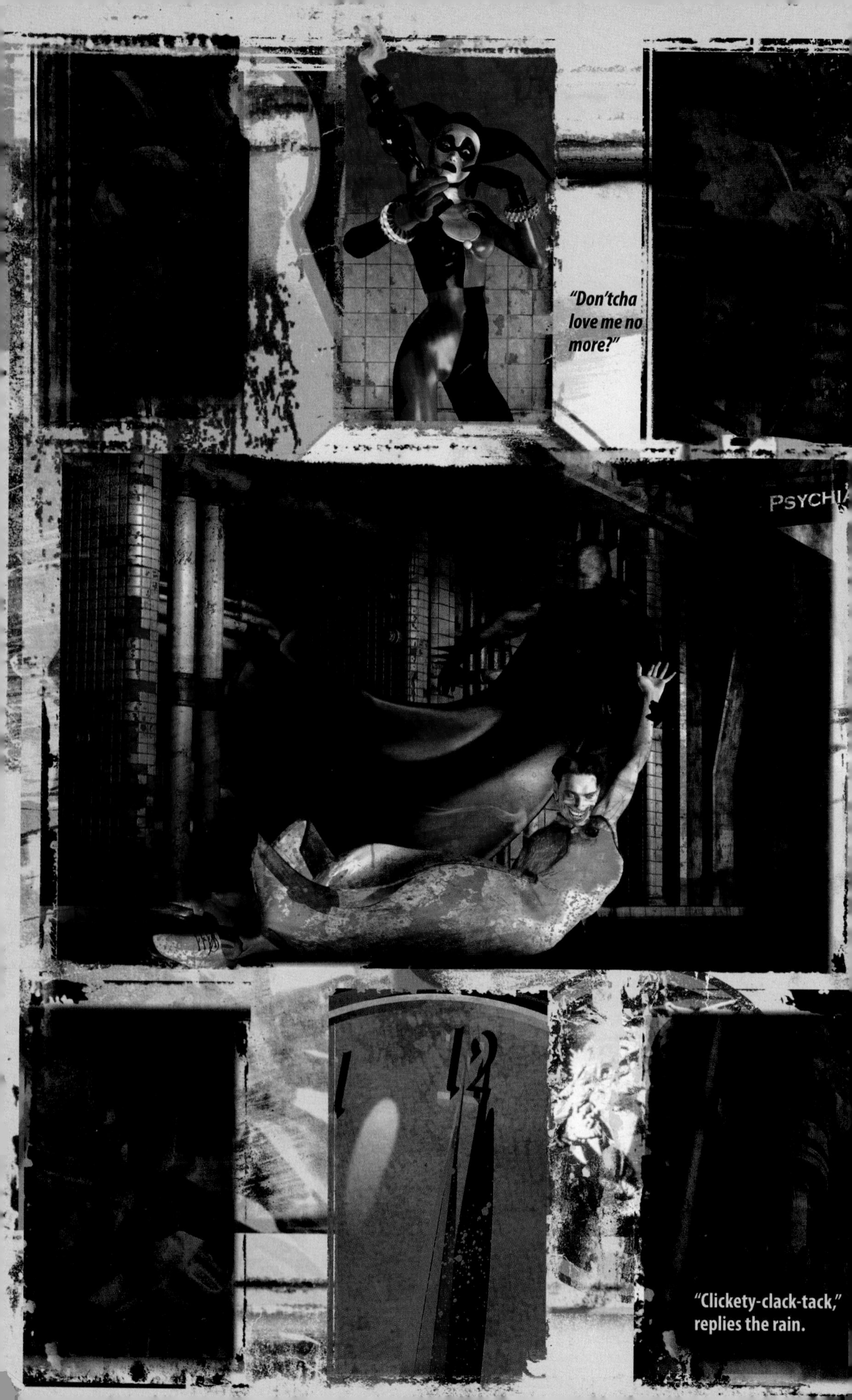
"Don'tcha love me no more?"
PSYCHI
"Clickety-clack-tack," replies the rain.

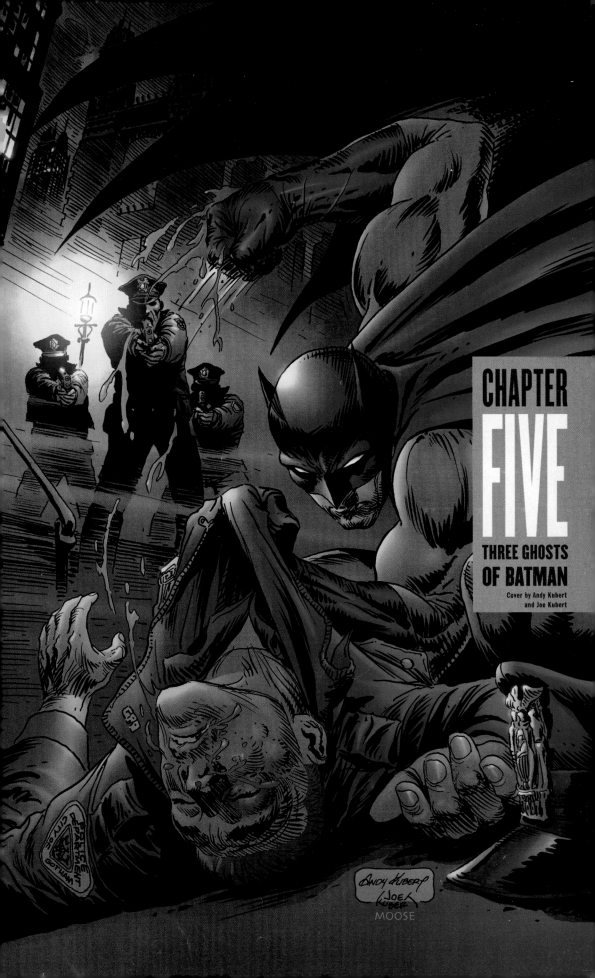

CHAPTER
FIVE
THREE GHOSTS
OF BATMAN
Cover by Andy Kubert
and Joe Kubert

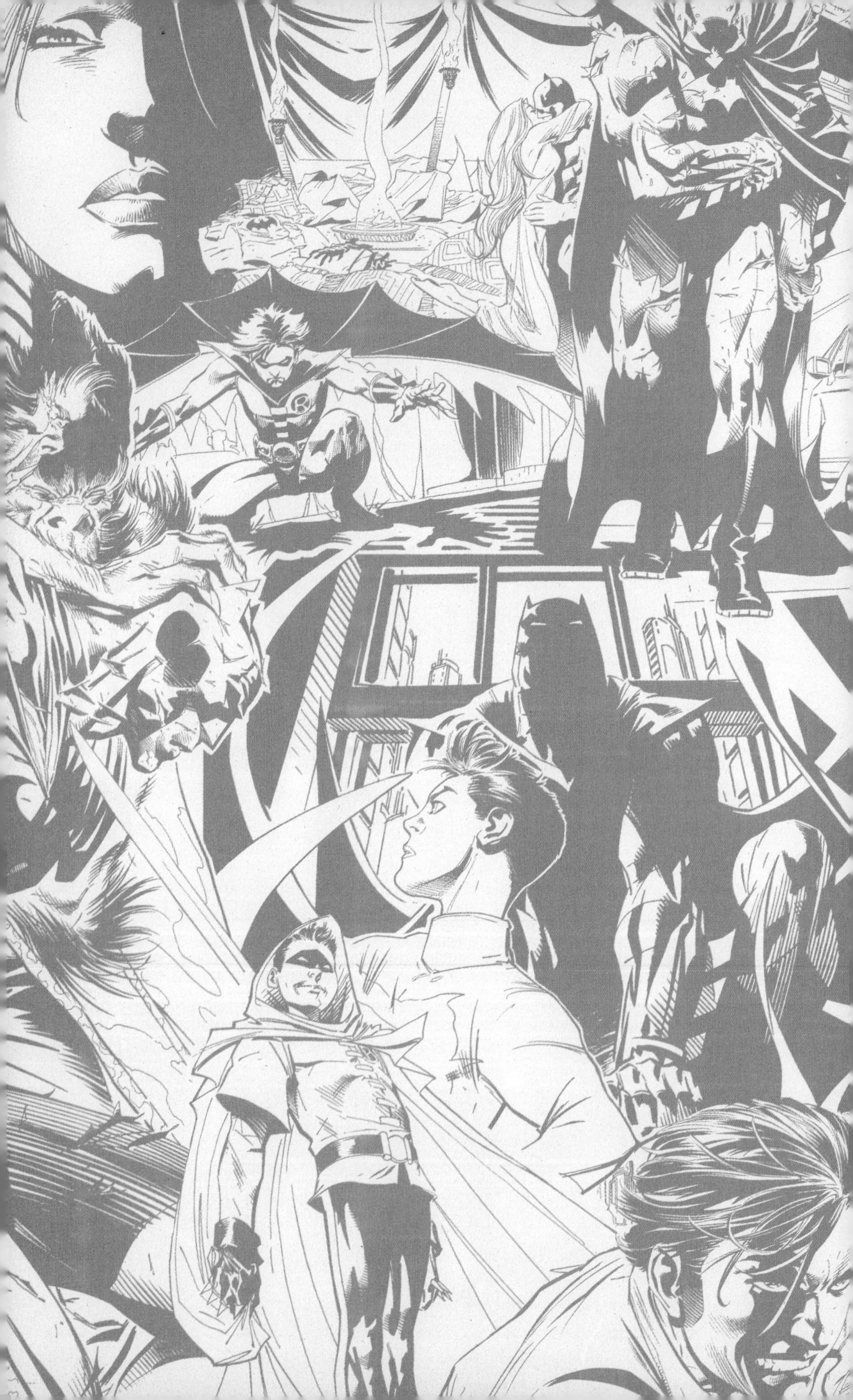

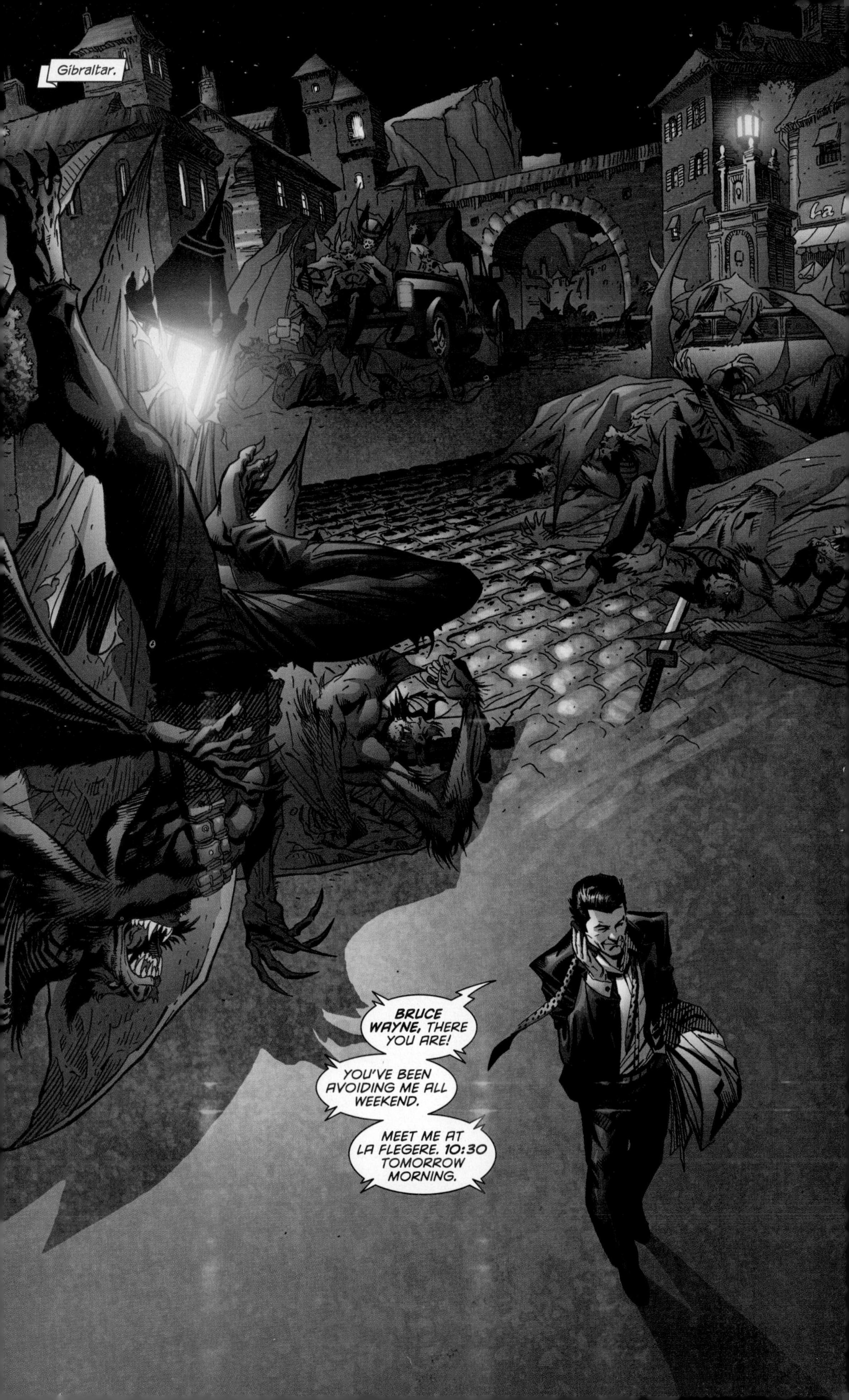
Gibraltar.
BRUCE WAYNE, THERE YOU ARE!
YOU'VE BEEN AVOIDING ME ALL WEEKEND.
MEET ME AT LA FLEGERE. 10:30 TOMORROW MORNING.

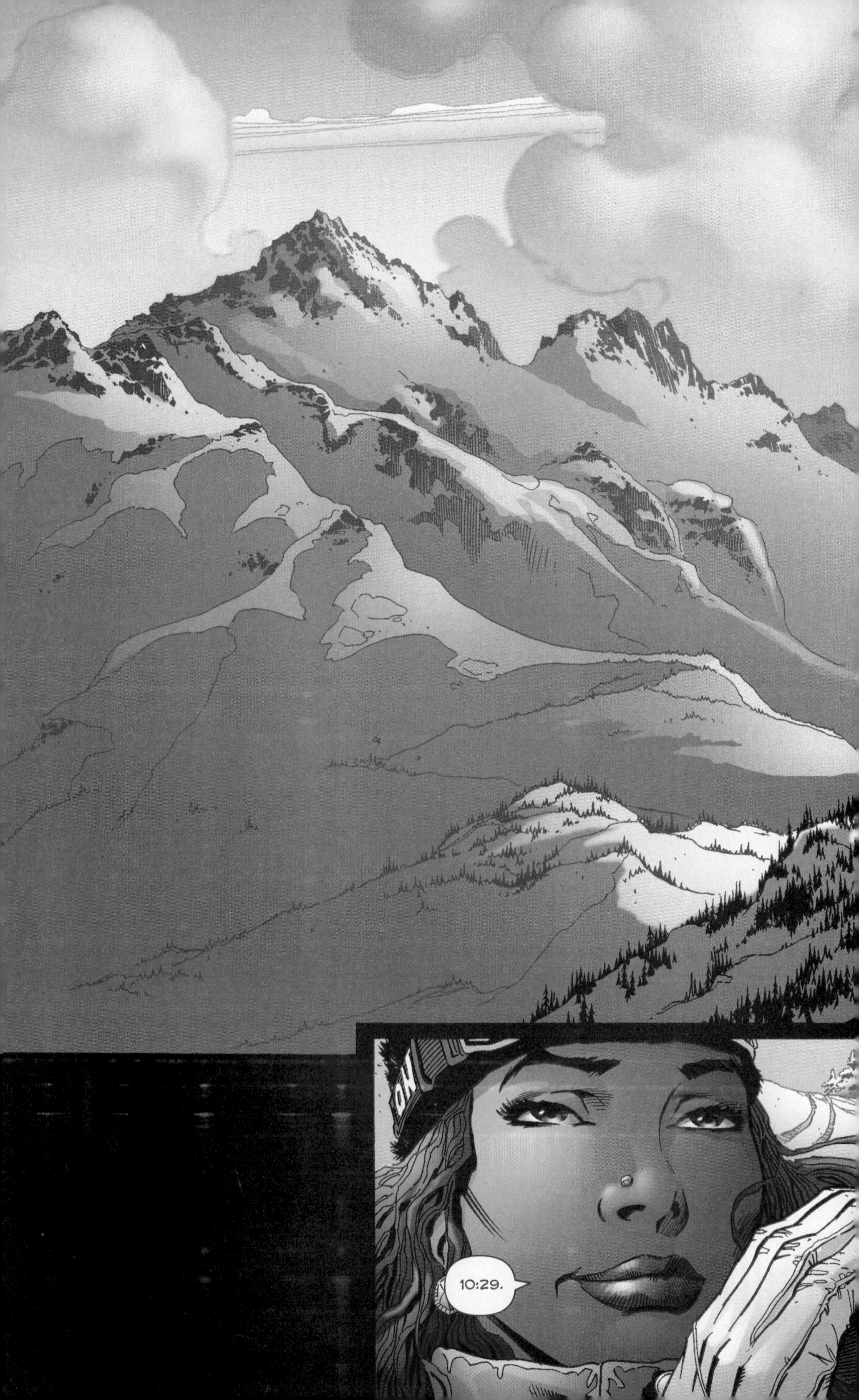
10:29.

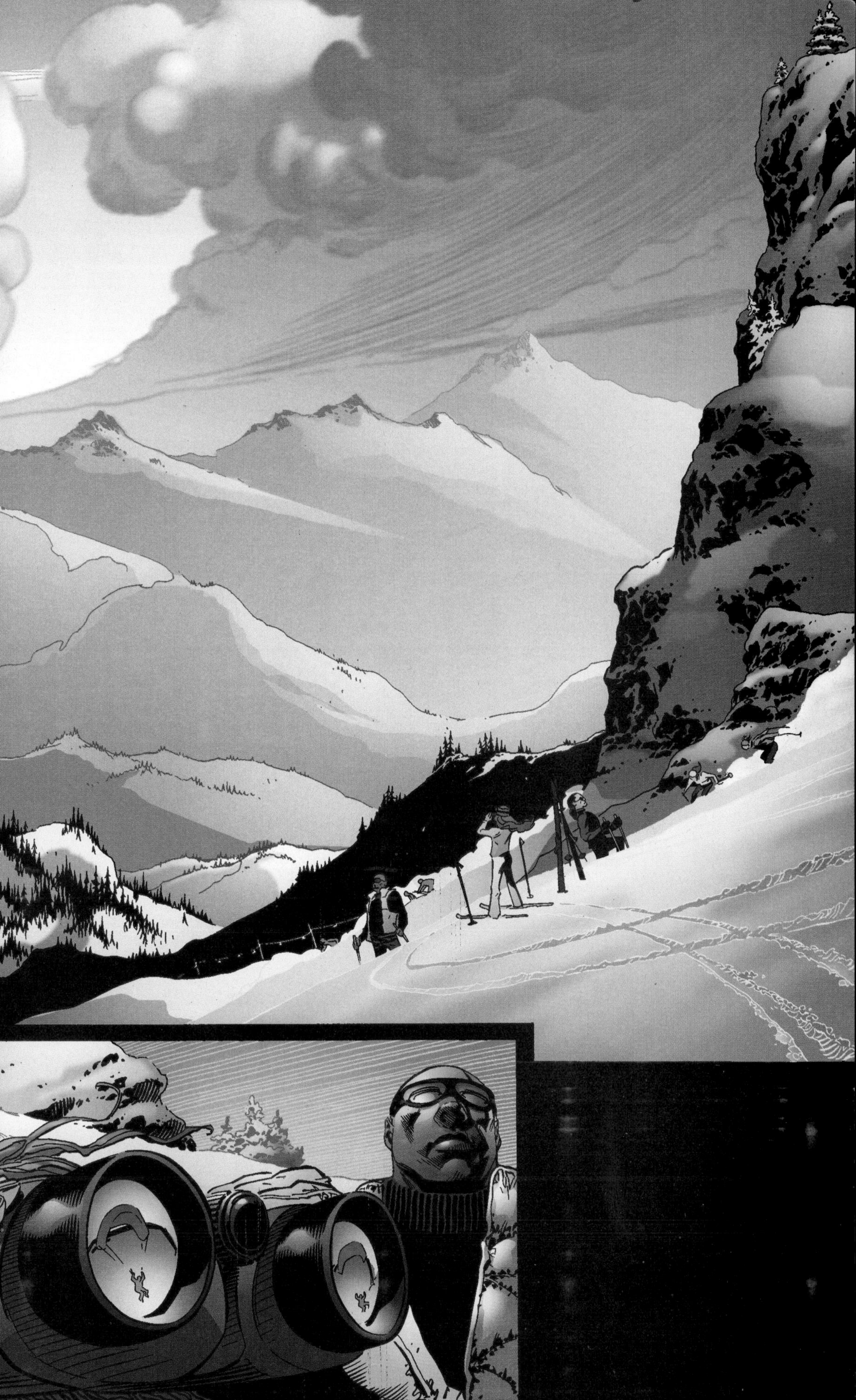

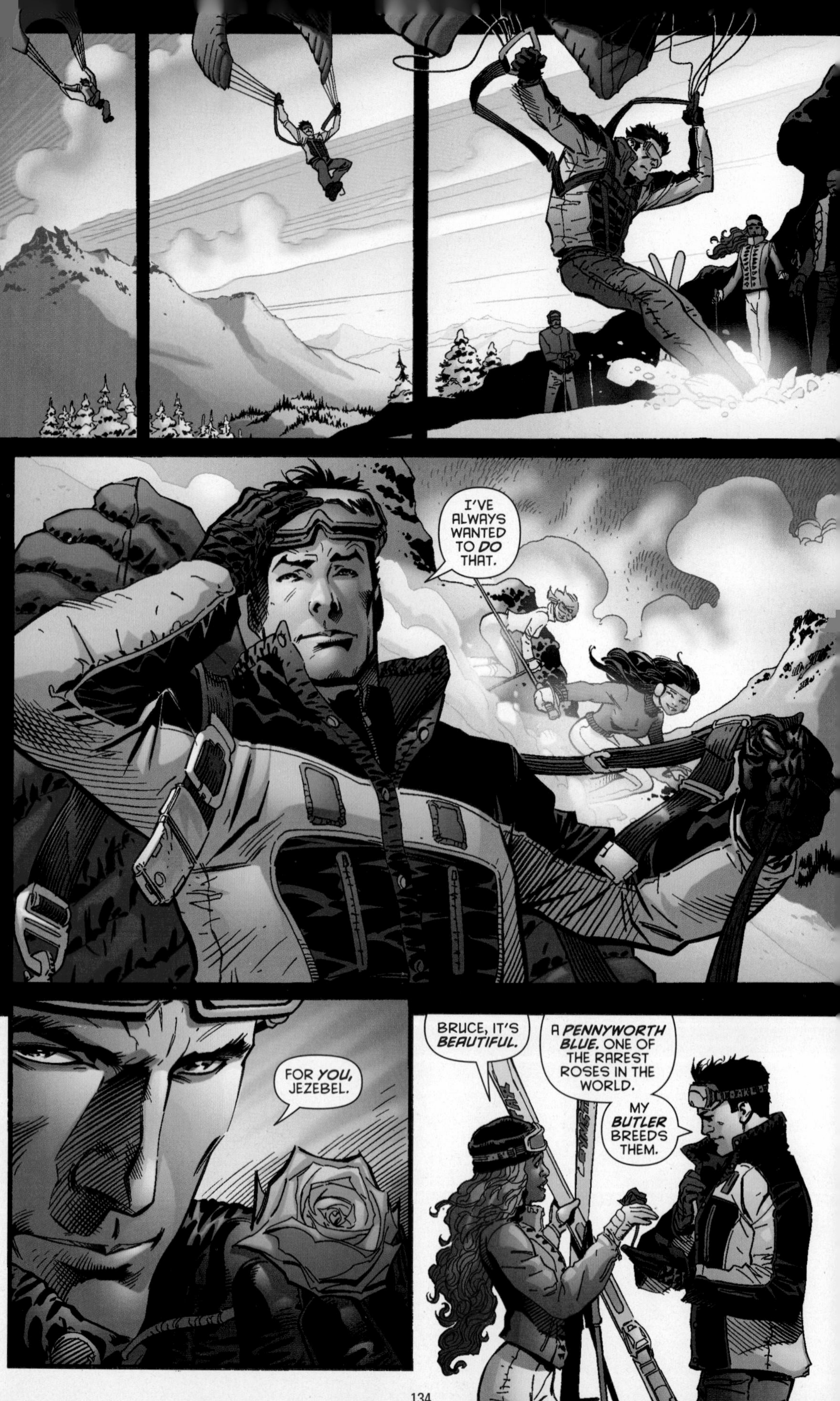
I'VE ALWAYS WANTED TO *DO* THAT.
FOR *YOU,* JEZEBEL.
BRUCE, IT'S *BEAUTIFUL.*
A *PENNYWORTH BLUE.* ONE OF THE RAREST ROSES IN THE WORLD.
MY *BUTLER* BREEDS THEM.

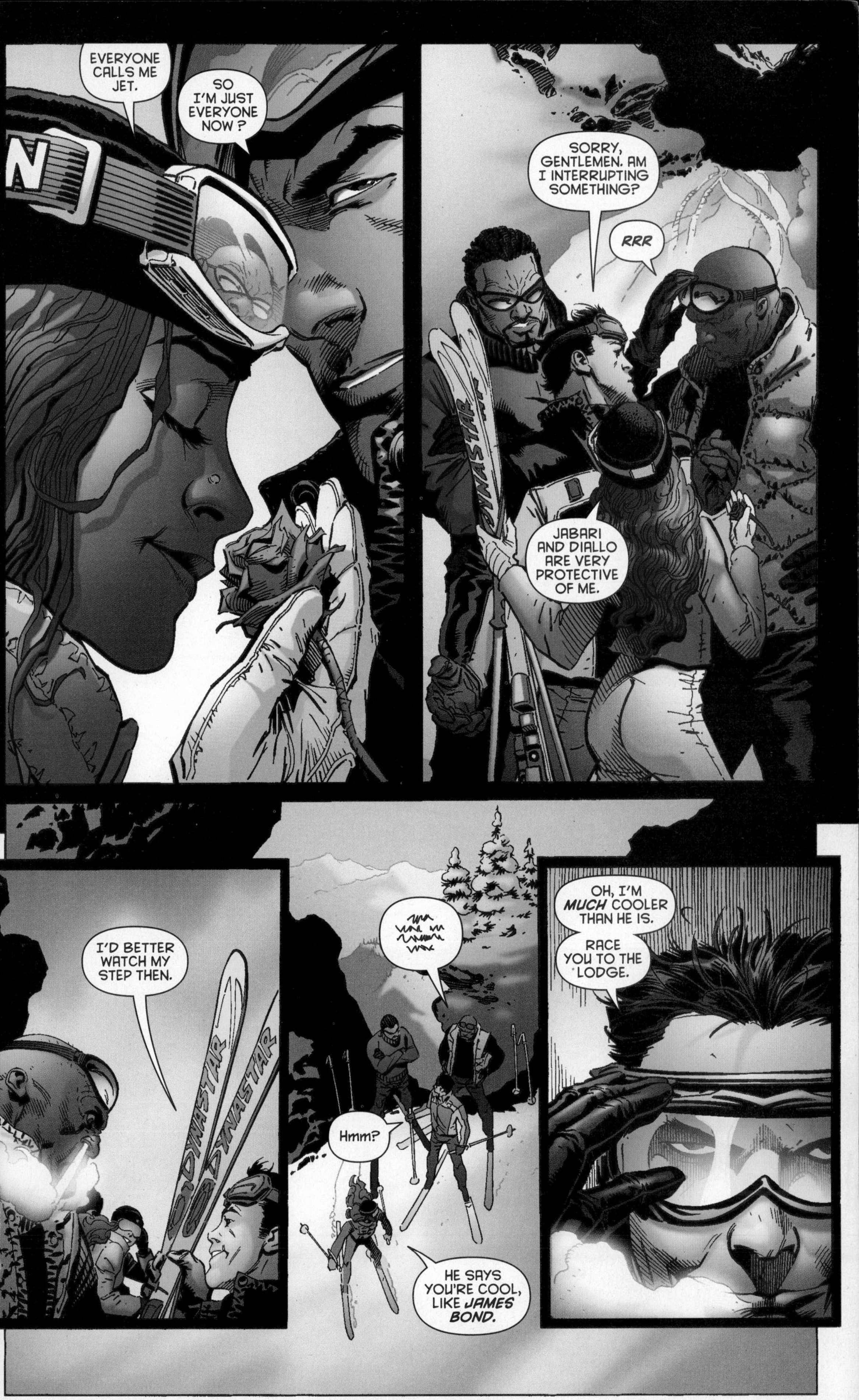
EVERYONE CALLS ME JET.
SO I'M JUST EVERYONE NOW?
SORRY, GENTLEMEN. AM I INTERRUPTING SOMETHING?
RRR
JABARI AND DIALLO ARE VERY PROTECTIVE OF ME.
I'D BETTER WATCH MY STEP THEN.
Hmm?
HE SAYS YOU'RE COOL, LIKE JAMES BOND.
OH, I'M MUCH COOLER THAN HE IS.
RACE YOU TO THE LODGE.

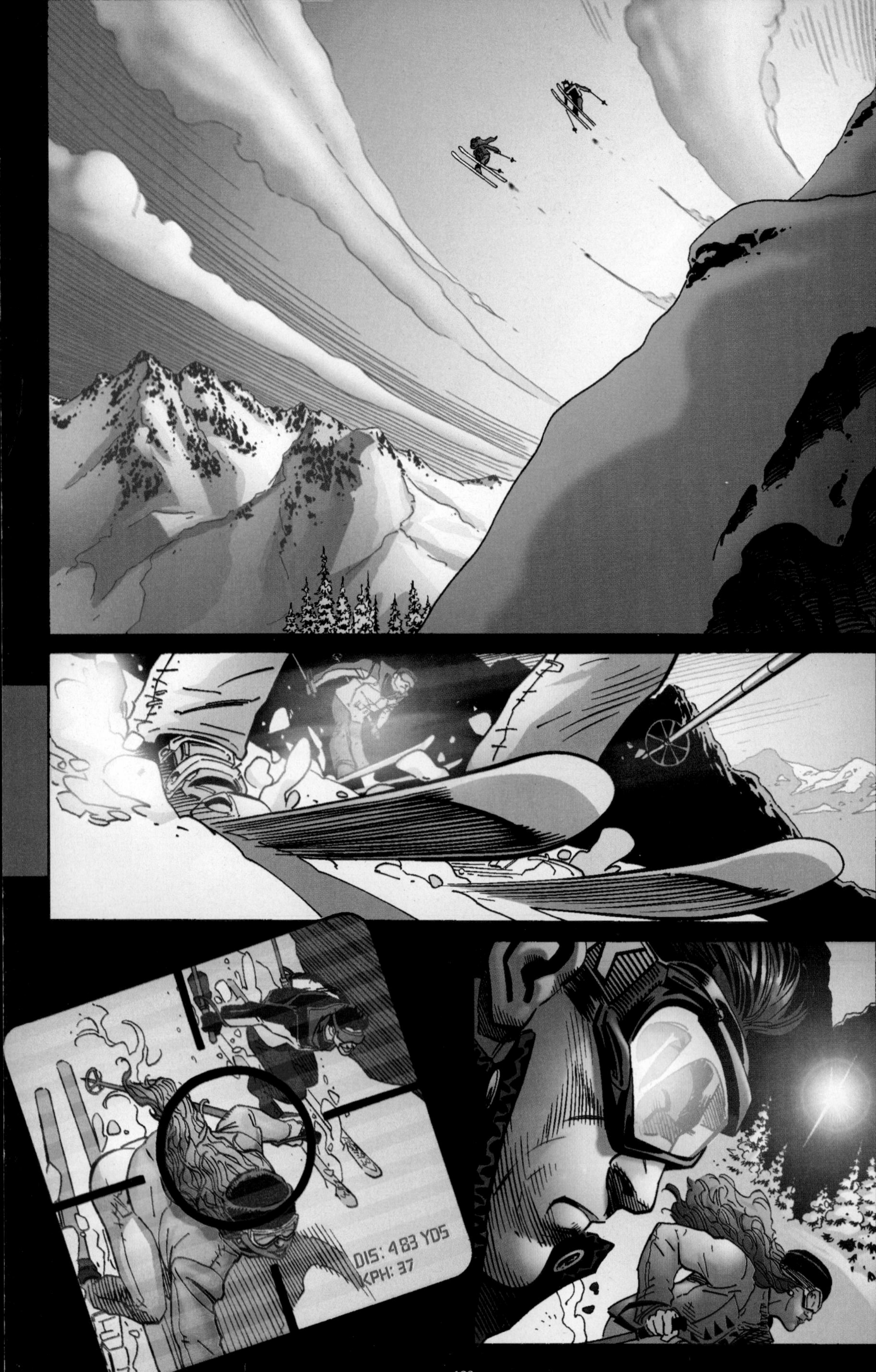
DIS: 483 YDS
KPH: 37

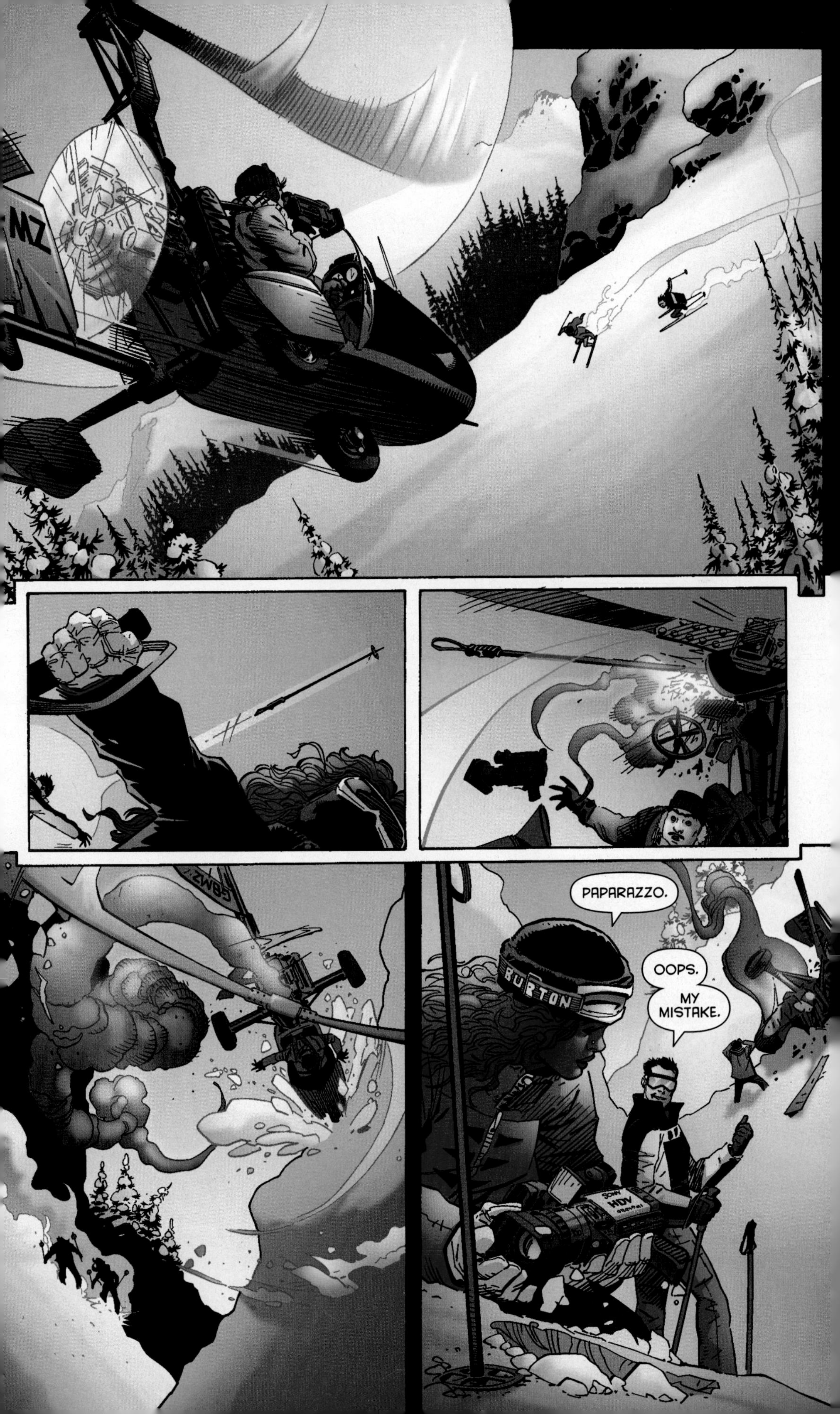
PAPARAZZO.
OOPS.
MY MISTAKE.

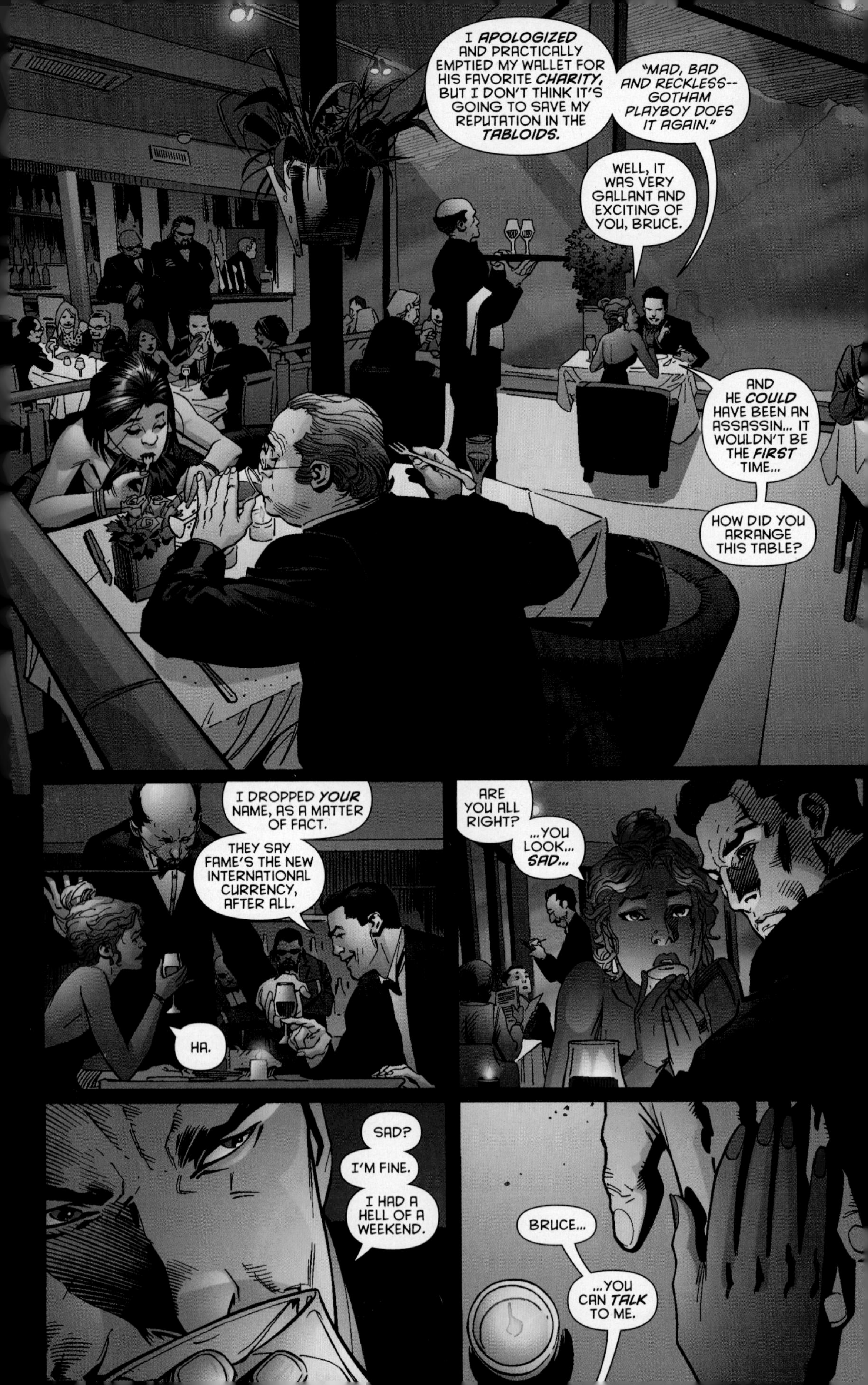
I APOLOGIZED AND PRACTICALLY EMPTIED MY WALLET FOR HIS FAVORITE CHARITY, BUT I DON'T THINK IT'S GOING TO SAVE MY REPUTATION IN THE TABLOIDS.
"MAD, BAD AND RECKLESS-- GOTHAM PLAYBOY DOES IT AGAIN."
WELL, IT WAS VERY GALLANT AND EXCITING OF YOU, BRUCE.
AND HE COULD HAVE BEEN AN ASSASSIN... IT WOULDN'T BE THE FIRST TIME...
HOW DID YOU ARRANGE THIS TABLE?
I DROPPED YOUR NAME, AS A MATTER OF FACT.
THEY SAY FAME'S THE NEW INTERNATIONAL CURRENCY, AFTER ALL.
HA.
ARE YOU ALL RIGHT?
...YOU LOOK... SAD...
SAD?
I'M FINE.
I HAD A HELL OF A WEEKEND.
BRUCE...
...YOU CAN TALK TO ME.

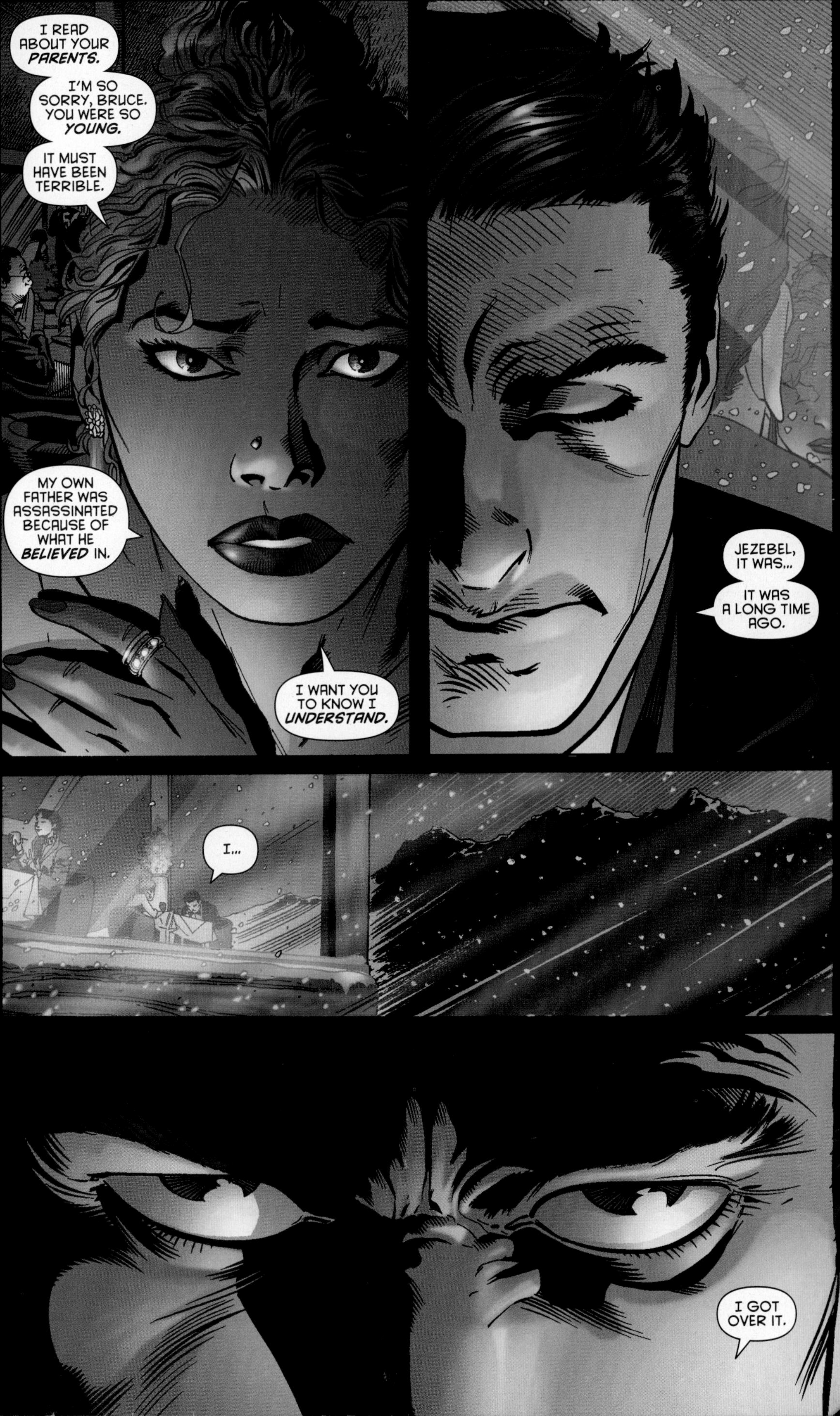
I READ ABOUT YOUR *PARENTS.*
I'M SO SORRY, BRUCE. YOU WERE SO *YOUNG.*
IT MUST HAVE BEEN TERRIBLE.
MY OWN FATHER WAS ASSASSINATED BECAUSE OF WHAT HE *BELIEVED* IN.
I WANT YOU TO KNOW I *UNDERSTAND.*
JEZEBEL, IT WAS...
IT WAS A LONG TIME AGO.
I...
I GOT OVER IT.

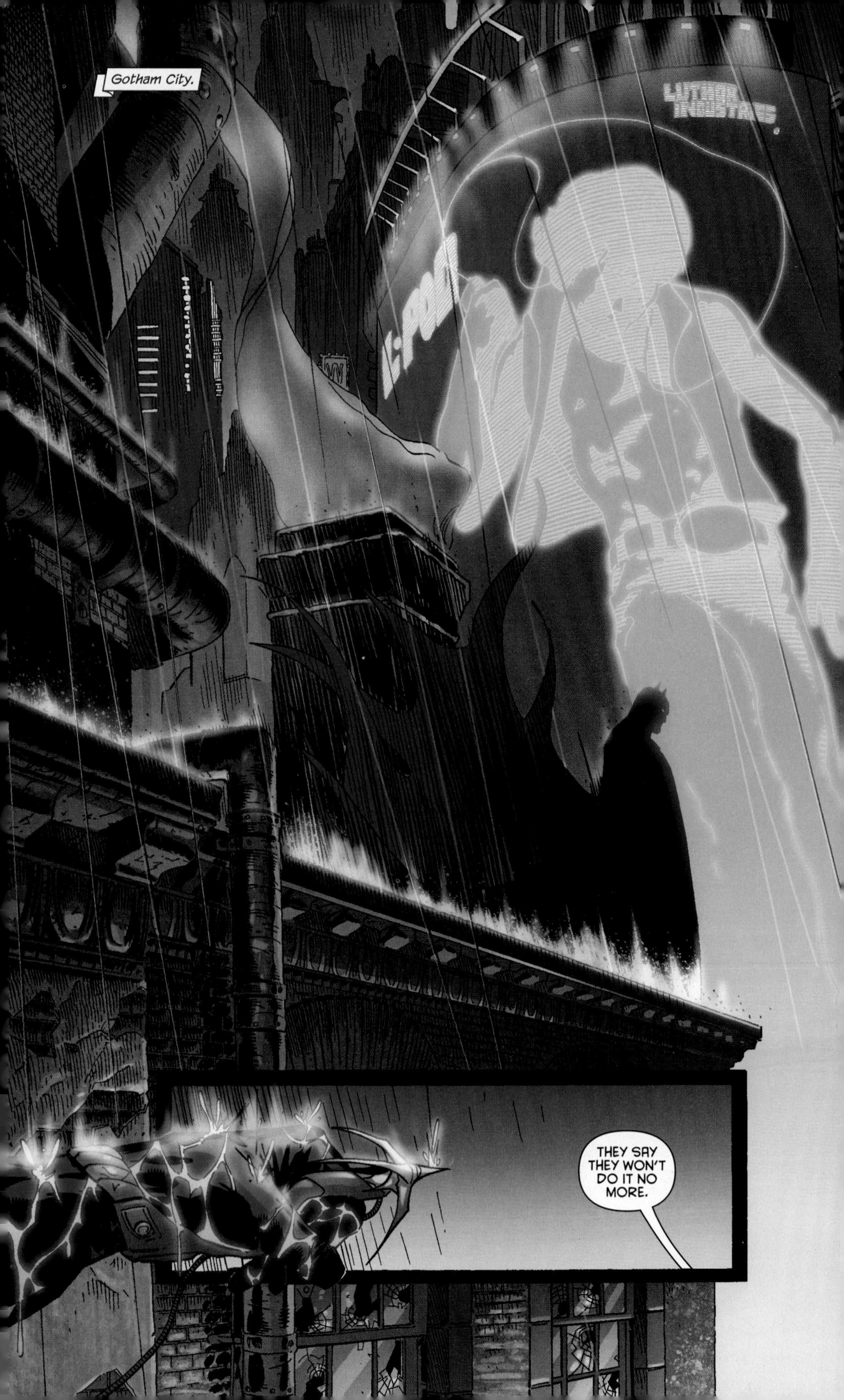
Gotham City.
THEY SAY THEY WON'T DO IT NO MORE.

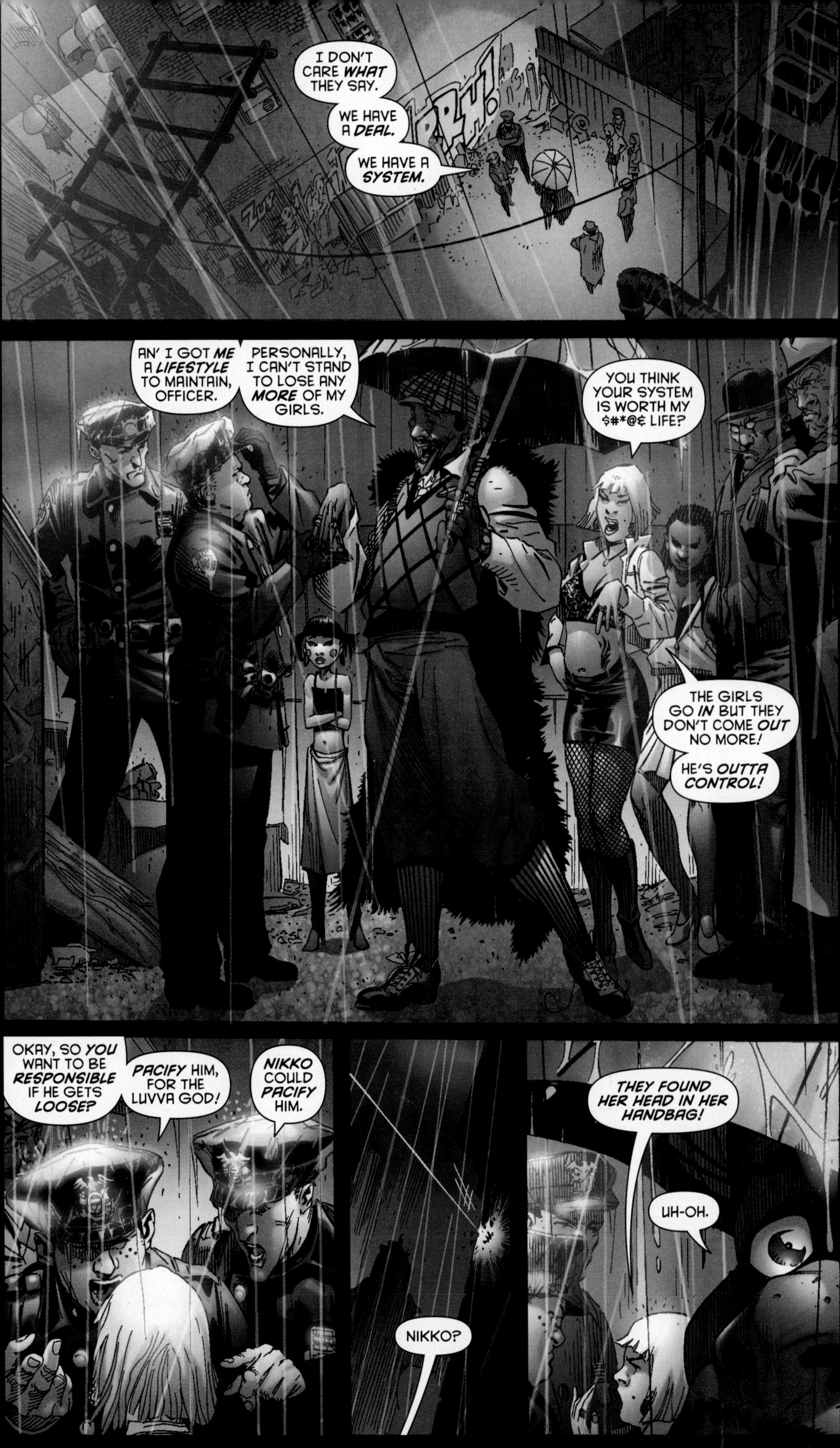
I DON'T CARE WHAT THEY SAY.
WE HAVE A DEAL.
WE HAVE A SYSTEM.
AN' I GOT ME A LIFESTYLE TO MAINTAIN, OFFICER.
PERSONALLY, I CAN'T STAND TO LOSE ANY MORE OF MY GIRLS.
YOU THINK YOUR SYSTEM IS WORTH MY $#*@¢ LIFE?
THE GIRLS GO IN BUT THEY DON'T COME OUT NO MORE!
HE'S OUTTA CONTROL!
OKAY, SO YOU WANT TO BE RESPONSIBLE IF HE GETS LOOSE?
PACIFY HIM, FOR THE LUVVA GOD!
NIKKO COULD PACIFY HIM.
NIKKO?
THEY FOUND HER HEAD IN HER HANDBAG!
UH-OH.

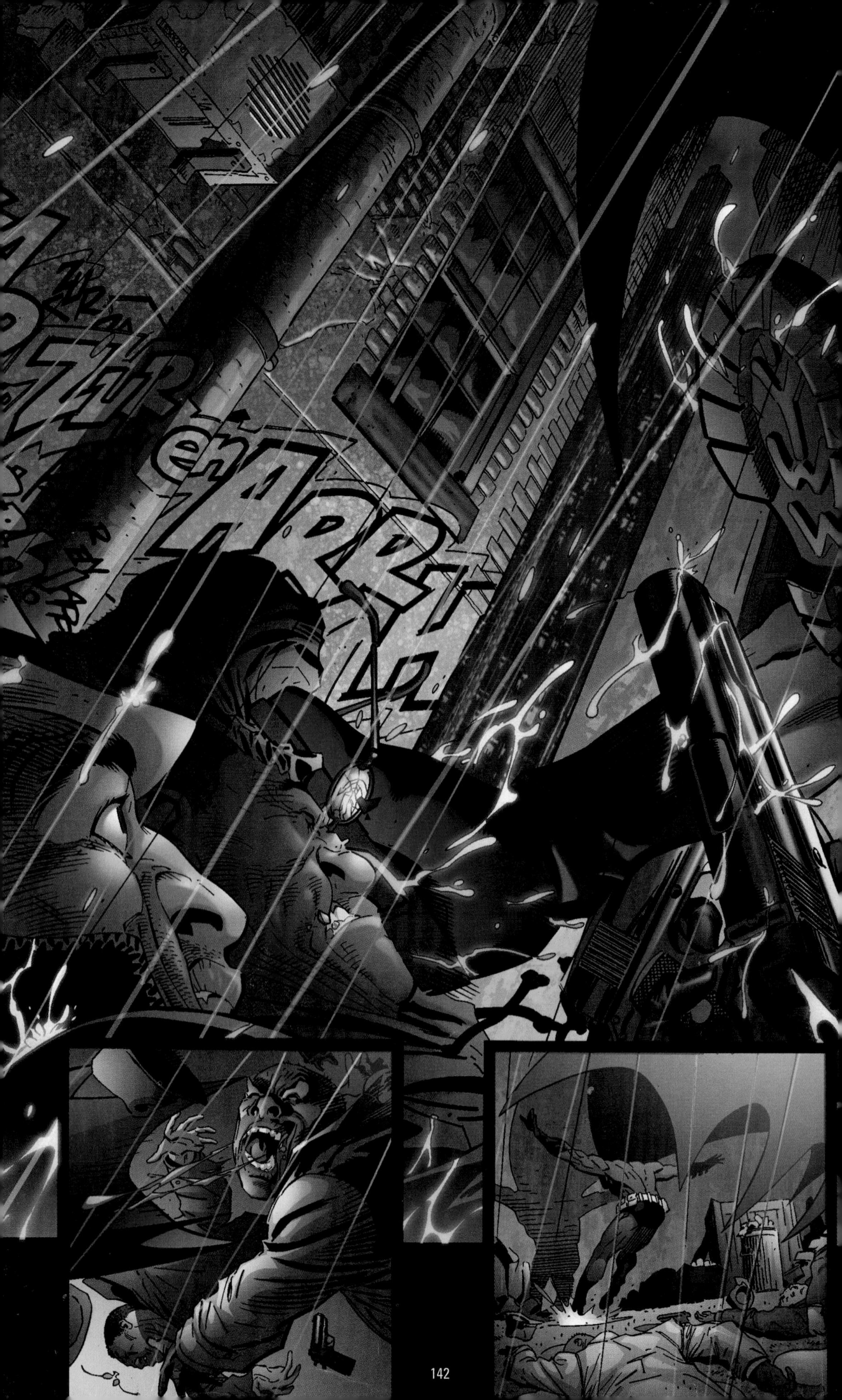

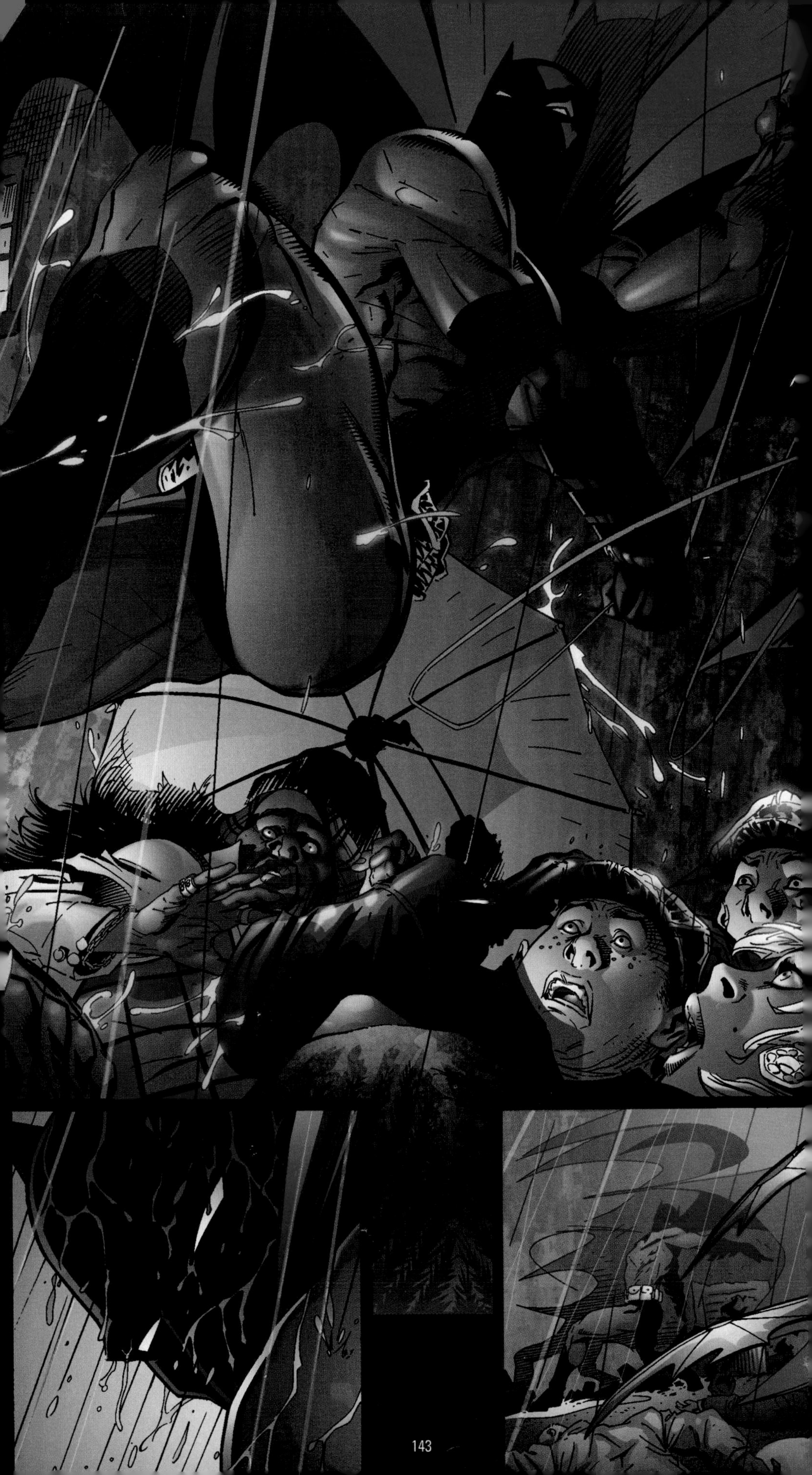

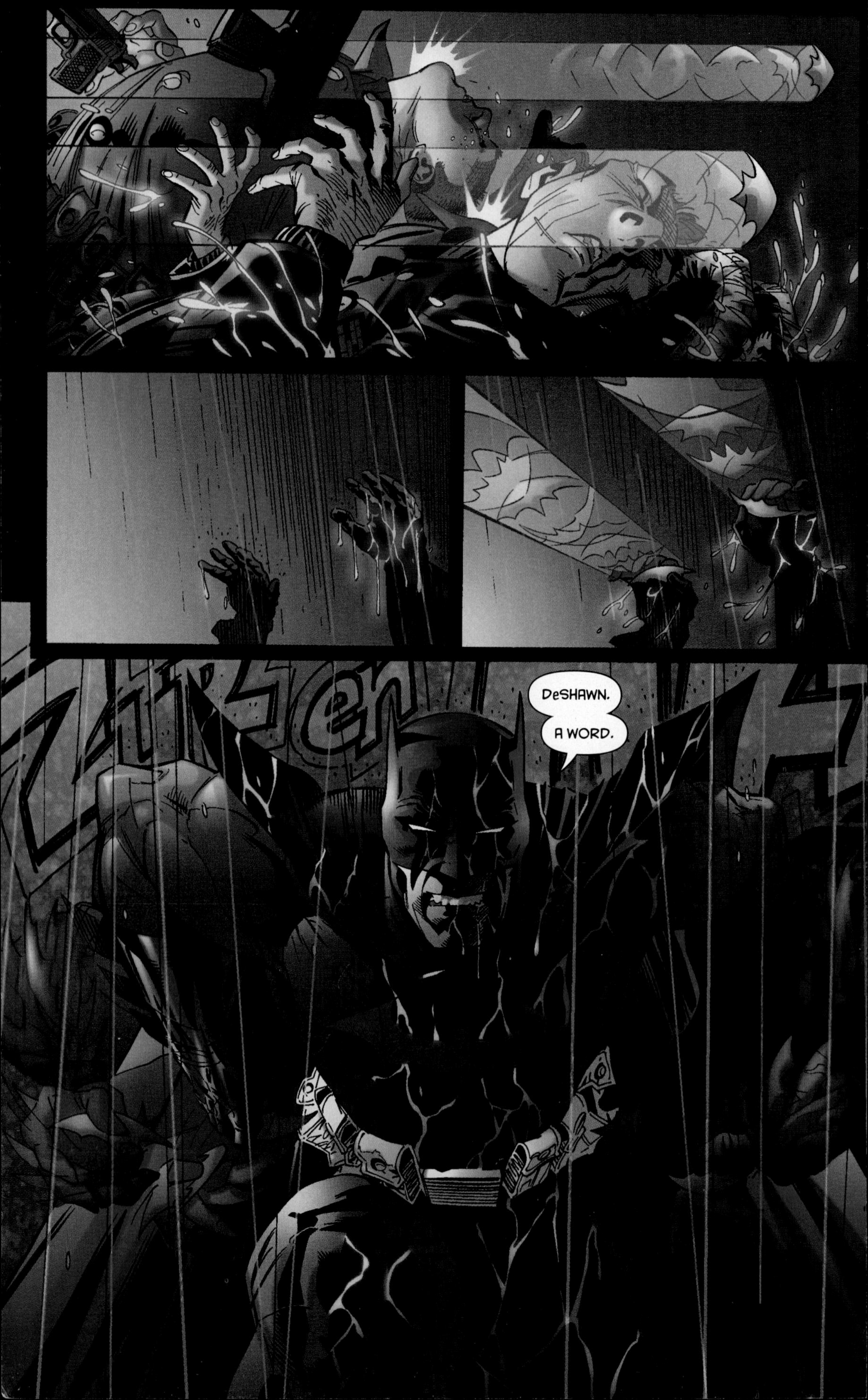
DeSHAWN.
A WORD.

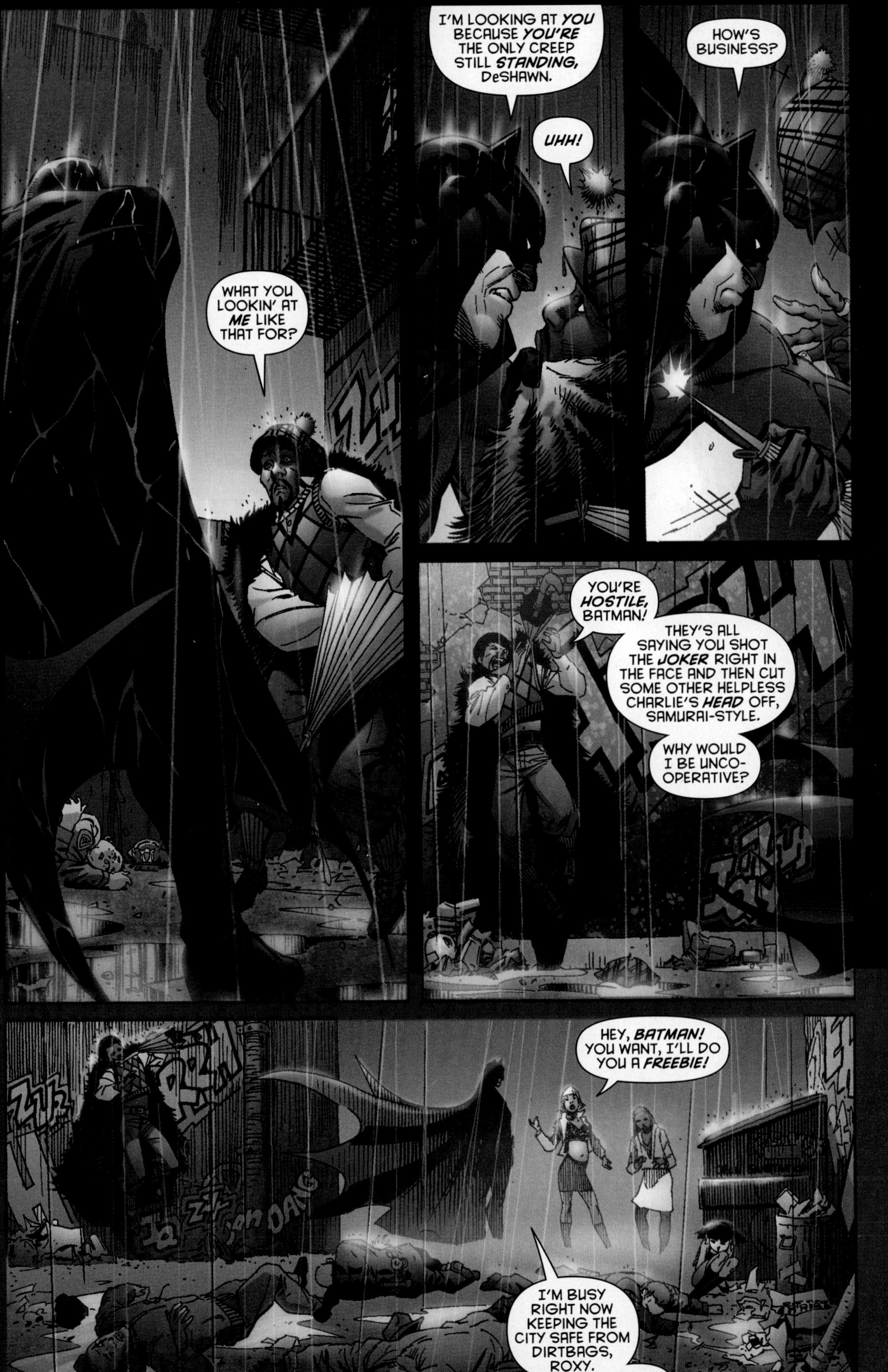
WHAT YOU LOOKIN' AT ME LIKE THAT FOR?
I'M LOOKING AT YOU BECAUSE YOU'RE THE ONLY CREEP STILL STANDING, DeSHAWN.
UHH!
HOW'S BUSINESS?
YOU'RE HOSTILE, BATMAN!
THEY'S ALL SAYING YOU SHOT THE JOKER RIGHT IN THE FACE AND THEN CUT SOME OTHER HELPLESS CHARLIE'S HEAD OFF, SAMURAI-STYLE.
WHY WOULD I BE UNCO-OPERATIVE?
HEY, BATMAN! YOU WANT, I'LL DO YOU A FREEBIE!
I'M BUSY RIGHT NOW KEEPING THE CITY SAFE FROM DIRTBAGS, ROXY.
WHAT'S UP?

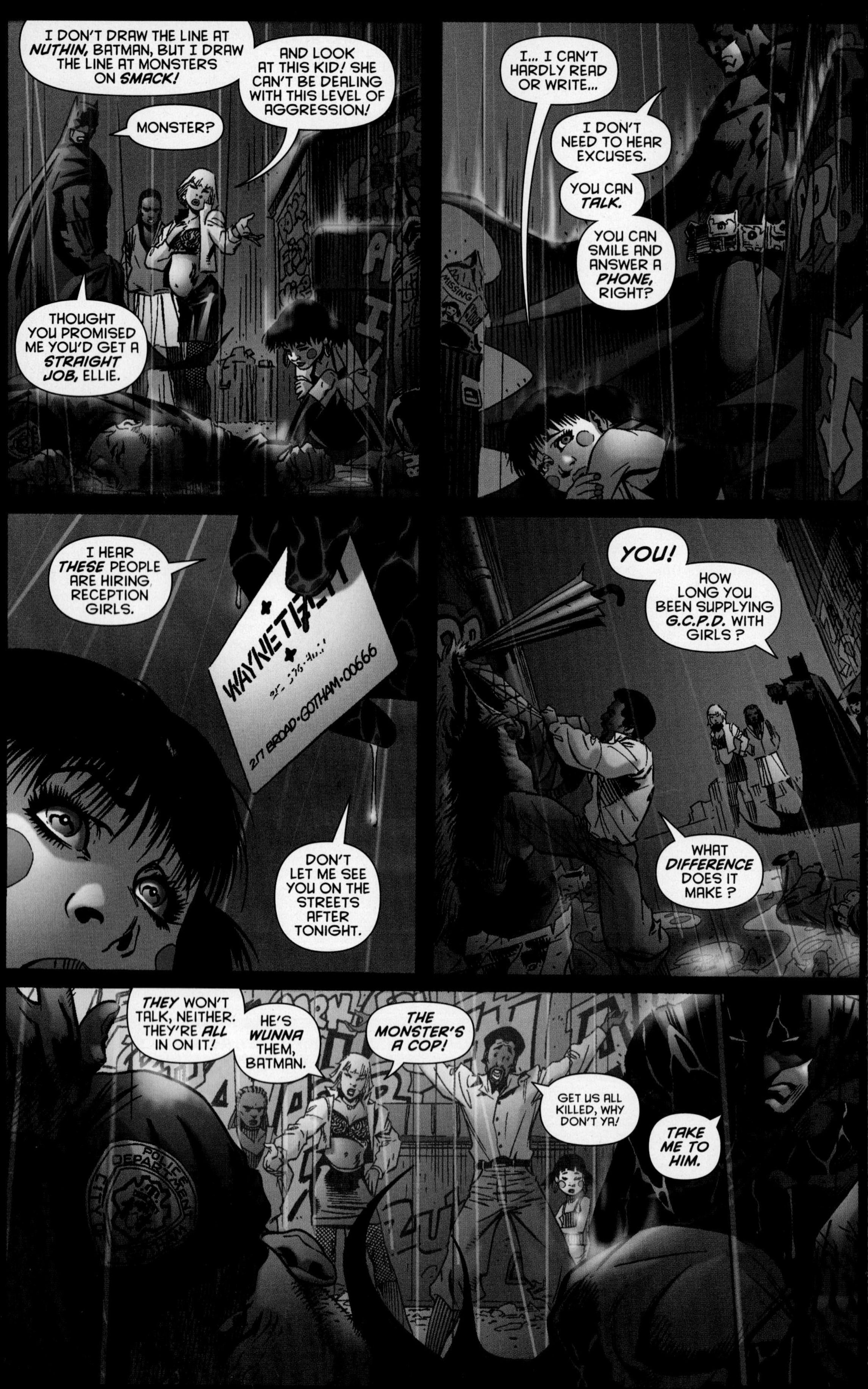
I DON'T DRAW THE LINE AT NUTHIN, BATMAN, BUT I DRAW THE LINE AT MONSTERS ON SMACK!
AND LOOK AT THIS KID! SHE CAN'T BE DEALING WITH THIS LEVEL OF AGGRESSION!
MONSTER?
THOUGHT YOU PROMISED ME YOU'D GET A STRAIGHT JOB, ELLIE.
I... I CAN'T HARDLY READ OR WRITE...
I DON'T NEED TO HEAR EXCUSES.
YOU CAN TALK.
YOU CAN SMILE AND ANSWER A PHONE, RIGHT?
I HEAR THESE PEOPLE ARE HIRING RECEPTION GIRLS.
WAYNETECH
217 BROAD • GOTHAM • 00666
DON'T LET ME SEE YOU ON THE STREETS AFTER TONIGHT.
YOU!
HOW LONG YOU BEEN SUPPLYING G.C.P.D. WITH GIRLS?
WHAT DIFFERENCE DOES IT MAKE?
THEY WON'T TALK, NEITHER. THEY'RE ALL IN ON IT!
HE'S WUNNA THEM, BATMAN.
THE MONSTER'S A COP!
GET US ALL KILLED, WHY DON'T YA!
TAKE ME TO HIM.

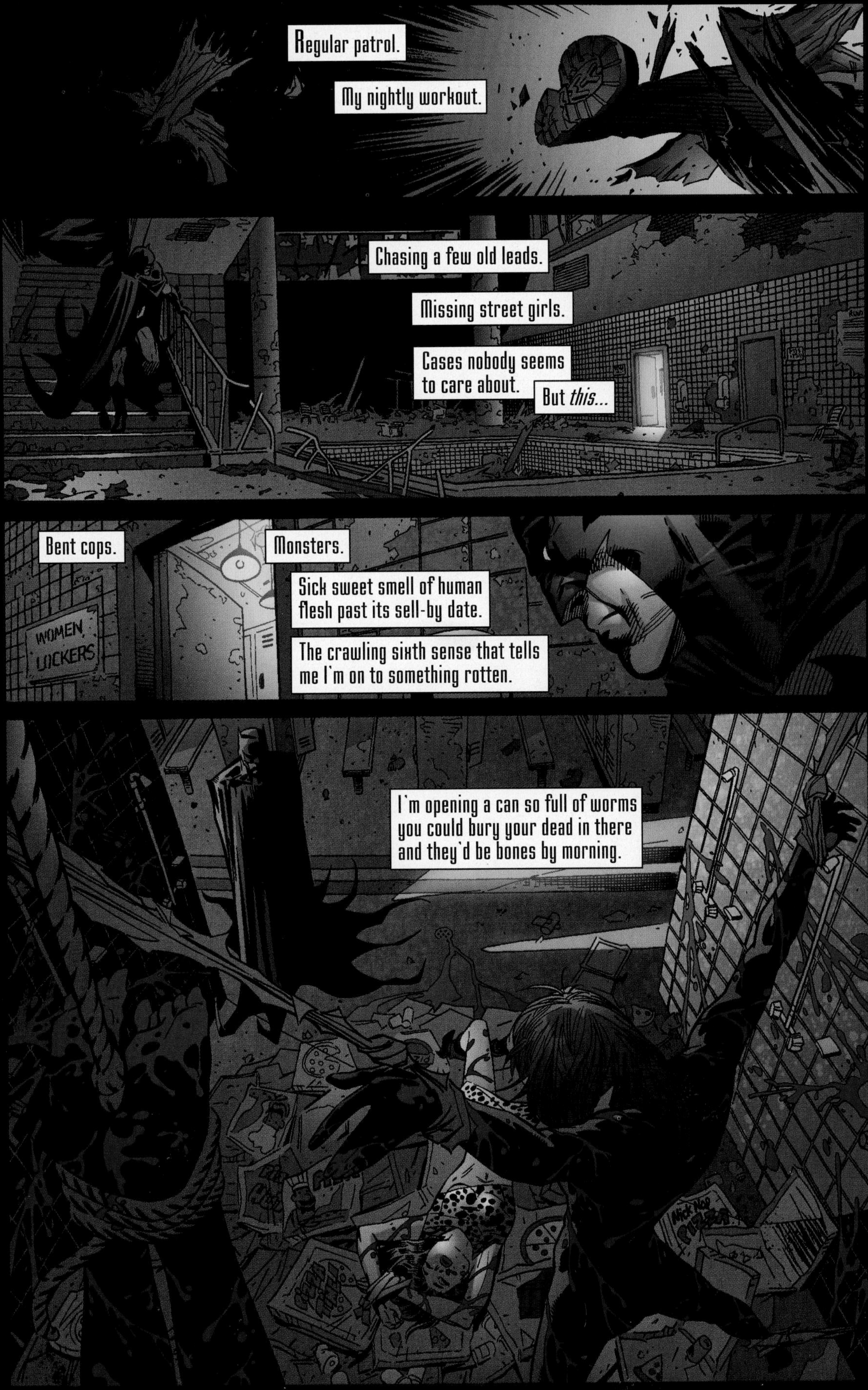
Regular patrol.
My nightly workout.
Chasing a few old leads.
Missing street girls.
Cases nobody seems to care about.
But *this...*
Bent cops.
WOMEN LOCKERS
Monsters.
Sick sweet smell of human flesh past its sell-by date.
The crawling sixth sense that tells me I'm on to something rotten.
I'm opening a can so full of worms you could bury your dead in there and they'd be bones by morning.

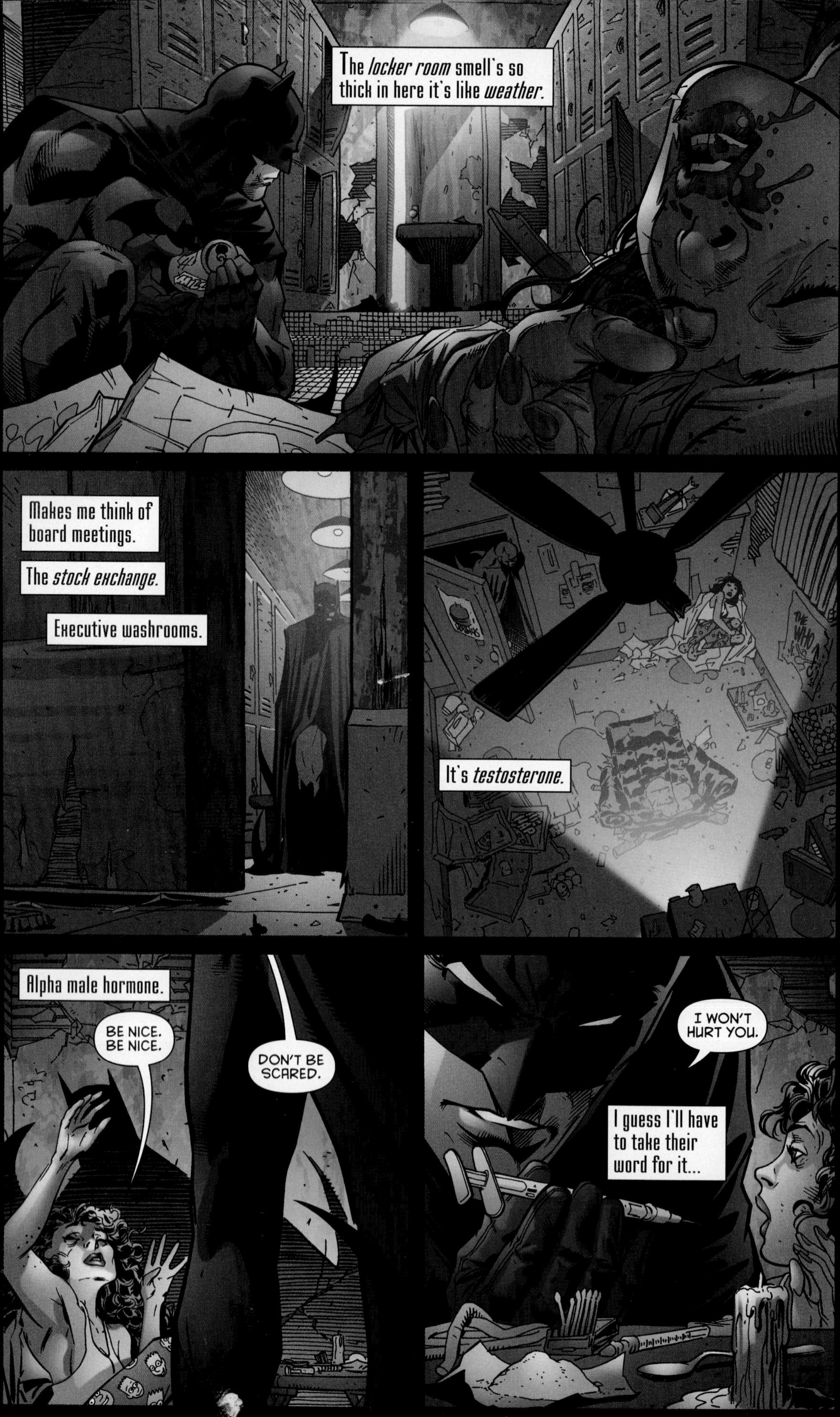
The locker room smell's so thick in here it's like weather.
Makes me think of board meetings.
The stock exchange.
Executive washrooms.
It's testosterone.
Alpha male hormone.
BE NICE. BE NICE.
DON'T BE SCARED.
I WON'T HURT YOU.
I guess I'll have to take their word for it...

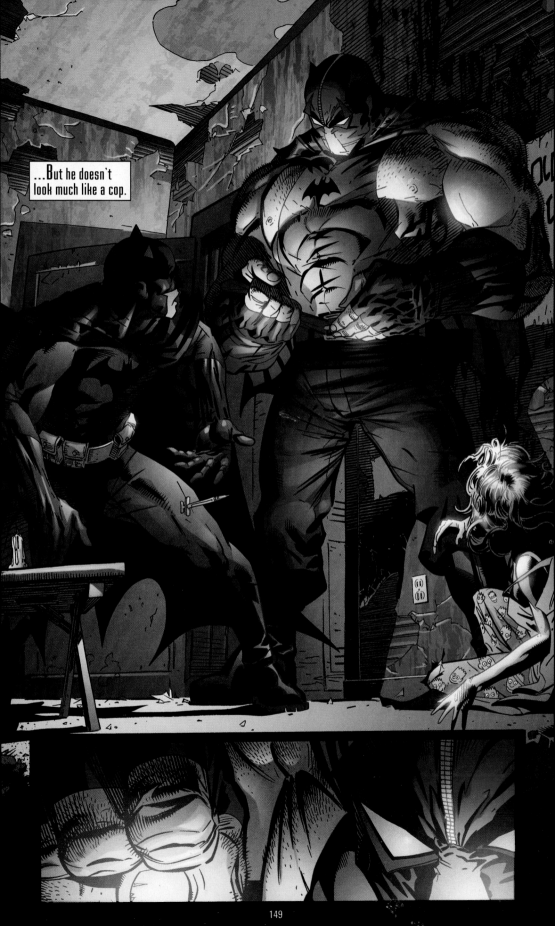

...But he doesn't look much like a cop.

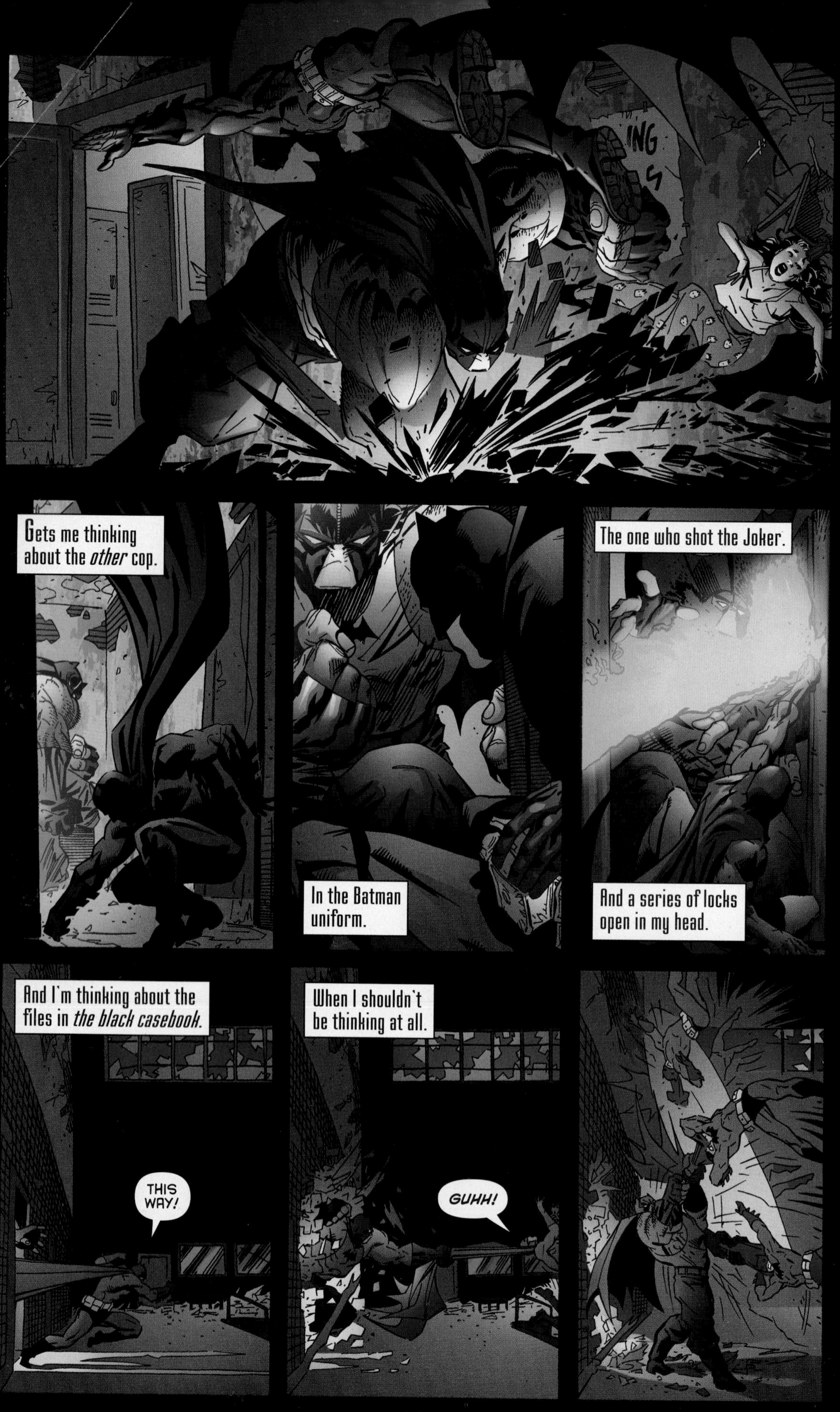
INGS
Gets me thinking about the *other* cop.
In the Batman uniform.
The one who shot the Joker.
And a series of locks open in my head.
And I'm thinking about the files in *the black casebook.*
THIS WAY!
When I shouldn't be thinking at all.
GUHH!

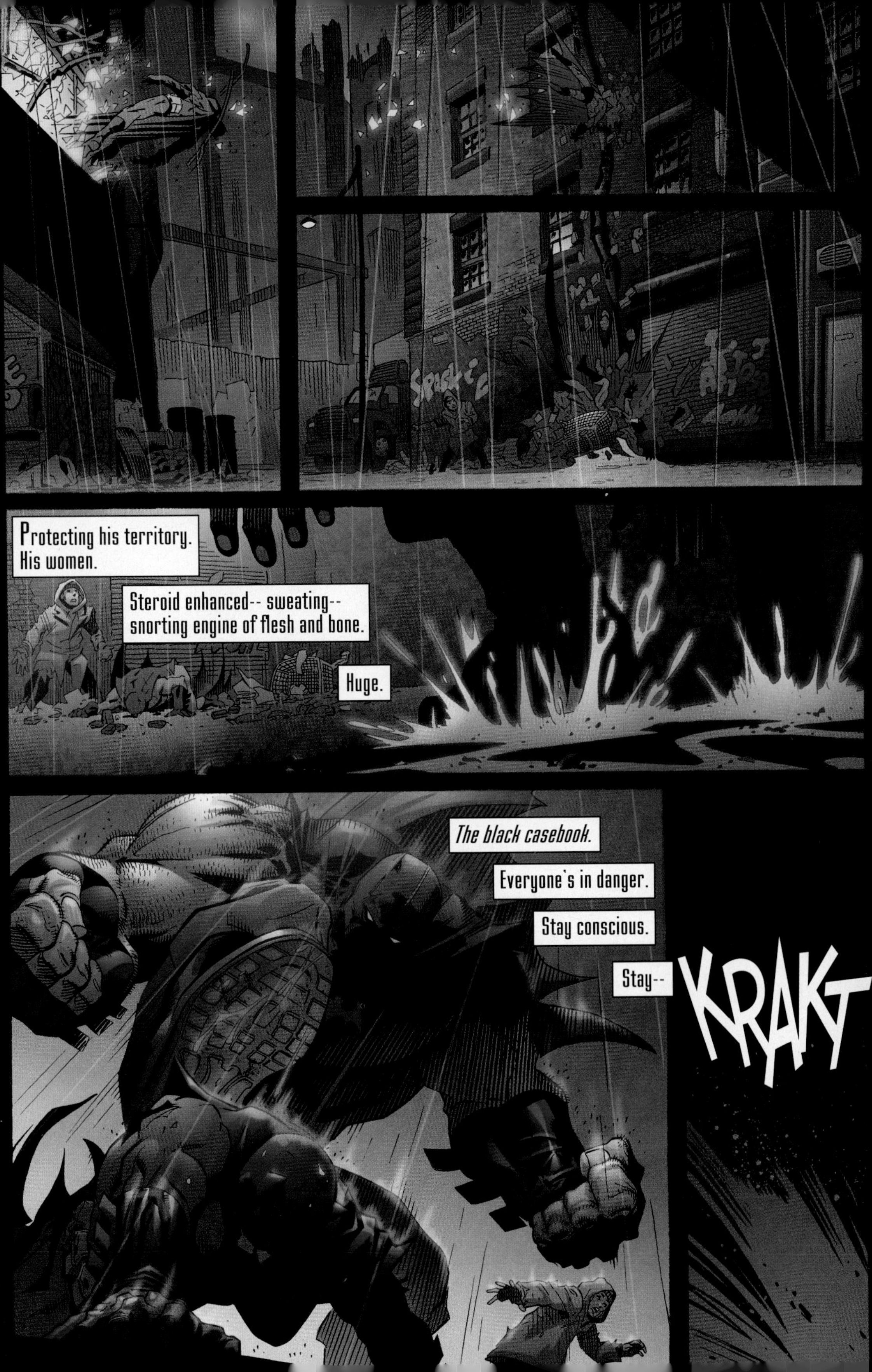
Protecting his territory.
His women.
Steroid enhanced-- sweating-- snorting engine of flesh and bone.
Huge.
The black casebook.
Everyone's in danger.
Stay conscious.
Stay--
KRAKT

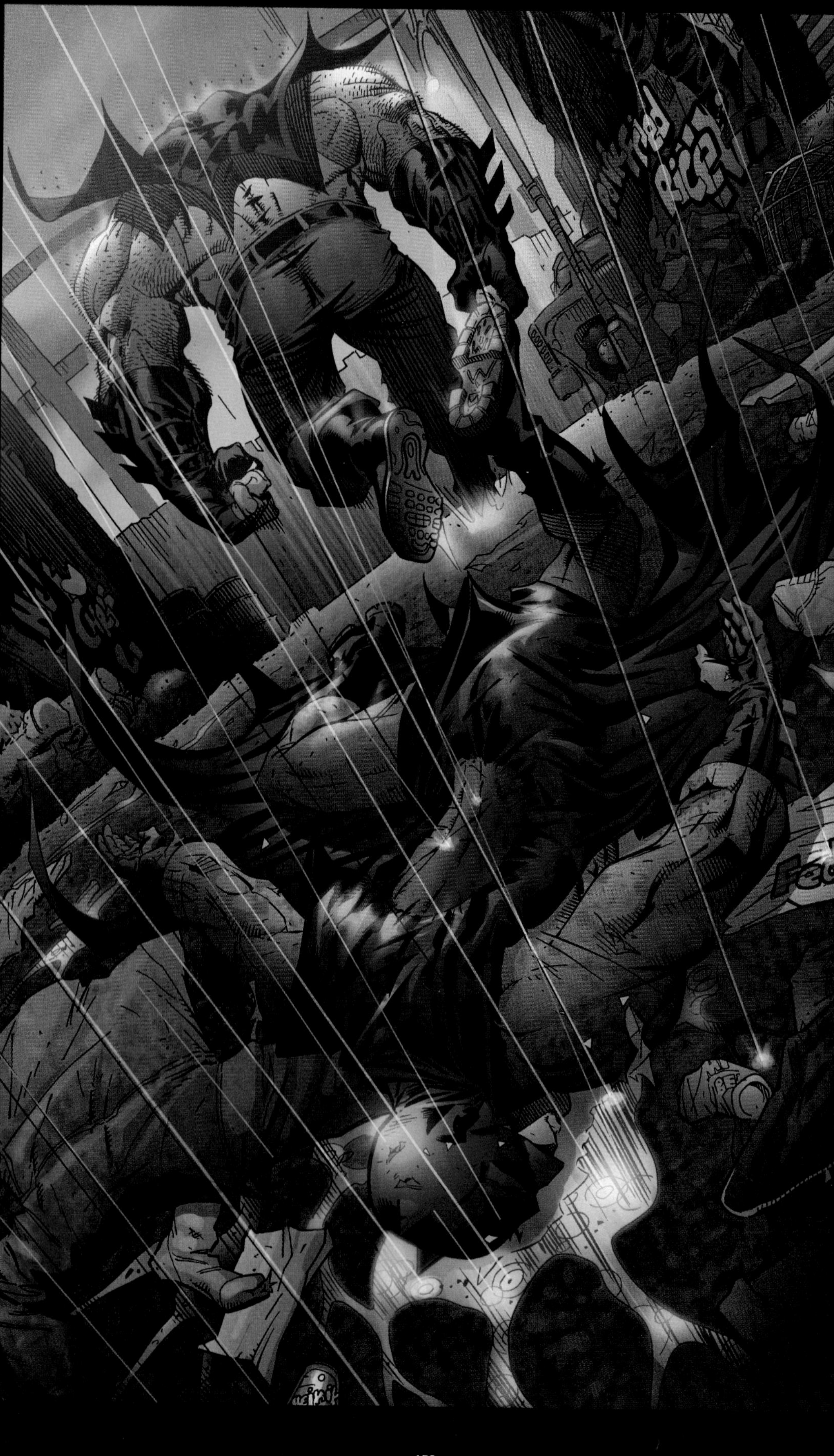

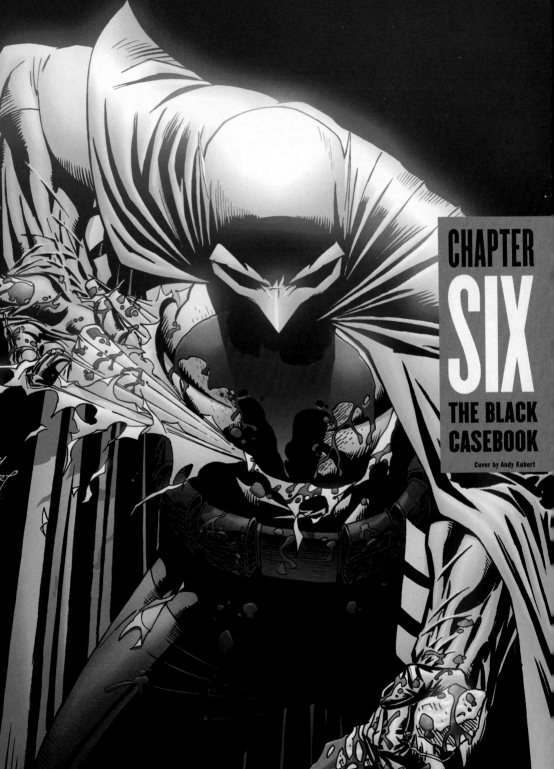

CHAPTER
SIX
THE BLACK
CASEBOOK

Cover by Andy Kubert

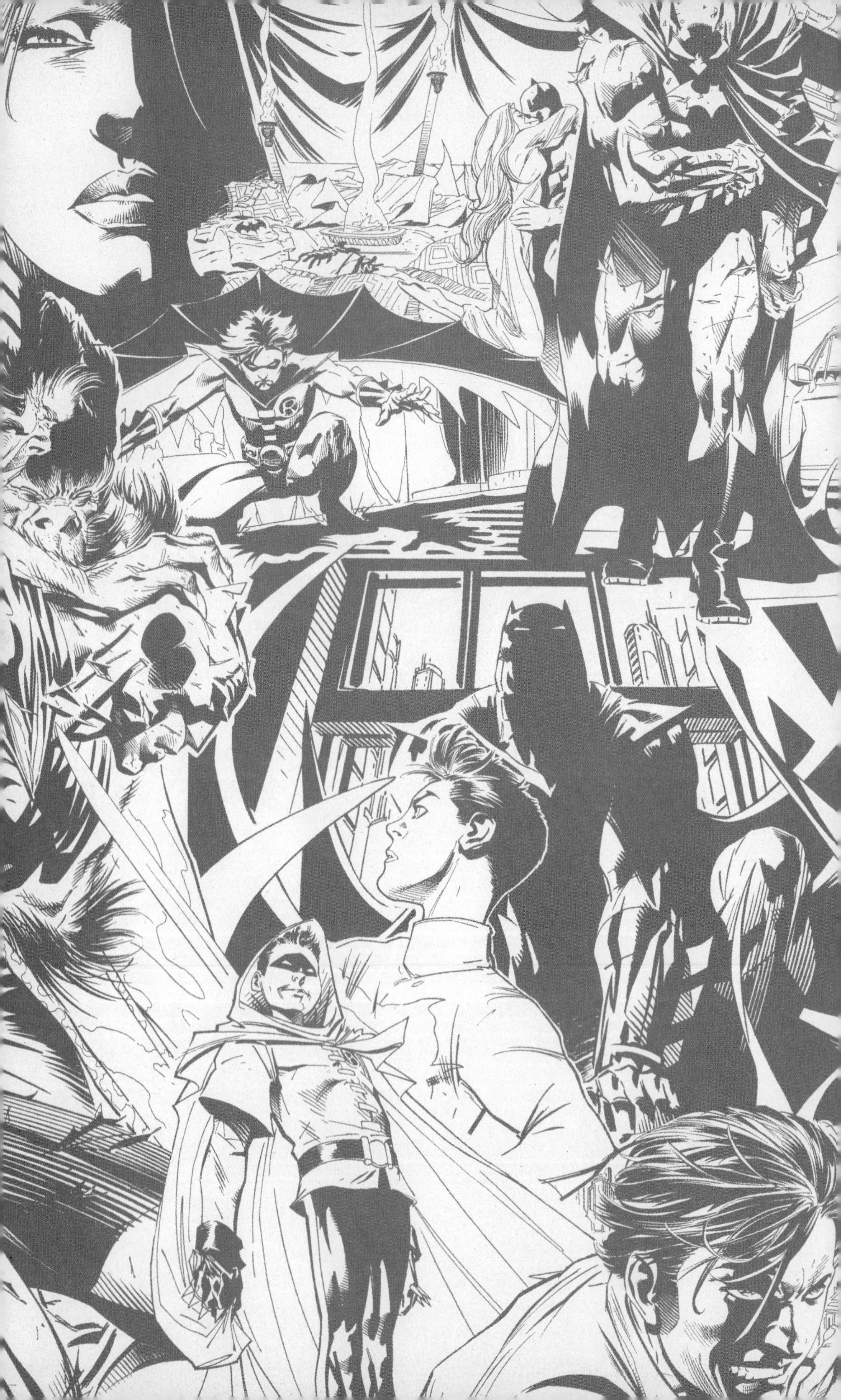

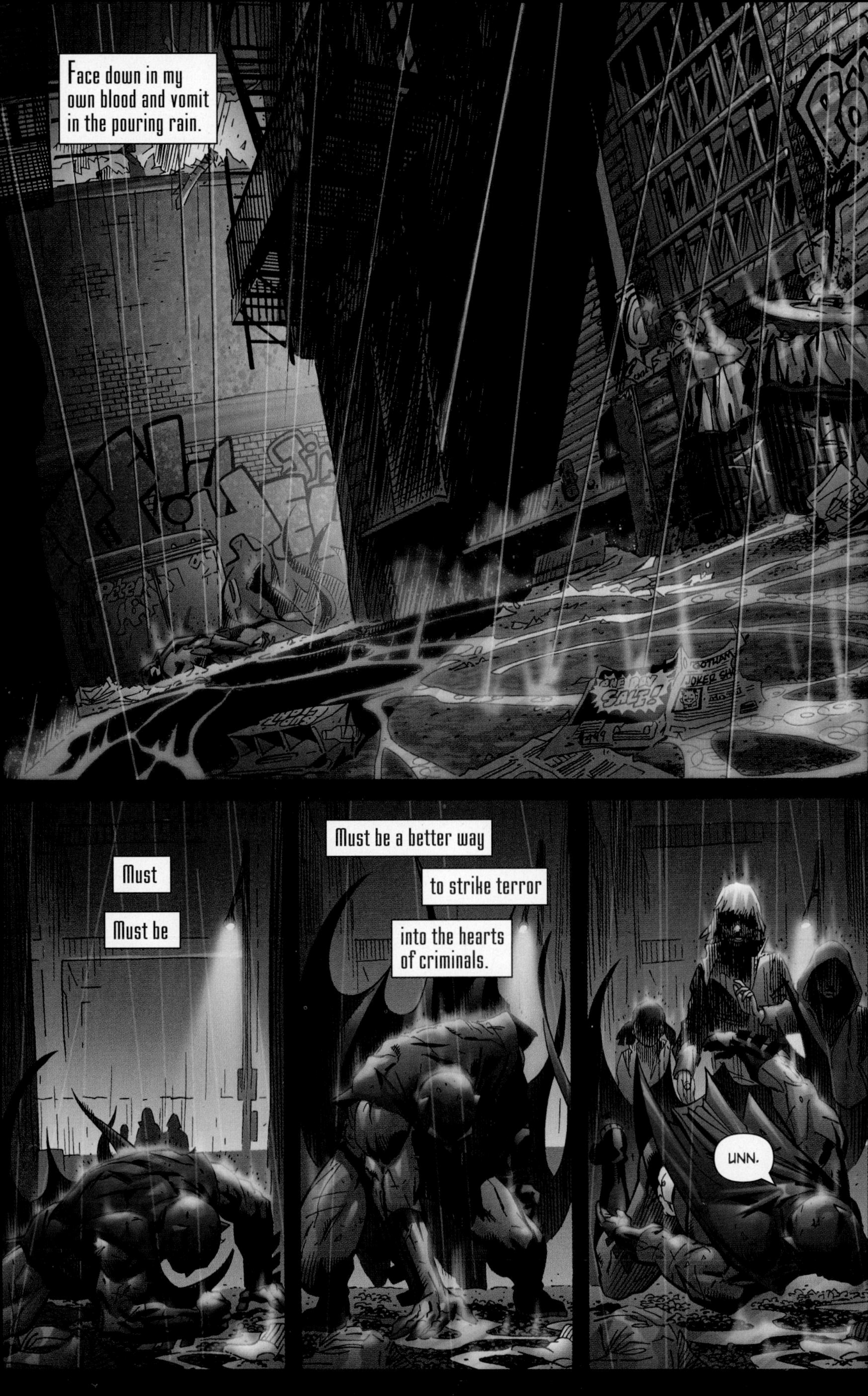
Face down in my own blood and vomit in the pouring rain.
Must
Must be
Must be a better way
to strike terror
into the hearts of criminals.
UNN.

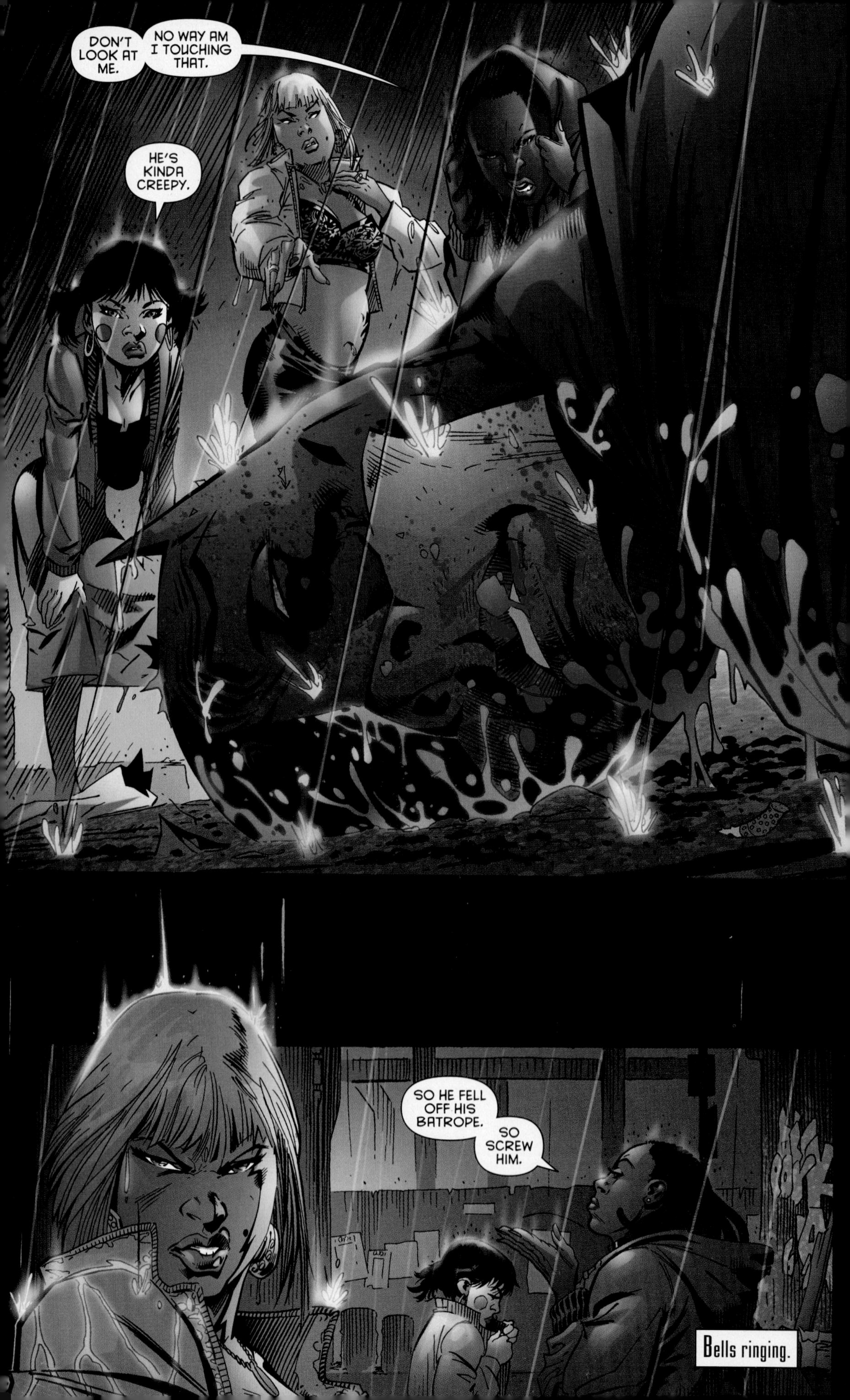

DON'T LOOK AT ME.
NO WAY AM I TOUCHING THAT.
HE'S KINDA CREEPY.
SO HE FELL OFF HIS BATROPE.
SO SCREW HIM.
Bells ringing.

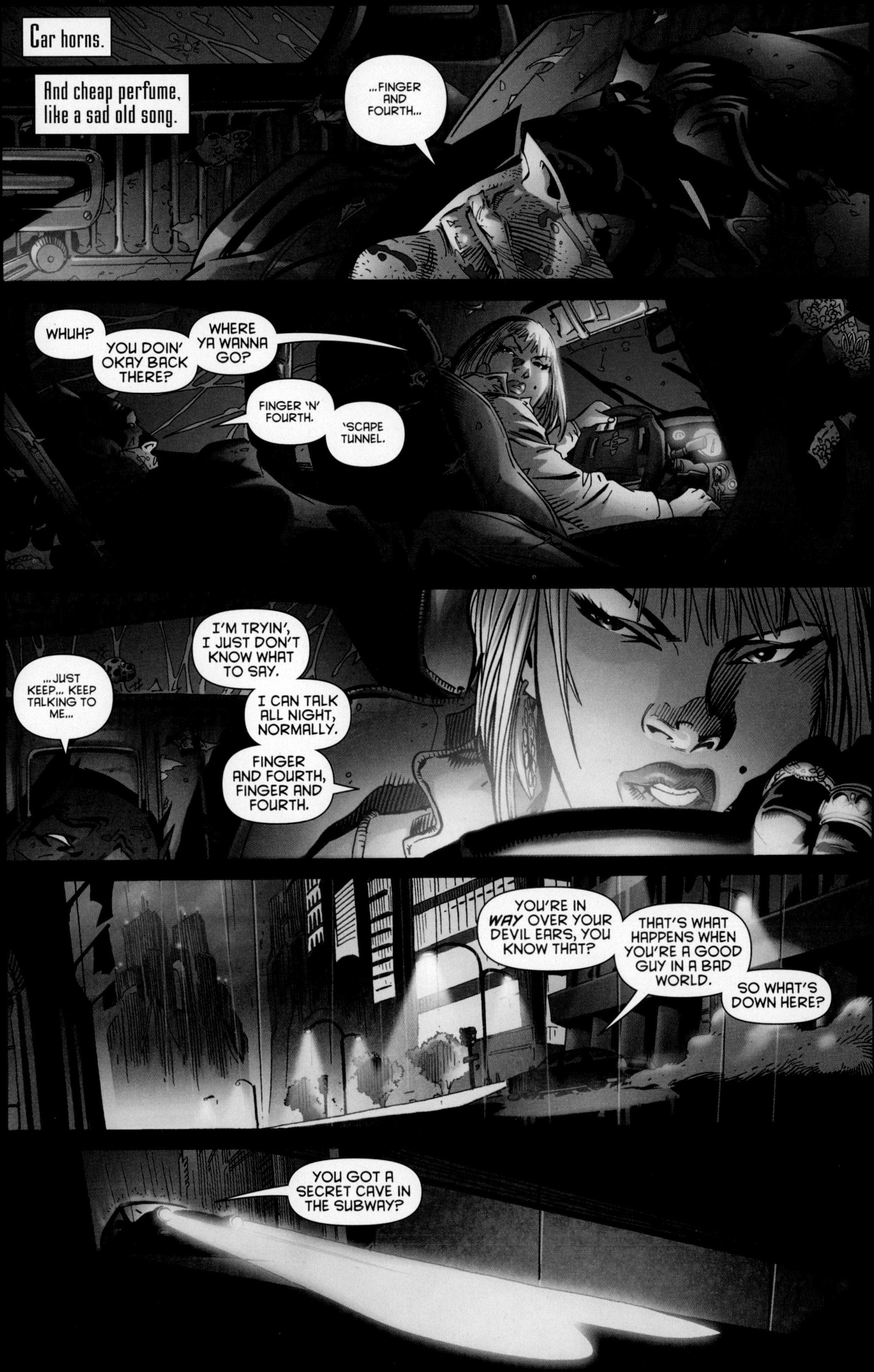
Car horns.
And cheap perfume, like a sad old song.
...FINGER AND FOURTH...
WHUH?
YOU DOIN' OKAY BACK THERE?
WHERE YA WANNA GO?
FINGER 'N' FOURTH.
'SCAPE TUNNEL.
...JUST KEEP... KEEP TALKING TO ME...
I'M TRYIN', I JUST DON'T KNOW WHAT TO SAY.
I CAN TALK ALL NIGHT, NORMALLY.
FINGER AND FOURTH, FINGER AND FOURTH.
YOU'RE IN WAY OVER YOUR DEVIL EARS, YOU KNOW THAT?
THAT'S WHAT HAPPENS WHEN YOU'RE A GOOD GUY IN A BAD WORLD.
SO WHAT'S DOWN HERE?
YOU GOT A SECRET CAVE IN THE SUBWAY?

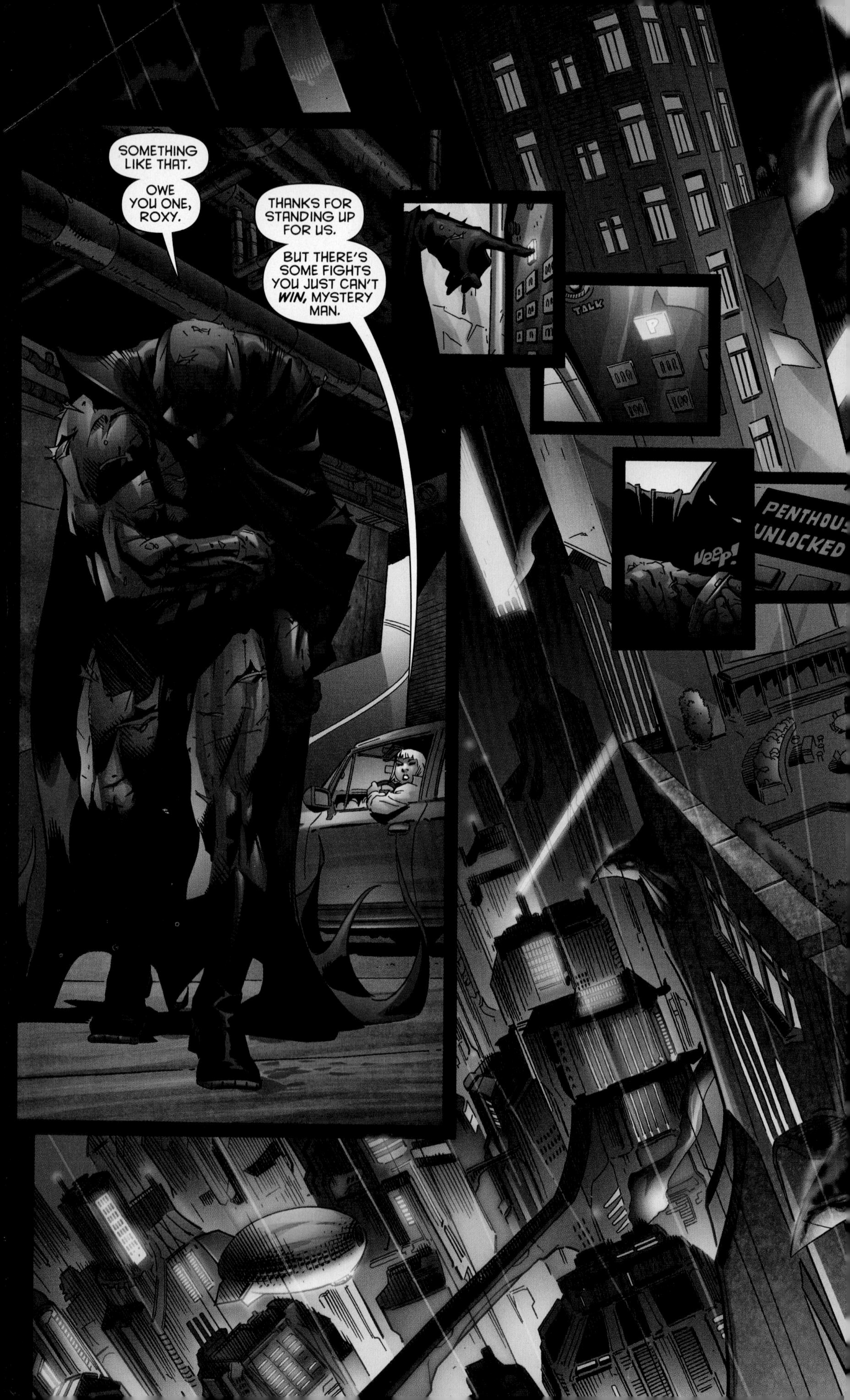
SOMETHING LIKE THAT.
OWE YOU ONE, ROXY.
THANKS FOR STANDING UP FOR US.
BUT THERE'S SOME FIGHTS YOU JUST CAN'T *WIN,* MYSTERY MAN.
TALK
P
VEEP!
PENTHOUS UNLOCKED

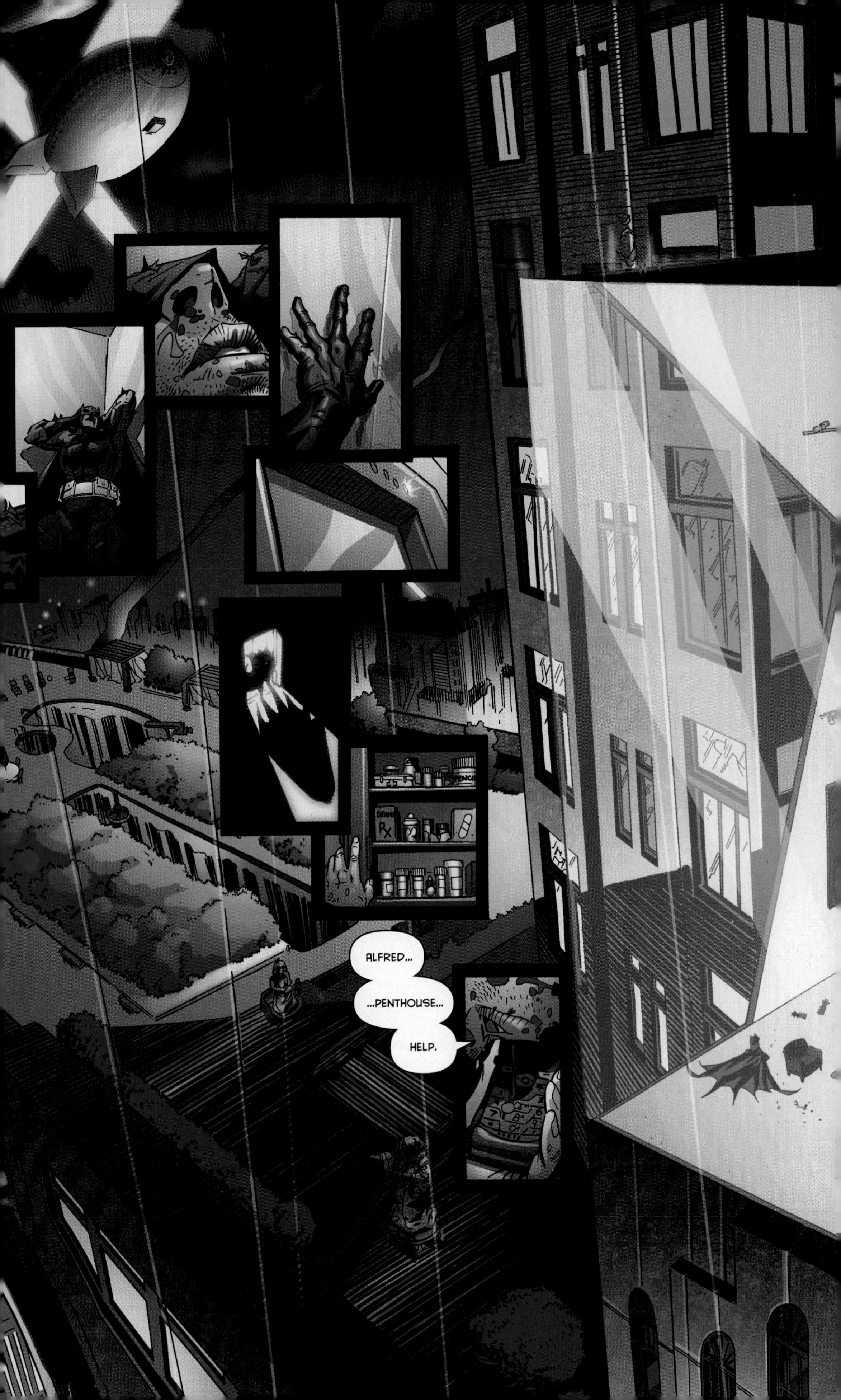
ALFRED...
...PENTHOUSE...
HELP.

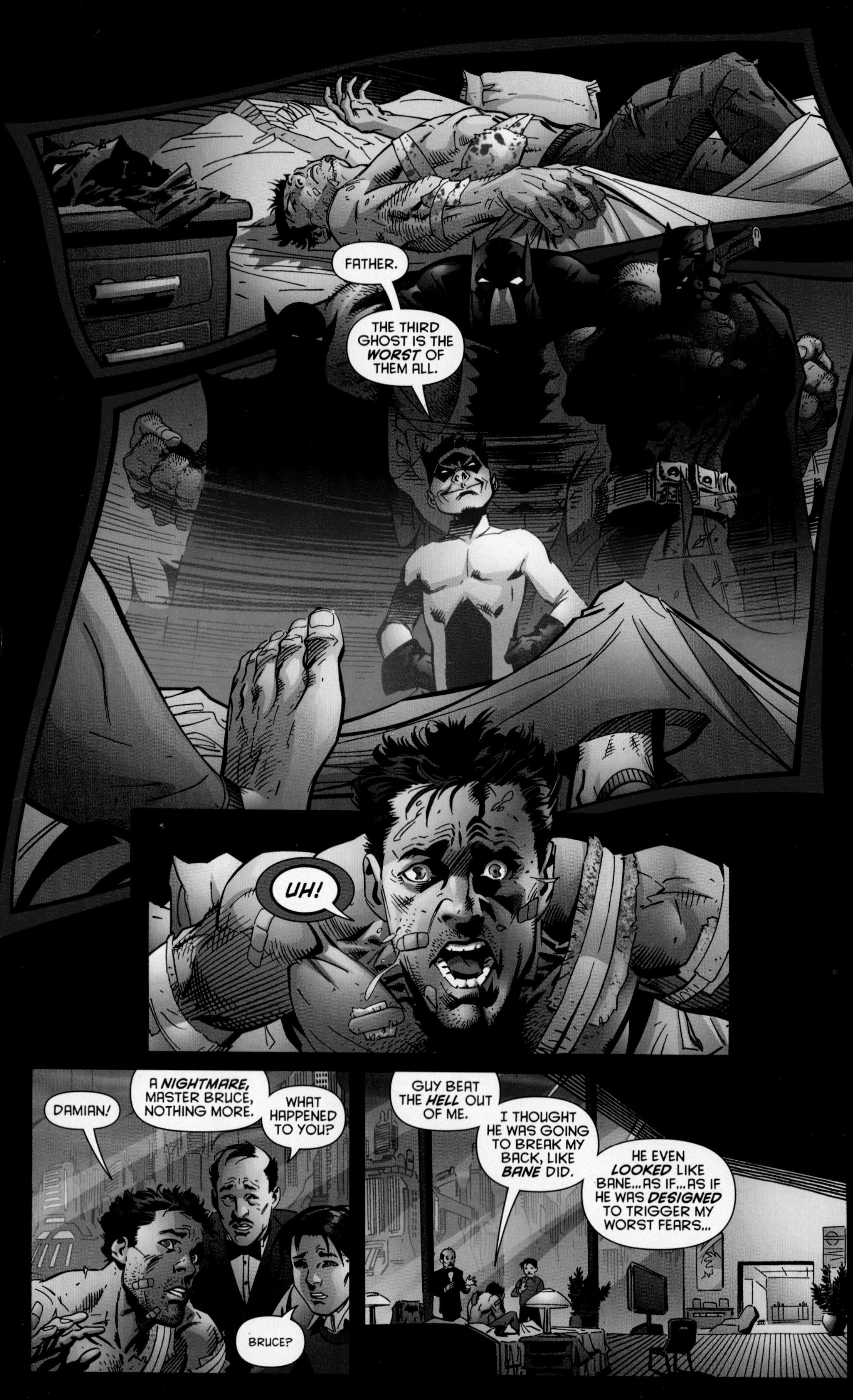
FATHER.
THE THIRD GHOST IS THE WORST OF THEM ALL.
UH!
DAMIAN!
A NIGHTMARE, MASTER BRUCE, NOTHING MORE.
WHAT HAPPENED TO YOU?
BRUCE?
GUY BEAT THE HELL OUT OF ME.
I THOUGHT HE WAS GOING TO BREAK MY BACK, LIKE BANE DID.
HE EVEN LOOKED LIKE BANE... AS IF... AS IF HE WAS DESIGNED TO TRIGGER MY WORST FEARS...

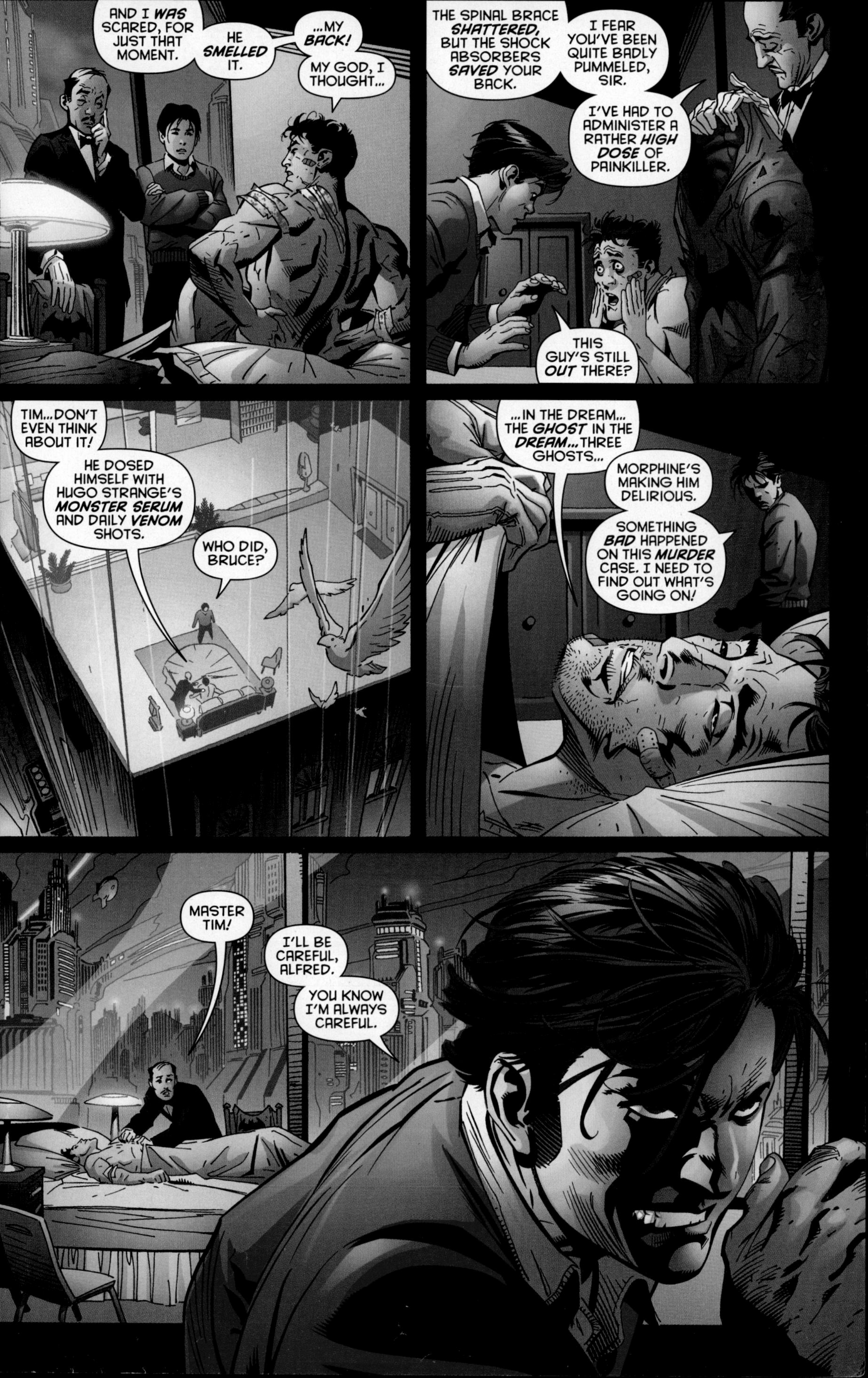
AND I *WAS* SCARED, FOR JUST THAT MOMENT.
HE *SMELLED* IT.
...MY *BACK!*
MY GOD, I THOUGHT...
THE SPINAL BRACE *SHATTERED,* BUT THE SHOCK ABSORBERS *SAVED* YOUR BACK.
I FEAR YOU'VE BEEN QUITE BADLY PUMMELED, SIR.
I'VE HAD TO ADMINISTER A RATHER *HIGH DOSE* OF PAINKILLER.
THIS GUY'S STILL *OUT* THERE?
TIM...DON'T EVEN THINK ABOUT IT!
HE DOSED HIMSELF WITH HUGO STRANGE'S *MONSTER SERUM* AND DAILY *VENOM* SHOTS.
WHO DID, BRUCE?
...IN THE DREAM... THE *GHOST* IN THE *DREAM*...THREE GHOSTS...
MORPHINE'S MAKING HIM DELIRIOUS.
SOMETHING *BAD* HAPPENED ON THIS *MURDER* CASE. I NEED TO FIND OUT WHAT'S GOING ON!
MASTER TIM!
I'LL BE CAREFUL, ALFRED.
YOU KNOW I'M ALWAYS CAREFUL.

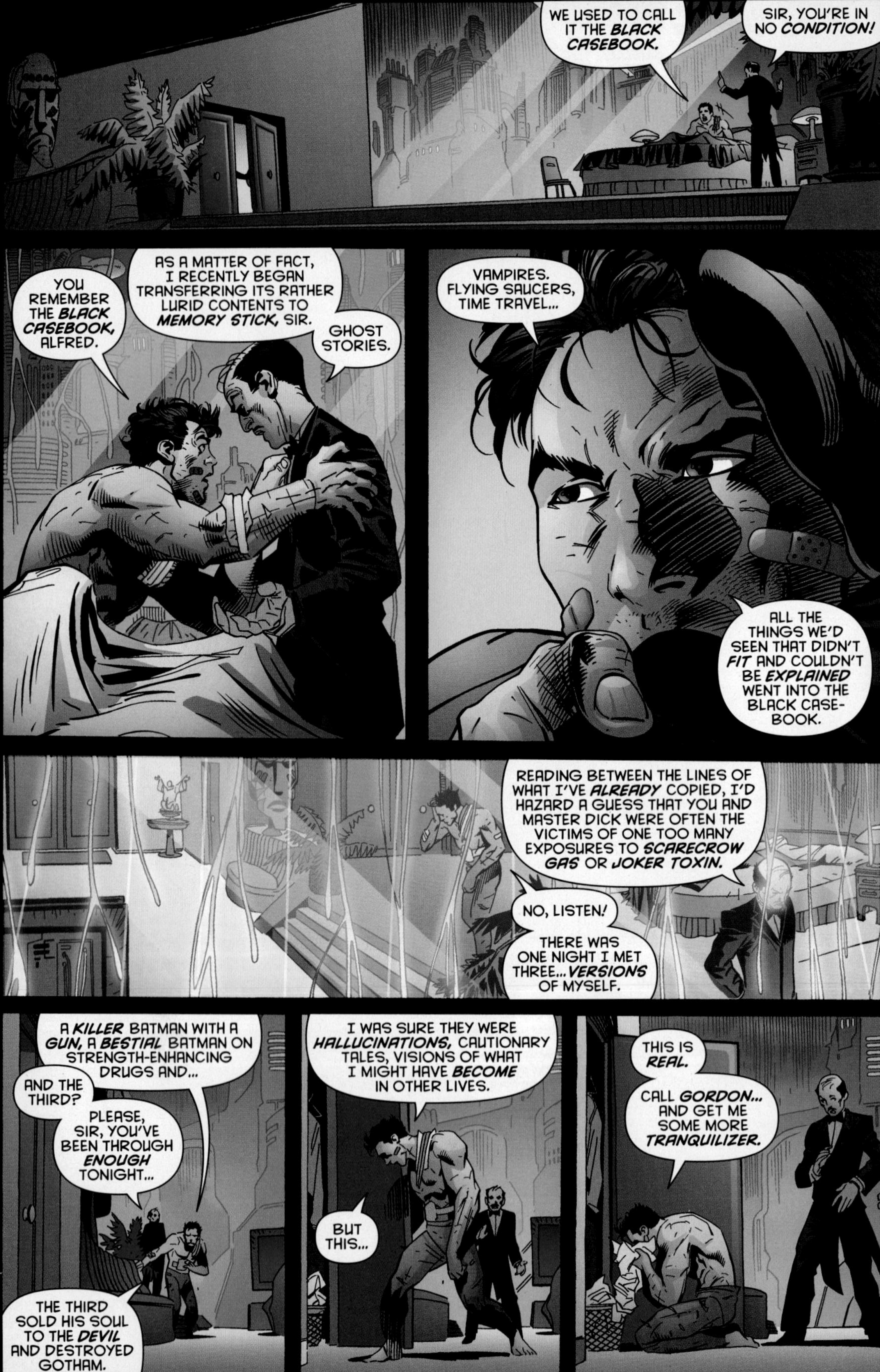
WE USED TO CALL IT THE *BLACK CASEBOOK.*
SIR, YOU'RE IN NO *CONDITION!*
YOU REMEMBER THE *BLACK CASEBOOK,* ALFRED.
AS A MATTER OF FACT, I RECENTLY BEGAN TRANSFERRING ITS RATHER LURID CONTENTS TO *MEMORY STICK,* SIR.
GHOST STORIES.
VAMPIRES. FLYING SAUCERS, TIME TRAVEL...
ALL THE THINGS WE'D SEEN THAT DIDN'T *FIT* AND COULDN'T BE *EXPLAINED* WENT INTO THE BLACK CASE-BOOK.
READING BETWEEN THE LINES OF WHAT I'VE *ALREADY* COPIED, I'D HAZARD A GUESS THAT YOU AND MASTER DICK WERE OFTEN THE VICTIMS OF ONE TOO MANY EXPOSURES TO *SCARECROW GAS* OR *JOKER TOXIN.*
NO, LISTEN!
THERE WAS ONE NIGHT I MET THREE...*VERSIONS* OF MYSELF.
A *KILLER* BATMAN WITH A *GUN,* A *BESTIAL* BATMAN ON STRENGTH-ENHANCING DRUGS AND...
AND THE THIRD?
PLEASE, SIR, YOU'VE BEEN THROUGH *ENOUGH* TONIGHT...
THE THIRD SOLD HIS SOUL TO THE *DEVIL* AND DESTROYED GOTHAM.
I WAS SURE THEY WERE *HALLUCINATIONS,* CAUTIONARY TALES, VISIONS OF WHAT I MIGHT HAVE *BECOME* IN OTHER LIVES.
BUT THIS...
THIS IS *REAL.*
CALL *GORDON...* AND GET ME SOME MORE *TRANQUILIZER.*

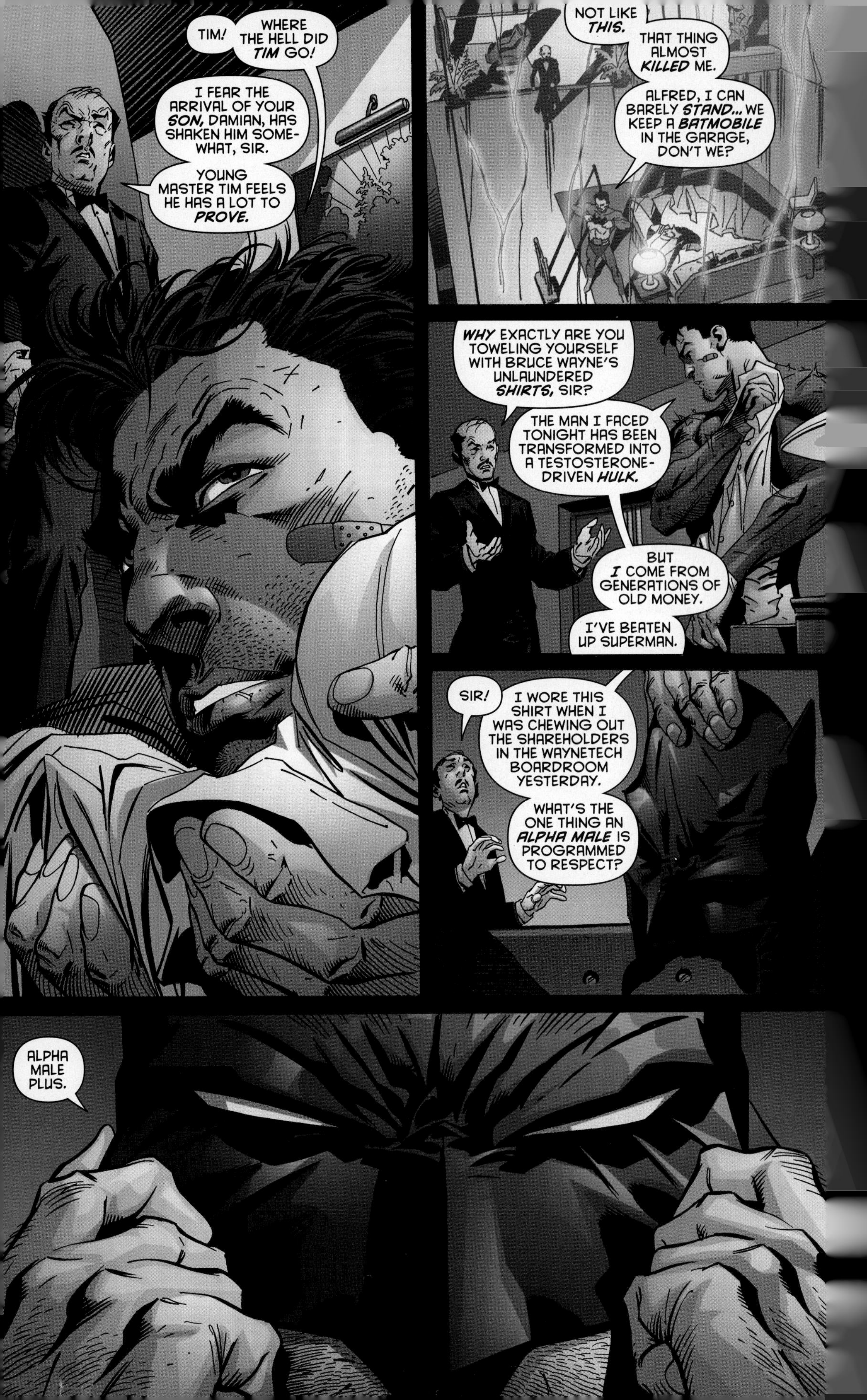
TIM!
WHERE THE HELL DID TIM GO!
I FEAR THE ARRIVAL OF YOUR SON, DAMIAN, HAS SHAKEN HIM SOME-WHAT, SIR.
YOUNG MASTER TIM FEELS HE HAS A LOT TO PROVE.
NOT LIKE THIS.
THAT THING ALMOST KILLED ME.
ALFRED, I CAN BARELY STAND... WE KEEP A BATMOBILE IN THE GARAGE, DON'T WE?
WHY EXACTLY ARE YOU TOWELING YOURSELF WITH BRUCE WAYNE'S UNLAUNDERED SHIRTS, SIR?
THE MAN I FACED TONIGHT HAS BEEN TRANSFORMED INTO A TESTOSTERONE-DRIVEN HULK.
BUT I COME FROM GENERATIONS OF OLD MONEY.
I'VE BEATEN UP SUPERMAN.
SIR!
I WORE THIS SHIRT WHEN I WAS CHEWING OUT THE SHAREHOLDERS IN THE WAYNETECH BOARDROOM YESTERDAY.
WHAT'S THE ONE THING AN ALPHA MALE IS PROGRAMMED TO RESPECT?
ALPHA MALE PLUS.

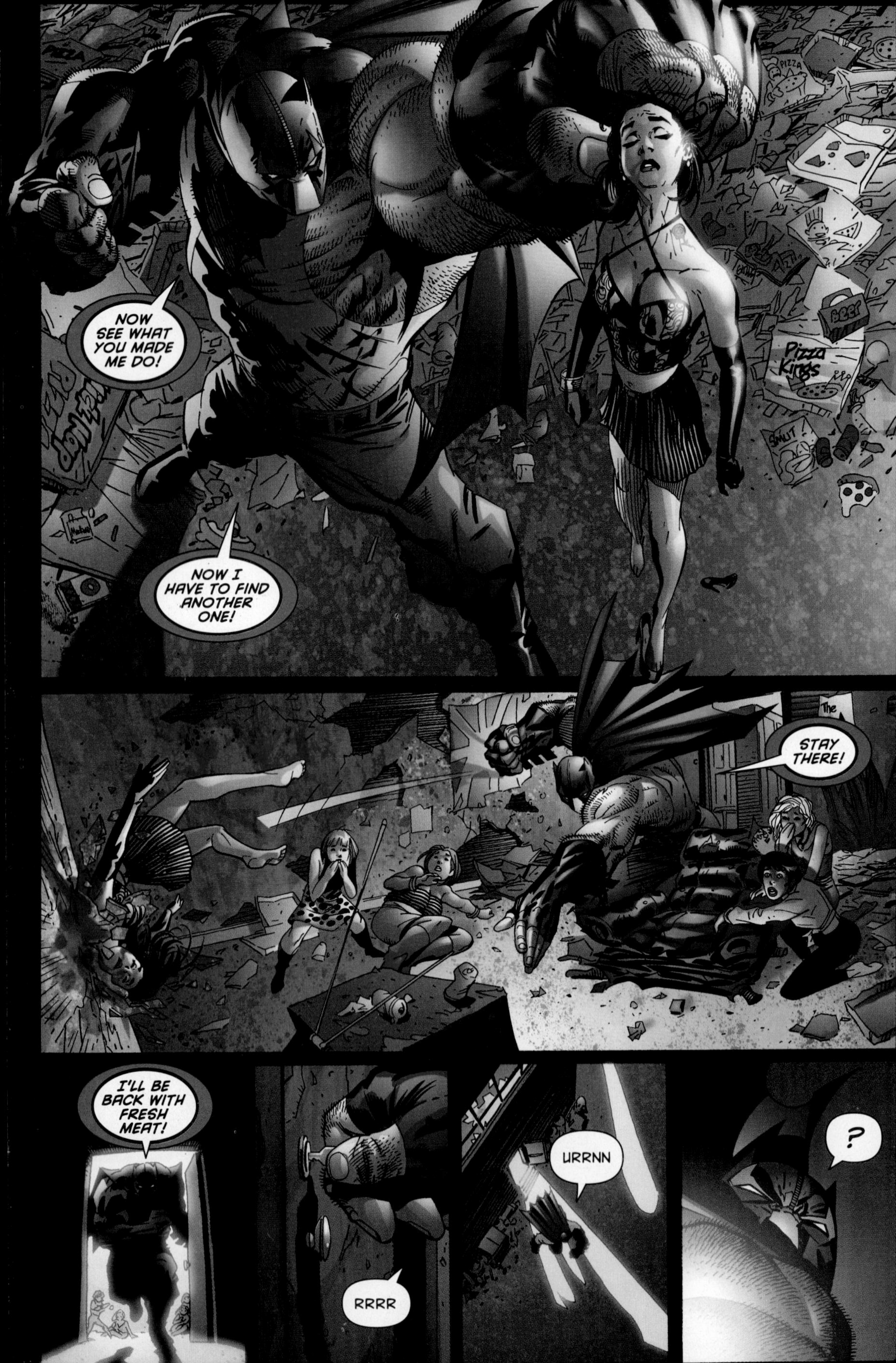
NOW SEE WHAT YOU MADE ME DO!
NOW I HAVE TO FIND ANOTHER ONE!
STAY THERE!
I'LL BE BACK WITH FRESH MEAT!
RRRR
URRNN
?

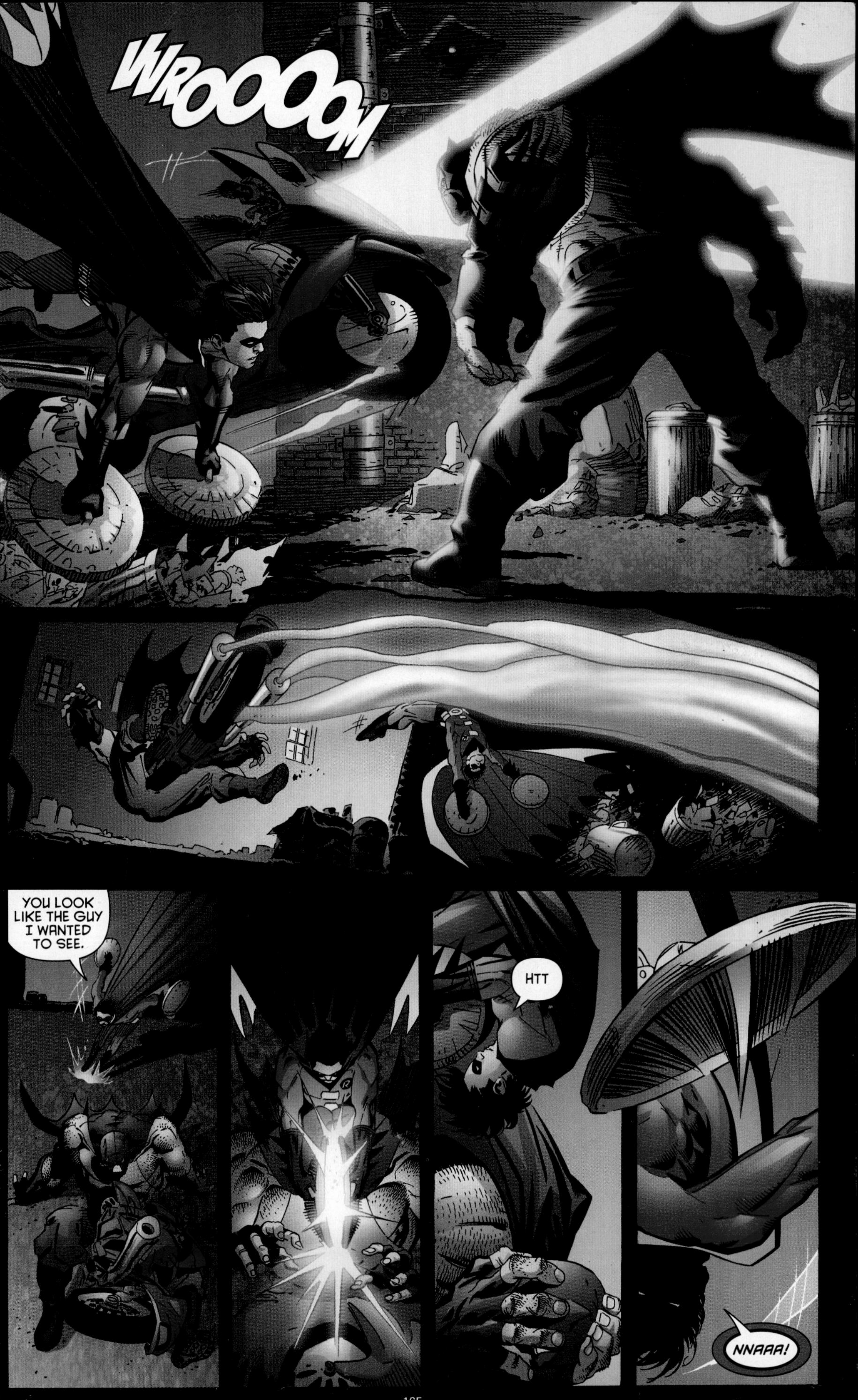
WROOOOM
YOU LOOK LIKE THE GUY I WANTED TO SEE.
HTT
NNAAA!

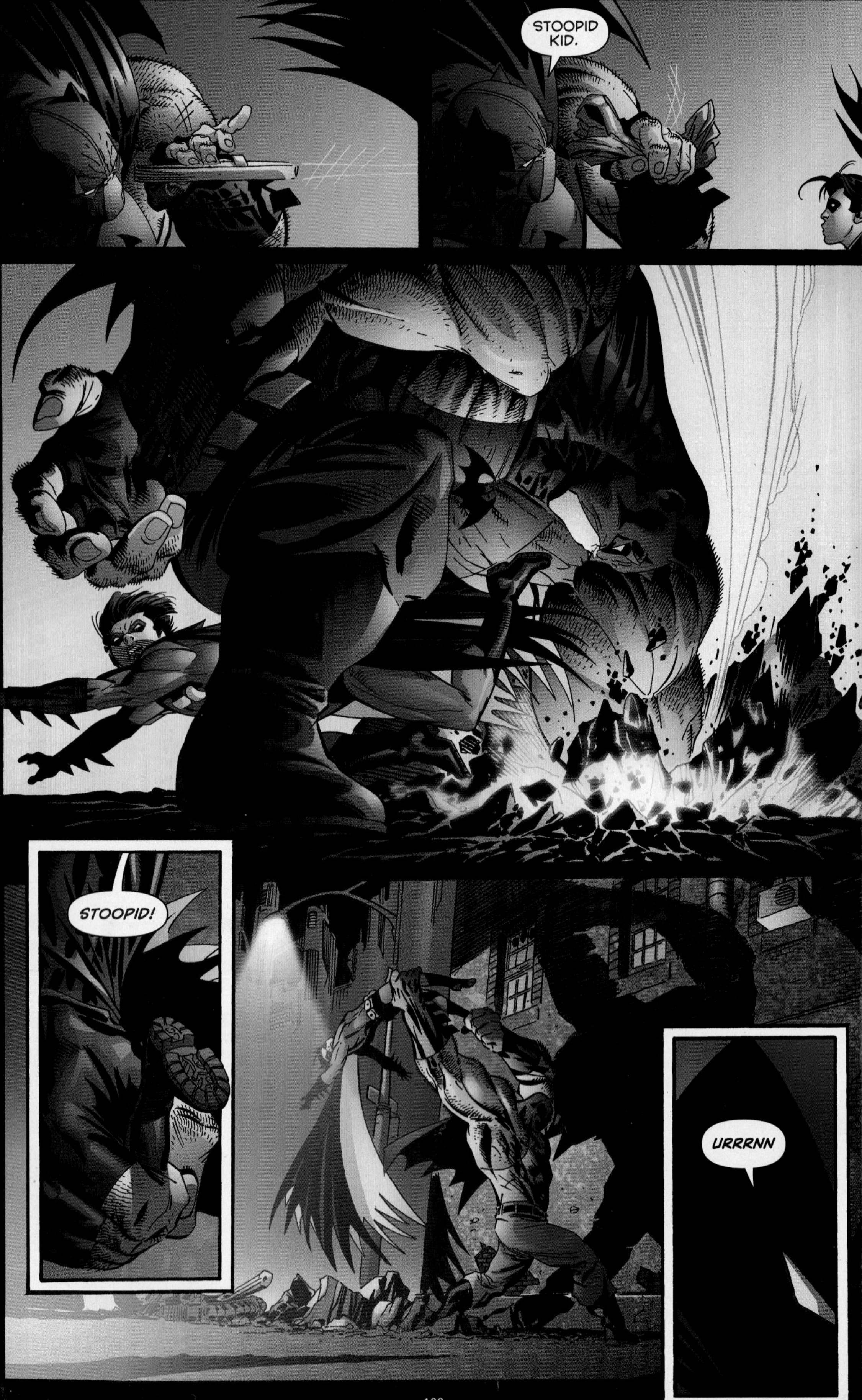
STOOPID
KID.
STOOPID!
URRRNN

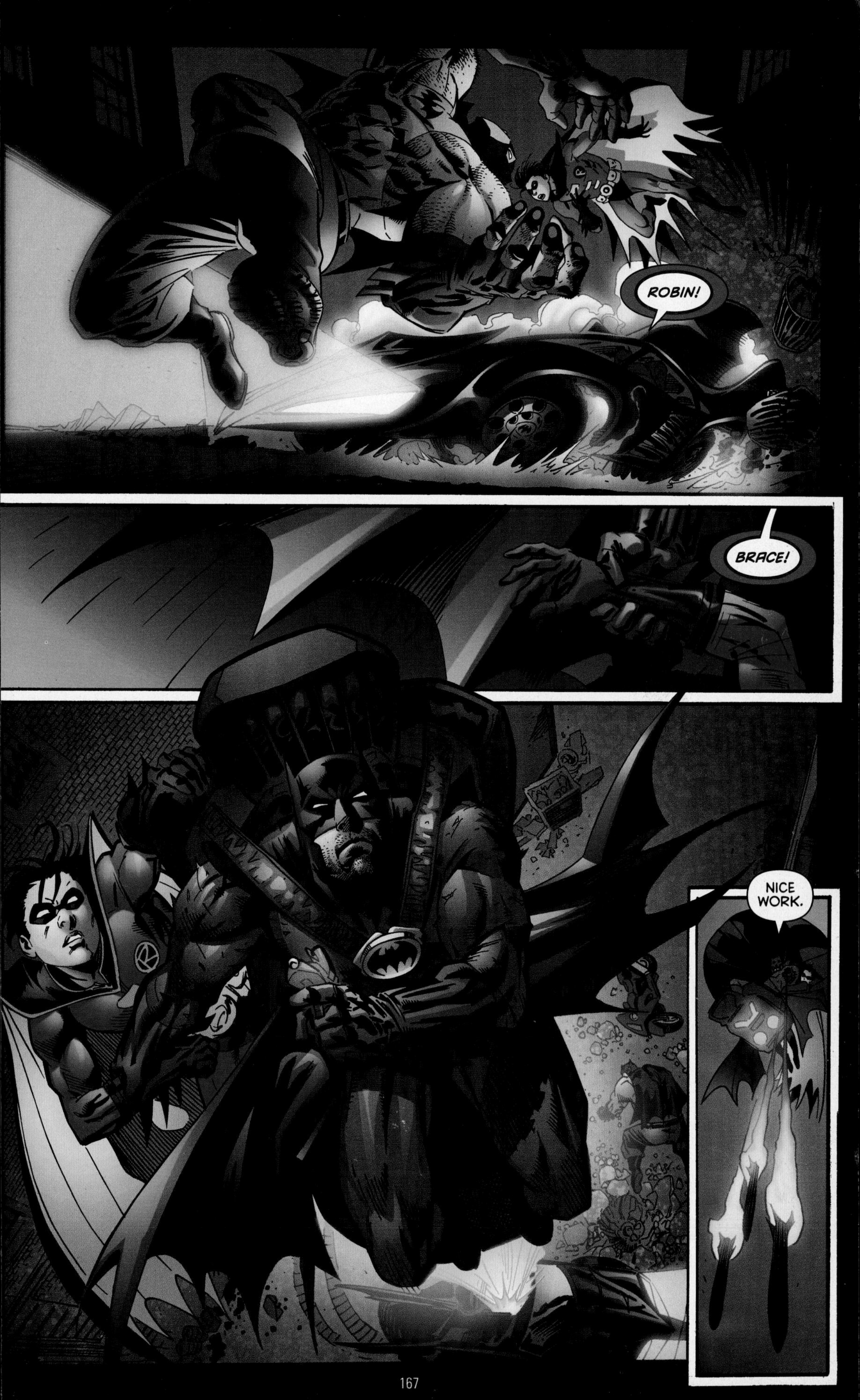
ROBIN!
BRACE!
NICE WORK.

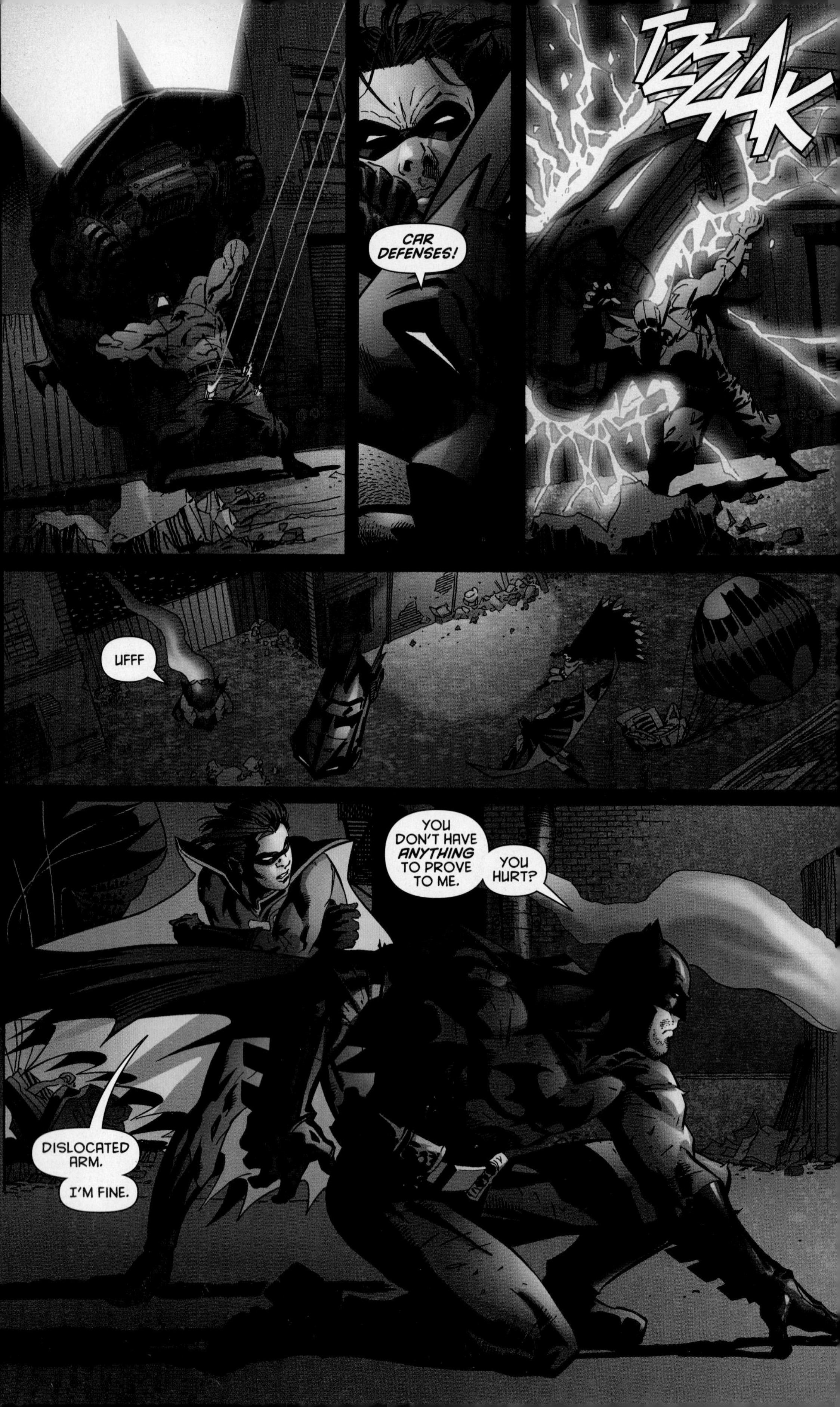
CAR DEFENSES!
TZZZAK
UFFF
YOU HURT?
DISLOCATED ARM.
I'M FINE.
YOU DON'T HAVE *ANYTHING* TO PROVE TO ME.

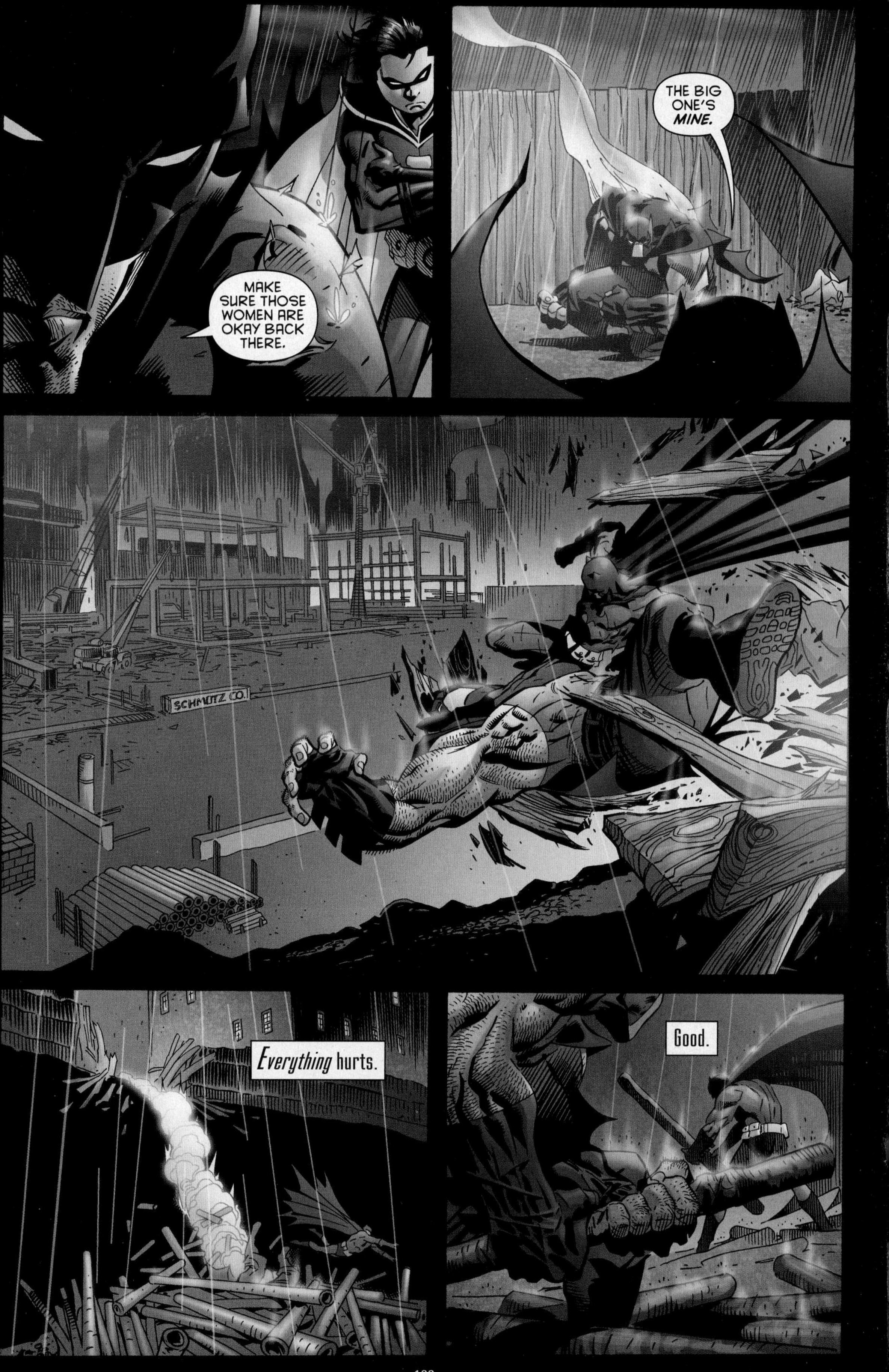
MAKE SURE THOSE WOMEN ARE OKAY BACK THERE.
THE BIG ONE'S *MINE.*
SCHMUTZ CO.
Everything hurts.
Good.

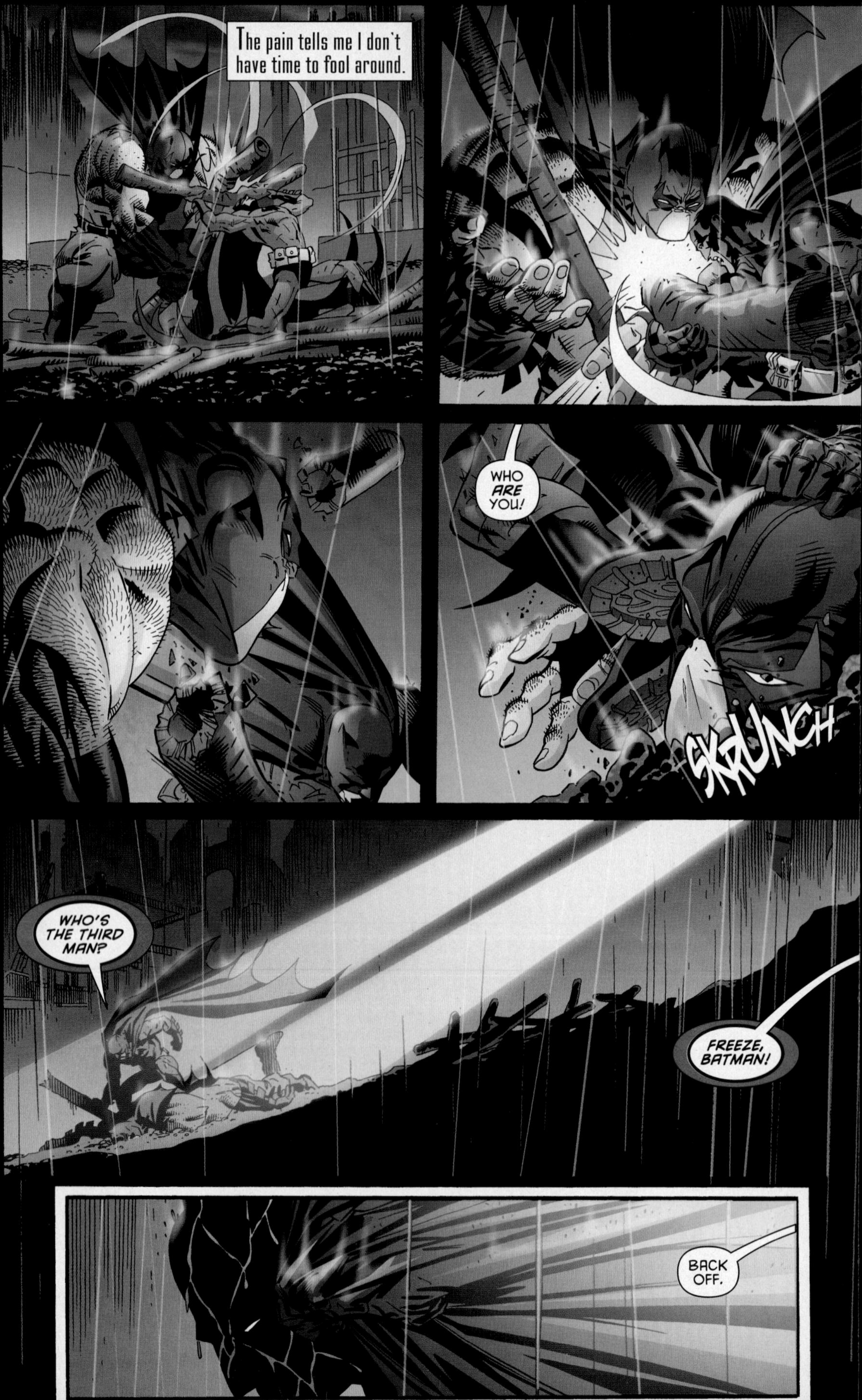
The pain tells me I don't have time to fool around.
WHO ARE YOU!
SKRUNCH
WHO'S THE THIRD MAN?
FREEZE, BATMAN!
BACK OFF.

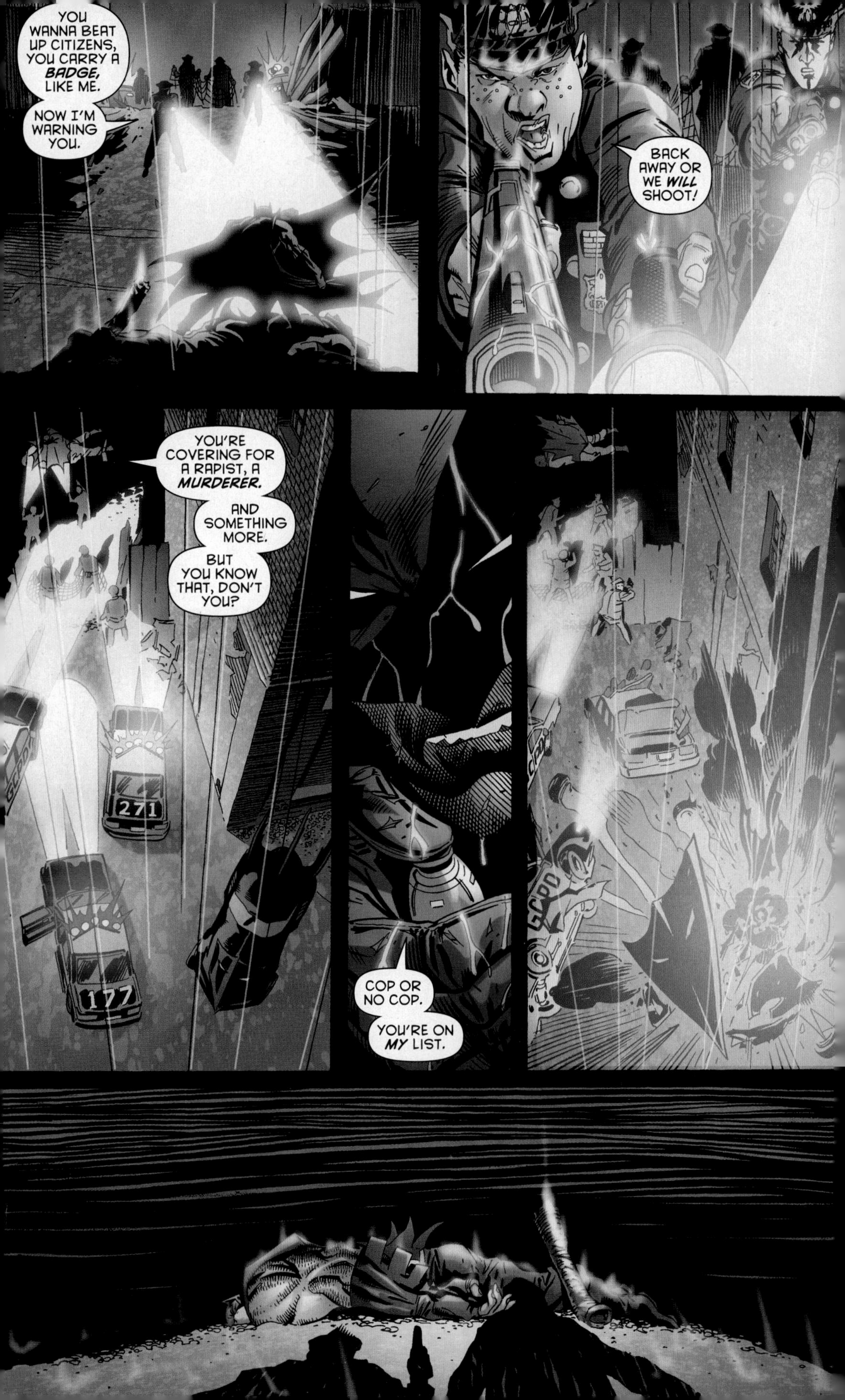
YOU WANNA BEAT UP CITIZENS, YOU CARRY A BADGE, LIKE ME.
NOW I'M WARNING YOU.
BACK AWAY OR WE WILL SHOOT!
YOU'RE COVERING FOR A RAPIST, A MURDERER.
AND SOMETHING MORE.
BUT YOU KNOW THAT, DON'T YOU?
271
177
COP OR NO COP.
YOU'RE ON MY LIST.
GCPD

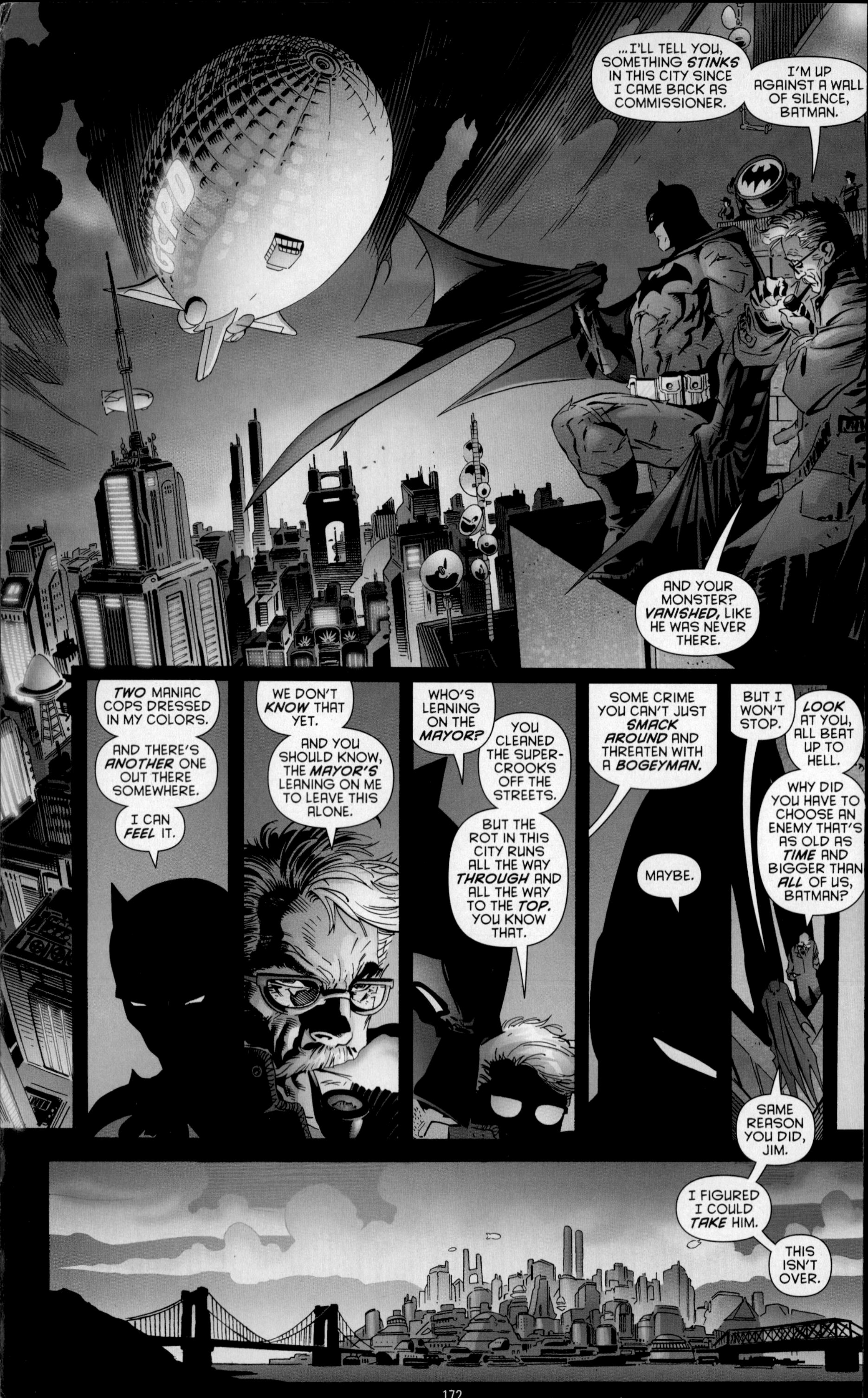
...I'LL TELL YOU, SOMETHING STINKS IN THIS CITY SINCE I CAME BACK AS COMMISSIONER.
I'M UP AGAINST A WALL OF SILENCE, BATMAN.
AND YOUR MONSTER? VANISHED, LIKE HE WAS NEVER THERE.
TWO MANIAC COPS DRESSED IN MY COLORS.
AND THERE'S ANOTHER ONE OUT THERE SOMEWHERE.
I CAN FEEL IT.
WE DON'T KNOW THAT YET.
AND YOU SHOULD KNOW, THE MAYOR'S LEANING ON ME TO LEAVE THIS ALONE.
WHO'S LEANING ON THE MAYOR?
YOU CLEANED THE SUPER-CROOKS OFF THE STREETS.
BUT THE ROT IN THIS CITY RUNS ALL THE WAY THROUGH AND ALL THE WAY TO THE TOP. YOU KNOW THAT.
SOME CRIME YOU CAN'T JUST SMACK AROUND AND THREATEN WITH A BOGEYMAN.
MAYBE.
BUT I WON'T STOP.
LOOK AT YOU, ALL BEAT UP TO HELL.
WHY DID YOU HAVE TO CHOOSE AN ENEMY THAT'S AS OLD AS TIME AND BIGGER THAN ALL OF US, BATMAN?
SAME REASON YOU DID, JIM.
I FIGURED I COULD TAKE HIM.
THIS ISN'T OVER.

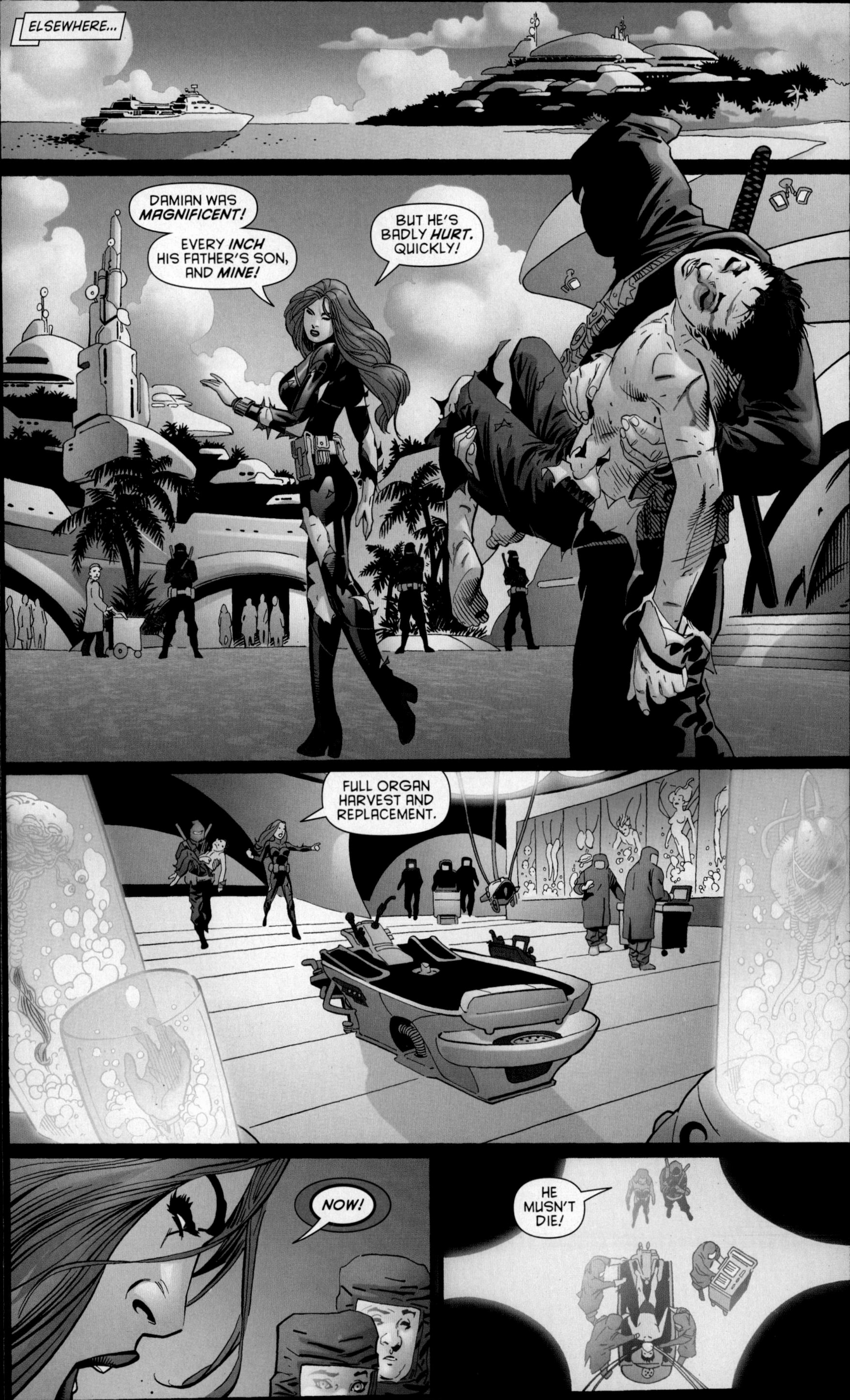

ELSEWHERE...
DAMIAN WAS MAGNIFICENT!
EVERY INCH HIS FATHER'S SON, AND MINE!
BUT HE'S BADLY HURT. QUICKLY!
FULL ORGAN HARVEST AND REPLACEMENT.
NOW!
HE MUSN'T DIE!

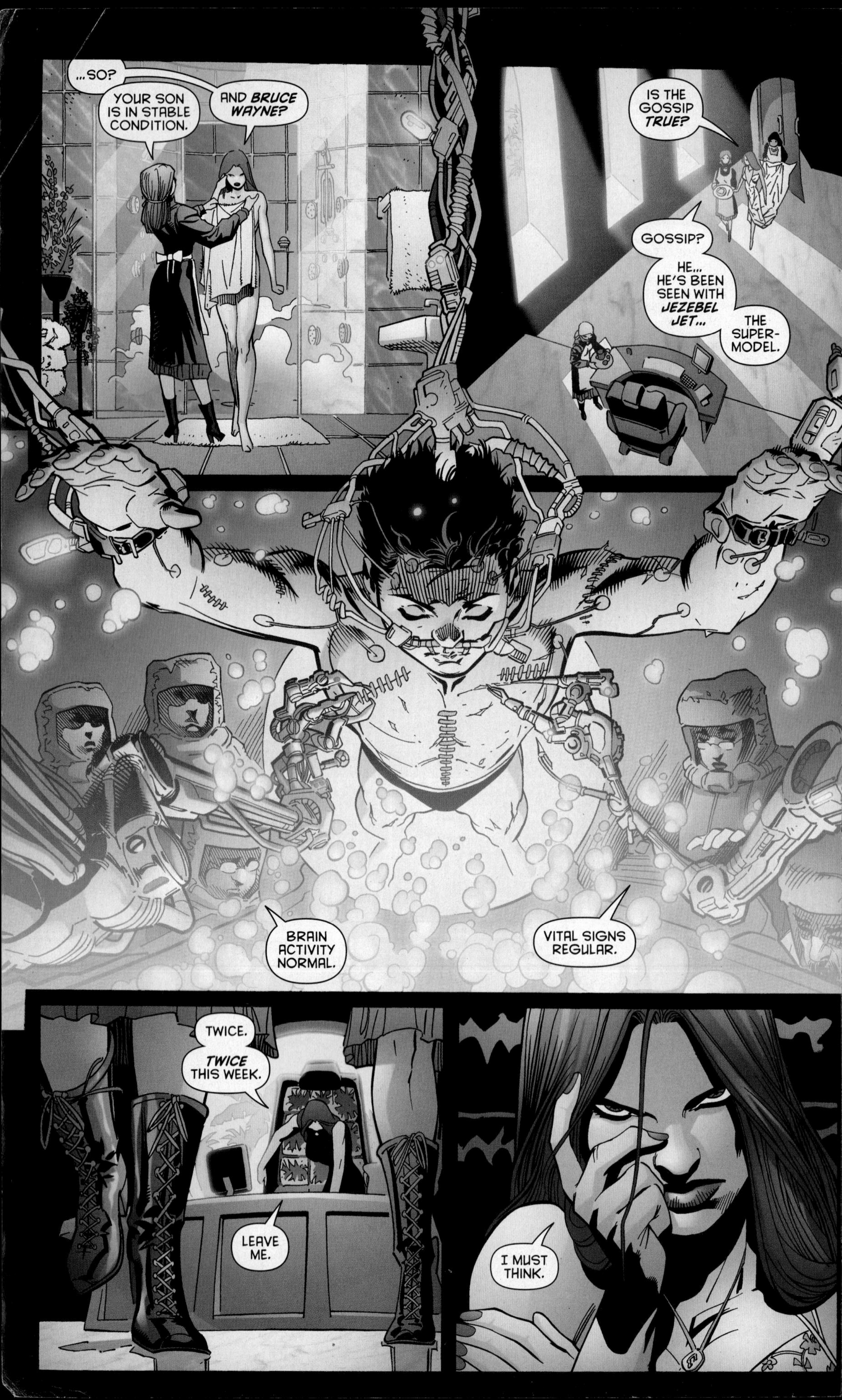
...SO?
YOUR SON IS IN STABLE CONDITION.
AND *BRUCE WAYNE?*
IS THE GOSSIP *TRUE?*
GOSSIP?
HE... HE'S BEEN SEEN WITH *JEZEBEL JET*...
THE SUPER-MODEL.
BRAIN ACTIVITY NORMAL.
VITAL SIGNS REGULAR.
TWICE.
TWICE THIS WEEK.
LEAVE ME.
I MUST THINK.

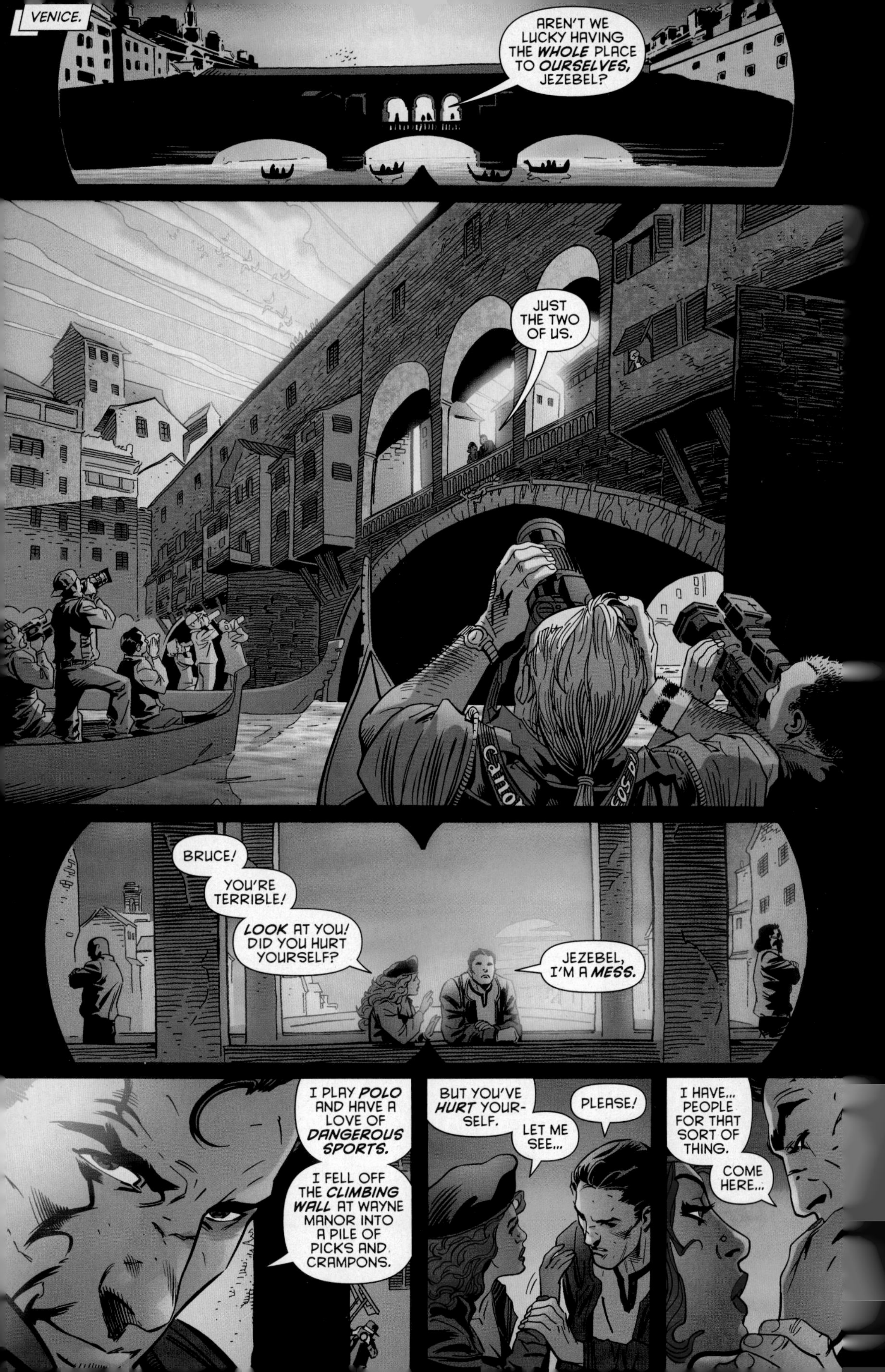
VENICE.
AREN'T WE LUCKY HAVING THE WHOLE PLACE TO OURSELVES, JEZEBEL?
JUST THE TWO OF US.
Canon
BRUCE!
YOU'RE TERRIBLE!
LOOK AT YOU! DID YOU HURT YOURSELF?
JEZEBEL, I'M A MESS.
I PLAY POLO AND HAVE A LOVE OF DANGEROUS SPORTS.
I FELL OFF THE CLIMBING WALL AT WAYNE MANOR INTO A PILE OF PICKS AND CRAMPONS.
BUT YOU'VE HURT YOURSELF.
LET ME SEE...
PLEASE!
I HAVE... PEOPLE FOR THAT SORT OF THING.
COME HERE...

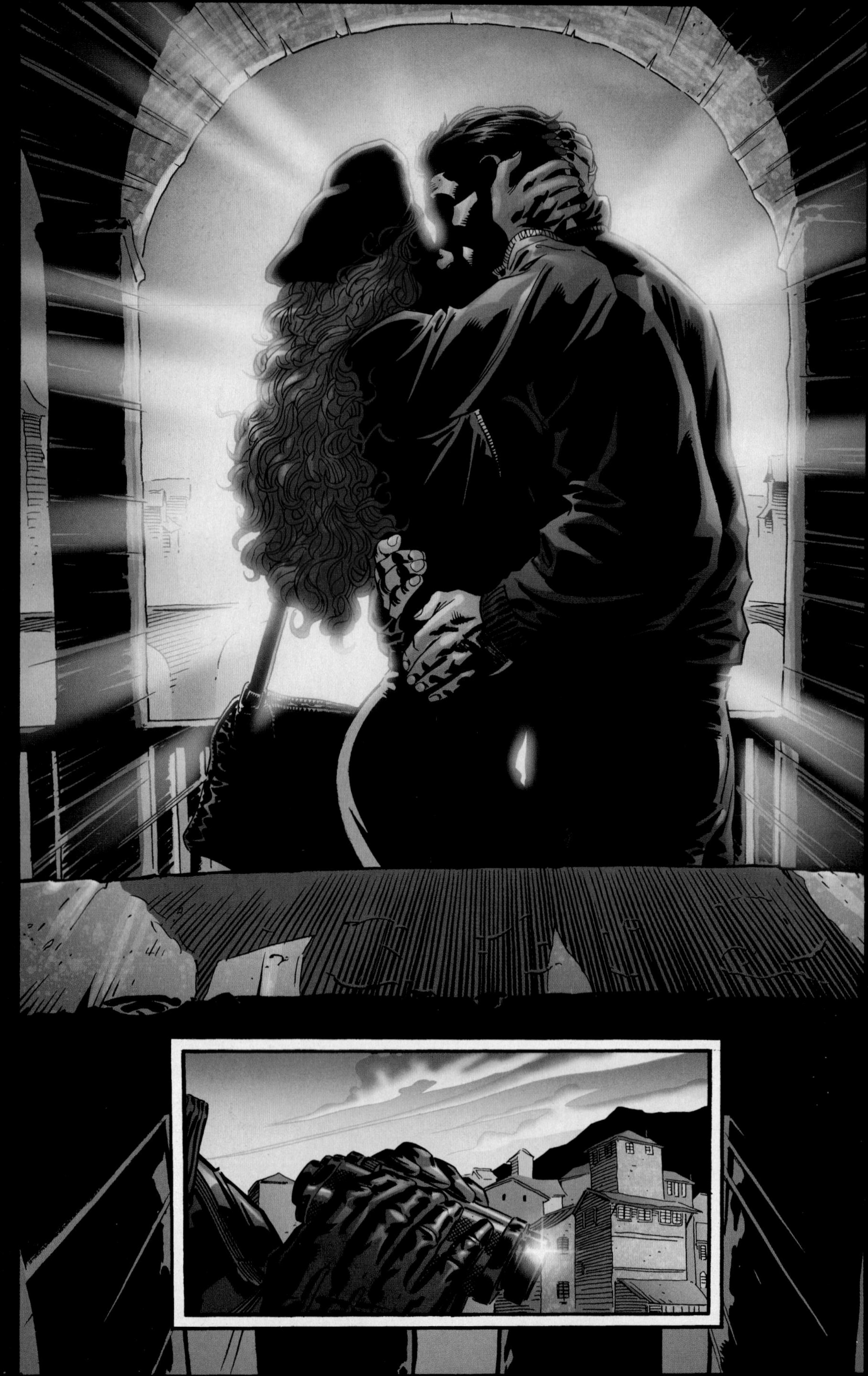

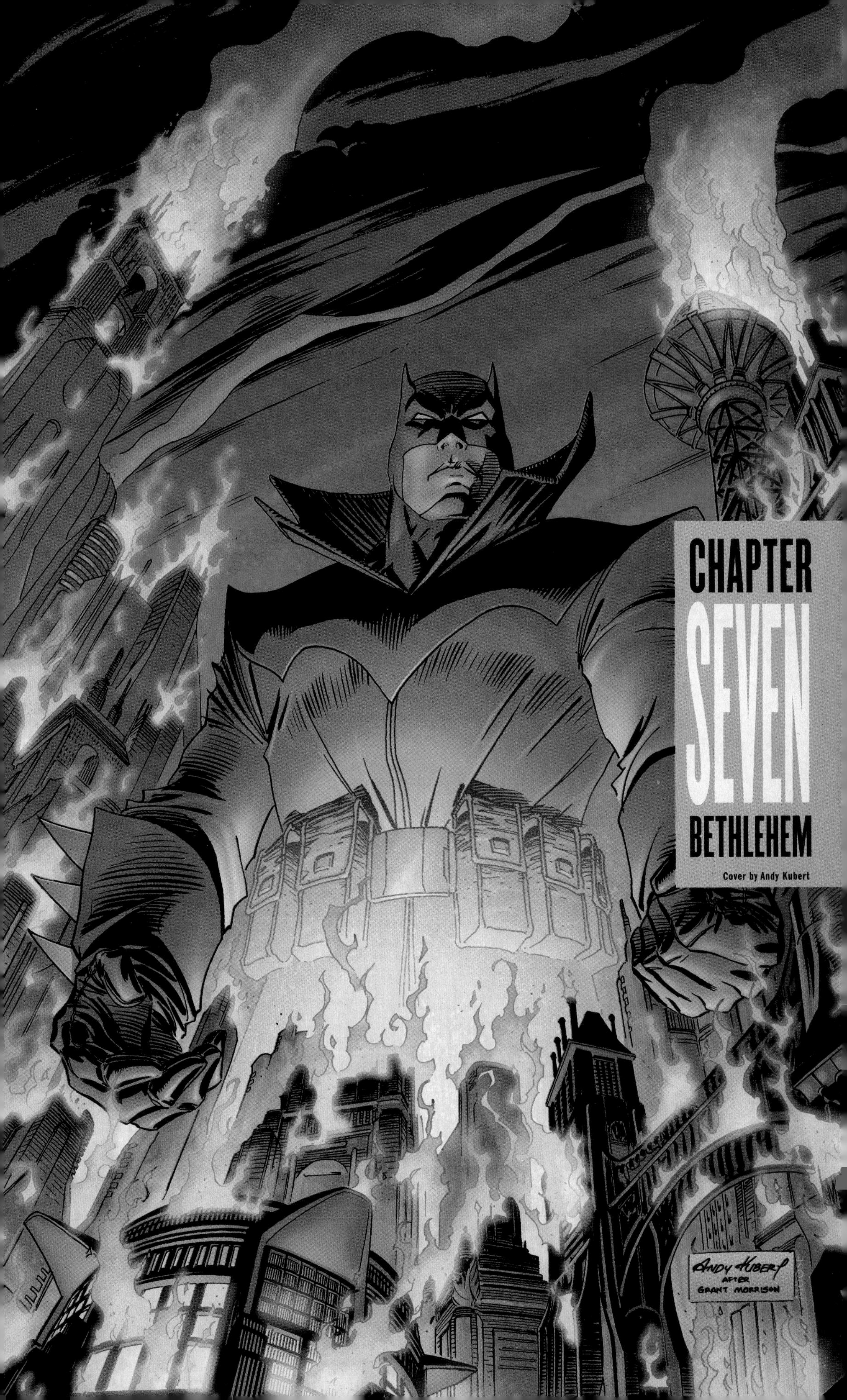
ANDY KUBERT
AFTER
GRANT MORRISON

CHAPTER SEVEN
BETHLEHEM

Cover by Andy Kubert

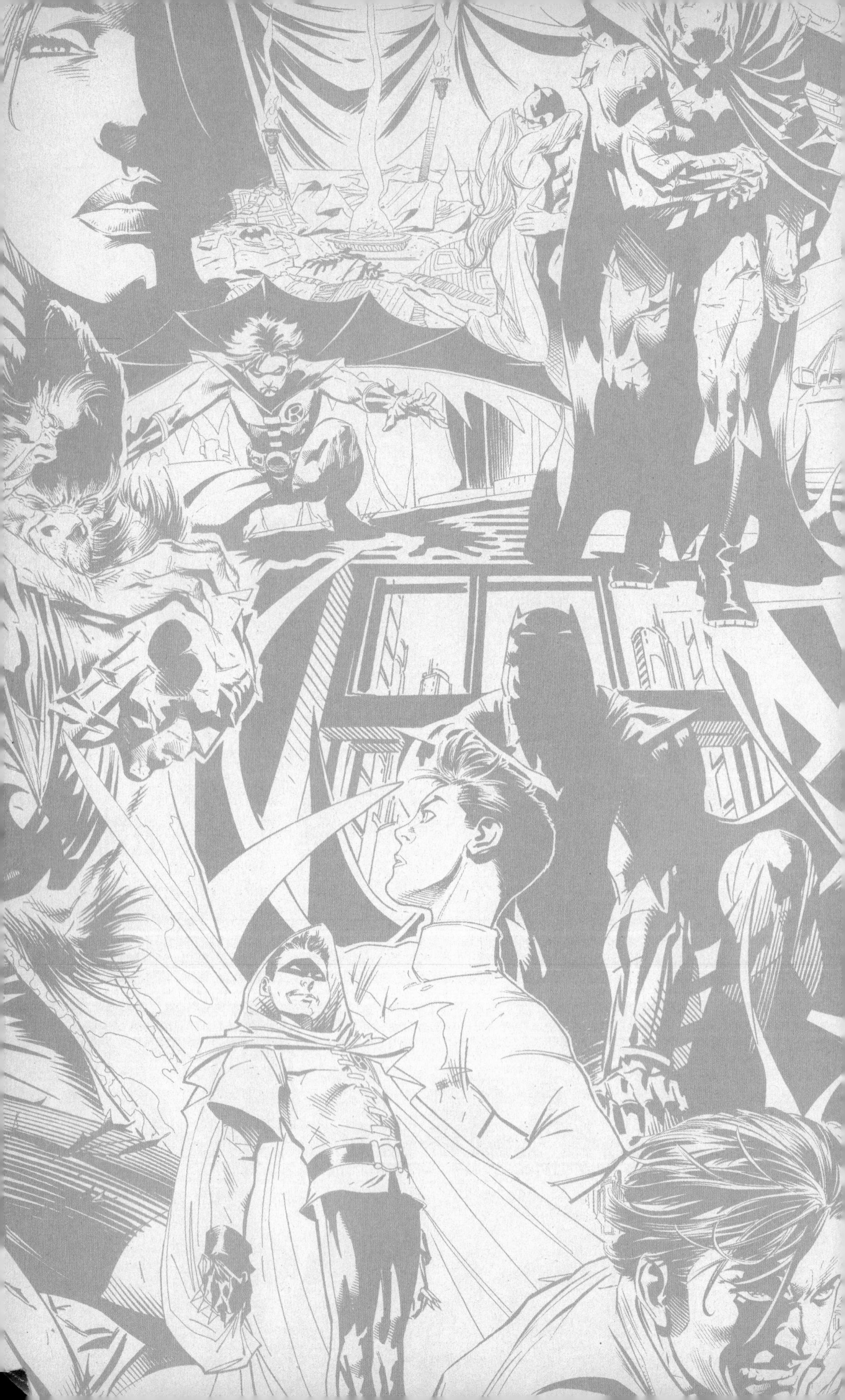

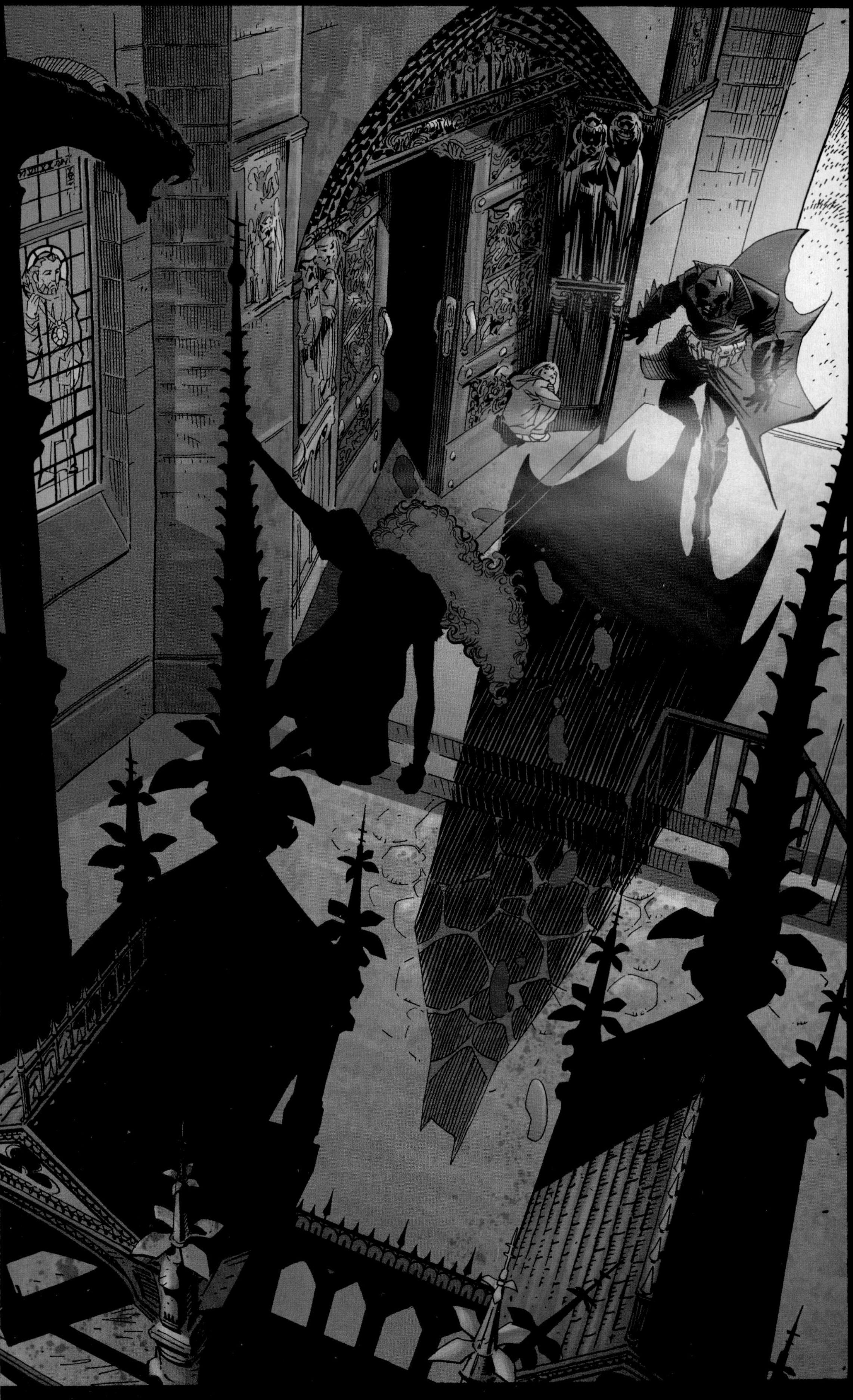

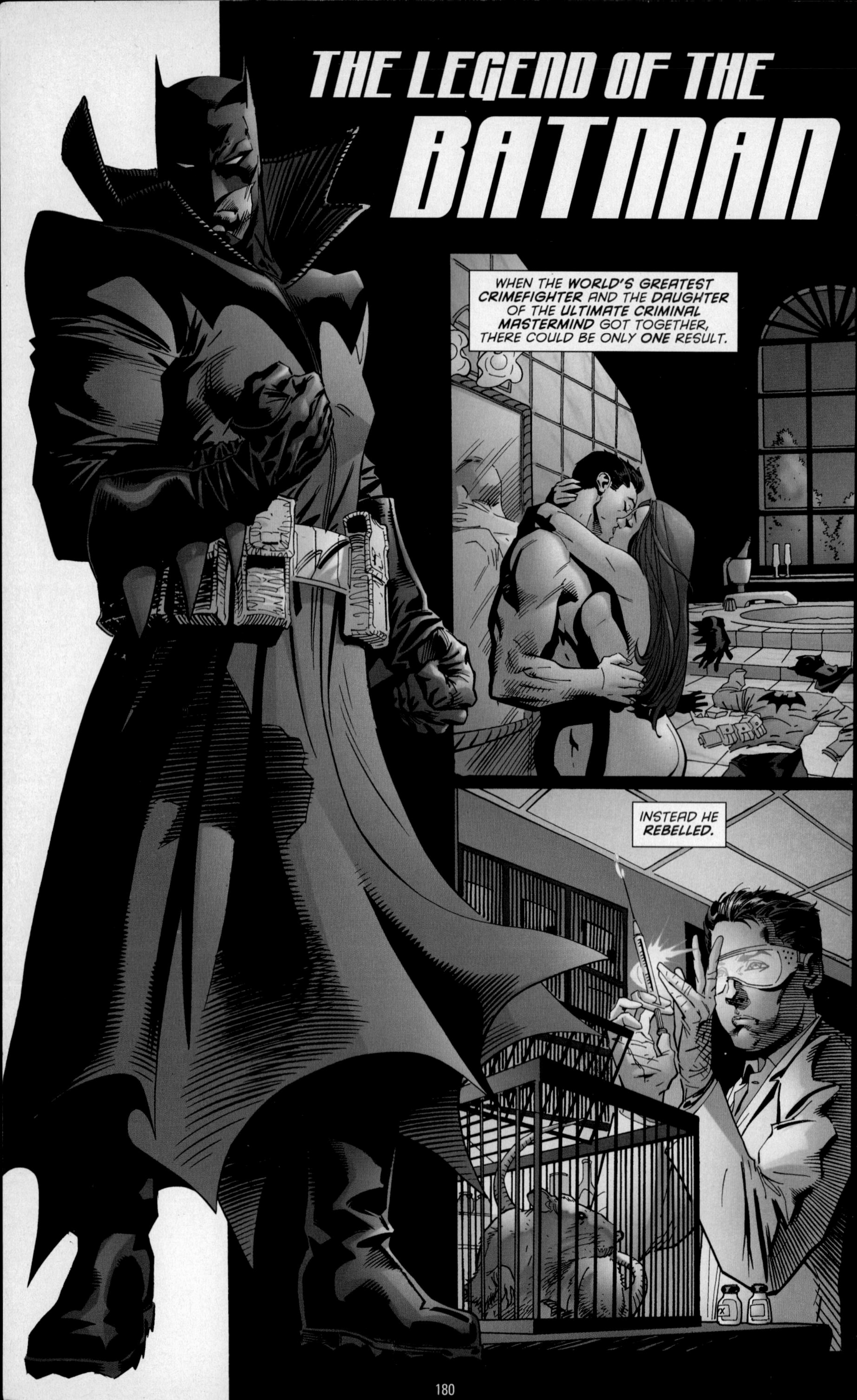
THE LEGEND OF THE BATMAN
WHEN THE WORLD'S GREATEST CRIMEFIGHTER AND THE DAUGHTER OF THE ULTIMATE CRIMINAL MASTERMIND GOT TOGETHER, THERE COULD BE ONLY ONE RESULT.
INSTEAD HE REBELLED.

WHO HE IS AND HOW HE CAME TO BE...

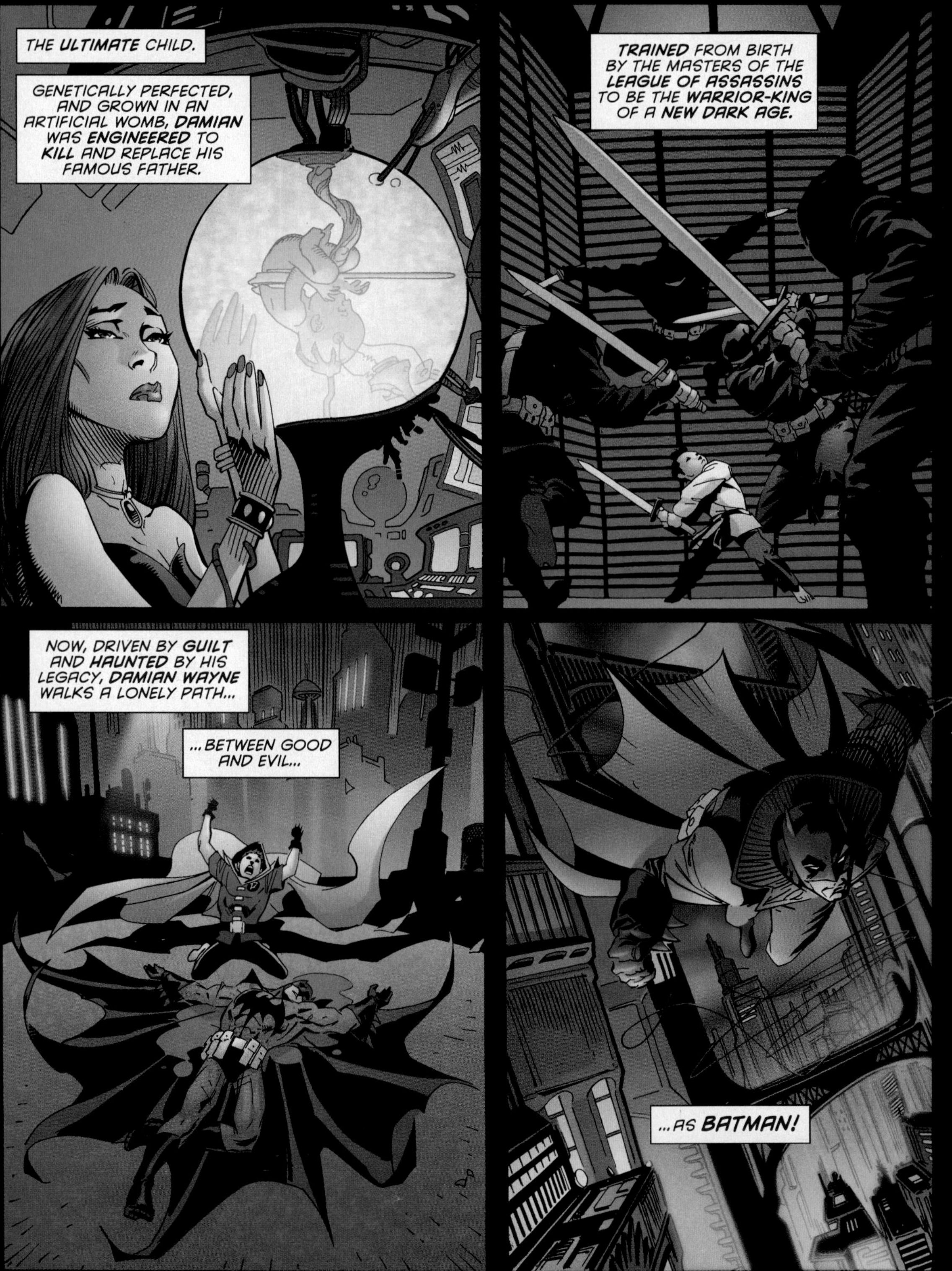
THE ULTIMATE CHILD.
GENETICALLY PERFECTED, AND GROWN IN AN ARTIFICIAL WOMB, DAMIAN WAS ENGINEERED TO KILL AND REPLACE HIS FAMOUS FATHER.
TRAINED FROM BIRTH BY THE MASTERS OF THE LEAGUE OF ASSASSINS TO BE THE WARRIOR-KING OF A NEW DARK AGE.
NOW, DRIVEN BY GUILT AND HAUNTED BY HIS LEGACY, DAMIAN WAYNE WALKS A LONELY PATH...
...BETWEEN GOOD AND EVIL...
...AS BATMAN!

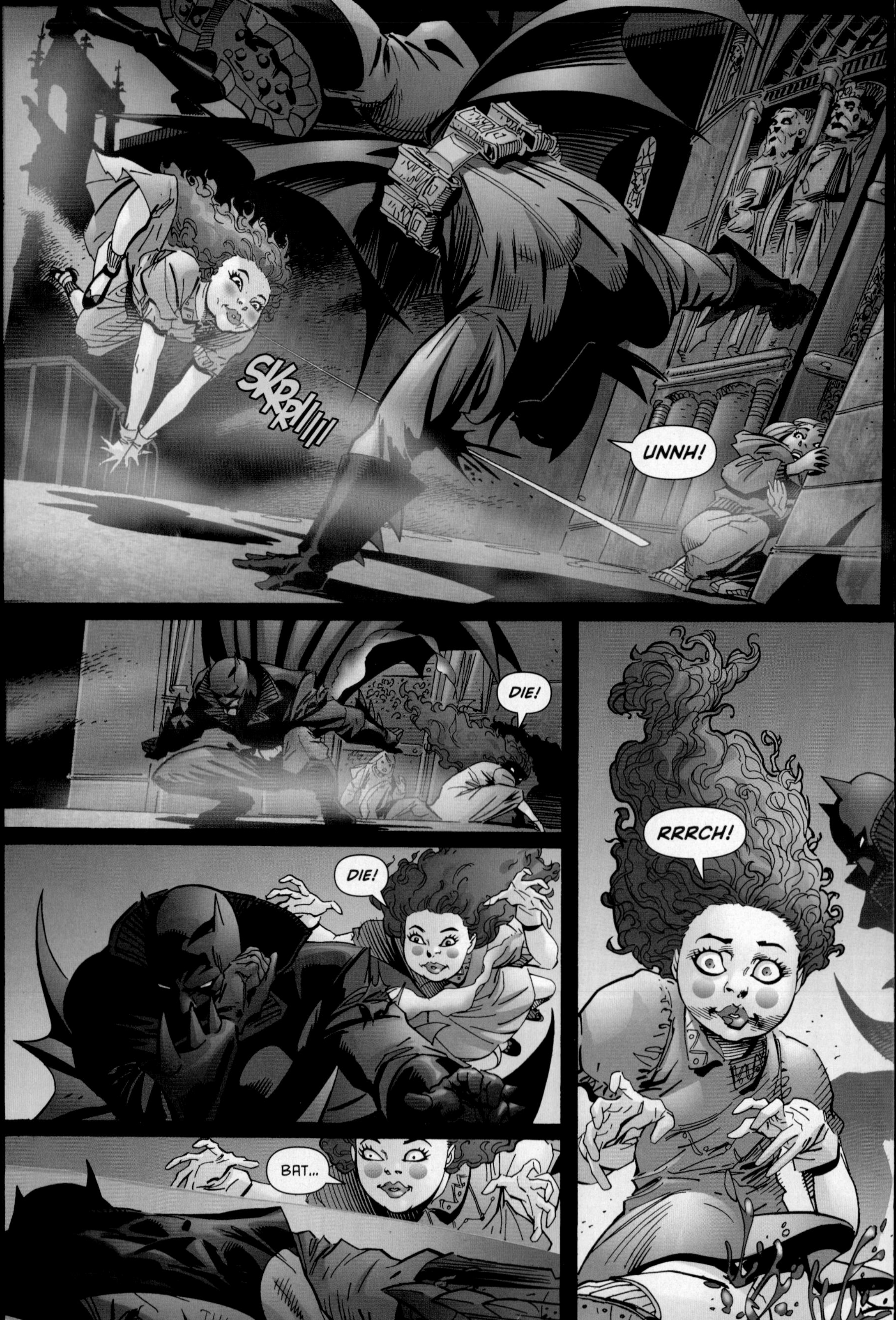
SKRRIII
UNNH!
DIE!
DIE!
BAT...
RRRCH!

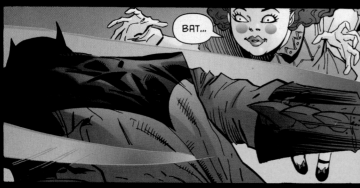

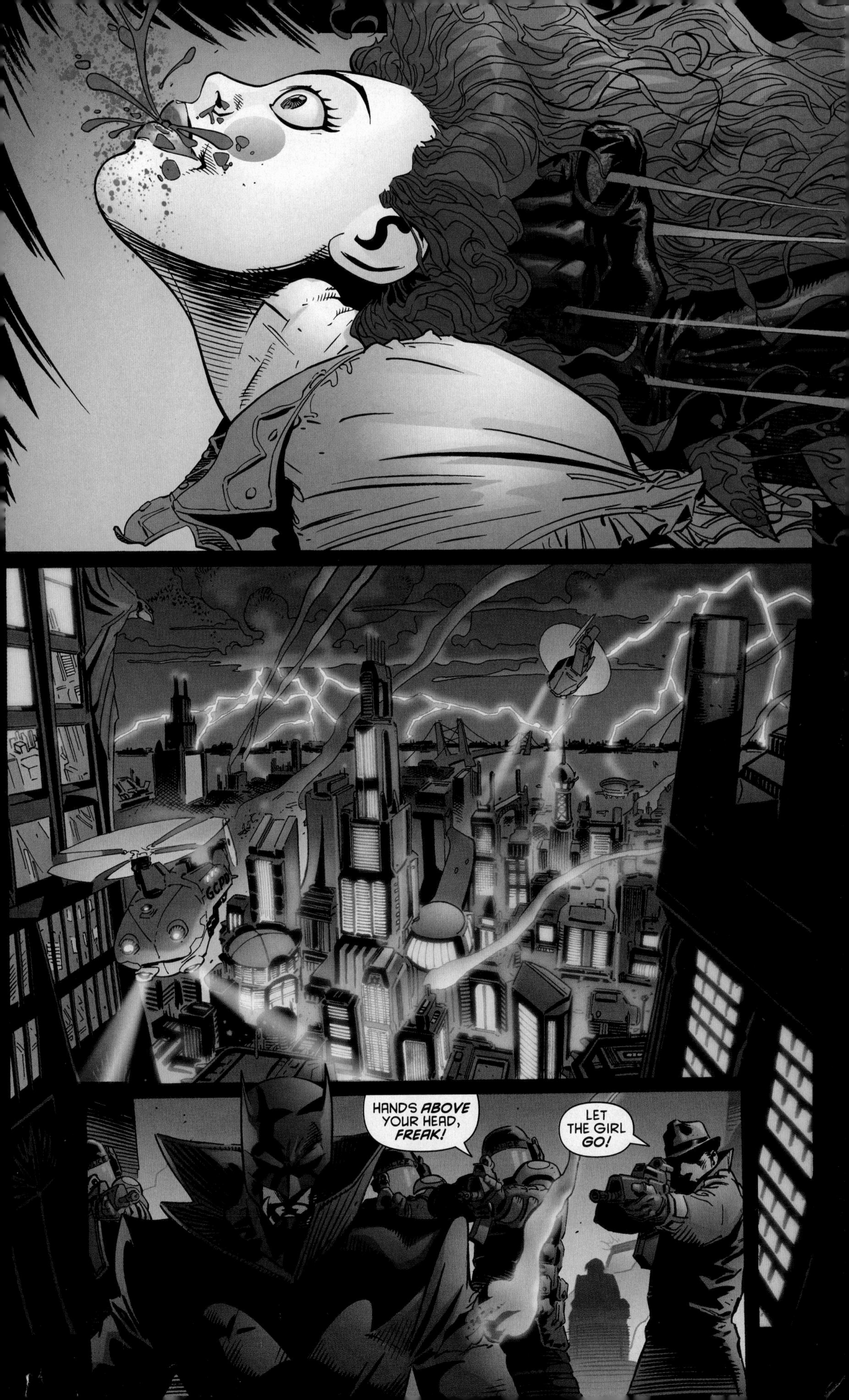
HANDS ABOVE YOUR HEAD, FREAK!
LET THE GIRL GO!
GCPD

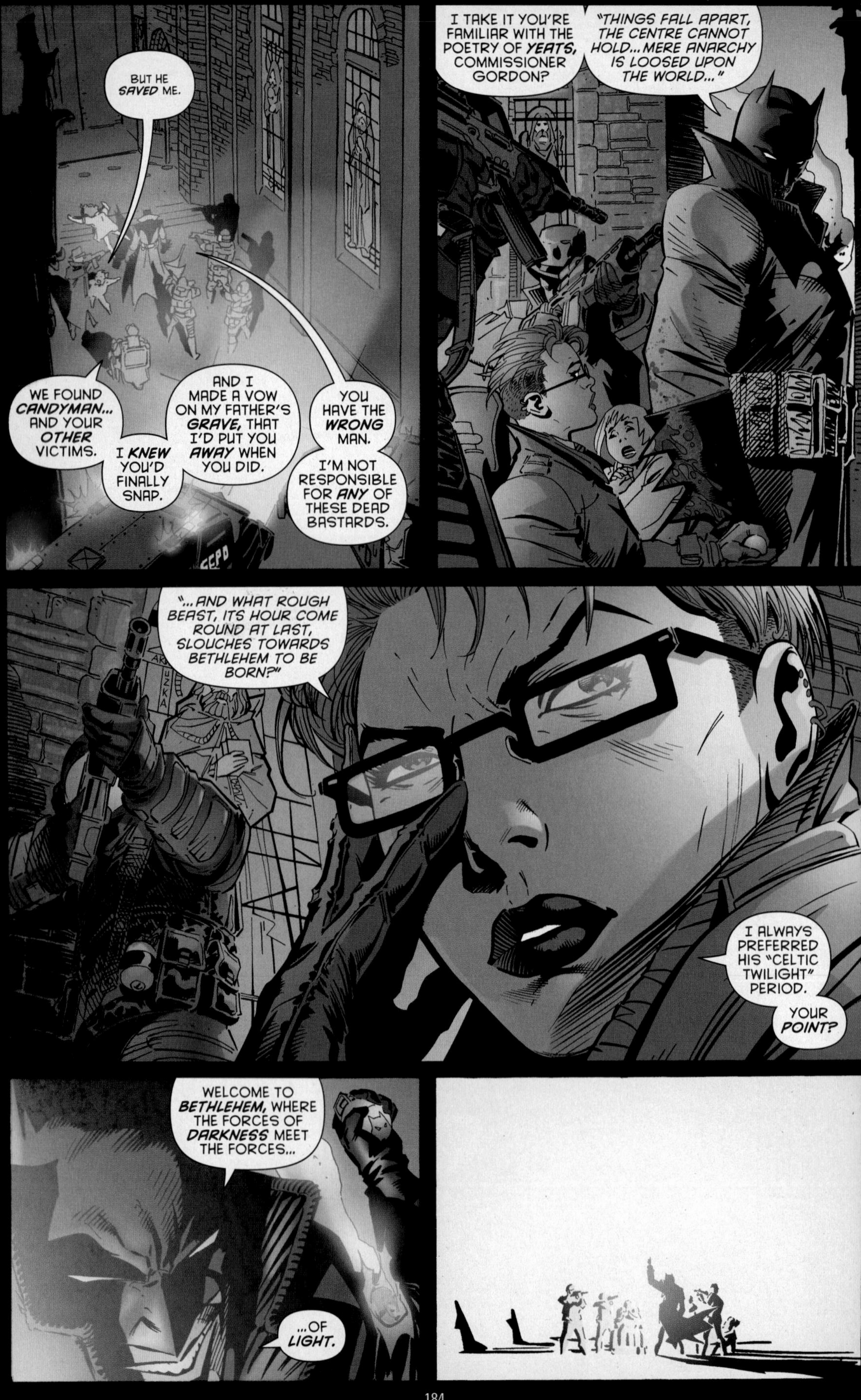

BUT HE SAVED ME.
WE FOUND CANDYMAN... AND YOUR OTHER VICTIMS.
I KNEW YOU'D FINALLY SNAP.
AND I MADE A VOW ON MY FATHER'S GRAVE, THAT I'D PUT YOU AWAY WHEN YOU DID.
YOU HAVE THE WRONG MAN.
I'M NOT RESPONSIBLE FOR ANY OF THESE DEAD BASTARDS.
I TAKE IT YOU'RE FAMILIAR WITH THE POETRY OF YEATS, COMMISSIONER GORDON?
"THINGS FALL APART, THE CENTRE CANNOT HOLD... MERE ANARCHY IS LOOSED UPON THE WORLD..."
"...AND WHAT ROUGH BEAST, ITS HOUR COME ROUND AT LAST, SLOUCHES TOWARDS BETHLEHEM TO BE BORN?"
I ALWAYS PREFERRED HIS "CELTIC TWILIGHT" PERIOD.
YOUR POINT?
WELCOME TO BETHLEHEM, WHERE THE FORCES OF DARKNESS MEET THE FORCES...
...OF LIGHT.

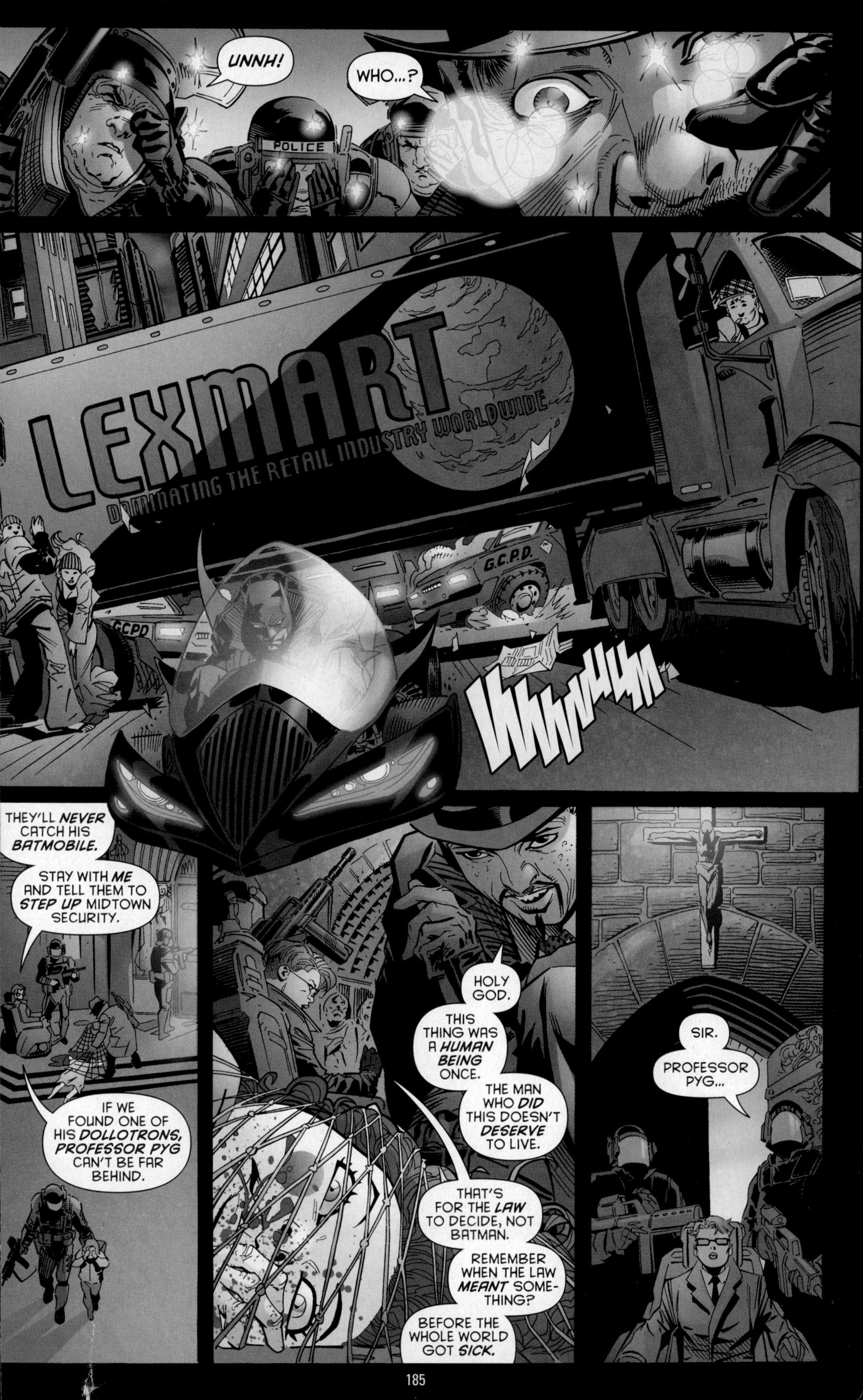
UNNH!
WHO...?
LEXMART
DOMINATING THE RETAIL INDUSTRY WORLDWIDE
G.C.P.D.
GCPD
VVVVVVUUM
THEY'LL NEVER CATCH HIS BATMOBILE.
STAY WITH ME AND TELL THEM TO STEP UP MIDTOWN SECURITY.
IF WE FOUND ONE OF HIS DOLLOTRONS, PROFESSOR PYG CAN'T BE FAR BEHIND.
HOLY GOD.
THIS THING WAS A HUMAN BEING ONCE.
THE MAN WHO DID THIS DOESN'T DESERVE TO LIVE.
THAT'S FOR THE LAW TO DECIDE, NOT BATMAN.
REMEMBER WHEN THE LAW MEANT SOME-THING?
BEFORE THE WHOLE WORLD GOT SICK.
SIR.
PROFESSOR PYG...

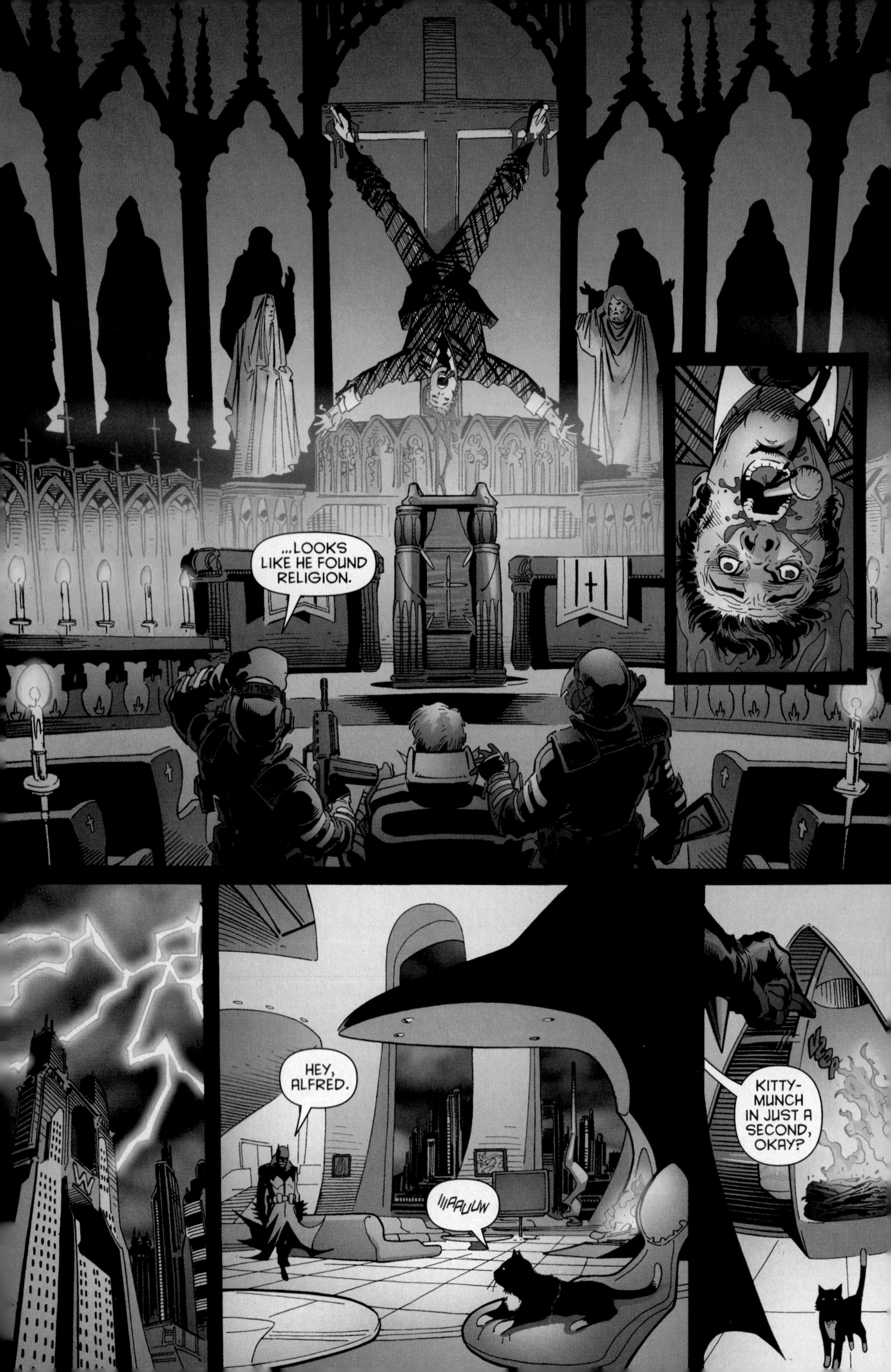
...LOOKS LIKE HE FOUND RELIGION.
HEY, ALFRED.
IIIAAUUW
KITTY-MUNCH IN JUST A SECOND, OKAY?

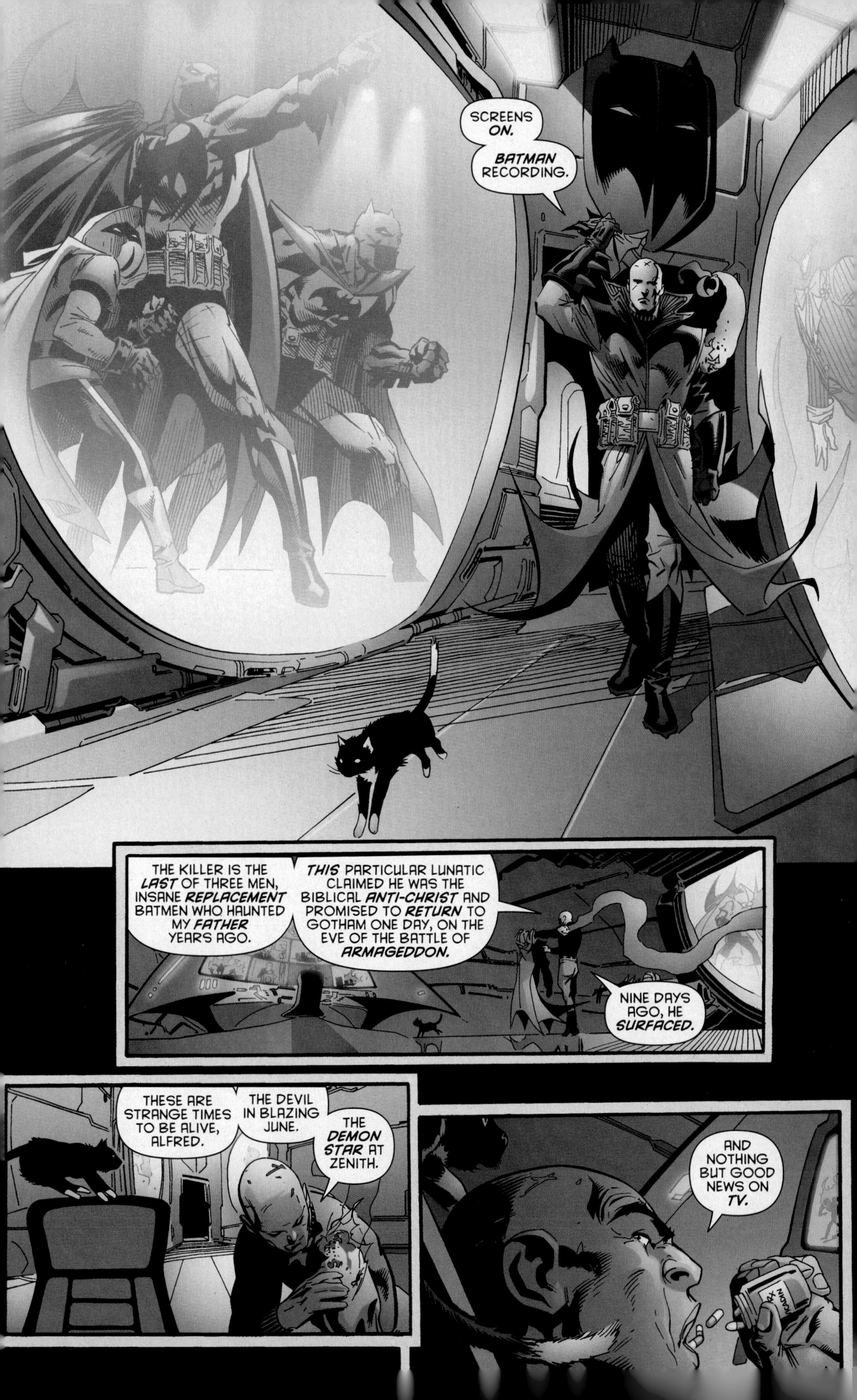
SCREENS ON.
BATMAN RECORDING.
THE KILLER IS THE LAST OF THREE MEN, INSANE REPLACEMENT BATMEN WHO HAUNTED MY FATHER YEARS AGO.
THIS PARTICULAR LUNATIC CLAIMED HE WAS THE BIBLICAL ANTI-CHRIST AND PROMISED TO RETURN TO GOTHAM ONE DAY, ON THE EVE OF THE BATTLE OF ARMAGEDDON.
NINE DAYS AGO, HE SURFACED.
THESE ARE STRANGE TIMES TO BE ALIVE, ALFRED.
THE DEVIL IN BLAZING JUNE.
THE DEMON STAR AT ZENITH.
AND NOTHING BUT GOOD NEWS ON TV.

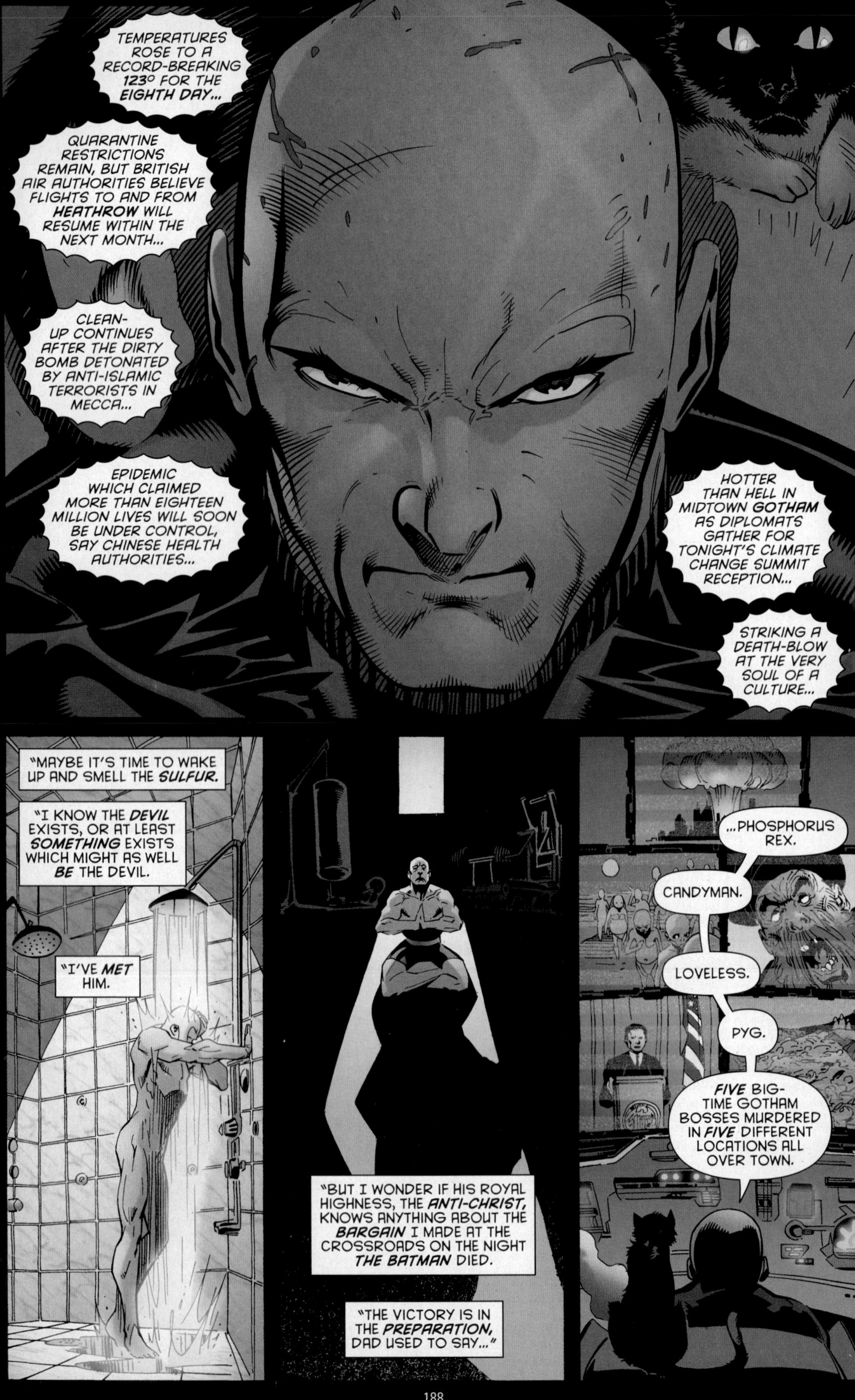
TEMPERATURES ROSE TO A RECORD-BREAKING 123° FOR THE EIGHTH DAY...
QUARANTINE RESTRICTIONS REMAIN, BUT BRITISH AIR AUTHORITIES BELIEVE FLIGHTS TO AND FROM HEATHROW WILL RESUME WITHIN THE NEXT MONTH...
CLEAN-UP CONTINUES AFTER THE DIRTY BOMB DETONATED BY ANTI-ISLAMIC TERRORISTS IN MECCA...
EPIDEMIC WHICH CLAIMED MORE THAN EIGHTEEN MILLION LIVES WILL SOON BE UNDER CONTROL, SAY CHINESE HEALTH AUTHORITIES...
HOTTER THAN HELL IN MIDTOWN GOTHAM AS DIPLOMATS GATHER FOR TONIGHT'S CLIMATE CHANGE SUMMIT RECEPTION...
STRIKING A DEATH-BLOW AT THE VERY SOUL OF A CULTURE...
"MAYBE IT'S TIME TO WAKE UP AND SMELL THE SULFUR.
"I KNOW THE DEVIL EXISTS, OR AT LEAST SOMETHING EXISTS WHICH MIGHT AS WELL BE THE DEVIL.
"I'VE MET HIM.
"BUT I WONDER IF HIS ROYAL HIGHNESS, THE ANTI-CHRIST, KNOWS ANYTHING ABOUT THE BARGAIN I MADE AT THE CROSSROADS ON THE NIGHT THE BATMAN DIED.
"THE VICTORY IS IN THE PREPARATION, DAD USED TO SAY..."
...PHOSPHORUS REX.
CANDYMAN.
LOVELESS.
PYG.
FIVE BIG-TIME GOTHAM BOSSES MURDERED IN FIVE DIFFERENT LOCATIONS ALL OVER TOWN.

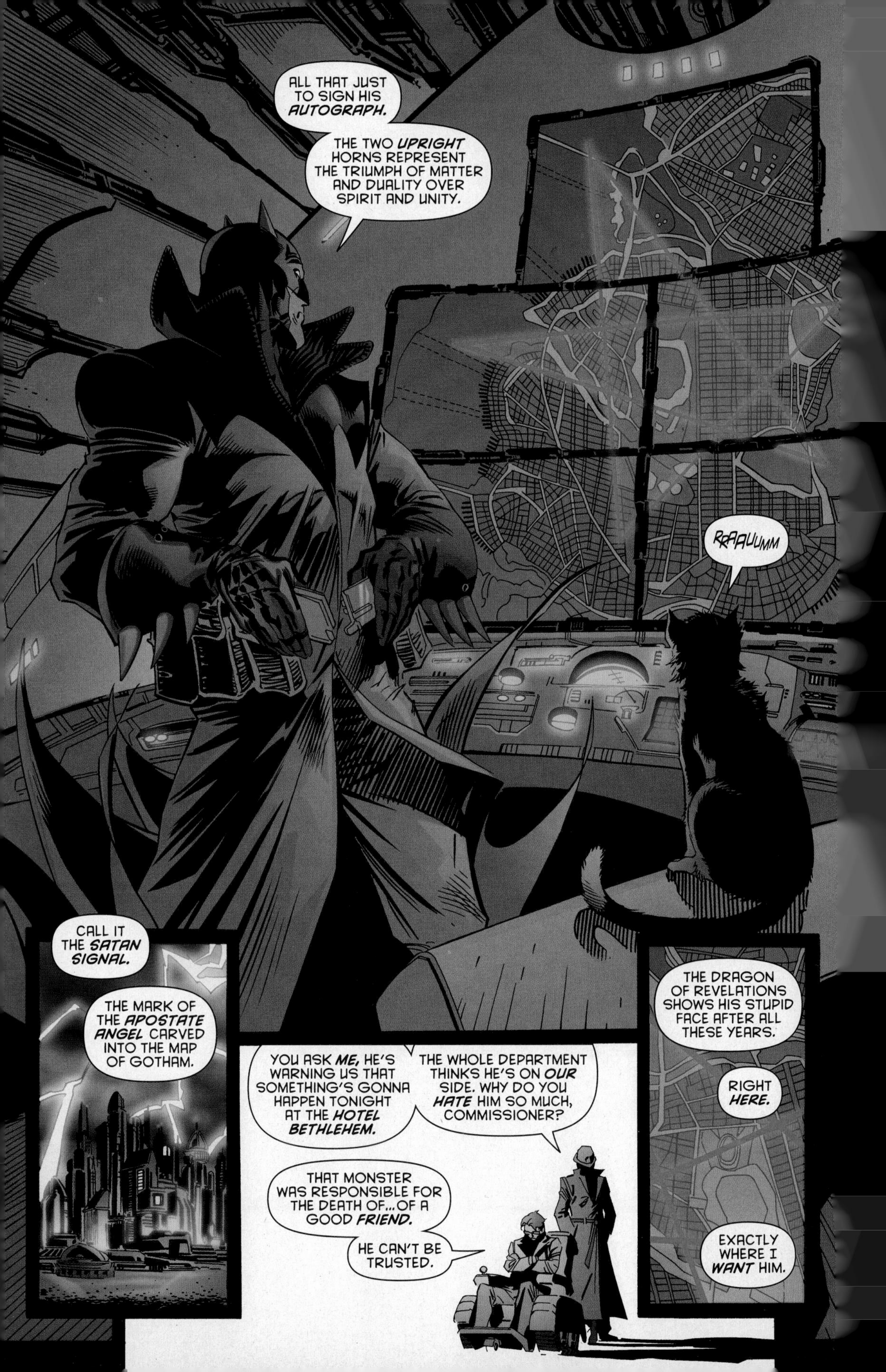
ALL THAT JUST TO SIGN HIS AUTOGRAPH.
THE TWO UPRIGHT HORNS REPRESENT THE TRIUMPH OF MATTER AND DUALITY OVER SPIRIT AND UNITY.
RRRAUUMM
CALL IT THE SATAN SIGNAL.
THE MARK OF THE APOSTATE ANGEL CARVED INTO THE MAP OF GOTHAM.
YOU ASK ME, HE'S WARNING US THAT SOMETHING'S GONNA HAPPEN TONIGHT AT THE HOTEL BETHLEHEM.
THE WHOLE DEPARTMENT THINKS HE'S ON OUR SIDE. WHY DO YOU HATE HIM SO MUCH, COMMISSIONER?
THAT MONSTER WAS RESPONSIBLE FOR THE DEATH OF...OF A GOOD FRIEND.
HE CAN'T BE TRUSTED.
THE DRAGON OF REVELATIONS SHOWS HIS STUPID FACE AFTER ALL THESE YEARS.
RIGHT HERE.
EXACTLY WHERE I WANT HIM.

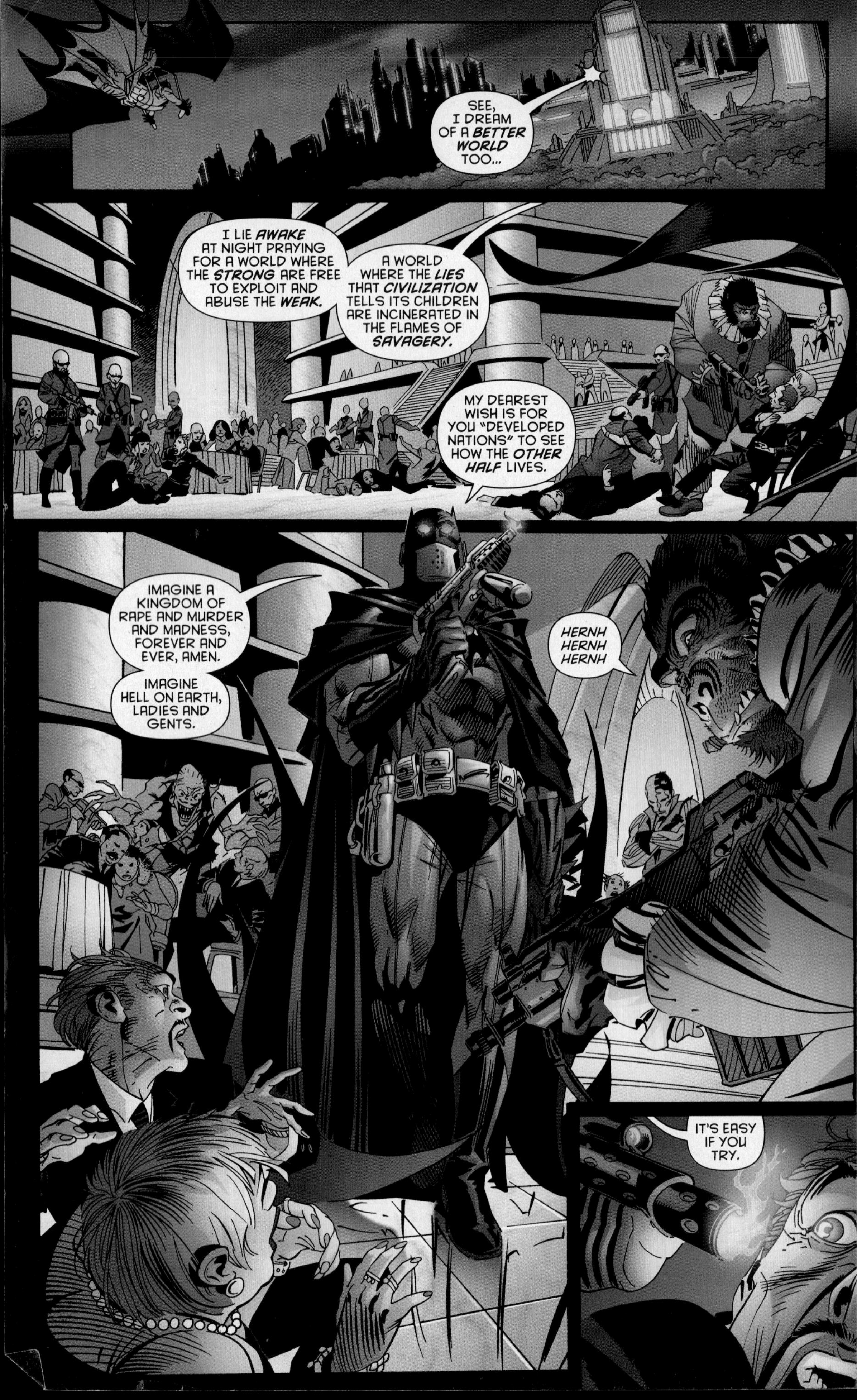
SEE, I DREAM OF A BETTER WORLD TOO...
I LIE AWAKE AT NIGHT PRAYING FOR A WORLD WHERE THE STRONG ARE FREE TO EXPLOIT AND ABUSE THE WEAK.
A WORLD WHERE THE LIES THAT CIVILIZATION TELLS ITS CHILDREN ARE INCINERATED IN THE FLAMES OF SAVAGERY.
MY DEAREST WISH IS FOR YOU "DEVELOPED NATIONS" TO SEE HOW THE OTHER HALF LIVES.
IMAGINE A KINGDOM OF RAPE AND MURDER AND MADNESS, FOREVER AND EVER, AMEN.
IMAGINE HELL ON EARTH, LADIES AND GENTS.
HERNH HERNH HERNH
IT'S EASY IF YOU TRY.

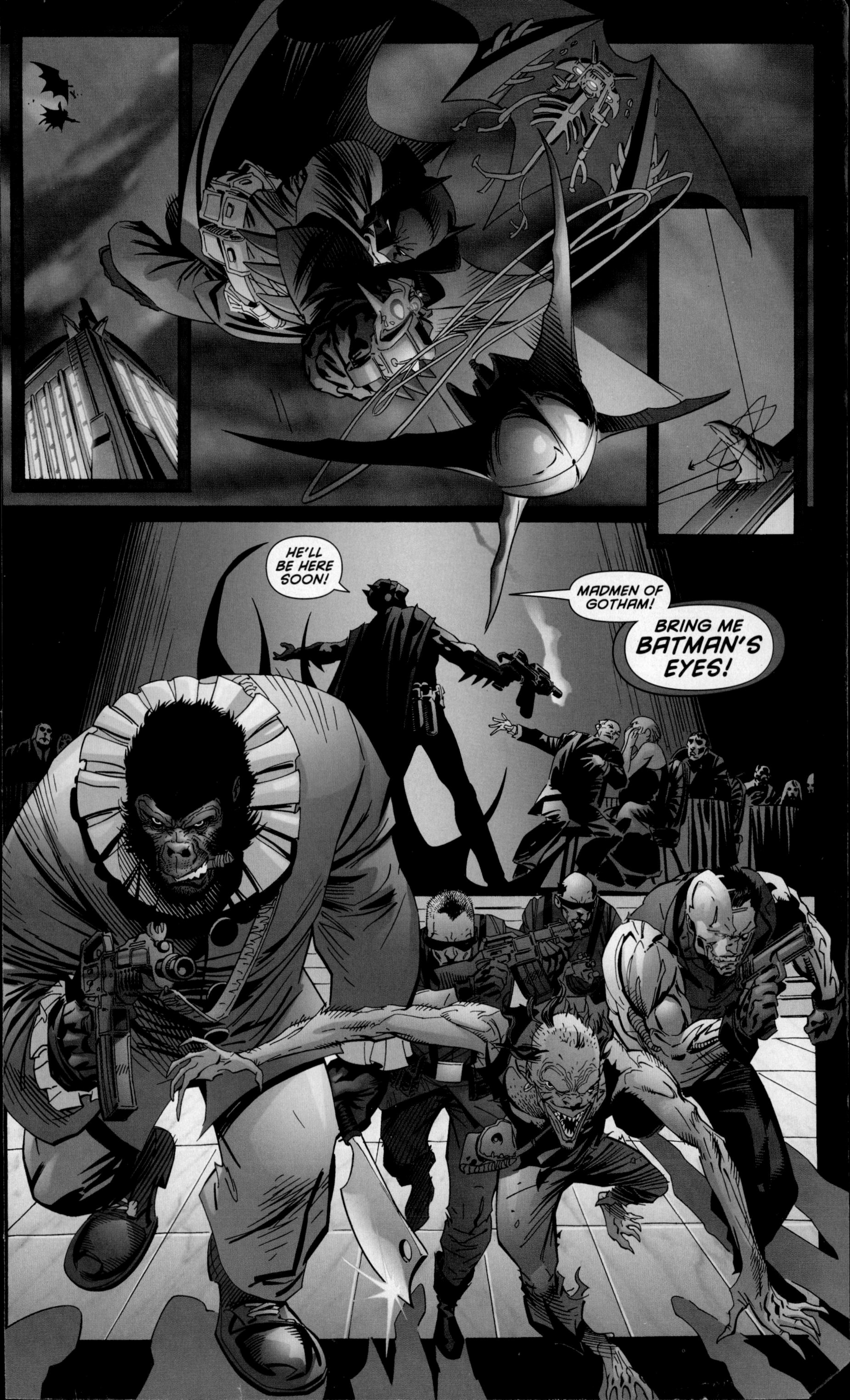
HE'LL BE HERE SOON!
MADMEN OF GOTHAM!
BRING ME BATMAN'S EYES!

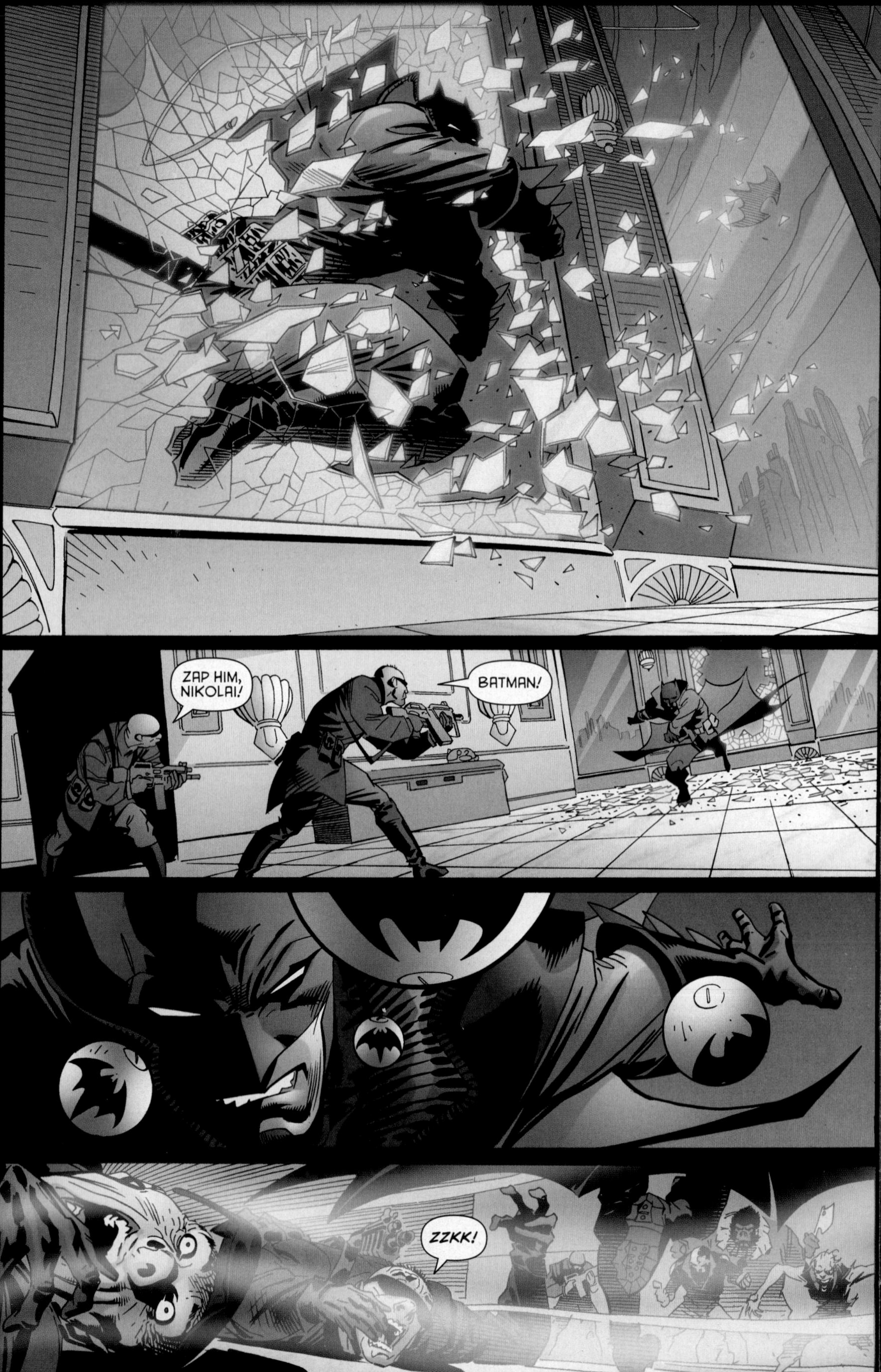
ZAP HIM, NIKOLAI!
BATMAN!
ZZKK!

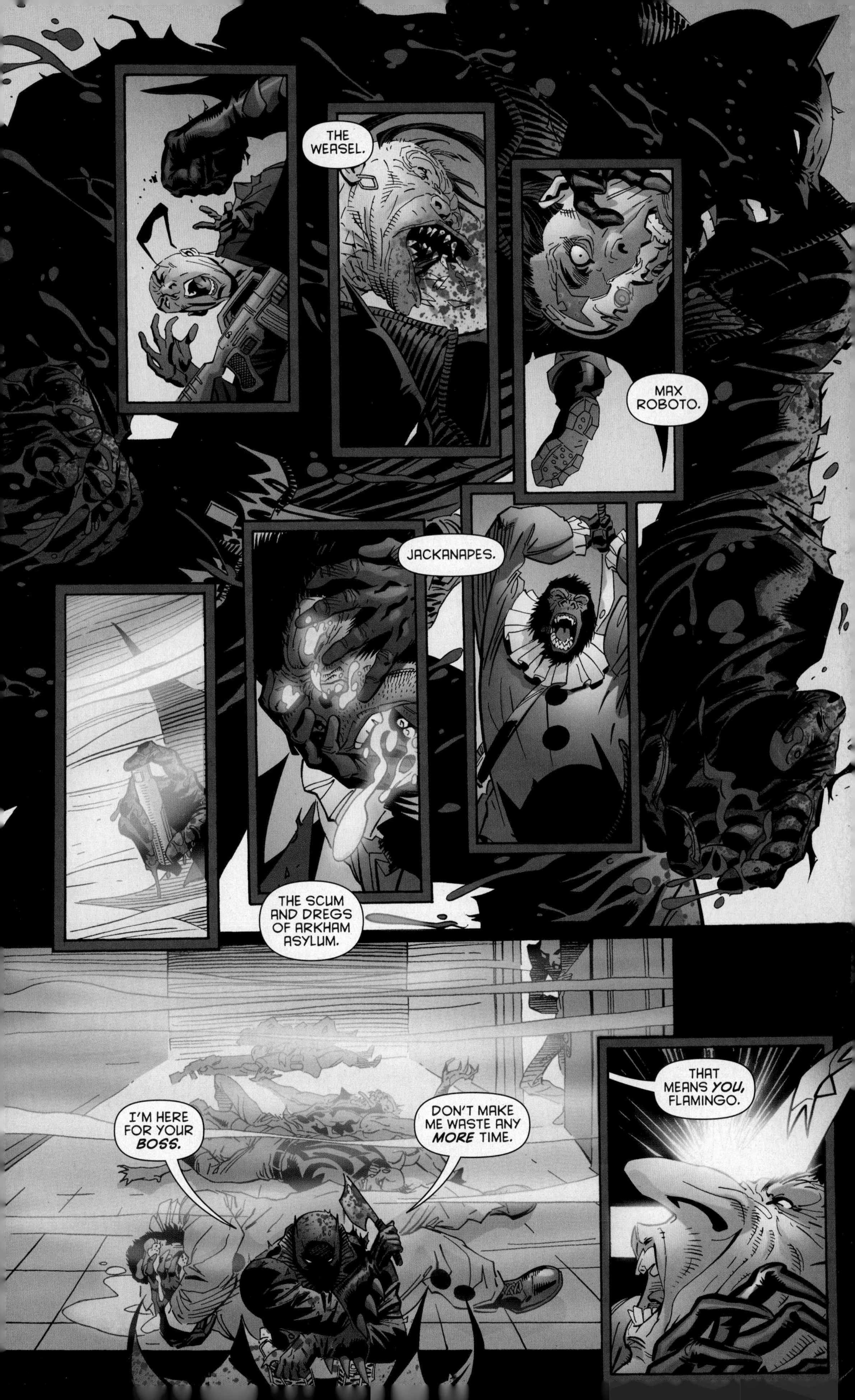
THE WEASEL.
MAX ROBOTO.
JACKANAPES.
THE SCUM AND DREGS OF ARKHAM ASYLUM.
I'M HERE FOR YOUR *BOSS.*
DON'T MAKE ME WASTE ANY *MORE* TIME.
THAT MEANS *YOU,* FLAMINGO.

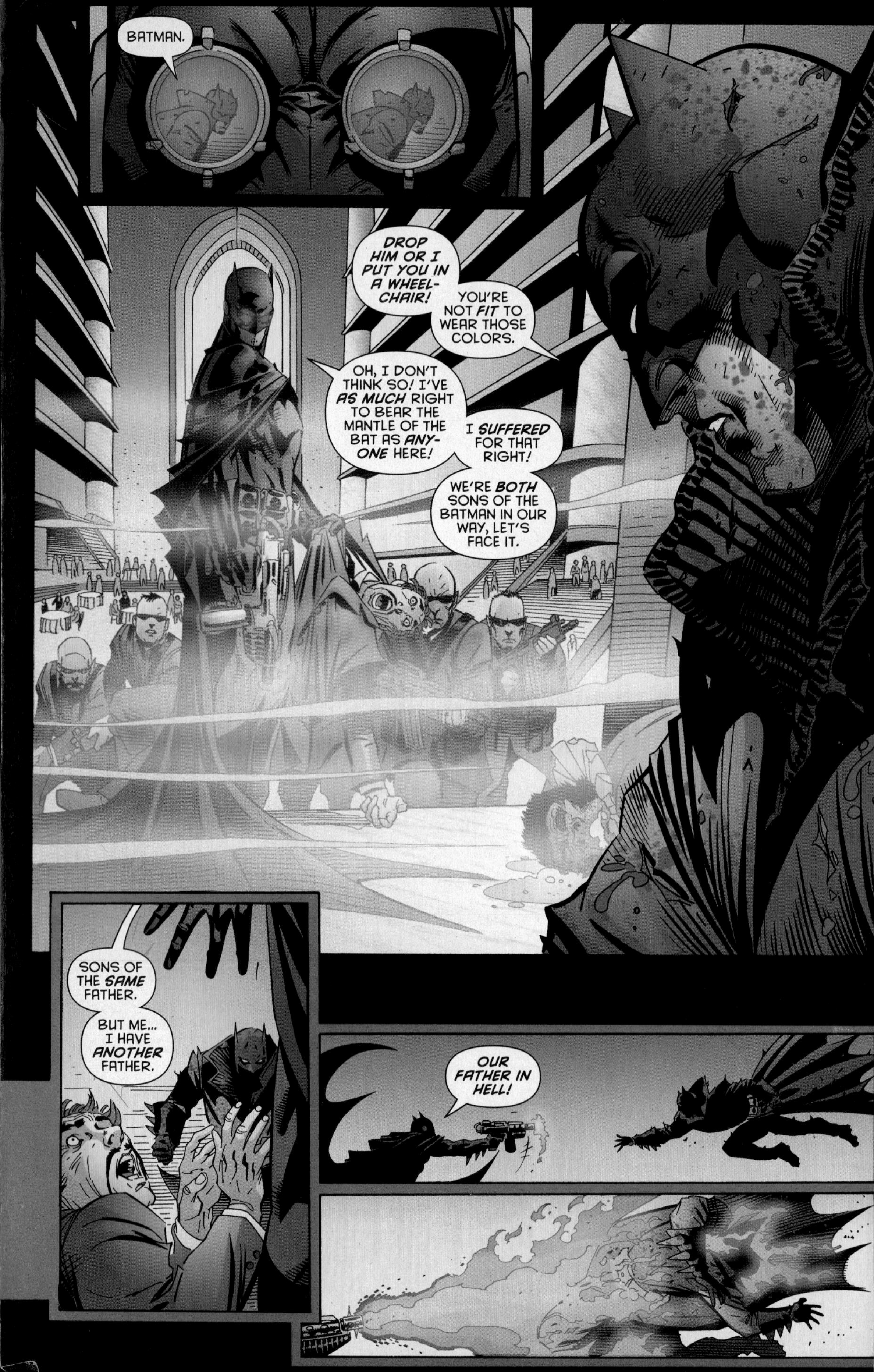
BATMAN.
DROP HIM OR I PUT YOU IN A WHEEL-CHAIR!
YOU'RE NOT FIT TO WEAR THOSE COLORS.
OH, I DON'T THINK SO! I'VE AS MUCH RIGHT TO BEAR THE MANTLE OF THE BAT AS ANY-ONE HERE!
I SUFFERED FOR THAT RIGHT!
WE'RE BOTH SONS OF THE BATMAN IN OUR WAY, LET'S FACE IT.
SONS OF THE SAME FATHER.
BUT ME... I HAVE ANOTHER FATHER.
OUR FATHER IN HELL!

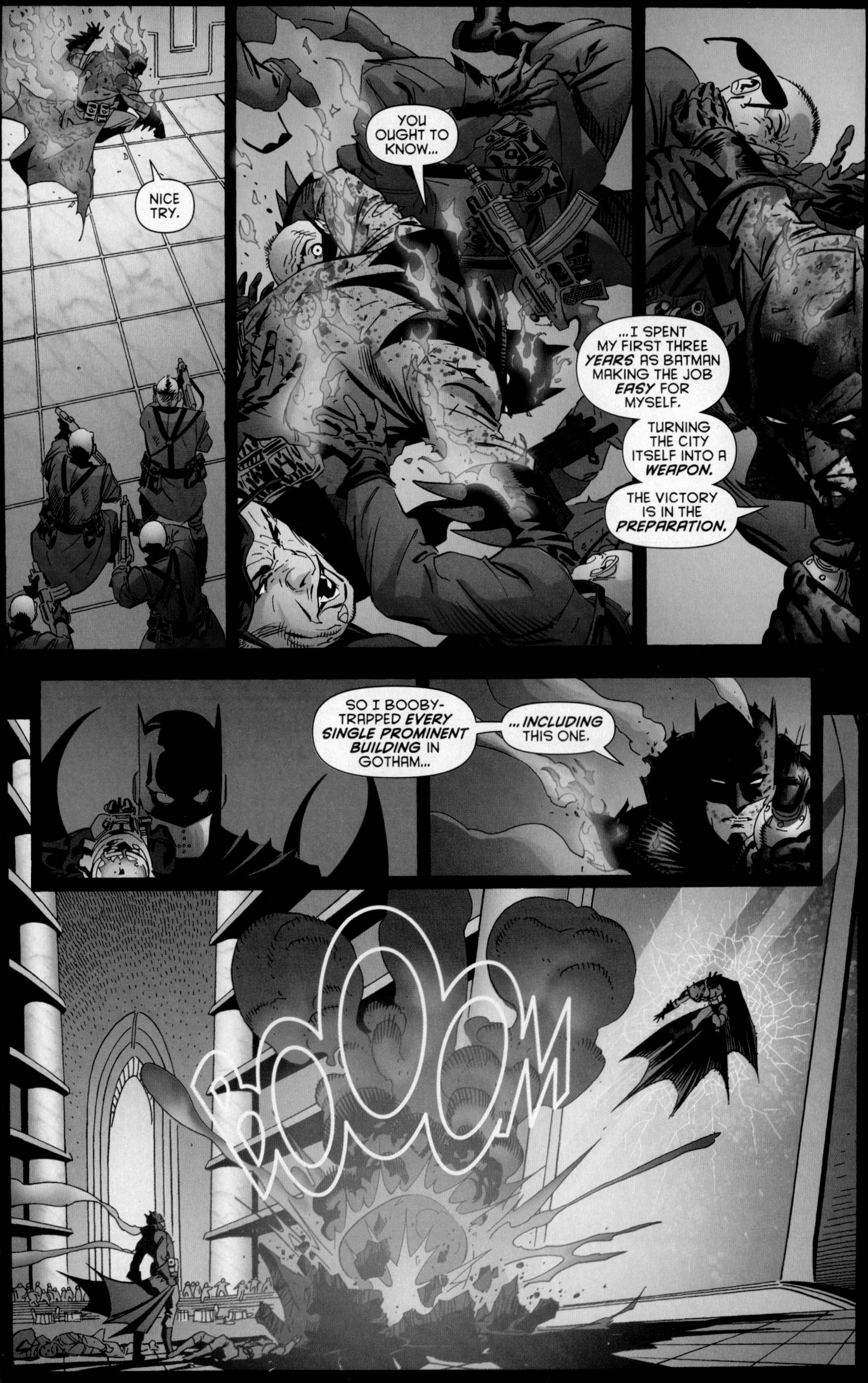
NICE TRY.
YOU OUGHT TO KNOW...
...I SPENT MY FIRST THREE YEARS AS BATMAN MAKING THE JOB EASY FOR MYSELF.
TURNING THE CITY ITSELF INTO A WEAPON.
THE VICTORY IS IN THE PREPARATION.
SO I BOOBY-TRAPPED EVERY SINGLE PROMINENT BUILDING IN GOTHAM...
...INCLUDING THIS ONE.
BOOOM

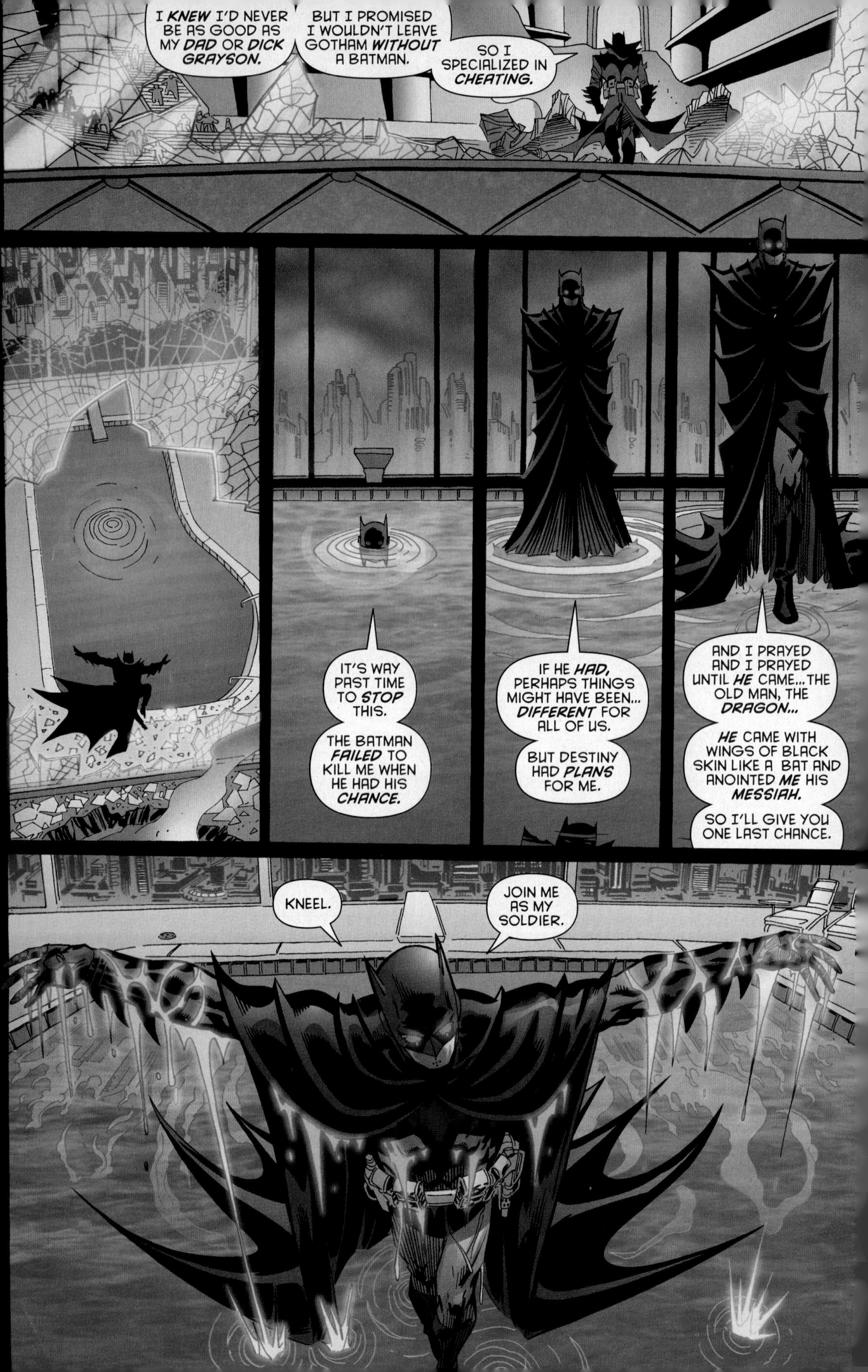
I KNEW I'D NEVER BE AS GOOD AS MY DAD OR DICK GRAYSON.
BUT I PROMISED I WOULDN'T LEAVE GOTHAM WITHOUT A BATMAN.
SO I SPECIALIZED IN CHEATING.
IT'S WAY PAST TIME TO STOP THIS.
THE BATMAN FAILED TO KILL ME WHEN HE HAD HIS CHANCE.
IF HE HAD, PERHAPS THINGS MIGHT HAVE BEEN... DIFFERENT FOR ALL OF US.
BUT DESTINY HAD PLANS FOR ME.
AND I PRAYED AND I PRAYED UNTIL HE CAME... THE OLD MAN, THE DRAGON...
HE CAME WITH WINGS OF BLACK SKIN LIKE A BAT AND ANOINTED ME HIS MESSIAH.
SO I'LL GIVE YOU ONE LAST CHANCE.
KNEEL.
JOIN ME AS MY SOLDIER.

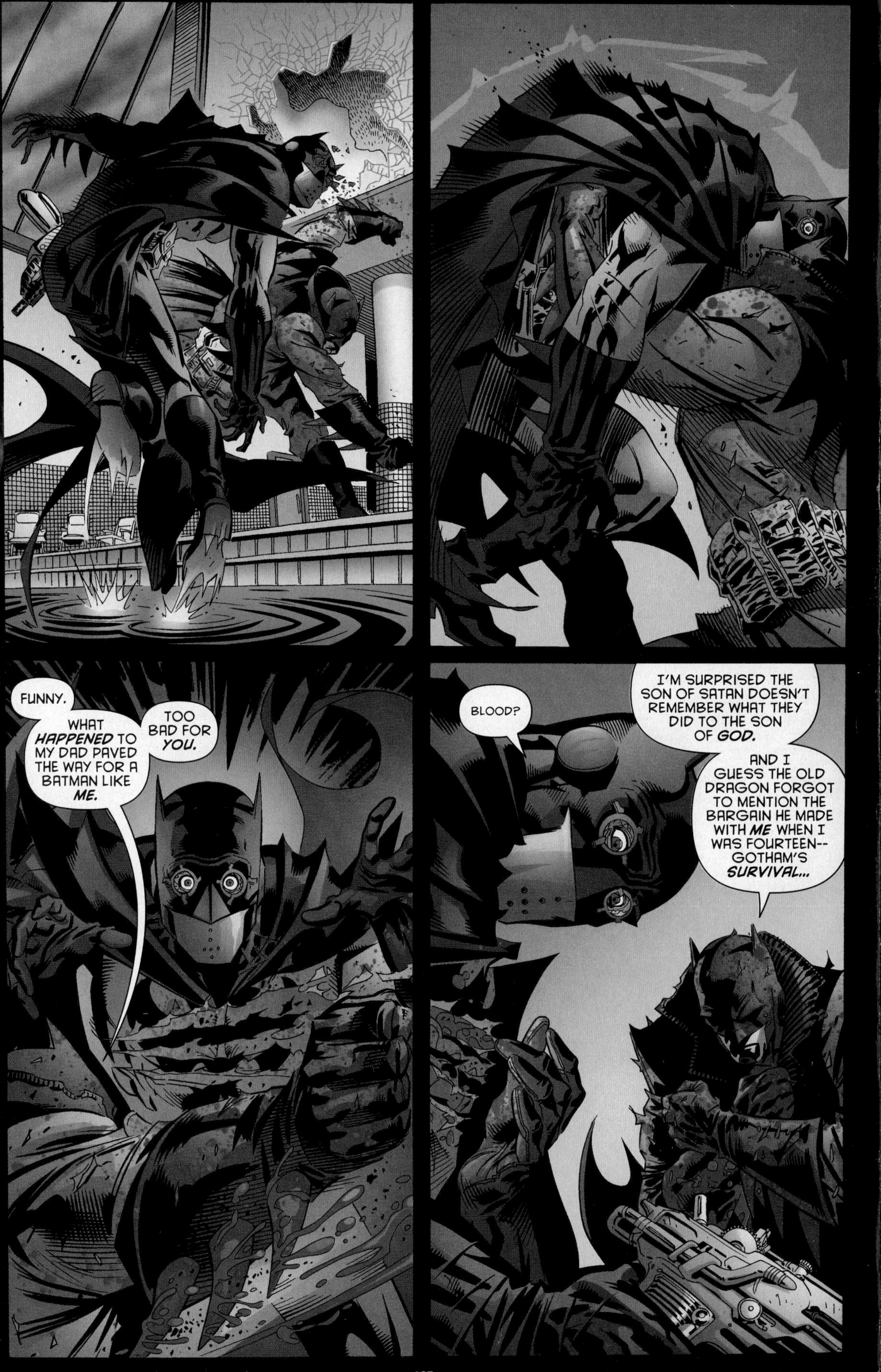
FUNNY.
WHAT HAPPENED TO MY DAD PAVED THE WAY FOR A BATMAN LIKE ME.
TOO BAD FOR YOU.
BLOOD?
I'M SURPRISED THE SON OF SATAN DOESN'T REMEMBER WHAT THEY DID TO THE SON OF GOD.
AND I GUESS THE OLD DRAGON FORGOT TO MENTION THE BARGAIN HE MADE WITH ME WHEN I WAS FOURTEEN-- GOTHAM'S SURVIVAL...

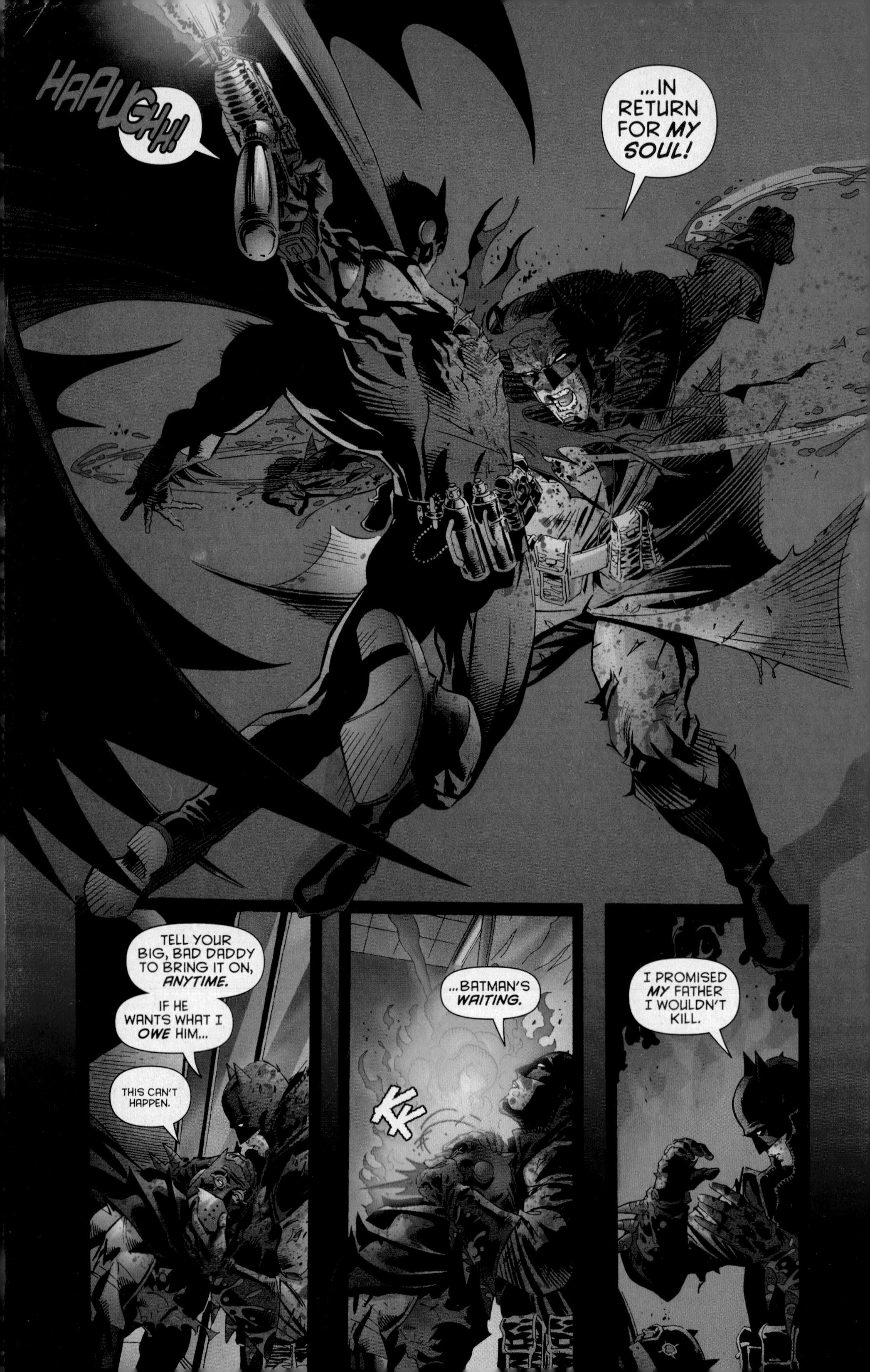
HAAUGHH!
...IN RETURN FOR MY SOUL!
TELL YOUR BIG, BAD DADDY TO BRING IT ON, ANYTIME.
IF HE WANTS WHAT I OWE HIM...
THIS CAN'T HAPPEN.
...BATMAN'S WAITING.
KK
I PROMISED MY FATHER I WOULDN'T KILL.

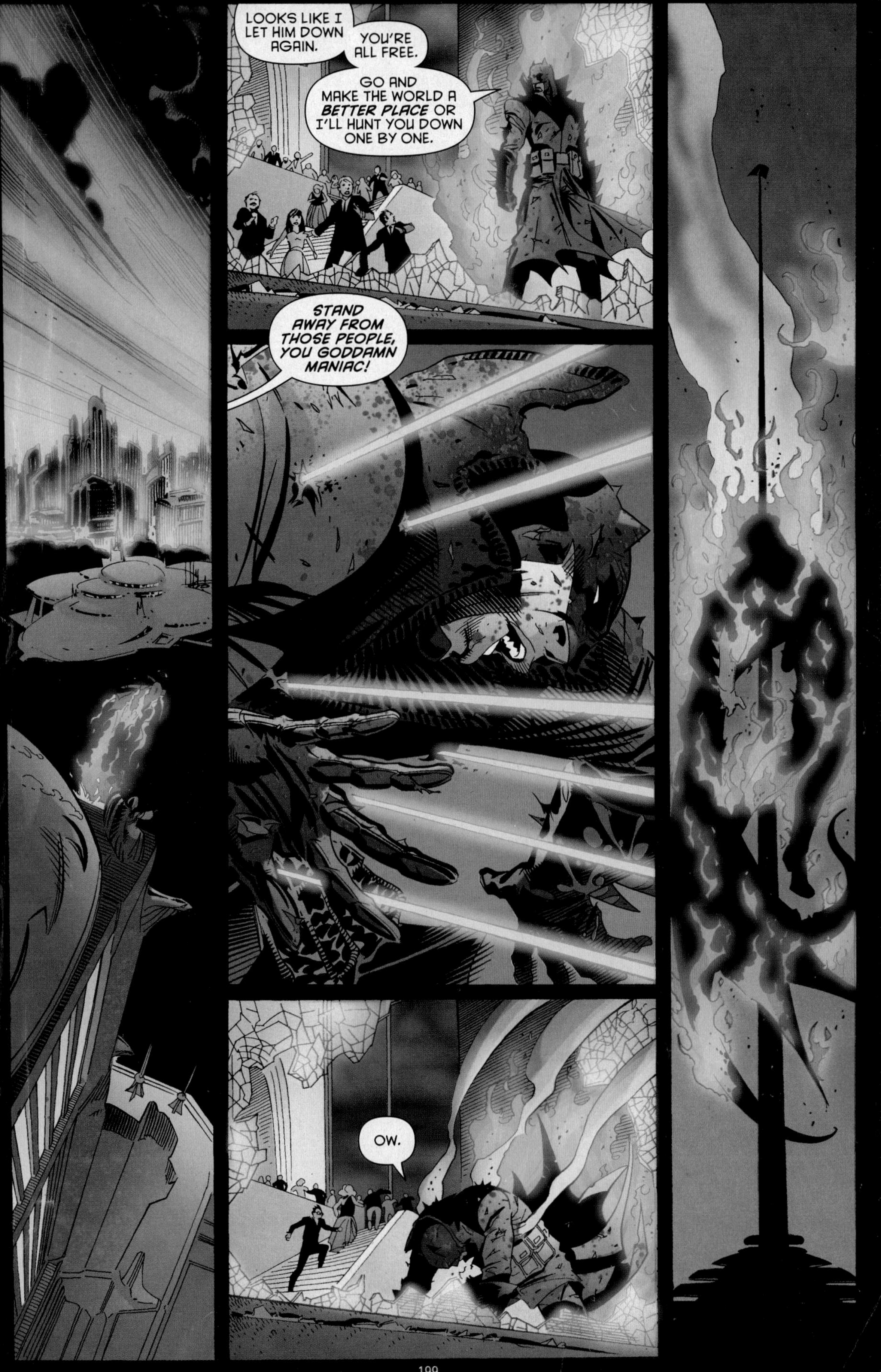
LOOKS LIKE I LET HIM DOWN AGAIN.
YOU'RE ALL FREE.
GO AND MAKE THE WORLD A *BETTER PLACE* OR I'LL HUNT YOU DOWN ONE BY ONE.
STAND AWAY FROM THOSE PEOPLE, YOU GODDAMN MANIAC!
OW.

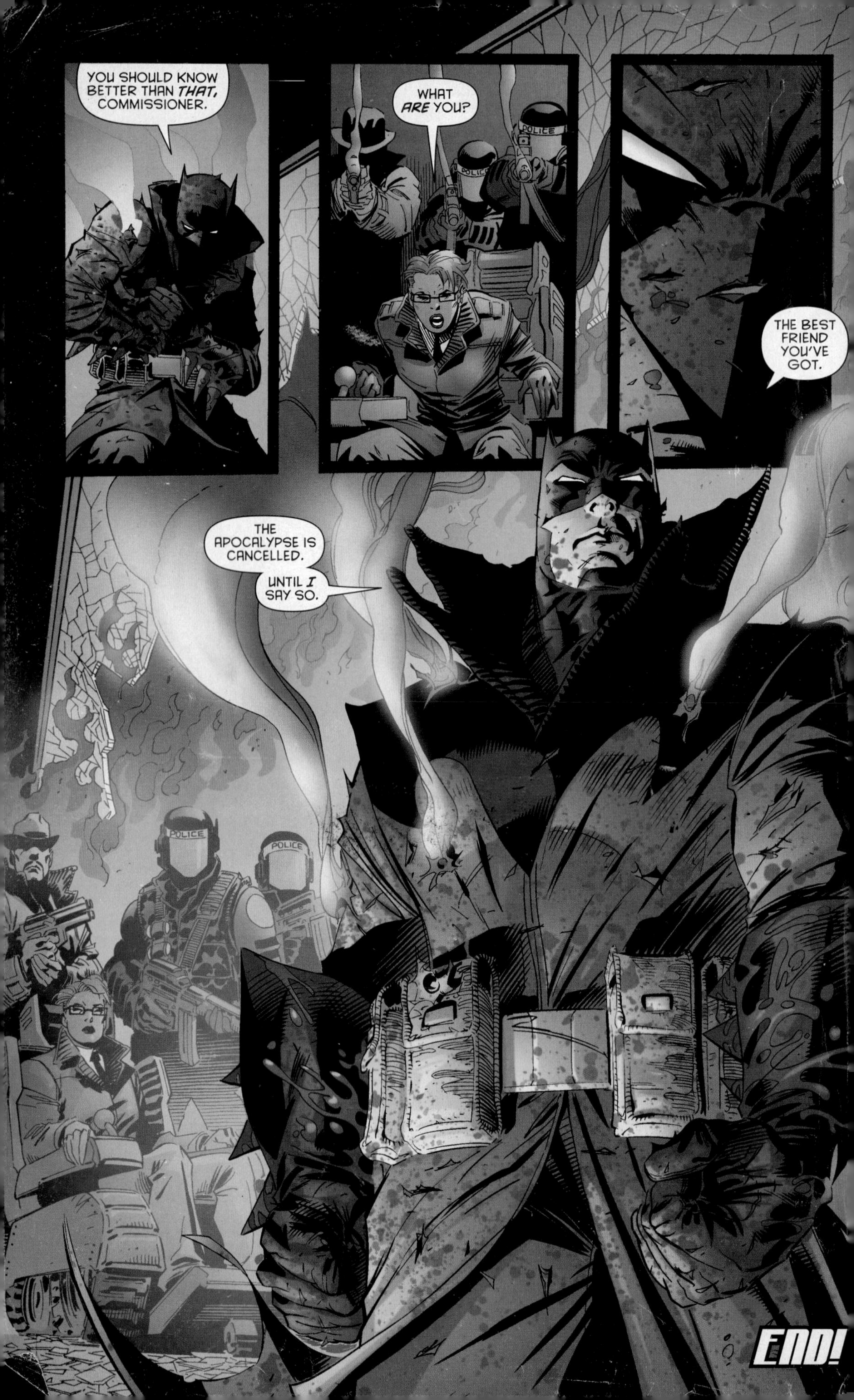

YOU SHOULD KNOW BETTER THAN *THAT*, COMMISSIONER.
WHAT *ARE* YOU?
THE BEST FRIEND YOU'VE GOT.
THE APOCALYPSE IS CANCELLED.
UNTIL *I* SAY SO.
END!